ROUTLEDGE LIBRARY EDITIONS:
GERMAN HISTORY

Volume 25

THE GERMAN FIFTH COLUMN IN THE SECOND WORLD WAR

THE GERMAN FIFTH COLUMN IN THE SECOND WORLD WAR

LOUIS DE JONG
TRANSLATED BY C. M. GEYL

Routledge
Taylor & Francis Group

NEW YORK AND LONDON

First published in English in 1956 by Routledge & Kegan Paul Ltd.

This edition first published in 2020
by Routledge
52 Vanderbilt Avenue, New York, NY 10017

and by Routledge
2 Park Square, Milton Park, Abingdon, Oxon OX14 4RN

Routledge is an imprint of the Taylor & Francis Group, an informa business

© 1956 English translation Routledge & Kegan Paul Ltd

British Library Cataloguing in Publication Data
A catalogue record for this book is available from the British Library

ISBN: 978-0-367-02813-8 (Set)
ISBN: 978-0-429-27806-8 (Set) (ebk)
ISBN: 978-0-367-24628-0 (Volume 25) (hbk)
ISBN: 978-0-367-24637-2 (Volume 25) (pbk)
ISBN: 978-0-429-28359-8 (Volume 25) (ebk)

Publisher's Note
The publisher has gone to great lengths to ensure the quality of this reprint but points out that some imperfections in the original copies may be apparent.

Disclaimer
The publisher has made every effort to trace copyright holders and would welcome correspondence from those they have been unable to trace.

The German
Fifth Column
in the Second
World War

by
LOUIS DE JONG

Translated from the Dutch by
C. M. GEYL

Routledge & Kegan Paul
LONDON

De Duitse Vijfde Colonne in de Tweede Wereldoorlog
First published in Holland 1953

Revised edition, translated into English and first published 1956
by Routledge & Kegan Paul Limited
Broadway House, Carter Lane, E.C.4
Printed in Great Britain
by Butler & Tanner Limited
Frome and London

Preface

★

In 1949 the International Council of Philosophic and Humanistic Studies, a body affiliated to Unesco, requested the State Institute for War Documentation at Amsterdam to contribute to a history of national socialist Germany and fascist Italy, to be written by historians from various countries. The subject was to be the so-called German Fifth Column. The request was acceded to; the Board of Directors of the Institute entrusted me with the task of writing the required study, which (a comparatively short piece) was finished in the last half of 1951.

At first I had confined myself to forming an idea of the intrigues carried out by the Germans outside Germany (usually summed up under the term 'Fifth Column work'), first from the literature on the subject and afterwards from other sources as well. At a later stage it struck me that, especially as regards the war years, the contrast between the activities *ascribed* to the German Fifth Column and its *actual* work constituted a problem in itself of general importance.

Thus a book came about that fell into three parts almost of its own accord.

The *first part* ('Fear') sketches how, after 1933, those outside Germany began to become increasingly afraid of sinister operations on the part of German agents and the partisans of national socialism; how this fear developed into a veritable panic each time Hitler passed on to a fresh deed of aggression; and finally how the conceptions born of fear and panic were embodied in what was written later on.

Numerous examples will be found later in this book of the mysterious omnipotence ascribed to the German Fifth Column. Here, however, I should like to quote a description given by a level-headed American journalist in order to conjure up a picture of what was, I believe, a fairly generally accepted view in most of the Western countries in the years in which Hitler, dizzy with success, stood at the very height of his power. It came from the pen of Otto Tolischus in the

v

week in which—after Poland, Denmark, Norway, Holland, Belgium, Luxemburg—France in turn lay in her agony:

Functions of the fifth column may be divided into peacetime and wartime activities. In peacetime chief functions consist in creating propaganda which is not always merely pro-German or pro-Nazi, in supplying detailed information on commercial, industrial and political activities and national morale which, when collated in Berlin, gives a complete picture of every country's life; in maintaining surveillance of important citizens of the 'host land'; in outright espionage and, above all, in preparation for an 'emergency' to the point of training shock troops for the first blow. In this work the fifth column skilfully utilises all the social, political and idealistic ambitions and aspirations of various elements of the 'host land' to lull that land in a false sense of security, undermine its defence preparations and sow political, class and racial dissensions. . . .

Its wartime activities were disclosed with startling results . . . especially in Poland, Norway and the Netherlands. But for wartime activities the fifth column usually is reinforced with determined men from Germany herself, who come in many disguises, principally as tourists, sportsmen, commercial agents and cultural representatives, and often carry their uniforms in their suitcases. They take charge of previously organised resident armies, which, often in disguise or in the uniforms of the enemy's own forces, seize strategic points, reinforce parachute troops, organise espionage and sabotage behind the enemy's lines and throw confusion into the enemy army and population through false orders and reports. . . .[1]

This general picture which Tolischus sketched tallies with the ideas which had arisen about the German Fifth Column in all the countries which Hitler had successively attacked: Poland in September, 1939; Denmark and Norway in April, 1940; the Netherlands, Belgium, Luxemburg and France in May, 1940. But these ideas existed elsewhere too: in England, in the United States, in the republics of Central and South America, in the Balkans and, after the invasion at least, also in the Soviet Union.

How far were these ideas in keeping with reality? Was German propaganda really so all-powerful and their espionage really so omniscient? Had the Germans who lived in the states with which Germany was at war formed groups in order to attack the armies of those states in the rear, and were those groups reinforced by persons who arrived from Germany in disguise so as to be able to carry out deeds

---

[1] Otto D. Tolischus, 'How Hitler made ready. I. The Fifth Column', *New York Times Magazine*, June 16, 1940.

of sabotage, to spread false orders and to sow panic? Did this 'military' German Fifth Column actually exist during the war?

We shall look for the answers to these and similar questions in the *second part* of our book ('Reality').

The fresh problems that emerge here and the problems that come forward in the comparison between the first and the second parts of the book will come up for discussion in the *third part* ('Analysis'). There we shall have to go further into the position of the German groups which were living outside of Germany at the time that Hitler started his assault. A distinction should be made regarding these groups—it is best to point this out at once—between '*Reichsdeutsche*', German citizens living abroad, and the persons whom in Germany itself people had come to call '*Volksdeutsche*' (Minority Germans[1]), people who were citizens of other states, but who did speak German and in other ways shared in German culture.

This book mainly confines itself to Fifth Column work developed by *Germans*. Naturally I am aware that there were other Fifth Columns which moved forward in the international offensive of national socialism. Hitler found accomplices in every country. The time is not yet ripe, however, to give an accurate description of the activities of those multifarious 'native' Fifth Columns. There are no good monographs extant, reliable archive material is hard to come by, and the social and political diversities of those non-German groups who actively sympathised with national socialism is greater and even more confusing than of the German groups. In this study a unifying element lies in the fact that the activities described originated with Germans, whereas a comparative study of the 'native' Fifth Columns would become a tangle of groups of divergent natures, which would each have to be understood from the special angle of its own social and political environment.

I am mainly confining myself to the *German* Fifth Column.

I am fully aware that I have not been able to give anything like a complete picture of what this Fifth Column did. I was able to consult many sources; many others proved inaccessible; and still more have probably disappeared for good. It goes without saying that I do not for a moment pretend to have studied exhaustively the historical development of the German minorities in garlands of states twined

[1] '*Volksdeutsche*' is really one of those terms that are utterly untranslatable. It calls up a whole world of feeling in the minds of the Germans; no rendering can do it justice. Others have translated '*Volksdeutsche*' by 'national Germans', 'German nationals' or 'ethnic Germans'. I prefer 'Minority Germans' because the fact that the Germans in question formed a minority in the areas where they lived was characteristic for their situation as well as a determining factor in the attitude of the German people towards them.

round the globe from Estonia to Chile and from Australia to Canada. A lifetime of study would be too brief. As a matter of fact one's hair might well turn grey trying to trace to their starting points all the rumours about the German Fifth Column that went the rounds in one single country during the German occupation. *It is for this reason that this book bears a provisional character*. The picture presented here, if it is not blotted out, will certainly be amplified on numerous points and will be more or less radically corrected. Precisely that 'international' image, however, that I have tried to build up out of as varied material as possible, may perhaps come to constitute a standard whereby experts in other countries can measure or re-measure their 'national' situation.

An apology is called for here.

As McCallum says: 'Anyone who writes on this subject of public opinion' (and what, after all, is the first part of this book but a partial description of public opinion during the years 1933–45?) 'finds it difficult not to convey in the course of his analysis a slightly odious impression of assuming a superior wisdom, of having been wise not merely after the event but before it'.[1] I do not hesitate to admit that I too was a victim of the Fifth Column panic. Many people whose remarks (which I quote here) proved to be unfounded though under-standable, might wish to note that in 1941 the present writer described the 'masterly organisation' of the Fifth Column in his native town of Amsterdam with uneasy admiration.[2]

No; this study has rather convinced me of the limitation of human judgment and it has given me insight into the measure to which storms of feeling manage to drive rational thinking completely out of its course. This is all the more so when these storms, intensified into cyclones, first come from one and then from the opposite direc-tion: a situation we shall repeatedly come across in the disputed areas where Germans were active.

Aggression breeds counter-aggression.

My study only forms a variation on that ancient theme.

LOUIS DE JONG

---

[1] R. B. McCallum: *Public Opinion and the Last Peace* (London, 1944), Preface.
[2] L. de Jong: *Holland Fights the Nazis* (London, 1941), pp. 16–17.

Contents

★

Preface   v

List of Maps   xi

PART ONE: FEAR

Introduction: The approach of disaster   3

CHAPTER I   Panic in Poland   39

II   Denmark and Norway surprised   54

III   The invasion of the Netherlands   66

IV   The German offensive in Belgium and France   78

V   Tension in England   95

VI   The Americas in alarm   105

VII   1941—Germany attacks again   121

VIII   The fixed image   134

PART TWO: REALITY

IX   Poland   147

X   Denmark and Norway   158

XI   Holland, Belgium, Luxemburg and France   182

XII   England and America   207

XIII   Yugoslavia, Greece, the Soviet Union   228

XIV   The military Fifth Column   241

CONTENTS

PART THREE: ANALYSIS

xv The imaginary Fifth Column   249

xvi Historical summary   267

Conclusion   295

Glossary of German terms   298

Acknowledgments   300

Index   303

List of Maps

facing page

German settlement-areas in Latin America 28

Poland, September, 1939: the German attack 40

Uruguay, May–June, 1940 112

German settlement-areas in the Soviet Union 128

Germany's territorial losses after the first World War 268

Survey of factors that can further the rise of a political Fifth Column among *volksdeutsche* groups (1933) 292

Part One

FEAR

The approach of disaster

★

B Y the end of September, 1936, the Civil War in Spain had been going on for two months. The generals who in mid-July had given the signal for revolt against the government had gained important victories. With Spanish Morocco as their base they had occupied large parts of Southern Spain. Along the Portuguese frontier they had gained a firm foothold too, as well as in Northern Spain. The improvised government armies suffered one defeat after another. The rebels were approaching Madrid and the Spanish capital was threatened with encirclement. On September 28 the rebels, who had defended themselves in the Alcazar of Toledo for seventy days on end, were relieved; once more a road to the heart of Spain seemed to lie open. From the south, the south-west, the west and the north-west General Franco launched his troops upon Madrid—*four* columns in all.

It was in those days, perhaps immediately after the relief of Toledo, perhaps on October 1 or 2, that one of the most prominent generals of the rebels, Emilio Mola, threateningly pointed to the operations of the four columns in a broadcast talk he gave, adding that the attack on the government centre would be opened by the *fifth* column which was already *in* Madrid. 'He will launch four columns against Madrid, says the traitor Mola, but it will be the fifth that shall start the offensive.' Thus the communist paper *Mundo Obrero* of October 3, 1936.[1]

---

[1] I have not been able to trace the exact date nor the precise text of General Mola's words. An examination of all the works by him and about him remained without result. From Spain I have received information that no positive indications could be found in the nationalist press of those days either. Spanish experts, however, believe that there is little reason to doubt that General Mola—who died on June 3, 1937—uttered words of the above mentioned purport.

In August and September Madrid had already been buzzing with the rumour that the country was being betrayed. Real or supposed supporters of General Franco had been arrested by the thousand. Communists, socialists and anarchists systematically worked through their lists of suspect persons. Every morning there were found in the streets the bodies of dozens of victims who had been killed in the night. But it seemed as if the danger from within could never be wholly warded off. In the hot month of August no one would enjoy the cool of the evening, it was too dangerous out in the streets, 'because especially in certain well-to-do quarters shots would suddenly ring out of the roof-tops; because ghost cars would suddenly appear round corners and fire a few rounds from sub-machine guns and disappear again'.[1] Rumours that the cause of the republic was in a bad way were general. It was as if they were systematically being circulated. Consequently General Mola's chance saying only brought the confirmation of uneasy conjectures: Franco then had his obviously organised support *in Madrid itself*—a 'fifth column'.

'His feline movements can be felt. . . . It is the enemy who must be destroyed forthwith,' cried La Pasionaria.[2] Whole series of house-to-house searches followed. From October 8 both active military officers and those on retirement pay were arrested in large numbers in any case where they were not fully trusted. People were continually urged to be on the alert against 'spies, scare-mongers, defeatists—those who, concealed in their hiding-places, are awaiting the order to rush out into the streets . . . the *quinta columna facciosa*'.[3]

In the last half of October the 'fifth column' had become a term in Spain that was continually being used by the republican press, particularly by the left-wing papers. Its origin had already been half forgotten; not quite a fortnight after General Mola's broadcast its paternity was attributed to General Queipo de Llano by a Madrid newspaper, and to General Franco by the correspondent of the London *Times*. The vagueness that continued to surround the term was an impetus to its employment rather than a hindrance. Did it not point to an intangible enemy? So great was the fear for this opponent that General Mola's carelessly uttered, business-like words—a numeral plus a military term—had immediately become charged with emotional force. The *accidental combination* 'fifth column' was raised to the *conception 'Fifth Column'*. It was as if people had been waiting for it.[4]

---

[1] John Langdon Davies: *Fifth Column* (London, 1940), pp. 6–7.

[2] *Mundo Obrero* (Madrid), Oct. 3, 1936.

[3] *Ibid.*, Oct. 15, 1936.

[4] In this same way four years previously two words from the peroration of a speech of Governor Franklin D. Roosevelt's, with which he accepted the democratic candidateship for the presidency ('I pledge you, I pledge myself to a new

If one should wish to write the history of the use of that conception, one would have to follow it in its tortuous, often hidden course, turning up now here, now there, alone or in combination with other similar terms—the 'Trojan horse', the 'Nazintern'. It seemed to smoulder on like a heath-fire. But in the year 1940, when the whole of the Western world was in a blaze, it suddenly flared up high and clear.

That it had smouldered on had been no accident.

The term 'Fifth Column' met a need which existed not only in republican Spain but also outside it. This need was felt among all those people who had felt themselves threatened, for almost four years, by the powers that supported Franco: national socialist Germany and fascist Italy.

Even before the term had come into being, the actions of people who would later be stamped with that highly unpleasant connotation had given rise to great uneasiness in many countries. In the states surrounding Germany it happened once or twice that German agents who had violated the frontiers did away with their enemies. The murder of Theodor Lessing, the distinguished scholar, at Marienbad in Czechoslovakia in August, 1933, had received particular attention. It was at that same time that people in Austria and outside it, at least in many chancelleries, were becoming gravely concerned about the acts of aggression committed by the Austrian national socialists against the Austrian state. There one outrage followed another, and week in and week out the fugitive Austrian party leaders of the illegal NSDAP made use of German broadcasting stations to call upon their people to rebel against the Dollfuss government. On July 25, 1934, not quite a month after the world had beheld with abhorrence how Hitler had disposed of a number of his supporters and a few of his hated adversaries, a *Putsch* was carried out in Vienna. It came to nothing, but the insurgents let the Austrian chancellor Dollfuss bleed to death, without granting him any medical aid or spiritual ministrations.

What was happening in the very heart of Europe?

What jungle manifested itself there?

Beyond the German frontiers people didn't worry about whether the Vienna rebels, such as Planetta and Holzweber, had acted on direct orders from Berlin and Munich. The complicity of the German *Reich* was evident. In the German capital, just before the rising, foreign correspondents had heard that something was brewing in Austria; a few days later they showed each other copies of the

deal for the American people') had developed into 'New Deal' without the author or the speaker wishing or so much as suspecting it. Samuel I. Rosenman: *Working with Roosevelt* (New York, 1952), pp. 71–2, 78–9.

Deutsche Presseklischeedienst (German Press Matrix Service) which, dated July 22, 1934—three days before the fighting in Vienna—had circulated pictures of the 'people's revolt in Austria'. 'Chancellor Dollfuss' it was printed, 'received serious injuries during the fights at the chancellery, which led to his death.'

Thorough German organization! The revolvers were not yet loaded —but the text for the picture of the victim had already been printed.

The Austrian rebellion was perhaps the most obvious, but certainly not the only symptom of the degree to which German national socialism had called into being in other countries organisations permeated by its aggressive spirit. There was hardly a country where the Germans, after 1933, did not unite under the sign of the swastika. That applies in the first place to the *Reichsdeutschen*, German nationals living abroad. These formed national socialist associations which were obviously in regular contact with a central agency in Germany, a body whose only function was to lead their activities, and which in 1934 assumed the name *Auslands-Organisation der NSDAP* (Foreign Organization of the NSDAP).

The nature of this contact was not made public—but nevertheless the newspapers frequently were able to publish items about the deportation by wakeful and suspicious governments of members of the *Auslands-Organisation*, usually on the grounds of having exercised unlawful pressure on some compatriots. National socialism apparently had introduced a new principle, demanding unconditional obedience from every German, wherever he be.

That was not the only danger threatening.

In all parts of the world there were millions of people of German origin, who, despite being nationals of the country they were living in, spoke German and still shared in German culture in many ways. Berlin called them *Volksdeutsche* (Minority Germans). National socialism proved able to get a hold on them quickly. Outside Germany more than one thousand five hundred newspapers using the German language appeared; very many of them commented with marked sympathy on Hitler's 'successes' in the field of foreign affairs. It was also reported that at an increasing number of German schools abroad—in 1936 there were about five thousand of them—the staff were instilling the pupils with a respectful devotion towards the *Führer*.

In the frontier regions which Germany had been forced to cede by the Treaty of Versailles, national socialism developed in strength. In 1935, in the Saar, a united front under the leadership of national socialists gained an overwhelming majority for going *heim ins Reich*, to the painful surprise of many people outside Germany. But even before then the French in Alsace, the Belgians in Eupen-Malmédy, the Danes in North Schleswig, the Poles in the Free State of Danzig, and the Lithuanians in Memel had been observing the growth of the national socialist organisations distrustfully. The Czechs in October, 1933, had banned the *Deutsche National-Sozialistische Arbeiterpartei* (German National Socialist Workers' Party), the DNSAP, which only differed from the party in Germany in the sequence of its initials; but soon they saw their three-and-a-half million Sudeten-Germans falling under the spell of a leader—Konrad Henlein—who, though protesting against being called a national socialist, had started a movement exactly resembling that self-same NSDAP, both in spirit and in organisation. The governments of Hungary, Rumania and Yugoslavia were not unaware of the increasing influence of the national socialist movement on the large German minorities in their countries. In 1933 such a movement in Rumania had already surpassed the old parties within the group of *Volksdeutsche* in that country.

Outside of Europe the same development could be observed.

Everywhere the swastika was being accepted by persons of German origin. Thus it was in South-West Africa, the only former German colony where a considerable number of Germans were still living; thus it was in Australia and New Zealand, where many German associations made Hitler a present on his first anniversary as State Chancellor, by uniting in the *Bund des Deutschtums in Australien and Neuseeland* (League of Germandom in Australia and New Zealand); thus it was particularly in the New World.

It looked as if the minds of all Germans the whole world over were being magnetically drawn towards the Third *Reich*. This impression was strongly encouraged by the German press. Proud of the response to the building up of the national socialist state amongst those who for years or decades had had no living contact with the country of their birth or that of their fathers, the press willingly published prosaic or poetic ebullitions praising the *Führer*:

> Where'er we Germans sing our verses under the wide firmament,
> There our call shall be resounding 'neath the foreign star-lit tent:
> Hail Thou, Hitler, Germany's Saviour, German star in need forlorn,
> Lead us through all stormy weather, till anew our Empire's born!

Thus it sounded from the Brazilian jungle in 1933.[1] And hardly three years later, just before General Mola called his Madrid 'fifth column' into action, the leader of the little group of national socialists in an East African village (Kitale, Kenya), at the annual congress of the *Auslands-Organisation*, 'with much applause' expressed his belief 'that the *Auslands-Organisation* would be the chosen instrument in

[1] *Der Auslanddeutsche* (Stuttgart), 1934, p. 12.

the *reichsdeutsche* orchestra on which the *Führer* would one day play a tremendous melody'.[1]

Generally speaking, before 1938 not much attention was paid to the spread of national socialism amongst the *Volks-* and *Reichsdeutschen* all over the world; but in one country after another a vague uneasiness grew, an irritated wondering as to the meaning of the symptoms of that aggressive spirit that manifested itself everywhere. True, in most countries the Germans constituted only relatively small minorities—but they were not the only groups threatening the existing order of society. Perhaps their growth would have remained almost unnoticed, but for the simultaneous development of 'indigenous' national socialist and fascist groups. Many of these had already started life in the twenties, but at the time they attracted little attention. The situation changed with the successful election campaign of the German NSDAP in 1930, when more than a hundred Nazis marched into the *Reichstag* with heavy step. Who had ever heard of Hitler? Who could remember the unsuccessful rebel of 1923? Now he was on the way to power in Germany.

His example had an inspiring effect on ambitious spirits: what was possible in Germany could also succeed in other countries. Even before Hitler (on January 30, 1933) made his entry into the Chancellery at Berlin, national socialist groups had been formed in a dozen countries and were aflame with the desire to conquer state power, convinced as they were of their ability to demolish the crumbling citadels of democracy with their small bands of picked and sworn followers. Eagerly they accepted the symbols of the German NSDAP: top-boot, shirt and swastika. In Sweden, the *Svenska National-socialistika Partiet* demonstrated under flags adorned with the swastika just as fervently as, in Denmark, the *Danmarks National Socialistika Arbejder Parti*, in the Netherlands the *Nationaal-socialistische Nederlandse Arbeiderspartij*, in France the Breton fascists, in England the Imperial Fascist League, in Latvia the 'Thundercrosses', in Hungary the *Magyar Nemzeti Szocialista Párt* (Hungarian national socialist party), in Rumania the 'Iron Guard'. As a mass, as a united front, they were by no means a negligible power. Although in many cases democracy retaliated by banning demonstrations and the wearing of uniforms and by prohibiting membership in such organisations for civil servants, in many countries an aspiring dictator succeeded in surpassing his competitors. Often with the support of parts of the anti-socialist bourgeoisie, such men could quickly build up a movement about which nobody could forecast whether it could soon be brought to a stand. Surly malcontents and short-sighted idealists would swell the ranks, and membership leaped up by

[1] *Fränkische Tageszeitung* (Nuremberg), Sept. 5, 1936.

8

tens and even hundreds of thousands. In the middle of the thirties there was anxiety in some circles in the Netherlands about the headway that Anton Mussert was making, in Belgium about Léon Degrelle, in Britain about Sir Oswald Mosley, in France about Colonel de la Rocque.

The 'fifth column' concept had then not yet been visualised, but fear of Hitler himself and of his followers and imitators abroad already existed. People were apprehensive of the activity of German national socialists in their countries just because such agents were organising the Germans living there in semi-military bodies, setting an inspiring example in this way for the indigenous enemies of democracy with whom—there could be no doubt—they apparently maintained a close co-operation.

Many governments took action against *Reichsdeutsche* who had misused the hospitality of their state, had them deported, and also in other ways attempted to stem the tide of activity of the German national socialists.

In order not to offend Germany unnecessarily, conflicts of this nature were usually treated behind closed doors. But even in the first years of the Third *Reich* incidents occurred in several widely separated countries, which—although not creating such a shock of horror in the civilised world as the murder of Dollfuss—attracted attention in many quarters, because they showed up the *internal* workings of the contacts Berlin maintained with the Germans abroad.

In South-West Africa the mandatory South African authorities had already noticed that *Reichs-* and *Volksdeutsche* were organising on a national socialist basis, with the special aim of having that former German colony given back to Germany. In the summer of 1934 an end was made to this activity. On July 11 it was decided to ban the *Hitler-Jugend* (Hitler Youth) and the next day a raid was carried out on the party offices of the *Auslands-Organisation*, where a great quantity of documents were confiscated. Their contents spoke for themselves. Four months later the NSDAP was declared illegal in South-West Africa. As the authorities announced,

the party strove to unite all the German-speaking people in the struggle for the realisation of the programme of the NSDAP with the aim of controlling the political and intellectual life of the German-speaking group. This aim was to be gained by ensuring that national socialists be placed in all strategic posts of the political, church and educative organisations. Resistance was energetically repressed by using every legal and illegal form of pressure, and this was made possible by an extensive system of espionage.[1]

[1] *Lüderitzbuchter Zeitung*, Nov. 27, 1934.

Another country where the growling of the approaching thunderstorm was to be heard—vaguely as yet, and far-off, but discernible to many—was Lithuania.

In 1923 the Memel territory, mainly inhabited by Germans, had been annexed by Lithuania. There, in 1933, two competing national socialist movements had seen the light of day; one was called: *Christlich-Sozialistische Arbeitsgemeinschaft* (Christian Socialist Action), the CSA, and the other: *Sozialistische Volksgemeinschaft* (Socialist Community) or *Sovog* for short. The latter was the stronger of the two.

Both movements, with a deadly hatred for one another, had their own SA organisations, whose members drilled on German territory and practised espionage in Lithuania. They lived with daggers drawn.

But there was more.

Before a court of law in Kaunas a sworn statement was read, dated January, 1934, which revealed that functionaries of the *Sovog* had at that time been instructed to keep themselves in readiness 'in order to join up with the SA units which were expected from Germany within a few days'.[1] Weapons had been confiscated belonging to members of both the CSA and the *Sovog*.

Partly because of the fierce German reactions this affair attracted international attention. Lithuania, however, was a far-off country—except perhaps for the Latvians, Estonians and Poles, who were similarly having trouble with their German minorities; and the names of all those organisations were so confusing! But in the same month which witnessed these trials in the little Baltic state, a simple case of political kidnapping happened in Switzerland, which attracted much more widespread attention.

A well-known German refugee, Dr. Berthold Jacob, who as a journalist had for two years been denouncing German secret rearmament, suddenly disappeared during a visit to Basle. His friends warned the police. Jacob had kept company in Basle with another refugee, Dr. Hans Wesemann. Dr. Wesemann was arrested, and confessed to having organised and put through Jacob's abduction, in collaboration with the *Geheime Staatspolizei*—Gestapo! terrifying name at that time! Everything had happened on Swiss territory. For months news of this affair appeared in the press. The Swiss government finally succeeded in its attempt to have Jacob released. But who would be the next victim of the long-tentacled octopus operating from—where? The Columbia-House in Berlin? Fearful conjecture surrounded that term.

Less than a year after Jacob's abduction the attention of all the

---

[1] *Vier Dokumente zum Prozess Neumann, Von Sass und Genossen* (Kaunas, 1934), p. 16.

countries of the West was again drawn to the work of the Nazi organisations outside Germany by another incident in Switzerland. On February 4, 1936, Wilhelm Gustloff, leader of the *Landesgruppe* (Country group) in Switzerland of the *Auslands-Organisation der NSDAP*, was fatally shot by a Hungarian-born Jewish student, David Frankfurter, at Davos. Frankfurter's object was to demonstrate against the increasing persecution of the Jews in Germany, where, in September 1935, the so-called Nuremberg laws had been promulgated. The remarkable thing was, however, that the measures taken by the Swiss government after the assassination were directed against the *Landesgruppe*. The Swiss had had enough of German interference in their country. A fortnight after the murder all organisations of the NSDAP in Switzerland were banned. The German government lodged a protest; the Swiss government ignored it.

These and like reports and disclosures were not, in 1936 and 1937, usually seen in their generic relationships. There was, moreover, so much other news to read in the papers. The reports on the Berlin Olympic Games or the abdication-crisis in Britain were so much more interesting. Nevertheless it was in 1933 and following years that the foundations were laid for the steadily growing spectral structure of fear. Each of the above-mentioned incidents, every flaunting demonstration on the part of German or other national socialists, caused a slight repercussion. The increasing insecurity of life became more noticeable. What, exactly, was brewing? What ends were being served by all those plots?

Many people in other countries had no illusions as to what was happening in Germany itself. The German and translated editions of the *Braunbuch über Reichstagsbrand und Hitlerterror* (Brown Book on the Reichstag fire and on Nazi terrorism) had sold in tens of thousands. Socialists and communists knew that their German party comrades were undergoing torture in the concentration camps; pressure on the churches increased with the growth of a new paganism, and both Protestants and Catholics were well aware of this; to the tyranny of the national socialist state every refugee—Jew or Gentile —could testify, and their number topped 350,000 in 1938. But who, privileged by being able to lead a normal life outside Germany, came to the conclusion, because of all this, that his own existence was at stake? Who realised that the internal aggressiveness of national socialism must almost unavoidably lead to external aggression?

Most people dared not, *could* not realise this.

But there were others.

From 1933 onward voices were calling in the wilderness of indifference and self-deception. Not all such voices were addressed to the great masses, however. There were diplomats whose reports were full of warnings. Then, a number of publications appeared demonstrating not only the aggressive nature of the national socialist state, but also its intrigues in other countries. In France, in November 1933, the newspaper *Petit Parisien* created a sensation by publishing the contents of documents smuggled out of Germany by communists, containing a campaign plan for extensive German propaganda in the Americas. This propaganda was to be partly veiled; confidential agents were to cover that area; statistics were to be gathered of the degree in which the newspapers published news from Germany; a 'neutral' news agency was to be started with a view to the distribution of pro-German news; bogus news items were to be passed on to anti-German journalists, to compromise them; articles were to be distributed to the agents to be offered by them for publication, if needs be with the use of bribes, to all the newspapers from the Rio Grande to the Strait of Magellan. In this way public opinion was to be influenced to bring pressure on the governments of Central and South America, so that these would not hinder Germany in her attempt to recover territories with a German minority.

Political refugees were active as well. They passed on their warnings as and where they could—in Prague, Amsterdam, London, Paris. They collected information everywhere; a life-and-death struggle was carried on against Gestapo agents like Wesemann; attempts were made to get at the roots of every German intrigue and to uncover them; and finally, in 1935, a survey of all the German machinations in Europe was published in book form in Paris: *Das Braune Netz. Wie Hitlers Agenten im Ausland arbeiten und den Krieg vorbereiten.* (The Brown Network. The activities abroad of Hitler's agents and their preparation of war).

This book sketched the espionage being practised by 48,000 agents; it mentioned the minutes of a meeting held in March, 1935, at which Himmler had been present, 'attended by all the leading Gestapo functionaries concerned in work abroad';[1] those minutes made mention of 2,450 paid, and more than 20,000 'honorary' agents. It told also of German propaganda and of the work of a new, almost unknown institution: The *Aussenpolitische Amt der NSDAP* (Foreign-political office of the NSDAP), which, under the leadership of Alfred Rosenberg, chief editor of the *Völkischer Beobachter*, collaborated with international anti-semitic organisations and minority movements which undermined the position of other governments. It mentioned that the *Auslands-Organisation der NSDAP* had 400 local branches, called *Ortsgruppen* (local groups), all over the world.

---

[1] *Das Braune Netz. Wie Hitlers Agenten im Ausland arbeiten und den Krieg vorbereiten* (Paris, 1935), pp. 22–3.

It pointed to the *Verein für das Deutschtum im Ausland* (Association for Germandom abroad)—a body offering membership to all those Germans at home who were interested in the fate of Germans beyond the frontiers—which stood in regular communication with 'more than 8,000 German schools abroad' and counted 'more than 24,000' local groups.[1] It sketched the similar work of the *Deutsche Akademie* (German Academy) and the *Deutsches Ausland-Institut* (German Institute for Foreign Countries). It estimated that the Third *Reich* spent more than 250,000,000 *Reichsmark* on propaganda and espionage abroad.

It recounted cases of 'denunciation, provocation, abduction, murder, arms smuggling, assault, sabotage and economic espionage'. It described the German work of undermining the states in Northern, Eastern, Southern and Western Europe, alluded to Austria as the battlefield of the German *Reich*, considered Yugoslavia to be threatened by 'so-called tourists and terrorists'. It paid attention to the White Russian and national socialist actions in North and South America. It concluded with a list of 590 'propagandists, agents, informers and spies of the Nazis abroad', giving their names and functions.

All that work abroad was directed from one centre, according to *Das Braune Netz*. Its editors had made an impressive schematic diagram of the organisation of this work, as far as the political part was concerned. This showed how Hitler and the *Reichsleitung der NSDAP* (Party Directorate of the NSDAP)—themselves influenced by the vested interests of the captains of industry and the big landowners—were keeping in touch either directly or indirectly (through a liaison staff directed by Rudolf Hess) with twelve sub-centres which in their turn contacted clubs, local groups, schools, churches and agents:

In looking at the work they do abroad, or at the organ that conducts these efforts, it at first seems as if there was only a striving at cross-purposes, or even an utter confusion. In looking closer, however, it appears that these exertions that are seemingly at variance, are in reality part of a carefully thought-out and organised system. Certainly after the coming to power of national socialism ample time had been needed for all the institutions and organisations serving the work abroad to become properly linked up, before the exertion of labour in all the parts of this gigantic net had been co-ordinated. Since the middle of 1934, however, this has been fully achieved.[2]

The Germans certainly knew how to organise!

[1] *Ibid.*, pp. 66–7.   [2] *Ibid.*, p. 15.

A year after the copies of *Das Braune Netz* had come from the presses, civil war started in Spain. War was approaching Europe. Machine-guns were rattling now, not in the far-off valleys of the Yellow River or Yangtse-kiang, but along the banks of the Ebro; bombs were being dropped, not on Nanking, but on Guernica; not Shanghai, but Almeria was being shelled. Fear of a spreading of the conflagration grew in Europe. Many people had no doubts about Hitler's and Mussolini's direct intervention in Spain; others regarded the assistance given to the Spanish government by Stalin a greater danger. These others—mostly adherents of parties of the right, often Catholics—tended to regard the communist menace, at least as far as Western Europe was concerned, as greater than that from national socialism. During the furious struggle raging about whether republican Spain was to be given aid, which almost led to civil war in France, these others had no ear for talk about German intervention.

Proof of such intervention was not, however, lacking. In Barcelona and some other republican-held cities archives of the *Auslands-Organisation der NSDAP* were seized during the first days of the civil war. They contained thousands of documents. A small group of German anarchists started sorting them, and in 1937 the *Schwarz-Rotbuch—Dokumente über den Hitler-Imperialismus* (Black-Redbook —Documents on Hitler's imperialism) was published.

Of the documents more than 150 were printed in facsimile. Again the propaganda and espionage activities of the officials of the *Auslands-Organisation* were disclosed in all their ramifications; passages were quoted which proved, according to the editors, that several of those officials had been involved in Franco's revolt; methods by which their work was camouflaged were revealed; it was demonstrated that the German Nazis had had a 'Harbour Service' at their disposal, an organisation which served to smuggle national socialist propaganda into Spain, and in several specified cases had forcibly taken victims of the Gestapo aboard German ships.

The documents were damning proof. A second edition, in German, was published in Paris, an English edition in London. The general public, perhaps, was not much roused, but in police and judicial circles and in the secret services of many countries the publications were seriously studied. It was not often that one's enemy dropped a card; now his full hand had fallen on the table.

The increasingly obvious activity abroad of the national socialists, accentuated by such revelations as were contained in *Das Braune Netz* and the *Schwarz-Rotbuch*, caused people in many countries to regard all activity by Germans with gradually growing suspicion. Why should this sinister work of terrorisation and espionage be limited to Spain? Was there a single country where Hitler's agents were *not* abetting his preparations for an offensive? Surely the signs were discernible everywhere! In Denmark it appeared that the president of the German club in Copenhagen, Schäfer, had sent the members a questionnaire, in March, 1936, asking, amongst other things, how many cars, motor-cycles and motor-vans they had at their disposal. One of the thirty-seven other questions was: 'Do you possess a typewriter? Can you write shorthand?'

These questions may look innocent on the other side of the Atlantic, but they are not, for in the accepted Nazi jargon a typewriter is a gun and shorthand means shooting. Another of *Herr* Schäfer's 'enquiries' concerned his followers' knowledge of Danish lighthouses, their position and manning, the easiest way to approach them, etc.

These accusatory remarks were not quoted from a penny-pictorial. They were expressed a year after the outbreak of hostilities in Spain, in an authoritative American periodical in the field of contemporary history, *Foreign Affairs*.[1]

At about the same time there was some commotion in Norway on account of a disclosure in a socialist newspaper, to the effect that in 1935 a German Nazi, an enthusiastic visitor of Northern Norway, had been allowed to take photographs of soldiers of the 'Nordic type' on the principal military drill-grounds near the economically and strategically important port of Narvik. What had that German been up to? Why had the military commander, Lieutenant-Colonel Sundlo, given him permission? Was this Sundlo perhaps a supporter of the national socialist Quisling movement? A board of enquiry could find no grounds for these suspicions.

It is characteristic that although the *Auslands-Organisation der NSDAP* had organised demonstrative congresses in 1934, 1935 and 1936, the congress held in August, 1937, was the first to be covered by the international press.

Earlier in the year *The Times* had already commented on 'the first spectacular invasion by the National Socialist Party into the Conservative sanctuary of the Foreign Office'.[2] The head of the *Auslands-Organisation der NSDAP*, Ernst Wilhelm Bohle, had been appointed 'head of the *Auslands-Organisation* in the German Foreign Office'. The aim was 'to promote uniformity in the care for German nationals abroad'. In this new function Bohle was to be directly responsible only to the Minister, then Baron von Neurath; when

[1] Joachim Joesten: 'The Nazis in Scandinavia', *Foreign Affairs* (New York), XV, 4 (July, 1937).
[2] *The Times* (London), Feb. 3, 1937.

matters touching on his field of work came before the German cabinet, he was, however, to attend its meetings. This was ordained by Hitler by special decree of January 30, 1937.

What did his promotion signify?

For those people outside Germany who had been observing the work of the *Auslands-Organisation*, the matter was clear enough. The organiser of propaganda and espionage, intimidation and abduction had been appointed to the dignified Foreign Ministry, on the one hand to clean up amongst the gentlemen of the *Wilhelmstrasse* and the German foreign service, on the other to extend and intensify subversive work abroad under cover of diplomatic privilege.

In a pamphlet on the work of the *Auslands-Organisation* published in Germany at the time, it was stated, as if quite commonplace, that its office employed 700 persons;[1] abroad, the number of local groups and cells had reached 548.[2] The foremost socialist newspaper in the Netherlands wrote, in connection with this pamphlet, that 'in the regional groups' outside Germany 'about 3,000,000 Germans were enrolled'.[3]

Again: it was only a select few who noted these and similar facts. Most people simply could not comprehend in what an unconscionably subtle and cunning way they were being taken in. No other adventurer in the whole of world history had ever drawn so heavily on the bank where people, high and low alike, had deposited so much of their credulity and of their simple honesty. Alarmist agitators were kept out. Hermann Rauschning, who had moved in the highest Nazi circles for some years and whose eyes had been opened to the depravity of the leaders and their system, had finished a big manuscript in April, 1937, named: 'The Revolution of Nihilism'. This was after he had fled from Danzig. It took him a year to find a publisher for it. During that year many of the articles he wrote 'were returned with the comment that his disclosures were too fantastic to be true'.[4]

That a Swiss publishing firm dared to risk the publication of Rauschning's sharp analysis in 1938 was no accident.

The international atmosphere had undergone a decisive change. Hitler had marched into Austria.

People were startled when in the middle of February, 1938 the news came that the Austrian Chancellor, Kurt von Schuschnigg, had visited Berchtesgaden, where he had had a prolonged interview with Hitler. The communiqué that was published on the 13th of that

---

[1] Dr. Emil Ehrich: *Die Auslands-Organisation der NSDAP* (Berlin, 1937), p. 10.
[2] *Ibid.*, p. 11.
[3] *Het Volk* (Amsterdam), July 30, 1937.
[4] Hans L. Leonhardt: *Nazi conquest of Danzig* (Chicago, 1942), p. 225.

month appeared unimportant, but those who were familiar with Austrian relations, cocked their ears when a few days later the news came through that the Austrian ministry of the interior (which also saw to police affairs) was to be occupied by Dr. Arthur Seyss-Inquart. Seyss-Inquart, a Viennese barrister, was an advocate of the *Anschluss*. Scarcely had he been appointed to his new function when he paid a visit to Berlin, where he had a talk with Hitler. In Austria tension increased; the national socialists demonstrated more and more openly and flagrantly. Outside Austria there was no more than a vague unrest here and there. Even the news that came on Wednesday, March 9, to the effect that Schuschnigg was going to hold a plebiscite on the forthcoming Sunday when people were to pronounce for or against an independent Austria, was still not felt as evidence that a life-and-death struggle was going on behind the scenes.

On Friday, March 11, the outbreak came.

It was broadcast from Vienna at 6 o'clock in the evening that the plebiscite had been called off. At a quarter to eight Schuschnigg spoke. 'In the hearing of the whole world I declare,' thus his voice rang out, 'that the German government has to-day handed Federal President Miklas an ultimatum with a fixed time limit, ordering the nomination for Chancellor of a person designated by the German government, who was to form a cabinet satisfactory to that government; if this did not happen, then German troops would march into Austria.'

It was bewildering.

Later in the evening Vienna broadcast the news that a new government had been formed under the leadership of Seyss-Inquart, while Berlin announced that Seyss-Inquart had 'urgently' requested the German government in a telegram to Hitler—whom he designated as *Führer*—to assist him in maintaining order and quiet, and to send German troops 'as soon as possible'.

Those German troops marched into Austria on Saturday, March 12. A day later the *Anschluss* was a fact.

Once more Hitler had accomplished his purpose! Once more the swastika had triumphed! Once more tens of thousands of the opponents of national socialism, Jews and non-Jews alike, would be in danger! The feelings thus aroused found a focal point of spontaneous loathing for the treachery committed by one: Seyss-Inquart. His name became synonymous with traitor. However, in Austria it had also been possible to see for the first time and at its best the *technique* of an attack that started in the very heart of the country itself. So that was how they acted abroad, those Nazis! First they occupied strategic points in the apparatus of government, then they

17

undermined the whole state, and finally they forced a crisis in order to call in German troops by means of a pre-arranged telegram.

That one telegram of Seyss-Inquart's, in March, 1938, aroused more fear of the German Fifth Column than all the hundreds of documents that had been published in the years following 1933. Those documents had been written about in books that were little read and in press reports that had more often than not been passed over. But the conquest of Austria was front-page news—in Norway as well as in the Argentine, in the Netherlands as well as in Greenland. And this conquest had settled the matter. What had failed in countries like Lithuania, South Africa and Spain had succeeded in Austria. The danger that had developed into a catastrophe on the Danube had in former cases perhaps only been narrowly escaped. By simply pressing a button Hitler had wiped out the free state of Austria; were there elsewhere supporters as inconspicuous and unknown as that barrister from Vienna, digging fresh tunnels and laying fresh mines?

The answer to that question was not long in coming.

In Czechoslovakia, as has already been shown, a gymnastics teacher, Konrad Henlein, had succeeded in building up a political movement, the *Sudetendeutsche Partei* (Sudeten German Party). Two out of three Sudeten Germans had voted for its candidates at the election in May, 1935. Henlein had always contested the view that he had any connections with Berlin.

But what could be seen in 1938?

Hardly six weeks after the *Anschluss* of Austria that same Henlein came out with new demands in Karlsbad. These, if they were acceded to, would mean giving autonomy to the Sudeten Germans within the framework of the Czechoslovakian state in exactly those frontier districts where the Czechs had set up their fortifications. Henlein called on Hitler several times. Henlein continually made new claims in the almost endless negotiations with the Czechs. Henlein went to the party congress of the NSDAP at Nuremberg, and finally it was Henlein who fled to Germany when a revolt broke out against the Czechs in the Sudeten area by the middle of September; who called upon the three and a half million Sudeten Germans to rise in a general revolt; and who, so the German press and radio proclaimed, was forming a volunteer corps of Sudeten Germans for the military struggle against the Czechoslovakian republic—citizens of that republic, now its armed aggressors.

Henlein's function of political weapon in Hitler's hand attracted greater attention in 1938 than the launching of the revolt, the summons to rebel and the forming of the volunteer corps. Those events, which fell between September 13 and 16, were ousted from the front

18

pages of most papers and from the minds of most people by the all-important question: peace or war?

On Wednesday, September 28, war seemed inescapable. In France the arterial roads leading from Paris to the west showed a continuous stream of cars. A third of the population left the French capital.

In England gas-masks were being distributed, trenches were being dug in the parks, children were being evacuated; the first anti-aircraft guns stuck their pointed barrels into the air to defend London's nine millions against an attack which, according to the official estimate, would take a toll of fifteen thousand human lives in the very first days.

Four weeks later thousands of people on the other side of the Atlantic ran into the streets when a play was broadcast describing the landing of 'strange creatures, men from Mars, armed with deadly rays'; 'panic swept that night across the length and breadth of the United States'.[1] There once again, in a whirlpool of emotions, the fear that lay at the bottom of the soul had become visible.

The Munich Agreement had saved world peace. All that had gone before, however, had undermined people's belief in the *maintenance* of peace. By no means everyone would admit this, either to others or to himself. With an obstinate mixture of short-sightedness and despair some insisted that the fall of Czechoslovakia had been a turn for the better. 'Peace in our time'—with that slogan the English Prime Minister had come back from Munich. Three weeks later the world's most widely circulated daily paper prophesied 'that Britain will not be involved in a European war this year or next year either'.[2]

During the last months of 1938 and the first of 1939 the weight of events and the growing pressure Hitler brought to bear on the Western democracies had driven dissension to its highest pitch. 'Appeasers' and 'warmongers' fought each other with such fierceness that it was as if they had the real enemy bodily before them. Their struggle was in fact settled by Hitler himself when he marched into Prague on March 15, 1939.

Anschluss—Munich—Prague—war; three periods of about six months lay between each of those terms. They were the last milestones on the road covered between Hitler's coming to power and the outbreak of the second World War.

During that last year and a half a decisive change had set in, here stronger and there weaker. The uneasiness about *distant* wars

[1] Whitney H. Shepardson and William O. Scroggs: *The United States in World Affairs. An account of American foreign relations, 1938* (New York, 1939), pp. 2–4.

[2] *Daily Express* (London), Oct. 19, 1938.

19

(Manchuria, Abyssinia, Spain) made way in many nations for fear of one *near at hand*—the war in which people themselves would be involved, the new slaughter, the Armageddon, a *repetition* of the wholesale slaughter of 1914-18, made even more atrocious by the progress of technical science. The determination that had grown in the course of 1939 had as its counterpart fear of war—fear especially for the new and the unknown.

It seemed as if Hitler was always a jump ahead. He used means unknown to others, and he had applied a new method: the Fifth Column. Conquests for which others before him had needed armies and fleets he succeeded in gaining as if in play, by penetration through agents, by treachery in the country itself. Spies and political saboteurs were apparently his strongest soldiers. In what countries were they *not* burrowing? Everywhere lived German nationals, of whom in August, 1938, Bohle stated in public and 'with pride' that they 'formed a close following of national socialism and its *Führer*'.[1] Such utterances, listened to carefully by the secret services, escaped the observation of the public in the countries outside Germany. But in 1938 and 1939 other reports were to be found in the press, and many people drew the conclusion from them which the head of the *Auslands-Organisation der NSDAP* had put into words in his own way.

In September, 1938, a German photographer was arrested in Switzerland who had photographed other Germans on the sly while they were reading anti-national socialist papers. At least one of these had been arrested on his return to Germany.

In Sweden the minister for Foreign Affairs disclosed four weeks after the anti-Jewish pogrom in Germany (November 10, 1938) that German firms in Sweden were trying to oust Jews from economic life and that information was secretly being collected about the composition of their capital and personnel. This 'mercantile espionage' had also occurred, according to Mr. Sandler, in the Netherlands, Belgium and Switzerland.

Likewise in December, 1938, four Germans were sentenced in New York for military espionage; the most important of them had got away to Germany.

At the end of April, 1939, three Nazis were deported from England, and at the end of May six more, most of them officials of the *Auslands-Organisation*.

The correspondent of the *Völkischer Beobachter* in Cairo had to leave Egypt, and similarly the leader of the German colony in Bagdad had to leave Iraq.

The Brussels correspondent of the *Rheinisch-Westfälische Zeitung*

[1] Speech in Stuttgart, Aug. 28, 1938, *Jahrbuch für Auswärtige Politik*, V (Berlin, 1939), p. 24.

was deported from Belgium, likewise in the beginning of May. He had caused à scandal through appearing as a speaker at a meeting of German miners, working in Belgium, of whom a few had turned up in white socks—the symbol of Henlein's followers!

France, which had prohibited all national socialist organisations in Alsace at the end of April, 1939 (their leader, Dr. Karl Roos, had been arrested in February), deported the leading officials of the *Landesgruppe* of the *Auslands-Organisation*. On July 1 all the various party formations were disbanded. A few weeks later the chief of the news service of *Le Temps*, France's foremost daily paper, together with a member of the board of directors of *Le Figaro* were arrested. Had they been spying for Germany? This was generally assumed to be behind the action.

In that same summer great unrest arose in the Argentine through the publication of a document which seemed to point to Germany's wishing to occupy Patagonia by surprise, and on the East coast of the Southern Atlantic the South African government apparently trusted the Germans in South-West Africa so little that an armed police force was sent to the mandated territory.

Finally in Palestine, where German Nazis seemed to work in ever closer contact with Arabian terrorists, a German farmer (the Germans had a number of agricultural colonies there) complained in public of being 'constantly watched by a net of spies and Nazi officials'.[1]

The carryings-on of Seyss-Inquart and Henlein had the effect of making such reports which formerly would probably have been negligently passed over, front page news. Reporters, editors and the newspaper-reading public became more and more convinced of the existence of a spying German Fifth Column. It was particularly the New York trial that caught the full limelight. And who at that trial had been mixed up in espionage? A doctor, a steward, a translator, a corporal, an administrator, the proprietress of a rest-home, a woman hairdresser, a waiter, a technician, a designer—all inconspicuous people. A film was made of their cunning trade which drew an audience of millions. The chief detective of the Federal Bureau of Investigation wrote a book of breath-taking suspense devoted to how they traced these people. One could read in it how one of the organisers of the net of spies, a certain Dr. Ignaz Griebl, had confessed that the secrets of the American naval plans had been known in Germany 'before some of our high-ranking Navy officers knew them'; 'Griebl was able to describe in detail to me the U.S. Navy's plans for a fleet of new destroyers—their designs, tonnage, power, armament, and so forth—and when we checked up with the Navy

[1] *Palestine Post* (Jerusalem), Aug. 17, 1939.

Department there was great consternation, because Griebl was absolutely right!'[1] It was uncanny.

In Europe numerous books came out in which the authors summed up all the data that had appeared thus far about the Fifth Column, adding new disclosures. In Paris a writer recalled Himmler's twenty thousand agents; according to him Nazi 'tourists' had made secret arms dumps in Palestine; in France they worked with secret transmitters, some so small 'that they could easily be put into a waistcoat pocket or a coat pocket'.[2] A second French author said that there were Nazi agents 'of as many sorts as there were insects'.[3] A third Frenchman, still revelling in the beauty of a particular German spy—*une tendre jeune fille, si douce, si rêveuse, si innocente, si 'gemütlich'*—gave it as his opinion that the Third *Reich* had an army outside the Fatherland of 'twenty million Germans'.[4]

An English writer was able to say that in Northern Schleswig estates were being bought up by the Germans and that wells were being poisoned. And according to him there were 30,000 'avowed Nazis' in one state of Canada alone.[5] London's most widely read evening paper reported that 400 Gestapo agents were at work in England. Among them were Jewish refugees.[6] Throughout England there were rumours to the effect that German maid-servants had been smuggled into the houses of high-placed officers and civil servants as spies. Even the German boys who had visited English youth hostels in 1938 aroused suspicion. Some believed they had come to size up strategic points in order to map them.

Were there readers who shook their heads incredulously on reading some of these reports and opinions?

Perhaps.

There were certainly many more who accepted them without criticism. The shudders caused by all this mysteriousness repelled, but at the same time held the fancy. And what reason was there to doubt, after having beheld the fatal hollowing out of Austria and Czechoslovakia? The underhand plots that had been contrived there, the penetration that had been carried out, the internal aggression that had been practised—it was all looked upon in terms of the whole world.

This also held good for that part of the earth that was separated

[1] Léon G. Turrou: *The Nazi Spy Conspiracy in America* (London, 1939), p. 129–30. [2] Pierre Dehillotte: *Gestapo* (Paris, 1939), p. 83.
[3] Bertrand Gauthier: *La cinquième colonne contre la paix du monde* (Paris, 1938), p. 73.
[4] Paul Allard: *Quand Hitler espionne la France* (Paris, 1939), p. 98, p. 13.
[5] F. Elwyn Jones: *The Attack from Within* (London, 1939), p. 106.
[6] *Evening Standard* (London), Feb. 16, 1939.

from Europe, and so from Germany, by the full breadth of the Atlantic: America.

In the United States large groups of the population had reacted with great fierceness to the Nazi régime from 1933 onwards.

Nazis and fascists, like the communists, were considered to be un-American. There were plenty of fascist organisations, however. There was no part of the country where some warped character did not push its way to the fore in the shape of an ambitious little *Führer*. By the end of 1938 'at least 800' organisations could be pointed to 'which might be called pro-fascist or pro-Nazi', and they 'all sing the same tune—words and music by Adolph Hitler, orchestration by Dr. Paul Joseph Goebbels'.[1] They aroused a good deal of resistance.

That applied with even more reason to those organisations which were not only fascist but German as well. In Chicago a sort of SA had sprung up as far back as the twenties. After Hitler's coming to power, New York became the centre of a movement in which German nationals as well as American citizens of German origin took part. At first they formed what was called the Friends of the New Germany, later the German American *Bund*. This *Bund* was an exact replica of the German NSDAP. It developed considerable activity in 1937–8 that testified to a fanatic national socialist obsession. 'We stand here as the heralds of the Third *Reich*, as preachers of the German world-viewpoint of national socialism, which has displayed before the eyes of the world the incomparable German miracle, the miracle of national socialism.'

That might be read in the 1937 Year Book of the *Bund*.[2]

The authorities had not let the totalitarian threat pass unnoticed.

As soon as the American government saw that German nationals were developing unlawful activities in connection with the *Auslands-Organisation* of the NSDAP they protested. If the republic had ever allowed visitors or immigrants to keep up political connections with their mother country, then the quarrels of Europe and Asia would have been fought out anew on American soil. The German government promised to mend its ways. To that end the German ambassador was empowered in 1933 to inform President Roosevelt, in the name of Rudolf Hess (who deputised for Hitler in party matters) 'that the local groups of the *Auslands-Organisation* that have existed so far are disbanded, and that henceforth not a single party organ

---

[1] From a report of the Institute for Propaganda Analysis, quoted by Alfred McClung Lee: 'Subversive individuals of minority status', *Annals of the American Academy of political and social sciences* (Philadelphia), Sept. 1942, p. 164.

[2] Quoted in: *The German Reich and Americans of German origin* (New York, 1938), p. 42.

shall exist, neither for *Reichsdeutsche* nor for *Volksdeutsche*'. By the latter term were meant American citizens of German origin.[1]

There was no trace, meanwhile, of any real disbanding of the party apparatus. The ignorance of and contempt for the United States that characterized the Nazi leaders gave them the assurance that they might permit themselves any and every freedom of corruption and deception.

The exposure began in 1934.

In March of that year the House of Representatives decided to call into existence a committee of enquiry in order, among other things, to take stock of the 'extent, character and objects of Nazi propaganda activities in the United States'. Representative Mc-Cormack of Massachusetts was the chairman. Representative Dickstein of New York, member and also initiator, was its driving force. In Washington, New York, Chicago, Los Angeles and two other places the McCormack committee interrogated some hundreds of witnesses. The most important refused to answer, however. Many of the archives of incriminated organisations appeared to be burnt. Nevertheless, the committee was able to give an impressive picture in its report, published in the beginning of January, 1935, of the subversion that was going on. They recommended a few useful preventive measures.

Congress ignored these recommendations.

But not everyone was caught napping.

Anti-fascist organisations remained vigilant. A few private investigators like Richard Rollins and John Roy Carlson fearlessly cleared a way through the emotional wilderness of American fascism, reporting on it in periodicals and books. At every step they encountered German influences, the Nazi party, the *Bund*, that mysterious centre for anti-Jewish propaganda, the Erfurter *Weltdienst*, Rosenberg's nasty internationals, the Hamburg *Fichtebund*—all of them influences exercised on German nationals, Italian fascists,

---

[1] Ambassador Thomsen to *Staatssekretär* Weizsäcker, Oct. 20, 1940. Nuremberg document NG-4416, p. 4. The indication 'Nuremberg document' will henceforth be left out in the references to documents submitted to the International Military Tribunal and the American Military Tribunals, Nuremberg. The documents for the prosecution are identified by one or more capitals (for instance: L, C, NG, NO, PS, NOKW) followed by a number. The documents for the defence are identified with the name of the accused on whom they have a bearing, followed by a number (for instance: Krupp-25). There is hardly a subject concerning the Nazi régime about which a wealth of unique data cannot be found in these extensive collections, especially those of the American Military Tribunals. The trial against the German diplomats (Weizsäcker *et al.*, 'Case XI') was of most use to me. The trials against Flick *et al.* ('Case V') and against the directors of *I.G. Farben* ('Case VI') and of Krupp ('Case X') threw light on the intricate relations between national socialism and German big business.

White Russians, anti-semites, members of the Ku-Klux-Klan, 'Knights' of various 'orders', 'Aryans' and Catholic and Protestant extremists. The queerest birds of the most diverse kinds twittered in that wilderness, but it was a harmony of hate that rose up out of their throats.

In May, 1938, in the week in which the Czechs mobilised for the first time, a new committee was created by the House of Representatives, with Representative Martin Dies of Texas as chairman. In January 1939 this committee produced its first report. It attracted a great deal of attention, just as the interrogations had already done. The German network of spies was again held up for all to see. There was a detailed report on the *Bund*. One witness reported that the *Bund* leader of one of the Long Island sections had taught his men from German military textbooks, adding: 'In Germany the people finally rose up in resentment. This will happen here. It is inevitable. When that day comes, and it is probably not far-off, we must be prepared to fight for the right kind of government. We must win the masses to our side. There will be bloodshed and fighting. We shall have to do our part.'[1]

From July 1, 1937, to July 1, 1938, as many as 250 cases of supposed espionage were reported to the Federal Bureau of Investigation. The number increased to 1,651 for the period between July 1, 1938 to July 1, 1939. Whether there actually was so much more spying is not certain, but it is clear that the disquieted public had become more vigilant.

Disquietude and vigilance applied particularly to the countries south of the Rio Grande: Mexico and Central and South America.

Millions of people of Italian origin lived there and millions of Germans. The Italians were 'nearly all zealous partisans of Fascism',[2] wrote the best American Year Book for contemporary history. Was it probable that it would be different with the Germans? It was in 1938 that people began to ask themselves this question seriously, partly on account of the Integralist rising in Brazil that year, which was thought to have been inspired by Germany. People started to hunt for Seyss-Inquarts and Henleins in South America— and found them, too. Dailies, weeklies and monthly periodicals sent special reporters to the scene. In that same year, three editions appeared of one book, and indeed, Carleton Beals had quite enough alarming things to report!

Nazi propaganda was enormous, he wrote. In Brazil, in one state

---

[1] *Investigation of Un-American activities and propaganda* (76th Congress, 1st session, House of Representatives, House Report no. 2) (Washington, 1939), p. 92.
[2] Whitney H. Shepardson and William O. Scroggs: *The United States in World Affairs, 1937* (New York, 1938), p. 136.

alone (Rio Grande do Sul), sixty Nazi organizations had sprung up, all of them linked with some similar body in Germany. It was said that Hitler had concluded a secret treaty with the dictator of the Republic of San Domingo, on the strength of which an initial group of 40,000 Germans were to be settled near the frontier of Haiti. Although Beals spoke sceptically of the stories about every Japanese fisherman on the Panama canal being a Japanese naval officer and every barber an army spy, he nevertheless thought that the efficacy of 'the dread Gestapo secret service, under the evil-faced, shifty-eyed, jawless Heinrich Himmler' should not be doubted.[1]

The feeling of being threatened became stronger. Statistics showed that Germany was carrying on a continually more intensive trade with South America. In several of the republics a German military mission was at work. Had the Germans perhaps got U-boat bases on the Canary Islands? Washington anxiously put this question to London and Paris. Were there plans to destroy the locks of the Panama canal? One German bomb would be able to break that vital point of connection between the Pacific and the Atlantic Ocean. A large portion of the South American air line companies flew with German planes and German pilots. There were rumours that Germany's allies, the Japanese, had laid out rice-fields in Columbia and Costa Rica, two hours flying time from the Panama Canal, and they had made them so flat that they might very well be used for a landing field for airplanes. In April, 1939, a committee of American lawyers published the news that Germany possessed a naval base on the coast of Peru. 'German warships and submarines go in and out and rows of Nazi sentinels guard the concession boundaries.'[2]

Puzzling, alarming particulars!

In 1938 (the year of the *Anschluss* and the Sudeten crisis) the United States government took far-reaching measures. Reports containing a summary of disquieting diplomatic news about German and Italian propaganda and penetration in South America were submitted by the Department of State to the military authorities; as luck would have it (although in a deeper sense it was no accident) the first report of this nature was despatched on the day of Schuschnigg's conference in Berchtesgaden, and the second one on the day of the Austrian *Anschluss*. What was to happen if a German agricultural colony in Latin America 'would provide a ready-made bridgehead for intervention and later full-scale invasion from Europe'?[3]

[1] Carleton Beals: *The Coming Struggle for Latin America* (Philadelphia, 1938), p. 68–9.

[2] *Hitler over Latin America* (New York, 1939), p. 14.

[3] Mark Skinner Watson: *Chief of Staff. Prewar plans and preparations. (United States Army in World War II)* (Washington, 1950), p. 87. An extremely valuable study.

Once the Germans had got in it would be no easy matter to get them out again.

Nothing was ready in Washington, not even on paper, for countering this menace. In South America, so the Chief of the Army Air Corps said in public, there were 'German sympathisers who might establish aerodromes and who might have bombs and gasoline waiting for [the Germans] when they came there and then take over a certain section of South America'.[1]

Measures were taken.

Whilst the Sudeten crisis was reaching its culminating point a permanent board was formed in Washington for co-ordinating the defence of South America. It consisted of the Under-Secretary of State (Sumner Welles), the Chief of Staff of the American Army and the Chief of Naval Operations. It was decided to try to drive out the German military missions and pilots from South America. In order to be prepared for every eventuality new plans for military operations were drawn up. Early in 1939 the Army War College received the secret commission to make plans for offering military support to Brazil and Venezuela. In April 1939 President Roosevelt said that the United States 'would match force with force to defend the integrity of the hemisphere'. A month before war broke out in Europe the first so-called Rainbow-report had been adopted, according to which the American hemisphere would be defended down to 10° South Latitude. The grounds it gave were, 'the real danger that Axis powers might establish themselves on the bulge of Brazil'. There would be an 'absolute necessity for the United States to expel the enemy in such a contingency'.[2]

Meanwhile, how had the South Americans themselves seen the German Fifth Column in those years from 1933 to 1939?

In that part of the world there lived a good many people of German origin. According to the Germans themselves there were only some hundreds in Bolivia, Columbia and Ecuador, and some thousands in Venezuela, Peru, Paraguay and Uruguay, but for Brazil they themselves put the figure at over half a million, for the Argentine between 80,000 and 240,000, for Chile 30,000. They were not by any means all German citizens. By far the greater proportion had emigrated from Germany for good and had become citizens of one of the South American republics. That applied also to more than 100,000 immigrants from German agricultural colonies in Southern Russia, who had principally settled in the Argentine. They spoke German.

[1] *Evening Public Ledger* (Washington), Feb. 24, 1938.
[2] William L. Langer and S. Everett Gleason: *The Challenge to Isolation, 1937–1940* (New York, 1952), p. 135. This is a most useful survey.

That was sufficient for the statisticians in Berlin to consider them as 'Germans', and the propagandists of national socialism needed no further incentive to try systematically from 1933 onwards to use their influence on them.

Literature in which the Third *Reich* was called a heaven on earth was distributed in enormous quantities. The German radio broadcast special programmes daily. In every one of the republics formations of the *Auslands-Organisation der NSDAP* sprang up. After 1933 they became stronger and more numerous. Many newspapers appearing in German allowed themselves to be Nazified, and wherever that did not happen, the Nazis started newspapers of their own.

Now, national socialism as an ideology was unacceptable to the large masses in South America. The continent, steeped as it was in Spanish and Portuguese culture, and with French cultural influences also at work, did not fancy Prussianism. The glorification of *one* race was downright objectionable to peoples who were being formed through a *mingling* of races—a process which was becoming increasingly intensive. The principles underlying the Nazi movement were the opposite of those recognised by South and Central America. The brutish and harsh zeal of the Germans went against the grain of the somewhat indolent, ceremonious Latin Americans, who are so strongly imbued with ideas of personal honour. Those Latin Americans were all the more painfully struck by every kind of sign that showed that the national socialists not only kept themselves aloof from the growing cultural unity of that part of the world, but were even starting to form exclusive, *German* communities. What would remain of that unity if the Italians and Japanese were to do the same? 'All that South America asks of the immigrant is that he should assimilate; and newcomers are liked or otherwise in proportion to their willingness to forget the land of their parents.'[1]

But the Germans did *not* appreciate South America. They preferred Germany. They gave the Hitler salute and sang the Horst Wessel song. They opened their schools by hoisting the swastika flag. They organised a *Tag des Deutschen Volkstums* (Day of the German Nation) in Brazil and in the Argentine, celebrated for the first time on March 14, 1937. On May 1 of that same year 16,000 of them celebrated German Labour Day in Buenos Aires with 'exemplary order' and 'rigid discipline',[2] and in Rio de Janeiro they posted a sign on a German factory: *Unser Land ist ein Stück von Deutschland!*[3] ('Our country is a piece of Germany!')

The reaction did not fail to come.

[1] *The Times* (London), June 26, 1938.
[2] *Der Auslandsdeutsche* (Stuttgart), 1937, p. 501.
[3] *Las democracias americanas en peligro* (Buenos Aires, 1938), p. 11.

Based on Otto Boelitz: *Das Grenz—und Auslanddeutschtum* [2], p. 197.

GERMAN SETTLEMENT-AREAS IN LATIN AMERICA

People started seriously to observe the national socialists. The South Americans were not able to see through their game entirely, but enough was known to show them up.

In May, 1937, 'a certain Nazi agent named von Cossel' was exposed in the Brazilian Congress:

He is the leader of an espionage organisation, he propagates anti-semitic propaganda, and appoints and dismisses German diplomats. Besides this, with the help of Nazi Integralist leaders and Italian technicians he surveys the strategic areas, the wealth of the soil, the transport system and other military factors. In one province alone he had already formed over eighty Nazi organisations, all linked up with the *Turner Bund* (Gymnastic League) in Berlin.[1]

Two months later an inspector of schools in the Argentine Republic sounded a warning note when he said that the schools where German was used 'were weakening and killing the Argentine language. . . The pupils there say they are not Argentinians but Germans.'[2] 'The classroom walls in those schools', so another report said, 'are covered with maps and symbols of foreign countries. The practice is observed there of greeting with the outstretched arm, accompanied by an exclamation which invokes the name of a foreign leader.'[3]

The year 1938 brought the conquest of Austria, extensive reports of which appeared in the South American press. Papers like *La Prensa* and *La Nación* in Buenos Aires held their own with the *New York Times*. In April Hitler called upon all German nationals abroad to vote. In many of the republics German ships lay ready to take German nationals beyond the three mile zone. What an affront to the right of sovereignty! Governors of two Brazilian states forbade the ships to put out.

Brazil was at that time going through a grave crisis.

For some years past a native fascist movement, the *Accao Integralista Brasileira*, which had been set up in 1933, had taken on enormous proportions. The action, led by Plinio Salgado—he was descended from a military doctor who had immigrated from Baden in Southern Germany—had met with great response in the area round Blumenau in Southern Brazil, one of the centres of German agricultural colonisation. Eight of the municipalities were governed by

---

[1] *Las democracias americanas en peligro*, p. 18.
[2] Samuel Guy Inman: *Latin America, its Place in World Life* (Philadelphia, 1942), p. 342.
[3] *Hitler over Latin America*, p. 24.

Integralists. They formed 'a stronghold in the movement'.[1] Opponents of Salgado asserted that he had been financed by Germany for a long time.

Late in 1937 President Vargas banished the Integralists. The movement was continued notwithstanding. In March, 1938, a plot for murdering Vargas was said to have been defeated. It was reported that firearms and three thousand daggers marked with the swastika had been found among leading Integralists. As a result all societies that had been formed by foreigners were disbanded. The wearing of foreign political symbols was prohibited. All political newspapers were suppressed or subjected to censorship. Brazilian citizens were no longer allowed to be members of any organisations where foreigners were also admitted. In the schools the teaching of Portuguese was made compulsory, and foreigners were no longer allowed to teach. The teaching of a foreign language to children under fourteen years of age was forbidden. And besides all this, Vargas threw a number of prominent German Nazis into prison.

All these events took place in April and the first week of May, 1938.

On May 11 a new *coup* on the part of the Integralists occurred. For a few hours the situation was critical, and Vargas had to help defend his palace personally. The rising was put down. Again it was reported that German arms had been found. Vargas said there had been 'help from abroad'. A fresh group of Nazis was placed under arrest. Berlin was informed that the German ambassador was no longer *persona grata*.

It was no wonder that it was the Germans who were most heavily hit by what followed, even though people of other origin—Italians, Poles, Japanese—had to conform to the ruling of Portuguese Brazil too. They were pushed back all along the line. Hotheads even tried to make German inscriptions on graves illegible. That was done, a Brazilian officer declared, because, when the frontier had to be agreed upon in the case of the Sudeten territory, 'Hitler among other things had pointed to the inscriptions on the graves as proof of the German character of the country'.[2] War had not yet broken out, but 'the average Brazilian' was already 'inclined to see a "Nazi spy" in every German national and a traitor in every Brazilian of German origin'.[3]

In the Argentine there had been a similar development.

From the beginning of 1938 the rumour had been general that the Germans possessed secret bases in Patagonia. A parliamentary committee of enquiry could find nothing suspect there early in 1939. In the last week of March, however, an evening paper in Buenos

[1] *Der Auslandsdeutsche*, 1937, p. 19.
[2] *Deutschtum im Ausland* (Stuttgart), 1939, p. 585.
[3] *Ibid.*, p. 584.

Aires published a document delivered to it by a certain Enrique Jürges. It was the facsimile of a letter dated January 11, 1937, signed by an official of the German embassy, von Schubert, and by Alfred Müller, 'deputy leader of the Argentine country-group of the NSDAP', and directed to the head of the 'Colonial-political office' of the German Nazi Party. The letter[1] gave a survey of the spying that had been carried out on a large scale in the south of Argentine, on instructions from Berlin. The conclusion was reported to have been drawn that Patagonia 'might be looked upon as no man's land'.

This document brought about an explosion.

Alfred Müller was promptly arrested. The President of the Republic had one of the chief justices institute an enquiry into the authenticity of the document. His conclusion was that Jürges had foisted a false document upon the President and the press. Müller was released and Jürges locked up. Many people refused to believe, however, that the document was really spurious. Had not the NSDAP in Buenos Aires got 'thirty thousand members, twenty thousand of whom' belonged 'to the SA'?[2] Were there not '43,626 Nazis' in the Argentine?[3] The left insisted on further investigation. The socialist representative Enrique Dickmann maintained in the session of June 7, 1939, that the document was authentic. It simply could not be anything *but* genuine. As far as form and contents went it tallied exactly with the 'totalitarian German national socialist system'.

Radical measures had meanwhile been taken.

In the autumn of 1938 the teaching of Spanish and of the history of the Argentine was made compulsory for all schools. On May 15, 1939, in part of the country all the formations of the *Auslands-Organisation* were barred. But the general nervousness did not vanish. There were rumours that secret consignments of arms had been discovered. For safety's sake some barrels that had arrived from Germany were opened, but they proved to contain only honey.

Other republics reacted similarly.

In May, 1939 the German schools in Chile (where a fascist *coup d'état* had failed in September, 1938), were required to take on Chilean teachers, Chilean books and the use of the Spanish language. The head of the publicity office of the German railways, who had spread anti-semitic propaganda, was thrown out of the country.

---

[1] Text a.o. in *Argentinisches Tageblatt* (Buenos Aires), March 31, 1939. This was an anti-national socialist daily.

[2] Hugo Fernandez Artucio: *The Nazi Octopus in South America* (London, 1943), p. 76.

[3] *Berliner Tageblatt*, quoted by the *Prensa* (Buenos Aires) and the *New York Times*, Sept. 9, 1938.

Uruguay had taken measures against the teaching of German as early as 1938. In Bolivia President German Busch did the same.

The Germans had not offered effective resistance in any of the South American republics. They lacked the means to do so. However, they had been embittered, particularly by the 'nationalisation' of the schools. They were not trusted. A régime that had taken Prague so suddenly was considered capable of anything. Even though some South Americans might have the feeling that they had set bounds to the 'German danger', nobody dared say that it was completely warded off, and many thought that this Fifth Column, if it were to get the chance, would advance anew, 'in exemplary order' and 'with rigid discipline'.

If we pause for a moment in our survey and look back on the development of events, we see that the fear of the German Fifth Column, which sprang up after 1933, was pre-eminently an international phenomenon. The free press and the radio formed one organic whole in the regions from which we took our illustrative material—the countries surrounding Germany; Northern, Western and Southern Europe and their respective colonies; the British Empire, North and South America. The Soviet Union stood apart. There the press and the radio kept themselves strictly to directives given by the Kremlin, and how far these reflected public opinion it would be difficult to say. When our account approaches June 22, 1941, the day the German tanks crossed the Russian frontier, we shall return to this subject.

For the other regions mentioned above, the rule obtains that, as regards fear of the Germans, they influenced each other in ever greater measure. A suspect act in one country was noted in dozens of others. It was therefore not any separate fact or separate piece of news that truly influenced people's minds but their accumulation. Wherever there was anything like freedom of the press people had come across reports in the papers about the German Fifth Column or had heard them over the radio. At first these reports were only to be found a few times a year, but after the beginning of 1938 they came every week, if not every day. A great deal of it had sunk into people's unconscious minds; it was forgotten, but it had not vanished.

The rough idea we have given of the *general* development naturally does not mean that there were no notable differences between individuals, social classes and nations. There were people, for instance, who never allowed their armour of reckless optimism to be pierced by any alarming report whatsoever, while others were mesmerised by the danger of war. Those who looked upon Germany as the defender against communism, or who cherished the unspoken hope that national socialists and communists would annihilate each other (and these were to be found even, or particularly, in the highest circles of Western Europe) observed these symptoms of German expansion relatively calmly, perhaps even with a certain satisfaction. Leftish circles on the other hand had sounded the alarm since 1933.

Also, the characters of the nations and their histories played a part. In the Scandinavian states, the Netherlands and Switzerland, many believed that it would be possible to remain outside the conflict in the case of a second World War, just as in the first. The Englishman, safe on his island and phlegmatic by nature, reacted less violently than the Belgians and French who had learnt to know the *Hun* as a devastator and harsh master in the first World War. The violence of feeling was greatest where nations had in former times had to suffer for a lengthy period, both from the military aggression and from the social and political oppression exercised by the Germans; in fact, where they had had to fight the Germans for their own national existence in a struggle that had lasted for generations.

That was pre-eminently the case in the country we must look at, now that we are getting nearer to the war of which it was the first and perhaps the most sorely stricken victim: Poland.

Living as the Poles did, in a plain that has no natural boundaries either on the East or on the West, they had perforce lived from the very beginning in continual conflict with their chief neighbours, the Russians and the Germans. Often there was war, almost always there were struggles going on.

Poland entered the nineteenth century governed by the Russians, the Prussians and the Austrians. Savage risings would flare up, fail, but nevertheless keep the feeling of nationalism alive. That feeling was also directed against the Germans, who were hated as chauvinists, big landowners, industrialists, civil servants, schoolmasters, gendarmes, 'Lutherans' and heretics. Among the Poles the strong desire grew to become masters in their own house once more, and to drive out the Germans, whom they looked upon as unwelcome guests.

After the misery of the first World War, whereby the fronts had repeatedly swung from East to West and back again, carving up the land as they went, the Poles had seen their opportunity. In the last months of 1918 and the first of 1919 the Polish republic was established. Polish patriots wanted to penetrate as far as the Baltic and the Oder, but the Germans, after first giving way, stood their ground. When the frontier was settled at last the Poles had gained a Corridor to the Baltic. In so doing they had separated East Prussia from the rest of Germany. It is true they had not been able to get Danzig into their power, but they at least had been able to divide it off from

Germany by having it turned into a Free State. The Polish flag flew over the territory round Posen and over the Eastern half of Upper Silesia, one of the richest industrial centres of central Europe.

For most Germans it was an unbearable thought to have to acquiesce in those losses. German-Polish relations remained in a state of tension and the Germans living in Poland felt the repercussions. The Poles tried systematically to drive them out. Hundreds of thousands of Germans packed up their belongings and set off, other hundreds of thousands remained. How many they were exactly, no one knew. Berlin said: one million; Warsaw said: 750,000 at most.

Of these *Volksdeutsche* there were certainly many, especially among the farmers, who were inclined to resign themselves, together with the Ukrainians, White Russians and Jews, 13 million in all, to the inevitable supremacy of the more than 20 million Poles. The hot-tempered spirits among them, however, thirsted after revenge and longed for the return of the severe orderliness of the German administration.

As early as 1933 there were moments, as an experienced American observer wrote, when 'the tension seemed too great to be borne any longer'.[1]

Hardly any European nation was so unitedly, so passionately opposed to the Third *Reich* as that of the Poles. By its very nature and structure it could not do otherwise than rebel against the *Reich*. Polish nationalism burnt in the hearts of intelligentsia and farmers alike. In the top layers of Polish society was a strong relationship with France; the workers were socialists or communists; the Jewish middle classes feared German anti-semitism, which was even more ferocious than the Polish brand. All of these emotions were experienced in the atmosphere of a public opinion that 'catches fire with the rapidity of gunpowder'.[2]

After 1933, too, there was much difference of opinion among the *Volksdeutschen* as to the best course to take. The Poles did not see this internal struggle (we shall come back to it later in another connection). Every German spoke Hitler's language; that was enough. Moreover, the outward unity of the *Volksdeutschen* was growing. For the mass of the Polish people it was an established fact that these Germans were awaiting the coming of the *Führer* with impatience,

[1] William John Rose: *The Drama of Upper Silesia. A Regional Study* (Brittleboro, 1935), p. 318. A wholly admirable study which provides deep insight into the social aspects of German-Polish antagonisms.

[2] Letter, Dec. 20, 1938, from the High Commissioner of the League of Nations in Danzig, Prof. Burckhardt, to F. P. Walters, assistant secretary general of the League of Nations. *Documents on British Foreign Policy 1919–1939*, Third Series, Vol. III, p. 659. The volumes of this series will henceforth be referred to as: *Doc. Br. For. Pol.*, III, Vol. I, etc.

and that the active ones among them would not be averse from 'lending a hand'.

Active ones were not wanting.

From 1933 onwards the *Jungdeutsche Partei* (Young German Party) arrayed its young members in a uniform with the swastika. The uniform and the swastika were banned in May, 1936. Two months later 119 *Volksdeutsche* in Kattowitz (Eastern Upper Silesia) were put in the dock; they had formed a secret organisation and were accused of collaborating with German nationals and agents of the Gestapo for the purpose of preparing an uprising in Upper Silesia; 99 of them were sentenced. Six months later 42 members of a secret German youth organisation were condemned to long terms of imprisonment, and in the summer of 1937 48 boys and girls underwent the same fate, their transgression being that they had, among other things, celebrated Hitler's birthday too enthusiastically in their camp.

Each of the trials was looked upon by Polish public opinion as evidence of a sinister scheme.

The aversion for everything German was deep-rooted. When they wanted to call the *Volksdeutschen* names they called them '*hitlery*' or '*hitlerowcy*'; which was tantamount to 'devils' or 'children of the devil'. Deep down in the souls of a simple, emotional, tormented people this comparison lay ready to hand.

Seeing that this was the general frame of mind it stands to reason that the Polish-German non-aggression pact, dating from 1934, was of no real moment. Both the government and public opinion in Poland increased their pressure on the *Volksdeutschen*, because their senses, sharpened by painful experience, discovered in Hitler's most sugary words his aggressive spirit. Fights against *Volksdeutsche* frequently occurred.

In 1939 the tension rapidly rose.

It was clear that Hitler would make demands regarding Danzig and the Polish Corridor, now that Czechoslovakia was eliminated (the Polish Government had quickly made use of the opportunity to annex the contested frontier district of Teschen). At the end of October, 1938, von Ribbentrop suggested to the Polish minister for Foreign Affairs, Josef Beck, that the solution would be for Danzig to become German and that Germany should be allowed to build an extra-territorial motor-road right across the Corridor.

On March 25, 1939, ten days after Hitler's entry into Prague, trusting to the support of England and France, the Polish government decided definitely to reject the request. The draft reserves of three years were called up. Enthusiasm blazed high. That same day the windows were smashed in the houses of some *Volksdeutsche* in

Posen and Cracow, and those of the German embassy in Warsaw. For a whole quarter of an hour people demonstrated in front of the embassy building, shouting: 'Down with Hitler!' 'Down with the German dogs!' 'Long live Polish Danzig!'[1] It was rumoured that fighting had already begun in Upper Silesia. Many people considered war inevitable. Few doubted what attitude the *Volksdeutschen* would take in that eventuality.

On April 28, 1939, Hitler denounced the non-aggression pact with Poland.

Once more it was the *Volksdeutschen* who were the first victims of the inevitable Polish reaction. German agricultural co-operatives were dissolved and many of their schools—already few in any case—were closed down, while *Volksdeutsche* who were active in the cultural sphere were taken into custody. Around the middle of May in one small town where 3,000 *Volkdeutsche* lived among nearly 40,000 Poles, in many houses and shops household effects were smashed to bits. In the middle of June the remaining German club-buildings were closed down.

Meanwhile the German people were psychologically prepared for war. In April Hitler had definitely decided to launch his armies. Goebbels made his journalists use headlines of increasingly provocative content. From the beginning of August not a day went by in which the German papers did not cry piteously about the 'persecutions' the *Volksdeutschen* were undergoing, sometimes on genuine grounds, more often on the grounds of exaggerated or invented reports.

Was it possible for the Polish authorities to draw any other conclusion than that the Germans were preparing for war? They kept on taking more precautionary measures against the *Volksdeutschen*, who in their turn tried to cross the frontier by the thousand, not so much to escape the difficulties they were all exposed to, but rather because they foresaw what war would mean for them.

By mid-August the Poles proceeded to arrest hundreds of *Volksdeutsche* by way of preventive measure. Again they chose those who filled leading fuctions in the community life of the *Volksdeutschen*. Numerous house-to-house searches took place. German printing-shops and trade-union offices were closed. On August 24 eight *Volksdeutsche* who had been arrested in Upper Silesia were shot down during transport. A day later the Polish police found explosives in the houses of two *Volksdeutsche* in Lodz. At the same time it appeared from the statement of an arrested German that the German

---

[1] Telegram of Ambassador von Moltke to the *Auswärtige Amt*, Feb. 25, 1939. *Dokumente zur Vorgeschichte des Krieges* (Berlin, 1939), p. 135. As all 'coloured books' (Sir Lewis B. Namier) this source must be treated with reserve.

Sicherheitsdienst smuggled *agents provocateurs* into Poland in order to murder *volksdeutsche* farmers whose death Berlin could again lay at the door of the Poles.

German saboteurs were arrested along the frontier on the night of August 25 to 26—the night in which Hitler had originally wanted to attack Poland; they had tried to get through the Polish lines to the railways in the hinterland. On August 25 in Lodz a telegram from Germany drew attention: 'Mother dead. Buy wreaths.' It brought the police on the track of a resistance group who had hidden 45 kilograms of dynamite in food tins with Polish labels on them and in oil-containers with double bottoms. Dozens of revolvers were also found, and the mechanisms of clocks for bombs, and German wireless sets. Twenty-four people were taken into custody.

The news of the find and of the arrest went racing over the telegraph wires, and raised among police and judiciary authorities everywhere the nervous question of whether perhaps groups of *Volksdeutsche* were awaiting their chance in their own districts too. The lists of persons who were to be arrested in case of war were taken out of the files.

On Friday September 1, 1939, at a quarter to five in the morning, without an ultimatum or declaration of war, Hitler struck.

CHAPTER I

Panic in Poland

★

Before France and Britain would be able to take action on the Western front, Poland had to be crushed.

The German general staff, at Hitler's bidding, had made a good job of it. In four months' time a plan of action had been prepared, of which the guiding principles were surprise of the enemy and speed of operation, and the aim was to concentrate superior forces at all critical points. One-and-a-half million trained soldiers were standing by, when, on August 31, 1939, the order to attack was given. At both ends of the broad arc formed by the Polish frontier they stormed forward in the early dawn of September 1—nearly forty divisions in the first line, including all the available German mechanised and motorised units, thirteen reserve divisions close on their heels.

In most sections the Polish frontier defences were rapidly broken down; tank formations passed through these breaches and penetrated deeply into the hinterland. The Polish air forces were immobilised at the end of the first day of combat; the Germans were masters of the air. At points where the German divisions met Polish forces, fierce fighting frequently resulted; everywhere the superior armament and generalship of the Germans tipped the scales in their favour. Unit after unit of the Polish army was surrounded, scattered and annihilated. The German High Command had planned the attack with such foresight as to possible Polish counter-moves and consequently necessary variants in their own offensive, that during the first five days of the fighting no new orders needed to be issued by the German operational headquarters. Every German army group, every army, every division and regiment knew its task. At the end of those five days the power of the Polish army was broken.

Locally, fighting continued until the end of September; it was no more than a drawn-out death-struggle. When the echo of the last shot of the last Polish stronghold had died away, the Polish government and the commander-in-chief had fled to Rumania. Thousands of soldiers had been killed, near on seven hundred thousand had been made prisoner. An enormous prize had fallen into German hands, large parts of Warsaw lay in ruins, burnt villages and farms were the visible sign that the German tanks had ploughed the Polish plain and that the German Stukas had cleaved the air.

Looking back on the events one might say that Poland had lost the unequal struggle even before the first German mortar shell had exploded in the trenches along the frontier. This would have been so even if on September 17 the Russian armies had not proceeded to occupy Poland's eastern half. The Poles, however, had not felt things in this way. What would later be seen, in the matter-of-fact military accounts, to have been a constantly developing catastrophe that was inevitable from the very outset, had to the Poles been a whirl of the wildest emotions, despondency again and again rising to heroism, and pessimism to elation.

The hasty wish to attack and a boundless overrating of their own strength had led the Polish military leadership to draw up a plan of operations whereby the German offensives would be caught on their flanks and the Polish cavalry in the centre would advance triumphantly in the direction of Berlin, where they would be able to water their horses in the Spree and the Havel. Strong Polish forces were concentrated to that end in West Poland, but when war broke out only about half of the Polish divisions were lined up; other divisions were on the way to their places of destination, and of yet others the reservists had only got as far as the trains that were to take them to the localities where they were to report.

The transport system went wrong, bridges and railways were wrecked by German bombs, and thus it happened that by the side of the troops the Polish commanders had well in hand, there were also chance units made up of officers and men who did not know each other. In front of and partly alongside the German tanks and infantry, throngs of despairing refugees made their way east by train, on foot, sometimes in cars and especially in farm wagons, carrying with them some scanty and hastily packed belongings.

This zone of panic and confusion flowed from the frontiers to the centre of Poland, where nobody during the first few days was able to form any idea about the progress of the fighting. Liaison with many of the divisions had been cut off, and what was happening in the Corridor soon became guess-work in Warsaw. At first no tidings of defeat could extinguish the firm belief in victory. On September 1 and 2 there was terrible doubt as to whether England and France would remain true to their word, but when on Sunday 3 the glad news

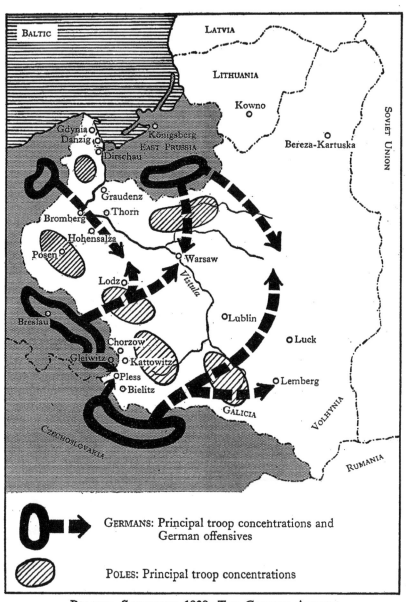

Germans: Principal troop concentrations and German offensives

Poles: Principal troop concentrations

POLAND, SEPTEMBER 1939: THE GERMAN ATTACK

spread of their double declaration of war on Germany, the general enthusiasm knew no bounds.

Newspapers no longer appeared in many places and letters were no longer delivered, but it was the news communicated by the radio that fostered a valiant optimism. By no means everyone owned a wireless set, but the news was passed on by word of mouth and rumour improved upon it. Thus it was possible for people to tell each other that Polish troops were everywhere on the offensive and that they were even nearing Königsberg in East Prussia. Whenever the air raids of the *Luftwaffe* held off for a time people said it was because the Germans had a shortage of petrol. Rumour had it that through lack of bombs the Germans had 'in some places taken recourse to throwing out pieces of rail bound together'.[1]

Every report that brought a confirmation of their confidence in victory was believed by the Poles.

But as the German operations advanced, this more and more spasmodic optimism at last turned into despairing prayers and cries for help and furious reproaches to allies who failed to fly at the throat of the German beast of prey. And from the very outset there had also been fear by its side. Fear of the brute force of war, of the German air squadrons that approached uninterruptedly from the West as if they were on a training flight, in fact, fear of the whole armed force of the Third *Reich* which attempted to ram open Poland's gates at its frontiers and—this bitter truth had to be recognised after a few days—had succeeded only too well.

Fear and hope were inextricably mingled. The rumour went that the Germans dropped poisoned chocolates and cigarettes from their planes as well as children's balloons filled with poison gas. According to other reports, they were said to strew tobacco leaves in the meadows so that the cattle, who could not endure the smell of the nicotine, would perish of hunger.

The German superiority that was manifest everywhere, the favourable reports that remained unconfirmed, the defeat that was gradually assuming a definite shape—not only did all this strike terror into the hearts of the Poles, it was utterly incomprehensible as well. It only became comprehensible when it was assumed that the reverses

---

[1] *Volksdeutsche Soldaten unter Polens Fahnen. Tatsachenberichte von der anderen Front aus dem Feldzug der 18 Tage. Zusammengestellt und bearbeitet von Dr. Kurt Lück, Posen* (Berlin, 1940), p. 34. All German publications about the sufferings of the *Volksdeutschen* in September, 1939, must be treated with caution but are not, it seems to me, unreliable in all details. On the whole the picture they give tallies with what the Poles reported in their own official publications. If one wishes to get some idea of persecutions, it would be a mistake to neglect what the victims have to say. They usually have a better memory than their persecutors.

were not attributable to the failure of their own troops in open combat—an unthinkable proposition anyhow—but that they were due to the cunning means the enemy used, to the operations of his agents.

Who were those agents?

The whole of Poland could point them out: all those who since 1918 had clung as strange intruders to Polish soil and to their own organisations, who since 1933 had tuned in every evening to the enemy broadcasting stations and who adorned themselves when at home with the symbols of national socialism: the accursed *Niemcy*, the *Hitlery*, the *Hitlerowcy*, in fact the German Fifth Column!

For years the Poles had been warned against them; even before war had broken out there had been posters pasted up with the admonition: 'Beware of spies! The German spy is listening!' Their vigilance had long since been concentrated on the *Volksdeutschen*. But obviously they had not been vigilant enough.

In the early morning of September 1 the Polish detachments in Danzig had been traitorously attacked by German units that had been smuggled into the town. News of the surprise attack reached Warsaw before the connections were cut off. In the industrial area of Upper Silesia German soldiers not belonging to the regular troops had tried to take the mines, factories and electricity stations with the help of *Volksdeutsche* who had a sound knowledge of local conditions. Bridges had been seized in the frontier area the night before the attack by mysterious enemies who could not be properly identified, but who had approached their objectives by sneaking through the Polish lines. In Kattowitz a group of *Volksdeutsche*, wearing bands round their arms with the swastika, tried to start a revolt. An American woman correspondent saw how thirty to forty of them (the oldest was not over twenty years of age) were led away heavily guarded, followed a few minutes later by two lorries: 'They were full of workmen, their clothes ripped, smeared with blood and dirt. They were crouching in a ring of soldiers, and every time one raised a head a rifle butt drove it down again. These men had been involved in another Nazi revolt.'[1]

Some of the *Volksdeutschen* who were mobilised in the Polish army —there were others who had simply not joined up but had gone into hiding—offered insufficient resistance to the German troops in many sectors, or even tried to run away. The watchword was circulated among them that under no circumstances must they shoot at Germans, but that they had to allow themselves to be taken prisoner as soon as possible. 'The Polish officers knew of this,' a *Volksdeutscher*

---

[1] Claire Hollingworth: *The Three Weeks' War in Poland* (London, 1940), p. 19.

wrote later, 'but they believed they could intimidate us by placing us in the front lines and by closely watching us.' [1]

Near Posen, in the centre of the area where most of the *Volksdeutschen* lived, a document was found on the crew of a *Luftwaffe* plane that had been shot down on the second day of the war. It was called a *Merkblatt zur Bekanntgabe an die gegen Polen eingesetzten Truppen* ('Instruction for the troops to be used against Poland'), in which might be read that 'the German groups and also other groups in Poland ... would support the operations of the German armed forces'; the 'actively fighting sections of the *Volksdeutschen* and other groups of the population' were to know the distinctive markings and watchwords carefully enumerated in the *Merkblatt*. The markings were to be a red handkerchief with a big yellow circle in the centre, a light blue band for the arm with a yellow centre, a beige overall with yellow tokens or bands for the arm adorned with the swastika. The password was to be 'echo', pronounced and written alike in German, Polish, Ukrainian, Russian and Czech.

All this information was to be found neatly typed on four foolscap pages [2] and duly signed: *Für die Richtigkeit, Prinz Reuss, Major* ('For copy conform: Major Prince Reuss'). There it was in black and white.

In Posen, where the *Merkblatt* had been discovered, twenty German agents were arrested, also on the second day of the war. They all wore the proper armlets and badges under their raincoats: 'They admitted that they had crossed the frontier during the night ... and that they had been charged with impeding the evacuation of the Polish army, carrying out diversionist work and destroying means of communication. They had all been through the appropriate course in Germany.' [3]

In various districts in the Polish Corridor military detachments came into action which consisted of *Volksdeutsche* or were helped by them. The French consul in the Baltic port of Gdynia, who rushed up to Warsaw during the first days of the war, saw that *Volksdeutsche* were taken into custody who had been caught in the act of cutting the telegraph and telephone wires. In one town the superintendent of police had indignantly told him 'that he was seriously beginning to ask himself whether everyone he spoke to was not a dangerous *Volksdeutscher* in disguise who ought to be arrested'.[4]

Elsewhere in Poland the routes for retreat had been obstructed by

---

[1] *Der Sieg in Polen, herausgegeben vom Oberkommando der Wehrmacht in Verbindung mit dem Aufklärungsdienst der SA* (Berlin, 1940), p. 127.
[2] Facsimile in *The German Fifth Column in Poland* (London, 1941), between pp. 148 and 149.
[3] Statement no. 4 of Major J. Z., *ibid.*, pp. 81-3.
[4] Notes of R. Chaulet, *ibid.*, p. 156.

trees cut down for that purpose. German agents might be encountered disguised as Polish military police, railway officials and officers. 'Their German documents were concealed in the lining of their clothes'.[1]

Behold—these were irrefutable facts. The *Merkblatt* of Prince Reuss could be read by all. The arrested German agents might be seen, their arms, clothes, pocket-torches and wire-cutters might be handled. And another definitely established fact was that in the Corridor and in Upper Silesia young *Volksdeutsche* had taken up arms. But a much wider application was given to these facts. The big masses of the Polish people did not expect otherwise than that the *Volksdeutschen* in large numbers would lend their lord and master Adolf Hitler a helping hand.

These expectations, so people felt, had come true. Everywhere and from the very beginning.

First of all, countless Poles believed that the *Volksdeutschen* had taken special steps to prevent their houses from being bombed or fired at. It was said that to that end they had made marks on their roofs, or had put heaps of straw in a certain position near their houses or had painted the chimneys white. 'At night,' a Polish lieutenant related, 'those chimneys were coloured with various colours in accordance with the agreed signal code.' [2] By day people also thought that they saw suspicious signs. Polish troops that had to pass the fields in regions where *Volksdeutsche* lived were often convinced that the *volksdeutsche* farmers had carried out special agricultural activities which, in accordance with their plan, contained signals for the German troops, particularly for the German air-force. Those signals were also noticed by Polish pilots. The grass had been cut 'according to plan'. Racks were placed 'in special arrangements'. In a field that had been ploughed a figure had been introduced 'according to a plan' by stamping on the ground.[3]

Whenever the Germans had carried out an air-raid the Poles would look in the neighbourhood of the bombed objects for accomplices who they thought must have lent the Germans a helping hand. *Volksdeutsche* were suspected of leaving on the lights in their rooms to help the *Luftwaffe*, or of letting the beam of light from their lanterns shine upwards through their chimneys, or even of showing the German planes the way by striking matches. In Western Poland it was declared that the owner of a stone-mason works not only possessed a radio transmitter but that he also had 'indicated the direction of the wind to German airmen, from his yard'. He was executed.[4]

[1] Statement no. 316 of an anonymous lieutenant, *ibid.*, p. 119.
[2] Statement no. 410 of Lieutenant Z., *ibid.*, p. 100.
[3] Statement no. 257 of Flight Observer S. K., *ibid.*, pp. 103–4.
[4] Statement no. 352 of Lieutenant S., *ibid.*, p. 100.

Between Posen and Warsaw two *Volksdeutsche* who had escaped arrest tried to do some cooking in a hut. Polish railway personnel heard them speak German, the soldiers were warned and the Germans were led away as prisoners. 'It was said that we made signals with smoke to German planes which kept on attacking the railway-yard.' [1]

How many were arrested on those grounds or were even killed for it?

Nobody knows, but in Thorn alone, in the Polish Corridor, 34 people were shot 'who had been caught in the act of making signals with mirrors or white material during attacks by German bombers'. [2]

Countless numbers of the *Volksdeutschen* were suspected of espionage or sabotage, for which purpose they had cunningly disguised themselves. They did this in Polish uniform and sometimes in civilian clothes 'as workmen, beggars, priests, members of religious orders' [3] or 'as women'. [4] But the German agents were by no means always dressed in a special garb from top to toe. They naturally had to have distinguishing marks, bands in special colours, for instance. There were others, however, so people thought, who made themselves known to each other in a much more inconspicuous way, through: 'buttons of distinctive shape, pullovers, etc.' [5] or by 'some peculiarity in their dress, by a band, a muffler'. [6]

What these agents were able to attain through espionage and sabotage had of course to be reported to German headquarters. Some reports, it was assumed, were passed on by means of signals that could be observed from the road. In other cases it was believed that there were numberless secret transmitters at work which sent a stream of data to the Germans. During the air-raids in the first days of the war the population in Warsaw was convinced that the *Luftwaffe* was in touch with agents in the town who were fitted out with transmitters.

It was also thought that such transmitters might be discovered in large numbers in the country. But they were cleverly concealed! They were to be found 'in the tomb of a well-known industrialist', 'in the house of a Protestant pastor', even 'in a hollow tree'. [7] In the Corridor alone, according to an officer of the Polish general staff, 'fifteen short-wave transmitters' were discovered [8] in house-to-house searches

[1] *Marsch der Deutschen in Polen. Deutsche Volksgenossen im ehemaligen Polen, berichten über Erlebnisse in den Septembertagen 1939* (Berlin, 1940), p. 65.
[2] Statement no. 72 of Dr. J. B., *The German Fifth Column in Poland*, pp. 120–1.
[3] *Ibid.*, p. 95.   [4] Statement no. 134 of Lieutenant R., *ibid.*, p. 96.
[5] Statement no. 185 of Lieutenant T. S., *ibid.*, p. 96.
[6] Statement no. 393 of Captain R., *ibid.*, p. 96.
[7] Statement no. 203 of Lieutenant-Colonel G., *ibid.*, p. 101.
[8] Statement no. 24 of Lieutenant-Colonel R., *ibid.*

among *Volksdeutsche*. Somewhere else a Polish lieutenant found a 'small short-wave wireless transmitter in a box not much bigger than a match-box'.[1]

Persons under whose roofs these and similar apparatuses were found were of course carried off as prisoners. As a matter of fact any strange object that looked typically German at once aroused suspicion. In Posen for instance two *Volksdeutsche* were shot 'as spies', because Polish soldiers had come across 'a stamp collection, an old German helmet dating from the first World War, a motor-bicycle lamp and a kilometer indicator' in their dwellings.[2]

There was not a ruse that could not be laid at the doors of those *Volksdeutschen*! 'Wherever Germans were to be found, they fired at the Polish soldiers at night, they burned down the buildings in which the troops were quartered, they cut the telephone wires. They signalled details of Polish dispositions with the aid of coloured rockets. They ambushed the Polish troops, and frequently mixed mustard-gas in the water they provided for washing purposes.'[3] And in order to give an example of that latter, most sinister German activity:

> I certify [wrote a Polish major after the campaign] that I saw the case of Lieutenant Kowalski who was stationed with me at a colony in Wolhynia, in which there were German inhabitants. He washed himself with water which the mistress of the house brought him in a bowl, and immediately his face was swelled up terribly. He was taken at once to the hospital at Luck, where it was diagnosed that his burns were due to mustard gas, fortunately in a diluted form.[4]

Fear of the German Fifth Column aroused by events and reports such as we have sketched above was far from being a local pheno-menon. After the war was over, the exiled Polish government was able to collect over five hundred statements from among the officers and men who had escaped abroad. Each of these witnesses related what he had seen with his own eyes and heard with his own ears about that Fifth Column. These statements had a bearing on the first just as much as on the last week of the war, and came from all parts of the country.

Months before the outbreak of hostilities the Polish government

---

[1] Statement no. 69 of Lieutenant G. D., *The German Fifth Column in Poland*, p. 113.

[2] Document 71 in *Die polnischen Greueltated an den Volksdeutschen in Polen*, (Berlin 1940), p. 118.

[3] *The German Fifth Column in Poland*, p. 48.

[4] Statement no. 70 of Major F. S., *ibid*, p. 117.

had given orders for drawing up lists of suspect *Reichsdeutsche* and *Volksdeutsche*. This was probably done in April and May, 1939, at about the time that Hitler denounced the German–Polish non-aggression pact. Some groups of *Volksdeutsche*, as we saw, were taken into custody before the outbreak of the war and were conveyed to internment camps. The majority were still left in peace. On the first day of the war, however, a special order was issued to Polish judiciary and police organs, via the Polish radio—so at least was said by the Germans—ordering them to work through the lists that lay in readiness. Immediately, on that very Friday, September 1, warrants were handed out in all the places where *Reichsdeutsche* and *Volksdeutsche* lived. There were warrants on red, pink and yellow paper. Those to whom a red paper had been handed out, had to be taken to the local prison, while their houses were at once to be searched. Those who received a pink paper (usually *Reichsdeutsche*) had to report to the police for internment. The yellow papers indicated that the people in question were to go to specified areas far from the German frontier in Central or East Poland. The Polish authorities endeavoured, therefore, not to molest the majority of *Volksdeutsche*, but only to remove elements they did not unreservedly trust from the probable field of action, and to imprison only those who were looked upon as the avowed enemies of the Polish state.

In practice all these distinctions did not come to much. The *Reichsdeutschen* who were to be interned could not be transported, and those who had to go to Central or East Poland (carrying provisions with them for four days) sometimes arrived at stations where there were no longer trains for civilians. So the end was that all those who had received any sort of paper, whatever the colour, landed in the local police-office, in prison or in an internment camp. On the way to these spots the Germans were 'treated to kicks, struck by rifle-butts, spat in the face and regaled to the vilest invective' [1] by the excited population. Crowds assembled before the houses of the people who had been arrested, and sometimes they took to smashing the windows.

What mattered was that beside the 'official' arrests 'unofficial' ones also took place. In many places Polish patriotic societies had drawn up their own lists of those whom they deemed untrustworthy. These lists too were worked through, and often in a very rough way. Cries sounded in the streets of: 'Seize them, kill them, those *Niemcy*, those *Szwaby*, those swine, those spies!' [2]

Fear and hatred were not directed only towards the Germans in the neighbourhood. Other people who were also Germans but who

---

[1] *Die polnischen Greueltaten an den Volksdeutschen in Polen*, p. 21.
[2] *Ibid.*, p. 22.

were not recognised as such were perhaps even more dangerous. In some places people who were not trusted were made to pronounce Polish words that were veritable tongue-twisters in order to show them up. In Upper Silesia where tension was greatest members of Polish societies were fitted out with rifles, and 'whoever answered to their shouts in German or not at all were shot down'.[1]

In this way large numbers of Germans, mostly *Volksdeutsche*, were arrested or otherwise put out of the way during the first three days of the war.

What was to be done with all these people?

It was clear that they must be withdrawn from the grasp of the Germans. The general slogan was: 'Shift them east!' In some cases separate trains were formed, in others they had to go on foot. It would also sometimes happen that those in the trains had to get out half-way and continue their journey on foot. All these ways of transport were meant to end in the big internment camps near the Russian frontier. In some cases they succeeded, in others they did not. The total number of *Volksdeutsche* who were marched off, whether interned or not, was estimated by the Germans at well over 50,000.[2]

The treatment in the camps was bad. But the prisoners had had to endure even worse things on the way there.

A procession of prisoners that left one village became a disorderly cluster of dust-coated individuals by the next. They were guarded;— so they must have something on their consciences! They were Germans, *Niemcy*, *Hitlerowcy*. *They* were responsible for the disaster that had befallen Poland. Crowds would walk along by the side of the prisoners, giving vent to their feelings. 'We thoroughly learnt what it is to have to run the gauntlet', a *Volksdeutscher* wrote afterwards:

> Wherever we passed through a town of any magnitude the street was lined by a frenzied crowd of every age and sex that became abusive and spat and threw stones or dung, hitting out freely with sticks. Run-away railway officials and deserters from the army went at us worst of all. The police accompanying us were hostile. They hardly allowed us one drink of water a day and hardly ever a rest on our journey. But in the towns they at least protected us from being beaten or trampled to death by the crowd, although all of us, especially at first, received injuries.[3]

The behaviour of the guards varied. Sometimes they drove back the Polish crowds with rubber cudgels, but it also happened that it

[1] *Volksdeutsche Soldaten unter Polens Fahnen*, p. 49.
[2] *Marsch der Deutschen in Polen*, p. 14.
[3] *Ibid.*, p. 59.

was not unpleasing to them to see the captives victimised. On the whole the police (who after all knew who they were accompanying) behaved better than the indifferent Polish soldiers who often took over their task. Quite a number of 'spies' were shot *en route* by these soldiers and often they did not offer any effective resistance to attempts on the part of the public to get some *Volksdeutsche* into their hands and kill them off. In various cases it came to a sadistic massacre. After the fighting was over bodies of *Volksdeutsche* were found that had been hideously mutilated, or that had been dropped into a pit with the carrion of a dog.

Meanwhile, in numerous places where the suspect *Volksdeutsche* had been led away, fresh irregularities arose. In the Fifth Column panic houses and farms belonging to *Volksdeutsche* were stormed and plundered. Sometimes whole families lost their lives. There too the expression of sadistic impulses was tolerated, even applauded. But there were also Poles who kept their heads cool. They cautioned against indulging in excesses, they sometimes even helped to protect *Volksdeutsche* and to conceal them in their own homes. There were also officers who forbade or stopped executions. Though the general opinion was that no German was worth standing in·the breach for, some Poles nevertheless did just this, with risk to their own lives.

It is impossible to say how great the total number really was of those who fell victim to the fury of the Polish people. German sources reported that by February 1, 1940, the bodies of nearly thirteen thousand murdered *Volksdeutsche* had been found and identified.[1] This figure must be treated with reserve. It is not unlikely, however, that the Fifth Column panic was responsible for the loss of some thousands of lives among the 750,000 to one million *Volksdeutsche* living in Poland.[2]

The Poles were not sorry for what had been done.

With what rejoicings did the *Volksdeutsche* welcome the German occupation forces! How zealously they busied themselves in the per-formance of a thousand-and-one services for the troops dressed in the uniform so hated by the Poles. They sat on top of tanks to show the Germans the way, they lined the roads, tossing flowers at the passing Germans, and did not tire of shouting '*Heil Hitler!*' They

[1] *Die polnischen Greueltaten an der Volksdeutschen in Polen*, p. 5.
[2] That much is admitted in a memorandum, dated June 14, 1954, '*Die Frage der volksdeutschen Verluste im September 1939*', written by Dr. K. M. Pospiezalski, of the Polish West Institute, Poznán, and in ' "Dokumenty Polskiego Okru-cieństwa" (Metody propagandy Hitlerowskiej)' [' "Documents on Polish atroci-ties" (Hitlerian propaganda methods)'], *Biuletyn główny komisji badania zbrodni Niemeckich w Polsce* [Bulletin of the general Commission for the Investigation of German atrocities in Poland], Vol. III (Warsaw, 1947), 147–71, a study edited by Prof. Dr. J. J. Bossowski.

ran to fetch jugs of milk from their houses. They handed out bread-rolls, coffee and bars of chocolate amongst the soldiers, and every-where 'the German greeting, the name of the *Führer*' was to be heard.[1] They decorated their houses with paper flags bearing the swastika, and placed flower-decked portraits of Hitler in the open windows. The women 'caught the soldiers by the hand and tried to embrace them';[2] they pressed their last cigarettes on the soldiers, their children climbed on the military vehicles and 'everyone was beside himself with joy'.[3]

But how painfully did such scenes impress themselves on the Poles, sorrowing for their lost freedom and, knowing the Germans, awaiting the future with terrible anxiety! Before the war people had suspected that the *Volksdeutschen* would commit treason if the occasion called for it; during the war that surmise had been proved right; after the war it was again confirmed. Not a single Pole doubted the reality of the *volksdeutsche* conspiracy, whether he lived at home or in exile.

It is curious that only a few people outside of Poland paid much attention to the misdeeds those *Volksdeutschen* were reputed to have perpetrated—apart from the Polish refugees, of course. The latter were full of stories. Reports about the outrages of the Fifth Column continuously reached their government in exile, which had been set up in France. Towards the end of 1939 it obtained possession, as well, of the significant *Merkblatt* which had been found near Posen, and which it passed on to the world press after an examination of its authenticity. Long extracts from it were published in the London *Times* on January 4, 1940.

The Polish refugee government also promoted the publication, in Paris, in April, 1940, of a book, *l'Invasion allemande en Pologne* ('The German invasion of Poland'), which gave a striking account of the sufferings of the Polish civilian population and of the activity of the Fifth Columnists. Others added to this story. The correspondent of the *Manchester Guardian*, escaped from Warsaw, reported that the number of German spies 'ran into thousands', that 'the million odd members of the German minority . . . were used to the utmost by the Nazis', and that *volksdeutsche* girls who had gone to Germany supposedly to attend a nurses' training course 'were sent to spying schools instead'.[4] A Swiss officer in March, 1940, spoke of 'the

[1] *Der Sieg in Polen*, p. 38.
[2] Document 75 in *Die polnischen Greueltaten an den Volksdeutschen in Polen*, p. 125.
[3] Document 74, *ibid.*, p. 122.
[4] *Manchester Guardian*, Oct. 21, 1939.

perfection with which the spy system of the German minority fulfilled its task'.[1]

Public opinion in the West paid little heed to such reports and commentaries. Poland was far away. Poland was Eastern Europe. And what else did the defeat of Poland prove other than that the 'republic of the colonels', no democracy after all, had already been mouldering? People shivered at the sight of the illustrations of devastated Warsaw, but refused to admit to themselves that the German military machine—which in a few weeks had over-run like a steamroller a brave army of more than a million strong—still existed, let alone that it had grown even stronger.

Or had fear of what might happen yet, deep down in people's minds, increased none the less? Ought one to ask oneself, if one dared to look the truth in the face, what surprises Hitler had up his sleeve for his remaining opponents?

The apprehensions of those who did set themselves such questions were certainly augmented by the disclosures published by Hermann Rauschning in that first unreal winter of the second World War. *Hitler Speaks* appeared simultaneously in a number of countries. In England alone three printings were on the market in one month's time. Hitler's own words could be heard from these pages, based on notes jotted down in the years 1932–4. Not only the destructive demonism of his being sounded clearly from his words, but also his far-seeing cunning as a would-be conqueror of the world intending to use his mastership of the attack-from-inside to the full. No means to this end would he neglect: mass air-attack, surprise, terrorism, sabotage, assassination—these and many more methods found a place in his plans. A card-system of all the statesmen in the world was going to be made, with notes as to their secret weaknesses; new poison gases were going to be used; agents, disguised as commercial travellers, were to smuggle bacteria into enemy countries.

'When I wage war, Forster', Hitler had expressed himself to the *Gauleiter* of Danzig and his henchmen,

in the midst of peace, troops will suddenly appear, let us say, in Paris. They will wear French uniforms. They will march through the streets in broad daylight. No one will stop them. Everything has been thought out, prepared to the last detail. They will march to the headquarters of the General Staff. They will occupy the ministries, the Chamber of Deputies. Within a few minutes, France, Poland, Austria, Czechoslovakia, will be robbed of their leading men. An army without a general staff! All political leaders out of the way! The confusion will be beyond belief. But I shall long have

[1] *Neue Zürcher Zeitung*, Mar. 7, 1940.

had relations with the men who will form a new government—a government to suit me. We shall find such men, we shall find them in every country. We shall not need to bribe them. They will come of their own accord. Ambition and delusion, party squabbles and self-seeking arrogance will drive them. Peace will be negotiated before the war has begun. I promise you, gentlemen, that the impossible is always successful. The most unlikely thing is the surest. We shall have enough volunteers, men like our SA, trustworthy and ready to any sacrifice. We shall send them across the border in peace-time. Gradually. No one shall see in them anything but peaceful travellers. To-day you don't believe me, gentlemen, but I will accomplish it, move by move. Perhaps we shall land at their flying fields. We shall be capable of transporting, not only men, but arms, by air. No Maginot Line will stop us. Our strategy, Forster, is to destroy the enemy from within, to conquer him through himself.[1]

And the man who spoke thus had laid hands on Austria, Czechoslovakia and Poland in one and a half years' time.

What was to be his next move?

[1] Herman Rauschning: *Hitler Speaks* (London, 1939), p. 17–18.

CHAPTER II

Denmark and Norway surprised

★

Denmark

IN the early hours of Tuesday, April 9, 1940, the inhabitants of Denmark's capital, Copenhagen, were aroused from their sleep by the roaring engines of an airplane squadron flying low over the town. What could this mean? What had happened?

With more haste than usual people dressed and went out in to the streets. At all the main crossings in the city they saw soldiers in unfamiliar uniforms, some of them manning threatening machine-guns——*Germans*! Unbelievable! Where had they sprung from? Was it war? An invasion? What was the government doing about it? Where were the defending troops? Was there no resistance?

People clustered together, at first in a nervous quest for an explanation of such baffling happenings, later in speechless despondency as the rumour spread that Denmark had been occupied by German troops, and that the government had capitulated in the face of such overwhelming odds, in order to avoid needless bloodshed. At first there was only rumour, but around 9 a.m. Radio Kalundborg, the national broadcasting station, confirmed the news.

By order of the Commander-in-Chief of the German occupation forces in Denmark a proclamation was broadcast to the effect that Germany, in order to prevent a British invasion, had occupied Denmark and Norway. Denmark's liberty, however, would be respected, and the population was urged to go to work as usual and to remain calm. Directly following, a message from King Christian and the government was also broadcast: yes, it was true. Posters were pasted up in the town, printed with the texts of the proclamations of both General Kaupisch and the King. Shortly afterwards a loud-speaker van cruised through the town, bawling the proclamations of General Kaupisch at the house-fronts.

It was bewildering.

How could those armed Germans have entered Copenhagen in the morning twilight? Had the forts by which their ships surely must have passed, not even fired at the attackers? What had moved the government to submit to this ignominy so quickly? Had the staffs of army and navy been caught napping?

As April 9 wore on it became known that not only Copenhagen had been occupied at daybreak. All the points in the country which were vital to its defence had fallen into the hands of the Germans.

Not everywhere had the Danish troops allowed themselves to be surprised; in Copenhagen the regiment of the Guards had counter-attacked the detachment of Germans which had taken the old fort near the port, the *Kastellet*, and in South Jutland as well clashes had taken place. But the slight firing had ceased after the news of the capitulation had been broadcast. Such resistance as there had been hardly influenced, however, the general picture of complete surprise; Denmark had been overwhelmed from one day, nay, from one hour to the next.

If one recalled the developments during the previous weeks, one had to admit that there had been no lack of disturbing signs. All through the winter of 1939–40 the Baltic region had been the scene of international tension. There had often been talk of Allied plans for a landing in Norway, since the British had rescued some of their countrymen, prisoners-of-war, from the German ship *Altmark*, in Norwegian territorial waters; the peace concluded between Finland and Russia had not really led to relaxation of the tension: London and Paris were too clear about their intention not to tolerate indefinitely the undisturbed transport of iron ore from the Swedish harbours on the Baltic or from Narvik in Norway to German ports. The Norwegian and Swedish governments would certainly be put under heavy pressure on this account, and what would then be the counter-measures on the part of the Germans? But apprehensions about these matters were of an abstract and general nature. The Danes were more afraid for the fate awaiting Norway and Sweden than for their own.

In the first week of April news had trickled through from Berlin, London and Stockholm that a crisis was impending. The Danish minister in Berlin had sent a telegram in code on Sunday, April 9: 'Learn that a fleet of transport ships has left Stettin on April 4. Course West. Destination unknown, but expected to approach it April 11.' [1]

[1] *Betaenkning til Folketinget afgivet af den af Tinget under 15. Juni 1945 nedsatte Kommission i Henhold til Grundlovens § 45* [Memorandum of the Commission of Enquiry, 1945, of the Danish Lower House], Vol. I (Copenhagen, 1945), p. 24. This source will in future be referred to as *Danish Parl. Enq.* The reports of this commission form a source of primary importance.

The Danish minister of Foreign Affairs, Dr. Munch, had promptly requested further information from the army and navy staffs; the navy had observed nothing suspicious—and the transport was supposed to have been under way for three days! The General Staff knew nothing about concentrations of German troops to the South of Jutland, nor about unusual activity in German ports, such as Kiel for instance. False alarm, then?

Or was something brewing none-the-less?

On Monday morning, April 8, it became known that the governments of Britain and France had delivered notes to Oslo stating that mine-fields had been laid in Norwegian coastal waters to prevent the transportation of iron ore to Germany. What would be the consequences of this action? The Danish cabinet did not rightly know what to do. Aerial reconnaissance showed that a German fleet was on its way northwards. Should mobilisation be proclaimed? The minister of Foreign Affairs spoke of this apprehension to the German Minister, von Renthe-Fink. The latter's opinion was that such far-reaching precautionary measures would create a most unfavourable impression in Berlin, in view of the pact of non-aggression between the two countries.

At 8 p.m. the Premier, Stauning, and the ministers of Foreign Affairs, Defence and Finance conferred with the leaders of the four most important political parties. They were of the opinion that in the case of a conflict about Norway, Germany would make certain demands of Denmark; and in view of the fact that the country was well-nigh unarmed, these would have to be conceded. These views were cautiously put to the German Minister.

That night at 4 a.m. von Renthe-Fink called the department of Foreign Affairs to say that he had been instructed to ask for an appointment with the Minister at 4.20. The Danish official in charge assumed that 4.20 p.m. was meant, but his error was quickly made clear to him. Not half an hour later, at the moment that the German Minister delivered the ultimatum to Dr. Munch, the operations of the German *Wehrmacht* were already begun. 'Despite the early hour of my call, which surely indicated something unusual, they were quite unprepared for the purport of my message,' stated von Renthe-Fink, before the end of the week, in a communication to Berlin. 'The news that German troops had already crossed the Danish frontier, and were about to land in Copenhagen was something they would not believe at first.' [1]

[1] Communication of von Renthe-Fink to the *Auswärtige Amt*, April 15, 1940. *Bilag til Beretning til Folketinget afgivet af den af Tinget under 25. Oktober 1950 nedsatte Kommission i Henhold til Grundlovens § 45.* [Supplementary Report of the Commission of Enquiry, 1950, of the Danish Lower House], Vol. XII, *Tyske Dokumenter* (Copenhagen, 1951), p. 214. This source will in future be referred to as *Danish Parl. Enq.*, Vol. XII (docum.).

Poor startled government!
Poor people, taken by surprise!
The population especially, surprised and overpowered in its sleep, sought an explanation for the baffling rapidity of the invasion. That the Government had failed was clear to all, and many bitter reproaches were spoken. But then, were the means used by those cunning Germans such that an ordinary society could prepare itself against them? How could the German troops have been at hand so soon? The rumour spread that they had been hidden in the holds of some German ships which had come into the harbour of Copenhagen some days before, and that on the ferry from Warnemunde to Gjedser they had hidden themselves in some freight-cars; but as soon as the ferry had put to sea, they had issued forth 'like the Greeks out of the Trojan Horse' [1] to take possession of the ship.

In the capital, numerous Danish offices were occupied by the Germans in the morning of April 9; German residents, zealous and enthusiastic, showed them the way and acted as interpreters. In no time the broadcasting, post, telegraph and telephone offices, the railways and the news agencies were placed under German supervision. The Germans knew exactly where to go. That could not have been improvised! It had required months of painstaking preparation!

Now and again the Danish press had given reports about espionage networks that had been rolled up. Not half a year before a group of nine German nationals had been arrested, having worked on shipping espionage under Horst von Pflugk-Hartung, correspondent of the *Berliner Börsenzeitung*; this was one group that had been unmasked—how many had been able to do their work undisturbed, helping and preparing the invasion of Denmark as a Fifth Column? The *volksdeutschen* Nazis (German-speaking Danes from North Schleswig) who had appeared in the streets fully armed almost as soon as the German troops arrived, had probably not been up to much good, either!

'The Government shoulders full responsibility for what has happened,' announced Premier Stauning, bent and aged, the same evening, in a session of parliament lasting but twelve minutes. When the assembly silently left the building it was cloudy, and in the blackout the city was so pitch-dark (according to a parliamentary correspondent) 'that we had to crawl down the steps of our parliament building on all fours.' [2]

In like manner the people of Denmark sought their way through

[1] *The Times* (London), April 11, 1940.
[2] Knud Secher: *Kampf ohne Waffen, Dänemark unter der Besatzung* (Zürich, 1945), p. 7.

the uncertain times ahead—baffled, sad, full of cares and self-reproach, but convinced that the Germans they had tolerated in their midst had been the vanguard and accomplices of the German *Wehrmacht*, which had quenched the light of Denmark's freedom in the space of a few hours.

Norway

What had happened in Norway on the same April 9, 1940?

In this country as well the first three months of the year had not passed without causing grave concern to its citizens. During the first week of April tension rose. With increased urgency the British and French Governments repeated their request to have an end put to the situation by which the Germans could obtain iron ore from distant Narvik by way of the Norwegian territorial waters; the Norwegian government, however, would not consider giving up the country's neutrality. This Government as well received reports of German convoys in the Baltic, but like the Danish Government, the Norwegian was not able to ascertain how true these reports were, nor what exactly they purported. The same can be said of the message from the Norwegian Minister in Berlin dated Friday, April 5, 1940, concerning rumours about the occupation of points in Southern Norway.

That Friday a large number of senior Norwegian officers had been invited to the German Legation to see the film *Feuertaufe* ('Baptism of Fire')—made at the instigation of Hitler himself to show the annihilation of the Polish republic. In silence and much depressed, the Norwegians looked on. They saw the German Air Force roar over the plains and destroy Warsaw. Less than three days later several of those who had attended the show were inclined to believe that the invitation had not been given without reason.

While Professor Koht, the minister of Foreign Affairs, was busy preparing the protest against the Allied note which had been received that morning, concerning the mine-laying off the Norwegian coast, information came through that large German units had been sighted off the west coast of Denmark; a few hours later news was received from the news agencies that lifeboats carrying hundreds of German soldiers, soaked to the skin, had reached land in the South of Norway, saying that they were from a German ship, the *Rio de Janeiro*, which had been on its way to Bergen on the west coast. The Norwegian Legation in London sent warning that according to the British Admiralty a German attack on Narvik was to be expected.

Premier Nygaardsvold called the Cabinet together and at 9.15 p.m. the decision was taken to order partial mobilisation for certain vulnerable areas; of the size and the extent of the coming German landing, however, the Cabinet had no idea.

That night at half-past one the Cabinet assembled again, had the brigades in South Norway mobilised, and decided not to succumb without recourse to arms. When the German Minister, Bräuer, called on the minister of Foreign Affairs at 4.20 in the small hours of the early morning, to present von Ribbentrop's demands, he was given the Cabinet's answer after a short deliberation: 'We shall not submit voluntarily; the struggle is already on.' [1]

Though not taken by surprise to the same extent as the Danish Government, the Norwegians were but so recently aware of the full extent of the dangers impending that they could not bring the country into an effective state of defence in time. The Norwegian people, however, were as much the victim of surprise as were the Danes. The press accounts of naval movements in the North Sea had been read with only half a thought as to their real meaning; it had been supposed that they indicated a second Battle of Jutland. War on their own soil? Unthinkable!

The members of the Reserve Officers Club had attended a lecture that evening on the subject of 'Table pleasures in Ancient Rome'. What the wailing sirens implied shortly after midnight, no one knew. Perhaps the naval battle was on, and some of the planes taking part had crossed the Norwegian coast-line. 'When a lieutenant in the Air Corps, a mere youngster, gave this theory with all the weight of his authority the majority agreed that this was probably right. None of us dreamed of a German landing in Norway'—thus Sigrid Undset described her own reactions and those of the people around here, in the then unusual surroundings of an air-raid shelter (of which the key had at first been mislaid).[2] Nothing further happened and everybody went to bed again.

On waking up in the morning, people read in the papers that heavy fighting was going on in the Oslo fjord and that the two airfields of the capital, Fornebu and Kjeller, had been bombed by the Germans. German bombers flew over the town at such a low level that the crews could be seen in their cockpits, their machine-guns chattering. People made their way to work, though inwardly trembling with fear: they had seen photographs of the fate that had befallen Warsaw —was the same fate awaiting Oslo? The shooting continued; then

---

[1] Bräuer to the *Auswärtige Amt*, April 9, 1940. *Innstilling fra Undersökelse-Kommisjonen av 1945, utgitt av Stortinget, Bilag* [Account of the Commission of Enquiry of the Norwegian Lower House, Supplement], Vol. II, p. 319. In future to be cited as: *Norw. Parl. Enq.* These reports are less voluminous than the Danish ones but they too, form a source of important information.

[2] Sigrid Undset: *Return to the Future* (New York, 1942), p. 11.

the louder reports of anti-aircraft guns were heard. Rumours were general that the city would be blitzed; at about 10 a.m. the broadcasting station announced that the population should leave the town immediately; German planes were still skimming over the roof-tops:

At the entrances to the underground the people were struggling madly to get down into the tunnel; there are no other public shelters in Oslo. Some people sought shelter in doorways, others ran into the park near the palace, all were distracted with fear, dismay and doubt. Others, again, fled or tried to flee from the town, trundling prams, on trucks, storming the stations where every bit of rolling stock was loaded to the limit and sent away from the town, to the country.[1]

While part of the population turned their backs on the town in panic, other beings were coolly and collectedly marching into the city: the first detachments of German troops from the airports on their way to the Government buildings. Around midday they reached their objective; and from the south, from the direction of the fjord, distant gunfire was still to be heard. No one knew what to do. How was it conceivable that these German troops, in broad daylight, nearly 400 miles from the nearest German port, could be marching into the capital and calmly occupying all the Government buildings? The remaining population looked on dumbly.

One hour after the other went by in ineffectual confusion until, early in the evening, a new voice was heard from the loudspeakers: Vidkun Quisling. About ten years before this man had been a Government Minister for a little while; later he had founded a national-socialist party, *Nasjonal Samling*, which had polled less than 2 per cent of the votes in the 1936 elections; and now he presented himself as Prime Minister of the country. He disclosed that the Nygaardsvold Government had proclaimed a general mobilisation, which decision he, Quisling, had annulled. People should co-operate with the Germans, and to that end they should rally round him—round Vidkun Quisling, Prime Minister.

People could hardly believe their ears.

But there were more surprises in store for them!

Where exactly the Germans had landed was not at first known. When, however the first German men-of-war were riding at anchor in the harbour before the capital one day later, it had become an established fact that the Germans had not only penetrated into Oslo, but also into all the other important ports along the lengthy Norwegian coast: Kristiansand, Egersund, Stavanger and Bergen in the

[1] *Nieuwe Rotterdamsche Courant*, April 14, 1940.

south, Trondhjem in the centre and Narvik in the extreme north. The Norwegians were trapped.

How had this happened? How had they been caught unawares like that? One might turn to the annals of history without coming across one instance of a surprise on so large a scale and so successful, and which was at the same time so mortifying and humiliating. There *could* have been no question of a fair struggle. The Germans *must* have thought out and used tricks which made resistance impossible. Surely they must have made much use-of helpers and accomplices, who, like Quisling, had stood ready in the early morning of April 9 to stab the Norwegian people in the back. Almost immediately a whole swarm of rumours came into being, all purporting to explain at least something of the miraculously successful German landings and the further progress of the German troops.

There had been a great deal of sabotage, so people told each other. False orders had been passed on by means of letters and the telephone, so that some Norwegian troops had stopped their resistance prematurely and wrongly. The wires connecting the mine barrage in the Oslo fjord had been cut. In all the occupied ports the Germans had smuggled in troops in ships beforehand, and they had stormed ashore on that fatal 9th of April with weapons that had been previously smuggled in too. Other Germans, disguised as tourists or as members of the crews of the German merchant navy, had already been staying some time in the ports that were to be taken by surprise.

In Oslo there had already been numerous Germans in readiness, travelling salesmen, agents who had known exactly what was expected of them on April 9. The German nationals who lived in Oslo and who were acting as interpreters and guides had been implicated in the plot to a man. Quisling and his partisans all had their instructions: in Oslo Quisling had been ready with his proclamation while in Narvik the town commandant, Lieutenant-Colonel Sundlo, had been ready with his offer of immediate capitulation. And, yes, it all came back now, many years previously he had allowed a German Nazi to photograph military targets. . . .

And these Germans seemed to know everything. Their knowledge of the country was staggering. They must have acted the spy on a perfectly gigantic scale for years. What had all those German attaché's, consuls, commercial agents, travellers, tourists, sailors and hikers done other than take good note of everything, and make drawings and snapshots of it all? All that information collected by stealth, by people who had been greeted as guests and strangers by the Norwegians, had laid the basis for the action of the military forces. And these were for the most part from Austria, as was only too clear from their accent. Then the Norwegians remembered that after the first World War they had nursed starving Viennese children by the thousand. How meanly, how basely was their generous hospitality being requited! Their foster-children, the *Wienerbarn* of 1920, had come back in 1940 because *they* already knew the people and the country.

There was a general outcry of horror. People felt as if defiled, caught in traps and snares that had been set everywhere one looked. Quisling, in coming to the fore, had thrown off his mask—but how many still wore theirs?

The attack on Norway had the effect of a bomb-shell on the whole of the western world. Once more Hitler had been too much for England and France. Not only had he occupied Oslo, but also Bergen and Trondhjem, Narvik even, while sailing right past the British battle fleet. At first people refused to believe that Narvik too had been occupied. Neville Chamberlain, who had expressed his view only a few days previously that 'Hitler would miss the bus', said in the House of Commons that he supposed it was not Narvik but Larvik that was meant, a small harbour at the entrance to the Oslo fjord.

That same Tuesday morning in Paris Prime Minister Reynaud sat bent over his map with his nearest fellow-workers for at least five minutes vainly looking for some other Narvik on the Norwegian coast, 'convinced as we were that the Narvik where the German troops were supposed to be could not possibly be the harbour for ore in the north'.[1]

Unfortunately, by the evening it had become a certainty. It was the real Narvik that had fallen into German hands. They had ensconced themselves strongly in Oslo as well. All the important harbours were in their power. Hitler had achieved what the *Kaiser* had failed to do: he had penetrated as far as the Arctic Ocean, just as if there were no such things as the British Navy or the French *marine de guerre*. How otherwise could this inconceivably bold enterprise be explained except by supposing that Hitler had large numbers of tools, Germans as well as Danes and Norwegian, in all the places he had meant to occupy?

The correspondent for Denmark of the London *Times* was not certain to what extent the operations of the Fifth Column had been decisive. It was a fact, however, that 'members of the large German colony undoubtedly played pre-arranged roles, as did a number of German reserve officers in civilian clothes who had obtained Danish visas in the guise of commercial travellers'.[2] The *Sunday Express*,

[1] Paul Baudouin: *Neuf mois au gouvernement: avril–décembre 1940* (Paris, 1948), p. 22.
[2] *The Times* (London), April 22, 1940.

one of England's biggest Sunday papers, was even more positive: 'All the Germans resident in Denmark were roped in for subversive work . . . the whole German colony in Sweden is mobilised for propaganda, corruption and spying.' [1]

And then look at Norway!

The false orders, the cut wires, the sabotaging officers, the soldiers and arms that had been smuggled in, the German fishermen, commercial travellers, tourists and foster-children who had one and all acted the spy, all these appeared in almost every article in the daily papers, first in the news reports and afterwards in the editorial commentaries. What Leland Stowe, reporter of the *Chicago Daily News*, had to say about Oslo once he had arrived in Stockholm, the Swedish capital, made the deepest impression of all. He had been on his return from Finland, and had lingered a bit in Norway. It began: 'I believe it to be the most important newspaper despatch I have ever had occasion to write. . . . It is crying to be told now'; for the first time all the sinister reports from Norway were to be found together in one arresting article. Leland Stowe gave the solution to all the riddles: treachery.

Norway's capital and great seaports were not captured by armed force. They were seized with unparalleled speed by means of a gigantic conspiracy which must undoubtedly rank among the most audacious and most perfectly oiled political plots of the past century. By bribery and extraordinary infiltration on the part of Nazi agents, and by treason on the part of a few highly placed Norwegian civilians and defence officials, the German dictatorship built its Trojan Horse inside Norway. . . . Absolute control by only a handful of key men in administrative positions and in the Navy was necessary to turn the trick and everything had been faultlessly prepared. The conspiracy was about 90 per cent according to schedule. . . .

Stowe's article was taken over by the world press and read with astonishment and dismay. An elderly American professor from the Middle West called what Stowe had written in Stockholm 'the only really enlightened despatches'. [2]

The source of all these reports and stories did not run dry so soon.

Ten days after Leland Stowe an English eyewitness of the occupation in Bergen recounted in *The Times* how he had heard from a German soldier 'that he and his comrades had been hidden on

---

[1] *Sunday Express* (London), April 14, 1940.
[2] Francis Neilson: *The Tragedy of Europe. A Diary of the second World War.* Vol. I, 1938–1940 (Appleton, 1940), p. 443.

board these ships in Bergen for four weeks before the invasion'.[1] The English troops who were evacuated from Norway after their abortive attack on Trondhjem in the beginning of May came back with similar information. They too had been powerless against an opponent working with diabolical means. 'The place was full of spies,' lamented a Scottish soldier of the Royal Engineers; 'every move we made was known to the Germans almost as soon as we had made it.' [2]

Where else were such traitors lying in wait?

The Fifth Column in Poland, had received but little attention in Western Europe and America, but with his attack on Denmark and Norway Hitler stood on the very threshold of Western civilisation. There he had not overrun a 'backward nation' like the Polish, but the orderly, decent communities of democratic Danes and Norwegians. Just as in Austria and Czechoslovakia, so also in Norway Hitler had found a citizen of the state he was going to conquer who was willing to play Judas. Quisling had only followed in the footsteps of Seyss-Inquart and Konrad Henlein.

In addition, however, the whole pattern of the German *military* attack, so people felt, had become clear in the two Scandinavian states for the first time: through spies, saboteurs, false orders and hidden arms. Was there one German national who could be trusted? In every German firm abroad there might be an arms depot, and every German traveller to get out of a plane in Sofia or Santiago, in Cairo or Brisbane, in Cape Town or Vancouver might be carrying the bacteria with him in his luggage with which Hitler hoped to infect the peoples he had in mind to subdue.

It was not only the nations who were at times assailed by these fears.

After the happenings in Denmark and Norway many governments felt themselves entitled and in duty bound to take far-reaching measures to ensure internal safety. They were stimulated in this by a nervous public opinion.

In Sweden strangers were forbidden to ride in private cars or taxis. Factories and public utility services were put under the supervision of dependable workers.

In Switzerland the government warned the people against incorrect information in time of war; if their country were to be attacked it would defend itself and any news of a possible capitulation would be a trick on the part of the enemy.

[1] *Daily Telegraph* (London), April 17, 1940.
[2] *The Times* (London), May 8, 1940.

The Rumanian Government placed a ban on arms and cameras for foreigners; they had to hand in their passports to the police, and if they failed to do so they were put across the frontier.

In Yugoslavia, where according to reports a secret Gestapo centre had been traced as early as February, 1940, a whole series of house-to-house searches was executed among *Reichsdeutsche* and *Volksdeutsche*. This brought documents to light from which it was thought to appear 'that in the case of a crisis in the interior 30,000 people were in readiness at special places scattered throughout the country. At a given order' they were to 'occupy certain posts and objects'.[1]

In the far-away Dutch East Indies reports about the German and Norwegian Fifth Column caused such agitation and such drastic measures were demanded from the government against the German nationals and the Dutch national socialists living there, that the Governor-General in one of his rare addresses defended himself against the reproach that the government did nothing. 'The unrest which is threatening,' he said, 'although psychologically it is easily accounted for, is not justified by the order of events.'[2] But then why, his listeners wondered, was there a house-search in a big German firm not two weeks later? Why was the *German House* in Batavia situated next door to the offices of the broadcasting company? Why did the new concrete office building of the German firm *Siemens und Halske* look as if it might be turned into a fortress in the twinkling of an eye?

These and similar reports, statements, rumours, questions and suppositions were eagerly snatched up by the press and the radio. People had become alarmed and they were not going to be outwitted. On all sides measures were conceived for heading off the national socialist Fifth Column, before it should resume its deadly advance. This process of preparedness was still going on when May 10, 1940, dawned.

[1] *Telegraaf* (Amsterdam), May 1, 1940.
[2] *Nieuwe Rotterdamsche Courant*, April 24, 1940.

CHAPTER III

The invasion of the Netherlands

★

The outbreak of the second World War had had little effect on the quiet national life in the Netherlands. People were sorry for Poland and admired Finland. There was general appreciation of the fact that France and Britain had declared war on Germany, and heartfelt hope that they would be victorious. How? That was another matter. Most people did not see the war as a conflict which could determine the course of their own lives directly. The country had remained neutral during the 1914–18 conflagration; now it was neutral again.

Nevertheless, one could not be altogether easy in one's mind.

In the winter of 1939–40 there was on several occasions an acute fear of a German invasion. On November 9, 1939, and again on January 15, 1940, all military leave was stopped; the first alert was thought to be connected with an incident at the frontier near Venlo, where some British intelligence officers were abducted across the frontier and a Dutch officer was fatally wounded; the second with the forced landing of a German plane in Belgium, which was reported to have had military documents aboard.

There were other signs as well, less important perhaps than the complete manning of the defence lines, but nevertheless increasing the nervous tension. In the first week of November, 1939, the discovery was made that a Dutchman, living close to the German frontier, had attempted to smuggle some trunks full of Dutch uniforms into Germany. The press was full of reports. The father of this man was known as a member of the NSB, the *Nationaal Socialistische Beweging*, the principal Nazi movement in the Netherlands. The would-be smuggler had ordered two complete uniforms from a second-hand store in Amsterdam, and also a postman's uniform 'quite complete', railwaymen's uniforms 'complete', and the uniform of a state policeman 'quite complete'.[1] All these articles were present in the trunks.

A few months later, in January and February, 1940, light signals of varying colours were observed in many parts of the country. Police and the army were alerted. Every evening patrols were sent out to investigate in all provinces; nowhere could a culprit be detected. The commander of the field-army had cross-bearings of the signals mapped out; but neither rhyme nor reason could be discovered in this way. Were German agents and accomplices practicing for the time that their signal system would be needed, say on the occasion of the German invasion? Or was the enemy, who was after all not such a fool as to alarm an intended victim, only trying to make the Dutch nervous?

The smuggling of uniforms, the light signals, and the frequently reported cases of espionage by foreigners, mostly Germans (though in one sensational case a senior civil servant of the Department of Social Affairs was involved), led to the realisation among a number of the Dutch that special caution was indicated. They knew NSB members and *Reichsdeutsche* in their own neighbourhood, and kept an eye on them. If they noticed anything suspicious, they warned the police. The Attorney-General at the Court of Justice at Amsterdam heard 'the most fantastic tales: "They are now here, Sir, please come immediately!" And when one of the best detectives was sent there, he could find nothing out of the ordinary. Perhaps only a trunk full of stage properties was being dispatched. And so on.' [2]

The occupation of Denmark and Norway, April 9, 1940, caused a tremendous commotion. Every new edition of the newspapers reported fresh and revolting details of the treachery of Quisling and his followers, and of the deeds of German spies and saboteurs. Immediately it was decided to improve the defences of some of the Dutch airfields, and to plough up others. On Thursday, April 11, the government issued a warning against passing on rumours 'lacking foundation in truth that were being circulated by unpatriotic elements'.[3]

It happened that a few days after the invasion of the two Scandinavian countries, a large German official envelope was found near The Hague by a passer-by; it was addressed to H. Cohrs, care of the *Auslands-Organisation der NSDAP* in Berlin. It obviously contained

---

[1] *Vooruit* (The Hague), Nov. 4, 1939.

[2] Interrogation of Mr. J. A. van Thiel, *Tweede Kamer der Staten-Generaal, Enquêtecommissie 'Regeringsbeleid 1940–1945'* [Second Chamber of the Netherlands Parliament. Commission of Enquiry into the Government's policy 1940–1945], Vol. Ic, p. 204. Reports, appendixes and interrogations of the Commission will henceforth be cited as: *Neth. Parl. Enq.* They are a source of unique importance.

[3] *Nieuwe Rotterdamsche Courant*, April 12, 1940.

a considerable number of documents. To be on the safe side the finder took the envelope to a police station, and a few hours later it lay on the desk of the Police Commissioner of The Hague, as yet unopened. The latter rang up the Secretary-General of the Department of Justice, and said: ' "I have an unusual bit of lost property; it is an official German letter." ' So I answered [the Secretary-General is speaking]: ' "There may very well be some kind of bomb in it. You must always be careful with such things." ' [1]

It was decided to open the envelope.

Eight separate papers appeared, fifteen pages in all, mostly typed, some with handwritten notes, several on note-paper with the heading of the German Legation and signed by a certain O. Butting, attaché, also head of the *Reichsdeutsche Gemeinschaft* (the organisation set up in 1934 after the Netherlands Government had banned the country-group of the *Auslands-Organisation der NSDAP*). The papers contained dozens of spy reports from all over the country; descriptions of fortifications, airfields and road obstructions; records of overheard telephone conversations; reports on the movements of troops. Apparently many agents were at work under the supervision of a certain 'Jonathan', whose signature also appeared on some of the documents.

The Netherlands authorities had often wondered what exactly Butting's work might be; the man was not conspicuous in diplomatic circles. That he might be the organiser of German espionage had 'simply not been considered by anybody'.[2] Now the irrefutable evidence lay exposed. He was given a few hours to leave the country.

On April 19 a state of emergency was proclaimed for the whole country, so as to enable the military command to take immediate steps if circumstances so demanded, in view of what had been reported about Norway. The government thought to have many persons of doubtful loyalty detained; however, the Commander-in-Chief of the army and navy, General H. G. Winkelman, regarded the detention of only twenty-one of them as sufficient for the time being. The authorities regarded Anton Mussert, the leader of the NSB, 'as too much of a nobody to do him the honour of belonging to the twenty-one persons considered dangerous enough to be run in'.[3] Mr. M. M. Rost van Tonningen, a fanatical NSB member, and main spokesman of the party in parliament, was one of those detained. 'Many people,' said the Premier in a broadcast speech, had not been detained 'because there was not sufficient evidence that their actions were dangerous.' [4]

[1] Interrogation of Mr. J. R. M. van Angeren, *Neth. Parl. Enq.*, Vol. IIc, p. 180.
[2] Interrogation of Mr. E. N. van Kleffens, *ibid.*, p. 323.
[3] Interrogation of Mr. J. A. van Thiel, *ibid.*, Vol. Ic, p. 202.
[4] *Nieuwe Rotterdamsche Courant*, May 4, 1940.

Apparently there were more suspects!

In this connection everybody thought of the NSB members.

For more than seven years the NSB had identified itself with national socialist Germany. Why, the people were asking themselves, should one not expect the same of Mussert as of Quisling? It was recalled that Quisling had visited a rally of the NSB in 1935. Mussert himself encouraged the general opinion of his traitorous intentions through his attitude during an interview with a correspondent of the Columbia Broadcasting System:

> Miss Breckinridge asked: 'In the case of a German attack on the Netherlands, would the Dutch Nazis accept German assistance to further their own end in the Netherlands, or would they fight for their Queen?' According to Miss Breckinridge the answer to this question, as given by the 'leader' was, that now that Nazis were no longer allowed to be officers of the armed forces, they (the Nazis) would do absolutely nothing more than sit like this, and at that he crossed his arms and sat back in his chair.[1]

Could his traitorous intention have been expressed more clearly?

On May 10 war came as a surprise.

The aim of German Headquarters was to reach the 'Fortress of Holland' by way of the southern part of the country, with armoured and infantry divisions, at the same time swinging round into Belgium, all as part of the general offensive on the Western front. To realise this aim the immediate capture of the bridges across the river Maas and the Maas-Waal canal would be imperative. At dawn that day attacks were launched on all the bridges from Maastricht to near Arnhem by people who looked like civilians and by persons dressed in the Dutch uniforms of mounted police, military police, railway personnel. In many places the ruse was not discovered in time, and the commands receiving news of this misuse of mufti and uniforms— the reason for the smuggling of uniforms in the previous November was now disclosed—had to take hurried measures to relieve the situation caused by this reverse.

In the west of the country a still greater crisis had to be faced.

German parachutists were dropped near the bridges at Moerdijk and Dordrecht; other troops, at Rotterdam, clambered out of sea-planes which had alighted on the river Maas, and occupied the bridge there; the airfield of Waalhaven, to the south of Rotterdam, was captured by parachutists and airborne troops; finally the Germans attempted to capture three airfields in the neighbourhood of

[1] *Nieuwe Rotterdamsche Courant*, April 30, 1940.

The Hague in a similar way, in order to occupy the government centre there, and capture Queen Wilhelmina, the Cabinet and the military high command.

The attacks on the three airfields near The Hague were only partly successful; Dutch troops fought back fiercely and one field was soggier than the Germans had expected. Before 7 a.m. aircraft of the later waves of the German attack were circling above the west of the Netherlands in search of suitable emergency landing strips; some landed on the sandy sea-shore, others on the highway between The Hague and Rotterdam, others again in the meadows near Delft. If people did not see the parachutists themselves, they at least could not fail to hear about them. The look-outs of the civil defence corps, which had no shortwave transmitters at their disposal, were linked to the ordinary radio stations, which broadcast their reports: time after time people heard that German bombers, fighters or transport aircraft were approaching or circling or dropping parachutists—undisturbed and masters of the air. There was no end to it. One scaring bit of news after another.

Rumours soon spread that only part of the parachutists wore German uniforms; others were said to be dressed as farmers, policemen, postmen, conductors, priests, even as women, especially as nuns. Who was friend, who enemy? The butcher-boy approaching there might well be carrying hand grenades in his basket!

In Rotterdam and The Hague, both large population centres and under immediate threat from the enemy, nervousness reached a high pitch.

Already in the early morning the Germans in Rotterdam held the Waalhaven airfield and the rail and road bridges across both arms of the River Maas. The capture of the airfield had been facilitated by the fact that the commander of the detachment responsible for the safety of the field had deployed part of his troops in the direction of Rotterdam, in expectation of an attack by Dutch Nazis. The inhabitants of South Rotterdam saw *Reichsdeutsche*, especially pupils of the *Deutsche Schule*, acting as guides to the airborne troops; German soldiers who had been made prisoner-of-war, proved to be in possession of 'sketches of an area of 200 by 200 metres in which they were to operate. The places where they had to report were marked.' [1]

Such tales and rumours spread like wildfire.

Similar stories were told about the bridges across the Maas. There as well the surprise of the attack had been complete. As the first German soldiers, after paddling to the shore from their planes in collapsible rubber boats, came walking across the bridge, civilians

---

[1] Interrogation of Lt.-Col. J. D. Backer, *Neth. Parl. Enq.*, Vol. Ic, p. 367.

'gaping with surprise' asked a passing messenger-boy: 'Whoever are they?' [1] The available Netherlands troops were unable to dislodge the Germans from the bridges; the latter were too heavily armed. A Dutch army captain who managed to get across the bridges when they had already been manned by the Germans, had seen (and that seemed to be the explanation of all that heavy armament): '. . . that from a Swedish ship, lying to the west of the Maas bridge, . . . mortars, motor-cycles with side-cars, radio sets and other army goods were being unloaded'. [2] On the island in the Maas (joined to both banks of the river by the bridges) several German firms had their offices and warehouses; it was generally assumed that German military goods had been hidden there, preparatory to their being put to effective use by the German troops.

At the Rotterdam district army headquarters the staff at first did not know what to do to fend off the deadly danger that had suddenly sprung up from nowhere.

Alarming reports 'poured in, by telephone as well as brought in by civilians, concerning supposed action by parachutists in different parts of the town, and shootings from houses by unknown persons'. [3] Houses were searched by the hundred, especially at those addresses where members of the Dutch Nazi party were known to live. Soldiers climbed down into cellars and up on to roofs; suspects were delivered up to the police.

In The Hague as well the nervous tension was great on that 10th of May.

Nobody had expected that the royal residence and seat of government would be so directly threatened; the defence of the town had not been prepared, clear-cut instructions were lacking. The troops consisted mostly of young recruits spread over a number of depots, the commanders did not know from which side the Germans, who were landing from the air on all sides of the town, would approach. Even before 6 a.m. defence cordons were thrown around the centre of the town; the minister of Foreign Affairs, Mr. E. N. van Kleffens, on his way to his Department to receive the German ultimatum, was obliged to 'parley' for twenty minutes, and to ring Dutch General

---

[1] *Historisch overzicht betreffende afwijkingen van normale regelingen, extra getroffen maatregelen, feiten, gebeurtenissen enz., welke zich van 10 Mei t/m 30 Juni 1940 bij het P.T. en T.-bedrijf hebben voorgedaan* (stencilled) (The Hague, 1940), p. 625. This source will henceforth be cited as: *Historisch overzicht PTT-1940.*

[2] Major-General V. E. Nierstrass: *De strijd om Rotterdam, Mei 1940* (The Hague, 1952), p. 33, note 2. This is one of the volumes on the German invasion, May 1940, prepared by the war historical section of the Netherlands army general staff.

[3] *Ibid.,* p. 49.

Headquarters before the nervous and suspicious sentries would let him pass.[1]

It was at about the same time, 6 a.m. in the early morning, that the commander of the air defences of The Hague came into the possession of a dossier found in the wreck of a German transport plane that had crashed in the centre of the town. Sketch-maps indicated how to proceed by the shortest route from one of the airfields to the royal palace, or alternatively to Scheveningen where the Queen had a private residence. The most alarming part, however, was a battalion order in which the following statement, among others, was found: 'In the battle-area German civilians under special orders are in readiness. They are in possession of passes of the accompanying type. They must be given every support they ask for by the troops. Intensive instruction on this point is imperative.' The specimen pass was lacking, but that the enemy was making use of civilian accomplices was obvious.

Cautionary measures were increased to the utmost. Some officers maintained that they had been shot at on their way to their posts; others had been forced to keep civilians who tried to lay hands on them at a distance by drawing out their pistols. The feeling of insecurity increased from hour to hour, augmented as it was by rumours that prominent public men—the president of the Royal Dutch Airlines, the Postmaster General—had been shown up as traitors.

The general nervousness was fanned by the relative isolation of the civilian population. Most telephone lines were cut, postal services were stopped; only the newspapers were still delivered. The news in the papers was all of the same tenor, scanty and disquieting. People sat by their radios and listened avidly to the discouraging reports of the civil defence corps. The radio further gave warning against persons spreading the rumour that the drinking water had been poisoned; these miscreants were to be arrested.

The first army communiqué—awaited with suspense—was broadcast on May 11, and was still hopefully worded. It confirmed the Fifth Column action by making mention of a German armoured train in which Dutch uniforms had been found, and by stating that in The Hague 'an attempt to take the main police station by surprise had failed completely'.

That same second day of war, General Headquarters announced that Germans living in The Hague had attempted to advance on the centre of the town from a house in the western part. They had been driven back to the house, where they had been subjected to gunfire, 'after which the surviving Germans had surrendered'. Furthermore,

[1] Interrogation of Mr. E. N. van Kleffens, *Neth. Parl. Enq.*, Vol. IIc, p. 292.

it was officially announced that a Dutch army unit 'had been fired at by persons, some of whom were dressed in mufti, others in Dutch army uniforms'.

It was obviously a first requirement that *Reichsdeutsche* and NSB members should immediately be put out of the way to prevent their doing further mischief.

From 1938 the Netherlands police had taken much trouble to register the names and addresses of all those persons who were to be regarded as unreliable: for the whole country it came to about 1,500 *Reichsdeutsche* and 800 Dutchmen, mostly members of the NSB. On the morning of May 10, at 5 a.m., code telegrams were sent out, authorising the Attorneys-General to have all these 2,300 persons arrested. The Commander-in-Chief of the Armed Forces ordered that all other Germans or 'aliens of German origin' were to remain within doors; this included some tens of thousands of Jewish and political refugees. Arrest parties were formed and police-cars began to move.

The fact that all persons considered dangerous had been taken into custody so soon was not generally known. But what did dangerous mean? Was not every NSB member a traitor, every *Reichsdeutsche* a Fifth Columnist! Whoever felt called upon to do so or felt qualified, helped arrest them. 'Everyone then thought they might as well start arresting them, soldiers, sergeants, lieutenants and burgomasters.' [1] The treatment differed locally; sometimes it was correct, sometimes not. Especially in the big population centres many were unable to control their feelings when they saw the followers of Adolf Hitler and Anton Mussert being led away. But their hatred of the Dutch Nazis was greatest:

> There was a shouting of: 'Hands up!' National socialists were being chased down the stairs with their wives and children. Then, with their hands up, they have to wait in front of their doors for everyone to see until the house-search is finished. Loaded revolvers and rifles with bayonets keep them covered. Every movement is considered an 'assault'. 'Take your hands out of your pockets!'— 'Hold your jaws or you'll get the bullet!'—'Dirty traitors, shut your heads!'—'They ought to drown the lot of you!' [2]

So many people were arrested that the whole plan went wrong. In the district of Amsterdam where they had counted on eight hundred being interned the actual number rose to over six thousand. Added to them were thousands more from other parts of the country.

[1] Interrogation of Mr. J. A. van Thiel, *Neth. Parl. Enq.*, Vol. Ic, p. 203.
[2] J. de Haas: *Vijf dagen terreur* (Amsterdam, 1940), pp. 13–14.

'During those five days there were indescribable scenes.'[1] Some of those who had been arrested were shot down by nervous soldiers.

It was curious that the arrests made in the first two days of the war did not bring any relief. Rather, the general state of mind became more nervous still. This was also a reaction to the fact that there was no favourable news. The troops suffered from this too. The baptism of fire they were awaiting at the hands of so formidable an opponent was bad enough! Every supposed sign of Fifth Column activity only increased the tension. They had the feeling that parachutists had landed everywhere and that there was no village or town where citizens did not shoot from houses or where light signals were not made at night.

In the army too rumours were rife.

On the very first day the rumour comes that the government has fled. People of note in our society have been murdered. The Germans have landed on the North Sea coast. . . . One cannot name a single commander in the Dutch army who, according to rumour, has not been killed at least once. Over the roads along which our troops are to march poison gas has been observed. Whenever chocolates are found they should be destroyed, because they are sure to be poisoned. In our grenades there was supposed to be sand instead of gunpowder, and the rumour went that casemates had crumbled at the first shot because the concrete was no good.[2]

Elsewhere one might hear that all the women's handbags had to be examined because they might contain hand grenades, or that one was to be on the look out for German soldiers in Dutch uniform 'but without puttees', or that a motor-car with a special number-plate was to be fired at forthwith. 'In the end you did not know *what* to believe.'[3]

In general the troops soon assumed that the retreat and the reverses were to be imputed to treachery and sabotage. If there were Fifth Columnists everywhere then why not in the army as well? Several officers and men were arrested on suspicion of belonging to the Fifth Column. At least two of them were shot out of hand.

The nervousness was greatest in the west of the Netherlands on Sunday and Monday, May 12 and 13. People had the feeling they were not equal to the Fifth Column danger. No sooner had the fire been stamped out in one place than it flared up in ten others. Rumour was rife once more: meat and drinking water were poisoned;

[1] Interrogation of Mr. J. A. van Thiel, *Neth. Parl. Enq.*, Vol. Ic, p. 203.
[2] E. P. Weber: *De vuurproef van het grensbataljon* (Arnhem, 1945), pp. 195–6.
[3] W. A. Poort and Th. N. J. Hoogvliet: *Slagschaduwen over Nederland* (Haarlem, 1946), p. 282.

Fifth Columnists handed round poisoned chocolates and cigarettes; whole towns had already been razed to the ground. Among those who distrusted these rumours there were yet many who believed them to be circulated by the enemy's tools.

It was on Whit-Sunday, May 12, 1940, that the rumour thus spread in Amsterdam, the capital, that the sirens of the aid-raid warning system were out of order. 'I still see,' a refugee from the Netherlands wrote, after arriving in England,

> I still see the man who shouted the alarming news running down the street. 'Who told you?' 'It is a warning from the police office! Tell it to others!' The spreading of this particular rumour was a wonderful piece of organisation on the part of the Fifth Columnists. It was 'issued' at different points in Amsterdam at about the same moment, and spread like wildfire. It was, of course, entirely false, but had its destructive effects on public morale.[1]

It was alleged that various German parachutists had got into Amsterdam but had fortunately been caught; that in a room in the *Hôtel de l'Europe* 'magnesium bombs' had been found by means of which light signals could be made to German bombers; that the Fifth Column had drawn lines in the streets and on walls which contained geographical indications—and in certain parts of the town those marks were already quickly being scrubbed away.

In The Hague the fear of the Fifth Column was still more acute: everyone was aware of the enemy's immediate proximity. On May 11 there was so much firing in the streets that the troops thought they were fighting a general rising of the Dutch Nazis. There was 'plenty of NSB hunting on roofs and in porches'.[2] The shooting was liveliest near a prominent flat-building in the centre of the town where Fifth Columnists were supposed to have entrenched themselves. But everywhere 'cars with carbines pointing out of the doors' were to be seen, 'and policemen, revolvers in hand, shouting: "Hands up!" '[3]

Nobody knew exactly where the enemy was, his presence was suspected everywhere.

On the third day of the war, Sunday, May 12, the situation in The Hague became more confused still. The police too were suspected of being untrustworthy. Youthful members of the civic guard started to disarm them. That day the military commanders came to the conclusion that they would have to take radical steps if they wanted to prevent general chaos. People were instructed to keep their doors

[1] L. de Jong: *Holland fights the Nazis*, p. 16–17.

[2] W. A. Poort and Th. N. J. Hoogvliet: *Slagschaduwen over Nederland* (Haarlem, 1946), p. 63.

[3] A. van Boven (PS. of A. van de Kemp): *Jan Jansen in bezet gebied* (Kampen, 1946), p. 6.

and windows closed; no one was allowed to stand still in the streets; the troops were taken more firmly in hand. The result was that there was considerably less irregular shooting.

But the military authorities, following up the find of the German documents on May 10, had received a similar but much larger dossier that had been found on May 12 under the body of a German near one of the airfields surrounding The Hague. It had belonged to the intelligence-officer of the 22nd German airborne division and it contained a whole series of German espionage reports, many coming from the German military attaché in The Hague, a list of people obviously considered fit for arrest, long lists of garages in The Hague, maps on which not only the most important public utility services were indicated by arrows but also the shelter of the Royal family and the dwellings of the Premier and the minister of Defence. There was also an order concerning the 'citizens' who had been thrown into the struggle 'with special tasks' assigned to them, and a pass that went with it, running as follows:

'Mr. . . .'

The rest of the line had been left blank for a name to be filled in; '. . . has the right to pass through the German lines in the execution of special duties. All the units in the army are requested to help him in every possible way. This pass is only valid when accompanied by an identity card with photo.' The copy that had been found, signed by General Count Sponeck, bore the high number of 206.

More evidence of the extent of the work of the Fifth Column, which, so people thought, the military forces in The Hague were hardly able to master!

The symptoms the Dutch thought they perceived in the invasion of the Netherlands, made the concept of the 'Fifth Column' attain its full strength. Its Spanish origin was forgotten and its content was vague. Everything was summed up in that term that was considered to be contrary to a 'normal', 'respectable' way of conducting a war: so espionage on a grand scale, the enlisting of supporters and the formation of military stores in the country about to be conquered. Or then during the actual attack, duping one's opponent by using his uniform or by operations of combatants in civilian dress, or by assaults not only at but behind the front by means of an air force that dropped parachutists by the thousand. Or again by sowing panic through poisoning foodstuffs, and by creating confusion through issuing false orders, false reports and false rumours.

All these Fifth Column actions were not looked upon as chance infringements, committed by an enemy who otherwise kept to the rules of the military game—*this enemy did not keep to any rules what-*

soever. Defenceless women and children, disarmed prisoners-of-war, he drove on before him whenever it suited his malevolent purpose. The Fifth Column weapon was pre-eminently his weapon for attack, the true form of the national socialist military aggression.

That had become even more clearly apparent in the Netherlands than in Norway, so people felt. In Norway it had been Quisling, Sundlo and a few highly-placed civil and military authorities who had betrayed the country to Hitler. There the *coup*, so one had been able to read, had succeeded thanks to the 'absolute control' exercised 'by a handful of key men in administrative positions and in the Navy'. But in the Netherlands Hitler had launched a Fifth Column on an enormous scale, embracing thousands. *Reichsdeutsche* and Dutch Nazis had shot at the troops from countless ambushes, working in close co-operation with parachutists who had jôined in the turmoil, dressed in inconspicuous disguises like baker's men, priests, farmers, tram conductors, postmen; in fact, there was no trade or profession the clothes of which had not been used to base advantage by the Fifth Column. Any friend might be a foe.

This was the picture that disclosed itself to the bewildered gaze of the Dutch nation during those fateful days of May 10–14, 1940. It was passed on to the free world at large by the press and the radio, by letter and by word of mouth, causing a tidal wave of fear and tension to rise up that flooded the hearts and minds of millions of human beings.

CHAPTER IV

The German offensive in Belgium and France

★

THE Netherlands had been neutral during the first World War. The Belgian nation, in 1940, on the other hand still recalled only too well the nightmare of August, 1914, when the brutal German had ordered his armies to march through Belgium; villages and towns had gone up in flames, civilians accused of shooting at the German troops had been themselves shot by the hundred. After that advance four years of harsh German occupation had followed—years of unrighteousness, moral oppression, misery and forced deportations.

On May 10, 1940, the same enemy was again advancing.

The Dutch did not know from experience what a German war and occupation implied. The Belgians did! All their old fears came to new life. Thank heavens—powerful allies had foreseen the German offensive and had prepared counter-measures!

Hardly had the wireless reported the outbreak of war, hardly had the 'all-clear' sounded after the first air-raid warnings, before the population, from the Ardennes to the North Sea coast, were out on the streets to welcome jubilantly the French and British troops, comrades from the last war. These troops wheeled into Belgium in perfect order, greeted boisterously by people singing the *Marseillaise* and *Tipperary*. The sight of them gave the people confidence that they would succeed in arresting the advance of the German invaders far to the east, and would quickly drive them back. *On les aura!*

But fear was the counterpart of that confidence.

Already on that first day pessimistic rumours were spreading: there was said to be revolution in Paris; Italy had attacked France; the Maginot Line had been broken through; all the villages round Liège were razed to the ground. The police and much of the public were convinced that enemy agents were purposely starting such rumours. In Courtrai, as early as May 10, twelve persons were detained 'suspected of being spies and spreading those rumours'.[1] People were on the look-out for the enemy's accomplices—'la cinquième colonne' as the Walloons (the French-speaking Belgians) called them, 'de vijfde kolom' as the Flemings (the Dutch-speaking Belgians) did.

On May 10 the minister of National Defence appealed to the people by wireless to report to the military authorities or to the organs of the police signs of 'suspicious persons' near military works or strategic points. All receiving sets in motor-cars were to be removed: were there, people wondered, agents of the enemy who had received instructions in this way? On the third day of the war new warnings by the government gave rise to further alarm. The security service made known that German parachutists, dressed as civilians, and in the possession of small radio transmitters had landed 'on several parts of Belgian territory' with the aim of spreading rumours and committing acts of sabotage. The next day it was officially announced that enemy agents 'dressed in light brown uniforms with buttons stamped with the swastika and badges with the letters D.A.P.' had repeatedly attacked the police. The security service requested that all the advertisement placards of 'Pasha' chicory attached to telegraph poles and the like be removed; 'on the back of the posters', it was explained, 'drawings have been found which can give the enemy valuable information about communications, etc.'

Those Germans had thought of everything! Not a single detail had escaped their attention! How long ago, in time of peace, had not those posters been put up, which must now be hurriedly removed to prevent parachutists from finding out where the nearest vulnerable viaduct lay! But how could one recognise those parachutists? They were disguised, as the government had made known on May 13, 'as workmen, priests or Belgian soldiers'; even women were employed by the enemy as spies and saboteurs.

Especially the capital, Brussels, was like a beehive in those first days of war, buzzing with rumours and fears. Reports of military successes were not forthcoming. On the contrary, it became known that the Germans had captured three vitally important bridges across the Albert Canal to the north-west of Liège. How was this possible? They lay under the enfilading fire of the forts round Liège! Had these been silenced? It was uncanny. Was Hitler using secret weapons, gases or deadly rays? Or was it a case of treason? Who could say? But despite the optimistic tone of official news-bulletins— 'Our position is improving hourly', said King Leopold on the 13th

[1] René de Chambrun: *I saw France fall. Will she rise again?* (New York, 1940), p. 119.

—people knew that their own troops were being steadily driven back.

Even on the 12th the French historian Marc Bloch had seen Belgian deserters on the road near Charleroi;[1] that same night an English war correspondent had heard a soldier knock on a door in Brussels and call: 'It's me, mother!'; 'he had returned from the front, where it had not been much to his liking'.[2] Perhaps the number of deserters was not so great, but each of them added to the story of the overwhelming force of the German attack. The first stream of refugees further augmented the tale of woe. In south-eastern Belgium they were cluttering up the roads as early as the 10th. The staffs of the railways and the postal service had received orders to leave before the arrival of the enemy, but tens of thousands, soon hundreds of thousands of the rest of the civilian population did the same on their own account. At least one and a half millions fled to the west of the country, hoping to be able to reach France from there if the need should arise—desperate, excited, uprooted people, nervously reciting the barbarities they had suffered at the hands of the Germans and the Fifth Columnists, or the tales they had heard about them.

The horror, when it became apparent that the route of the flight was blocked! For five days the French kept their frontier closed. When it was opened it was almost too late. German tank divisions, of whose operations the Belgians were unaware, proved to be nearing the Channel. From the mouth of the Somme they advanced irresistably northwards, and in the last ten days of May the civilian population, refugees, tired-out Belgian, French and British soldiers formed a human whirlpool that was driven coastwards by the German advance towards the only port, Dunkirk.

The changing course of war had its greatest effect on the troops which had been rushed to the succour of Belgium. Advancing confidently, they had already in the first days been hard put to it to ward off the heavy German attacks. A week after the start of the struggle their lines of communication and supply in the south had been cut off by a tank offensive that nobody had foreseen; there was nothing to do but to retreat slowly, fighting doggedly against an enemy holding all the aces. The French and British troops considered themselves to be among strangers, in Flanders especially, where they could not understand the people. Many French battalions did not even have military maps. It occasionally happened that battalions met head-on on the same road.

[1] Marc Bloch: *l'Etrange défaite. Témoignage écrit en 1940* (Paris, 1946), p. 31.
[2] J. L. Hodson: *Through the Dark Night. Being some account of a war correspondent's journeys, meetings and what was said to him, in France, Britain and Flanders during 1939–1940* (London, 1941), p. 184.

An intelligence section capable of dealing with suspected Fifth Columnists was not available to the French troops; there was only one way out: to make short shrift with spies and saboteurs. It was said that they were dropped by parachute from German planes, and tales were told of agents, dressed as refugees, passing through the lines. There were hundreds of thousands of refugees; the problem they presented was insoluble. News from elsewhere did not reach these troops, or if it did, the reports were about Fifth Column activities: traitors shooting at their comrades-in-arms; agents in cassock or uniform; Belgian railwaymen who, as Fifth Columnists, purposely hampered transportation, or threw the traffic into utter confusion.

On May 19 René Balbaud, a French soldier, threw himself flat on the ground near Dunkirk. There were shots 'from the window of a farm. Our men have already rushed the place, to break down the door. Parachutists? Fifth Columnists? Nobody knows. Probably once more nothing will be found!' [1] One day later he heard shooting from automatic weapons all around him. 'No one knows what is the matter, but we can't help thinking it must be parachutists. Apparently all telephone communications have been sabotaged.' [2] Two days later a boy of eighteen 'was caught in the act of spying' and shot out of hand; 'it isn't worth looking at'.[3]

The British troops, as well, had become convinced of the existence of the all-pervading Fifth Column.

War-correspondent J. L. Hodson tried to start a conversation with an English corporal, while *en route* for Brussels on May 12; the latter 'could answer nothing till he had seen my identity papers'. As they were talking, a young couple came along on bicycles, all of a dither, because they had seen a stranger hiding in the near-by woods, 'a small man with pink eyes'; they had never seen him before, and 'they were sure that he was a spy'. Furthermore, in that neighbourhood two parachutists with machine-guns had been dropped, one dressed in the uniform of a Belgian policeman, the other in mufti.[4]

Next day Hodson met a titled lady in Brussels, who told him with a frightened mien that the Germans were dropping explosive watches and pencils; through one German bomb not one house was left standing 'within 150 yards radius'.[5] On May 14 he was told by a Scottish soldier that the latter had helped capture some parachutists wearing Belgian uniforms. 'Four dressed as civilians,' the correspondent notes, 'came down yesterday in the heart of Brussels. One landed on a roof and broke his leg. One is still at large.' [6]

[1] René Balbaud: *Cette drôle de guerre* (London, 1941), p. 60.
[2] *Ibid.*, p. 61.   [3] *Ibid.*, p. 67.
[4] Hodson: *Through the Dark Night*, p. 181.
[5] *Ibid.*, p. 182.   [6] *Ibid.*, p. 187.

In Louvain, he heard later, Belgian Fifth Columnists had been arrested by the hundred; 'one man, much suspected, burnt the Belgian flag in the market-place, with loud protestations that he couldn't have it falling into German hands. Was the smoke a signal? Nobody knew.' [1] From the Royal Ulster Rifles Hodson heard that German spies in British uniforms had penetrated into several British headquarters, and that 'in a newly ploughed field an arrow had been found of the type used by the enemy to locate headquarters—a long pointer, fixed in the earth, with three gramophone records at the back'. [2]

On May 21 Hodson was staying in Boulogne:

To-night when the bombing started I stood for a while at the bedroom window over-looking the harbour. One could see two or three fixed lights like small stationary stars. They might, we thought, be signals outlining to the enemy the area to be bombed, and we shouted down to the military police calling attention to them. (It is reported to-day that Swastikas had been chalked up in the streets.) This war seems to be imbued with treachery. [3]

'Imbued with treachery'—that was the impression the soldiers had also. Frequently senior officers were arrested, because their identity was doubted and had to be verified, and 'every odd-looking civilian was immediately suspected to be an enemy agent'. [4]

Naturally in Belgium as well stringent action was taken against all persons suspected of belonging to the Fifth Column: *Reichsdeutsche*, members of the fascist *Vlaams Nationaal Verbond* (Flemish National League) and the Rexist Movement in the first place. It was known to the judiciary authorities that the *Vlaams Nationaal Verbond* received financial support from Germany; the military authorities were concerned about the defeatist propaganda directed by the VNV at the soldiers. The Rexist movement was anti-democratic and had continually agitated against France and Britain. The *reichsdeutschen* guests could not be trusted *per se*; some members of their *Landesgruppe* had been caught spying during the first days of war in 1939. In the German-speaking district of Eupen-Malmédy there were elements that were looked at askance; the troops from that district, as a precautionary measure, had not been armed, but were put to work as units, digging trenches. Mistrust of them did not abate.

On May 10, the first arrests were made. Lists had been compiled of those *Reichsdeutschen*, VNV members and Rexists who were to be locked up. The lists had not all been prepared with equal care; in

[1] Hodson: *Through the Dark Night*, p. 200.   [2] *Ibid.*   [3] *Ibid.*, p. 223.
[4] Nigel Nicolson and Patrick Forbes: *The Grenadier Guards in the war of 1939–1945*, Vol. I, p. 19.

THE GERMAN OFFENSIVE IN BELGIUM AND FRANCE

some places the police had taken the trouble to find out who were the ring-leaders, elsewhere they had only registered the regular readers of the VNV weekly paper; in some places nothing at all had been done. The leader of the Rexists, Léon Degrelle, was arrested on the 10th; the same happened to the principal leaders of the VNV, the most important of whom, Staf de Clercq, was set free on May 12 for unexplained reasons. Quite a number of front-rank communists were arrested at the same time, amongst them five members of Parliament.

All these early arrests went off in a relatively orderly manner. After a few days, however, an enormous new wave of arrests occurred, mainly at the instigation of the disquieted public, with the result that in a short time many prisons became over-crowded. Soldiers under arrest for minor misdemeanours were sent back to their units, and other prisoners were sent home to make room for newcomers. At the same time a decision was made to send the most dangerous of the suspects to France for safe keeping. The transports organised for this purpose were of a strangely-mixed nature.

Thus a train left Brussels with more than eleven hundred detained persons, 'nearly all of them *Reichsdeutsche*, but many Jews as well'; from Wallonia there were 'Rexists, communists, suspects from Eupen and the other German-speaking districts, publicans, police-men'.[1] There was also 'a Persian student, who had been removed from the University as a suspect',[2] and a Yugoslav engineer, who had aroused suspicion in Antwerp by going up and down in the lift of a flat several times—to move his things from the dangerous upper stores where he lived, according to him, but the population had believed he was signalling to the Germans.[3] Priests were arrested as well, because, on principle, 'all clergymen were suspected of being parachutists in disguise'.[4]

In Bruges, on May 15, three buses were loaded with seventy-eight other prisoners, handcuffed together in couples: 'Germans, Dutchmen, Flemings ....; besides Jews, Poles, Czechs, Russians, Canadians, Italians, a Dane, a Swiss, even Frenchmen.' [5]

They were first taken to the prison in Béthune, then to that in Abbeville. 'No more could be received there. The cells were bursting with Fifth Columnists.' [6] The population was in a panic, the military were at their wits' end—at any moment the silhouettes of German tanks might appear on the hill-tops in the east. Twenty-two of the prisoners were shot out of hand near the band-stand.

In Tournay two convoys composed of suspects converged: two

[1] René Lagrou: *Wij verdachten* (Brussels, 1941), p. 24.
[2] *Ibid.*, p. 29.   [3] *Ibid.*, p. 47.   [4] *Ibid.*, p. 109.
[5] *Ibid.*, p. 145.   [6] *Ibid.*, p. 148.

thousand of them from Antwerp, some hundreds from Ghent and environs. All the suspects concentrated here, nearly three thousand all told, were marched through the town on the 14th—the day on which the news spread of the fateful breach of the defences along the Albert Canal. Cries sounded of: 'Shoot them dead! Tear their guts out! What are your bayonets for? Scoundrels! Bastards! Where is your *Führer*? Huns! Swine! Riff-raff! Let them starve!'

'Women advanced on the prisoners to grin and spit at them. Men flourished jack-knives. Children made the sign of "heads-off".' [1] The people were beside themselves with fury.

How many Fifth Column suspects, arrested in Belgium, lost their lives, cannot even be approximately stated. There were shootings in other places besides Abbeville. At a later date it was alleged that of the two thousand *Reichsdeutsche* taken to France—including four officials of the German Embassy in Brussels—twenty-one 'were murdered or died as a result of maltreatment'.[2]

Generally speaking there was more reviling and maltreatment than beating or shooting to death. In most places the police and the law were able to protect the prisoners against the excited public. A large number of the prisoners, furthermore, was carried towards the south, as already mentioned in the case of the convoy from Brussels. For them this was the beginning of their worst sufferings, as they travelled into France under an unclouded sky, in padlocked cattle-trucks on which the words 'Fifth Column', 'spies' and 'parachutists' had been scrawled.

France

More than two months before, on March 7, 1940, the American Under-Secretary of State, Sumner Welles, had arrived in Paris after a tour through the principal capital cities of Europe. He met with a despondent people. 'One could almost sense in the very houses the feeling of sullen apathy which marked most of the faces that one passed in the nearly deserted streets. There was a sensation of general waiting; of an expectation of some dire calamity. Among the innumerable persons with whom I talked, only in the rarest instances, outside of a few governmental departments, did I obtain the impression of hope or vigour, or even, tragically enough, of the will to courage.' [3]

It was a worn-out France, a France exhausted by social and

[1] René Lagrou: *Wij verdachten*, (Brussels, 1941), p. 18.
[2] Julius Reinhard: *Kampfzeit im Ausland. Die Entwicklung der Auslands-Organisation der NSDAP in Belgien* (1941), p. 46.
[3] Sumner Welles: *The Time for Decision* (London, 1944), p. 98.

political strife, that had declared war on Germany that 3rd of
September, 1939. The majority of the nation realised that it was not
possible to let Hitler do as he pleased, and that the point at issue in
the outbreak of war—*Mourir pour Danzig?*—was not Danzig at all.
But how to win it?

In the early morning of May 10 the Germans attacked.

Something of relief passed through the country. At last! The nerve-
racking tension had snapped! The Germans would bleed to death on
the Maginot Line! In Northern France and in Belgium they would
be caught and hewn down. The plans for this were ready: French and
British armies were to march into Belgium together and, contrary to
what happened in 1914, to hold up the advancing Germans far from
French territory. Just as in Belgium the cry: *On les aura!* re-echoed,
giving vent to the desperate need to be rid of the cursed *Boche* at last.
'We are on the eve of a very great battle,' the Parisian *Temps* wrote.
'Its complications will extend over a long period of time and will
undoubtedly carry difficulties in its wake. But it can now already be
said that it has started under as auspicious circumstances as could
possibly be hoped for.' [1]

When these lines were read on May 12 the battle was already lost.

From the coast, the French Seventh Army, the British Expeditionary Force and the French First and Ninth Armies had wheeled
into Belgium on May 10. The French Second Army held the com-
municating link with the Maginot Line at Sedan. The Second and
Ninth Armies had to move into the line of fortifications along the
Meuse as far as Namur. The staffs had calculated that the Germans
would not appear on the Meuse until the fifth day after the beginning
of the offensive at the very earliest; where in the meantime the French
and British artillery would have been brought into position and
where the troops would have been refreshed after their tiring march.

But already on May 10 and 11 French scouts in the Ardennes had
come across disorderly processions of refugees and hastily retreating
soldiers, who told of endless lines of German tanks that were advancing. Part of the refugees came from Luxemburg where, they said,
a German Fifth Column of unprecedented dimensions had been at
work. The Germans had smuggled a great number of 'tourists' into
the country, over two thousand, some with a so-called circus whose
personnel consisted entirely of military men. All these people together with the *reichsdeutschen* citizens who had settled in Luxemburg had been mobilised and given marching orders in the night of
May 9 to 10. They had taken frontier stations and police offices by
surprise and had cut telephone wires. Mysterious cars, from which

[1] *Le Temps* (Paris), May 12, 1940.

shots had been fired, had driven through the country like mad. They had even seen a woman shoot; the very children had made signals from windows to German soldiers.

Before the onslaught of the German tanks the French scouts hurriedly fell back on the Meuse. On the 12th they crossed it again and on the left bank encountered the vanguard of the Ninth Army, who were starting to entrench themselves after the long march from the French frontier. That same day, however, three days before they had been counted on, the Germans started the attack from Sedan to Namur. Their dive-bombers, with sirens shrieking, roared down with a howling sound enough to freeze the blood in anyone's veins. An infernal cannonade burst forth. Infantry started crossing the river, and before night fell the first German tanks were creeping up the western bank of the Meuse valley. Some French units made a brave stand: with machine-guns, and even revolvers, they fired at the armoured coverings of those heavy monsters. The morale of other units was speedily broken.

Not a single plane of their own air force appeared.

The tale got round that the Germans had already crossed the Meuse in the south near Sedan, that Fifth Columnists were performing their work of destruction a long way behind the front, that parachutists were descending all over the place in the hinterland, that false orders were being circulated, that officers who should have seen to the blowing up of the bridges over the Meuse had been shot down with machine-pistols by Germans disguised as civilians and that yet other Fifth Columnists had fired from houses. At night you saw 'myriads of mysterious lights, now in the plain, then again in the woods'.[1] And it was said that the Germans in their assaults drove civilians and prisoners-of-war before them. Their material superiority was crushing.

The lines were shaken. The main body of the army started to fall back: how could anyone cope with *such* an enemy! Officers tried to intercept the fleeing soldiers and restore order. Sometimes they succeeded, more often not. First thousands, soon tens of thousands of soldiers streamed back from the divisions along the Meuse. Frightful rumours rushing ahead of them alarmed the staffs and units lying in reserve. There the same speedy process of disintegration was set in motion, fomented by the nerve-racking dives of the German bombers and the excited tales of endless files of refugees pressing forward over the rough cobble-stones, pale with fright, flurried and fearful— 'They're coming!'

[1] Georges Kosak: *Belgique et France 1940 avec la compagnie de génie du 4e D[ivision] L[égère de] C[avalerie] et 7e D[ivision] L[égère] M[écanique]* (Grenoble, 1946), p. 93.

'Back to the French border' was the new slogan.

Before the nerve-ridden, demoralised troops had reached the frontier fortifications most of the units already lying there had been infected by the general panic. In the sectors of the Second and Ninth Armies all the French frontier posts had been deserted on May 17. The German tank divisions droned westwards over the undulating roads of the farming country of northern France towards the Channel, cutting off the supply roads of the French and British armies in Belgium. In the territory between the lines of those tank divisions that ran westward and Paris a swarming chaos had come about. There were the hundreds of thousands of French citizens seeking safety in flight, the units brought from the Maginot Line out of which they tried to form a new army, and there were the officers and men who on May 12 and the days immediately following had been struck by the German offensive across the Meuse as if they had been hit with a sledgehammer.

The Ninth Army and a good part of the Second had ceased to exist.

For days Paris remained ignorant of this *débâcle*.

This was partly due to poor liaison; the military organisation was badly co-ordinated. Gamelin, commander-in-chief, first adviser to the government, was unable to give any direct order, and inversely he received no direct news. The War Ministry tried to get some idea as to where the Germans were by ringing up the post offices at given times in places they thought the Germans were approaching. Whether this crude sort of information reached Gamelin's headquarters is not definitely established. He had no means of communication of his own. There was no wireless transmitter.

The news that reached the commander-in-chief was always two days late. So the government and the high officials could expect no general survey of the situation from that quarter. Everyone groped in the dark after May 10.

In this state of nervous uncertainty the reports of Fifth Column activity in Belgium and the Netherlands that came in via news agencies and through other channels had a doubly perturbing effect. On May 11 the Parisian press announced that two hundred parachutists had landed near The Hague in English uniforms. On the 13th the French Government made it officially known that every enemy combatant who should be made prisoner-of-war and who was not wearing his own national uniform 'would be shot without further ado'. The parachutist arm was the most important German weapon, said the Belgian premier Pierlot on the 14th. 'Tens of thousands of [Germans] who took the advantage of the generous hospitality of the Dutch people have suddenly revealed themselves as ready for attack,' said the French minister of Information in a broadcast talk that same evening—and throughout the country the indignation was great. *Les salauds!* President Lebrun gathered on the 15th that '90,000' of the 300,000 Dutch soldiers 'had been killed'.[1] In the evening papers one could read that parachutists in the Netherlands were disguised as postmen, policemen and women. 'The variety of the disguises is unbelievable,' the Dutch ambassador in London said to the correspondent of *Le Temps*—he had heard this from the Dutch ministers. On the 16th the Dutch minister of Foreign Affairs, Mr. E. N. van Kleffens, informed the press in Paris that parachutists had descended 'by the thousand' in 'French, Belgian and British uniforms, in the cassocks of priests and in the garb of nuns or nurses'.

After the 15th, on top of all this enervating news, the first reports about the complete collapse of the Ninth Army reached Gamelin. They came to him in the night of the 15th to the 16th and in the morning of the 16th, in the fort of Vincennes where general headquarters were housed, 'a day sombre and endless, with a smell of corpses'.[2] The Germans then were quite close! It was reported that two or three German tank divisions were approaching. They might be in Paris by the evening!

Reserve divisions there were none. 'People are clearing out of Paris. Taxis are hard to get. There is panic in the air,' the English journalist Alexander Werth wrote in his diary.[3]

In the following days the German tank offensive proceeded towards the Channel. Soon the French, the British and the Belgians were hemmed in, but people still hoped they would be able to break through to the south. Day after day went by, however, without this hope being realised. Reynaud, in desperation, continued the fight, knowing that after the defeat in Belgium a *débâcle* in France would be all but inevitable. He added to his cabinet Marshal Pétain, the 'hero of Verdun', and Georges Mandel, close fellow-worker of Clemenceau-*le-Tigre*. Gamelin was replaced as commander-in-chief by Weygand, chief of staff of Marshal Foch. Spirits rose: the old names were expected to bring fresh glory.

The fortunes of war could not be turned, however. All the staffs were in confusion. If one visited the headquarters of General Georges, commander of the armies fighting in the north, one received the impression of 'a hopeless consultation of a hundred dazed medical

---

[1] Paul Reynaud: *Au coeur de la mêlée, 1930–1945* (Paris, 1951), p. 449.

[2] Jacques Minart: *P. C. Vincennes, secteur 4* (Paris, 1945), Vol. II, p. 163.

[3] Alexander Werth: *The Last Days of Paris* (London, 1940), p. 43. A book as fresh now as when it was written.

specialists who have been called in to the bed-side of a moribund invalid doomed to die'.[1]

'The situation is grave, but by no means desperate,' Reynaud said in a broadcast talk on May 19, 1940. But when two days later his classic cry of alarm resounded in the Senate of: '*La patrie est en danger*' ('Our fatherland is in danger!'), there was at least one auditor who felt his legs give way under him. 'If the bench with red velvet had not been there,' he confessed, 'I would have fallen headlong on the floor.' [2]

France in danger! In deadly peril from Hitler! Only a miracle could save her, so the premier had declared.

How was it possible? How had this state of things come about? What diabolical game had been played with the highest interests of the French people? Reynaud—this was the impression it gave people —lifted a corner of the veil. He said that as a result of 'inexplicable blunders' the bridges over the Meuse had not been blown up. He hinted at incorrect reports and false evacuation orders. He spoke of treachery, sabotage and cowardice. He mentioned the name of General Corap, commander of the Ninth Army, who had been removed from his command a week previously.

'*Le traître!*'

But there must be more traitors! Where were they hiding, those Fifth Columnists? Where was the *cinquième colonne*?

Measureless unrest arose throughout the country, a rapidly spreading disintegration. Under a sky that was ravishly, defiantly blue every day afresh, came the approach, as a poignant contrast, of unavoidable disaster. No longer was any music to be heard over the wireless. People's thoughts were being constricted to an ever smaller and gloomier compass. The newspapers were cut down first to four and then to two pages. In proportion as there was less concrete news people became more susceptible to rumour.

Wave after wave of refugees came up in force from the north-eastern part of the country. During the first few days the evacuation went off in orderly fashion. After May 13 it became a wretched *sauve qui peut*, prefects sometimes leaving their departments and burgomasters their municipalities. Trains full of refugees chugged towards the west, while the Paris buses conveyed hundreds of thousands.

How many refugees had set off on the roads was not known— millions, perhaps as many as six or seven millions. As early as the middle of May whole towns and villages between Paris and the

---

[1] Minart: *P. C. Vincennes, secteur 4*, Vol. II, p. 185.

[2] Paul Crouzet: '*Et c'est le même ciel bleu*', *Journal de guerre d'un maire de village 1939–1940* (Paris, 1950), p. 141.

northern frontier had become wholly or almost wholly depopulated. Normandy, Brittany and the south of France became chock-full. All those uprooted, despairing creatures infected each other with their fear. Reports about the Fifth Column over the wireless startled them, reports in the press of similar sinister content created alarm.

The civil defence corps that had been set up on May 17 erected barricades on the roads. There they asked after papers, looked at them suspiciously, checked them, and then hesitated—was it friend or foe? One could never be certain.

Fear of the Fifth Column soon began to play a part among the soldiers as well. Any strange phenomenon observed by them was written down to the mysterious actions of enemy agents. 'The Fifth Column really does exist,' an officer wrote; 'every night blue, green and red lights appear everywhere.' [1] The troops became highly suspicious of all this. Whenever they came across strangers who were unable to explain their presence in the area in question, they immediately took them for spies. The order went out that they were to be shot out of hand, 'no fuss or bother, merely keep an account of the total number dealt with', an officer stated.[2] 'As for the spy problem, we have solved that,' a youthful French military man declared to A. J. Liebling, correspondent of the *New Yorker*. 'We simply shoot all officers we do not know.' [3]

A great many foreigners thought to be Fifth Columnists went through some very unpleasant moments. The correspondent of the *New York Times*, Percy J. Philip, was dragged out of his train after the collapse of the Meuse front. His uniform of war correspondent, his blue eyes and fair hair, all gave rise to suspicion among the soldiers. The cry 'You're a dirty German parachutist,' was to be heard. Straightaway a furious crowd eddied round him. 'When he pointed out that he had the red ribbon of the Legion of Honour, they were aghast that even a German should have such effrontery; when he showed them his papers carefully supplied by General Gamelin's headquarters with numerous official stamps, they said that he was clearly suspect because he had too many papers.' [4] Philip was within an ace of being shot by the side of the railway. At length he was taken to a police office by rows of farmers hissing: '*Boche!* Murderer!' at him, and there his papers were found to be in order.

Millions of citizens also lived in this atmosphere of terror and uncertainty to which Philip had almost fallen a victim.

[1] D. Barlone: *A French Officer's Diary* (23 August 1939 to 1 October 1940) (Cambridge, 1943), p. 52. [2] *Ibid.*, p. 53.
[3] A. J. Liebling: 'Paris Postscript'. *The New Yorker book of War Pieces* (New York, 1946), p. 45.
[4] Gordon Waterfield: *What happened to France* (London, 1940), p. 48.

The frame of mind in the big towns, Paris especially, had been nervous from the very outset. As early as May 13 excitement mastered thousands: a parachutist was descending! It was a barrage balloon that had broken adrift and was floating down the sky. A week later the same thing happened; in the *Place de l'Alma* there was a traffic jam. 'Everybody apparently thinks they have seen a German parachutist and everybody is shouting "*à mort!*" ' [1] Time and again the rumour was rife that parachutists had descended in the Paris parks; 'Three children died of poisoned chocolate'; 'Gamelin has shot himself'; 'Arras was taken by parachutists descending at night from the sky with flaming torches in their hands'—these statements were noted down by Arthur Koestler.[2] Peter de Polnay, who in those days from his house on the *Butte* Montmartre was overlooking the metropolis at night, said: 'I saw signals in morse all over Paris. The Fifth Column was at work.' [3]

The blackguards!

It would happen quite often that citizens vented their rage on persons who in less than no time had suddenly fallen under suspicion of being tools of the enemy. Numerous priests and nuns were molested. English Cecily Mackworth, in fleeing from the Germans, was almost lynched when she arrived in Brittany in the garb of a nurse. In the village of Saint-Nicholas she was told that the mother superior of the local convent had already twice been taken for a parachutist and arrested by the inhabitants.[4] Barlone wrote that in the area round Rouen hundreds had been arrested as disguised priests and nuns—'and shot, I hope'.[5] Whatever dropped out of the sky was suspect. It sometimes happened that French and British pilots who descended with their parachutes were almost beaten to death by the farming population.

'The Trojan horse,' someone said, 'has become winged.' [6]

In that France, where people trembled with fear and indignation, cattle-trucks full of persons who had been arrested in Belgium rolled steadily southwards. The big convoy from Brussels took six days to reach Orléans. The 'Fifth Columnists' and 'spies' who, as it appeared from the chalkings, were being conveyed in it, received a draught of water now and again and once a day a lump of bread. It was unbearably hot. The captives—*Reichsdeutsche*, Flemish Nazis, Jews and

---

[1] Arved Arenstad: *Tapestry of a Débâcle* (London, 1941), p. 25.
[2] Arthur Koestler: *Scum of the Earth* (London, 1941), p. 172.
[3] Peter de Polnay: *Death and To-morrow* (London, 1942), p. 41.
[4] Cecily Mackworth: *I came out of France* (London, 1941), p. 52.
[5] Barlone: *A French Officer's Diary*, p. 107.
[6] Quoted by Alfred Fabre-Luce: *Journal de la France, mars 1939–juillet 1940* (Paris, 1941), p. 302.

communists—all lay mixed up together. Several died; one woman gave birth to a child. In Tours where the convoy of prisoners stopped in front of the station, an agitated crowd collected. 'Oil,' they yelled, 'we need oil to burn the skunks, the dirty lot of them!' [1]

Large parts of this Belgian convoy after many wanderings at last came to the internment camps near the Pyrenees.

Those camps were full even then because in France many tens of thousands of people had been robbed of their liberty on suspicion of being potential Fifth Columnists.

At the outbreak of war all the *Reichsdeutschen* living in France had been interned; first only the men, later on the women and children as well—altogether something like five thousand. A larger problem was formed by the thirty-thousand-odd refugees from Germany and Austria who had settled in France. Most of them wanted nothing better than to support the struggle against national socialism. They were not given the chance. The men were called up for internment in September, 1939, and put into improvised camps where they usually spent their time in idleness. They were continually being pressed to take service in the French Foreign Legion or in the military labour battalions. From time to time small groups were released. No damaging evidence had been found in their dossiers.

Socialists and communists of other than German nationality were taken into custody in great numbers together with the refugees, mostly Jewish, and were put away in the camp at Le Vernet, where Arthur Koestler (who was imprisoned there till about the middle of January, 1940) met with the sad remainder of the International Brigade from Spain. Koestler was arrested with 'anti-fascists from all over Europe, including adherents of the Croat Peasant Party, Spanish Syndicalists, Czech Liberals, Italian Socialists, Hungarian and Polish Communists, German Independent Socialists, and one Trotzkyist'.[2] Some of them had braved great dangers in order to reach France, where they wanted to take part in the war against Hitler.

The news from the Netherlands about the sudden rising of the enormous German Fifth Column had a fatal result on May 10 and 11, 1940. All persons of German origin, including those who came from Danzig and the Saar, if they were from 17 to 55 years of age and whether it was for the first time or over again, had to report for internment. In Paris the men were taken to the Buffalo stadium, and the women to the *Vélodrome d'hiver*. Some tens of thousands were deprived of their liberty. Some allowed themselves to be recruited for the Foreign Legion. Some joined the military labour battalions. Yet

---

[1] Lagrou: *Wij verdachten*, p. 70.
[2] Koestler: *Scum of the Earth*, p. 80.

others were sent to the mines and quarries in Morocco. Certain groups, added to the British army, were well handled; other groups, commanded by suspicious Frenchmen, were badly treated. Many others were shifted to the concentration camps near the Pyrenees, where, as we saw, part of the 'Fifth Columnists' arrested in Belgium also landed.

All the persons who had been arrested as Fifth Columnists in the weeks that people smelled dangers everywhere found themselves in those same camps. Mandel, who had been admitted to the Reynaud cabinet as minister of Home Affairs on May 18, a man of unbridled energy, an advocate of radical measures—thus the victory in 1918 had been gained!—had people run in right and left. In one week in Paris alone two thousand hotels were searched for spies, sixty thousand people were questioned, and five hundred were arrested. Numerous officials were dismissed. Various people were sentenced to terms of imprisonment on account of defeatist remarks. Every evening ten patrols went down into the Paris sewers in order to keep them under surveillance and if necessary to take suspect persons into custody. Thousands were arrested.

They too were usually sent on to the internment camps in the south. In the camp at Gurs there were from twelve to thirteen thousand prisoners, 'communists, anarchists, suspect Alsatians, Jews, Greeks, Russians, Armenians, Germans, Flemings, Dutch, and rats, lice and fleas'.[1] In the camp at Le Vernet six thousand persons were imprisoned; when Italy attacked France, thousands of Italians were added to the number, whom it had taken a week's journey in cattle-trucks to get there. A large group of Polish Jews found their way to that camp too; the Polish authorities in France had shifted them onto the French, who in turn had sent them on to Le Vernet. 'In this newly built tower of Babel all the nationalities of the Balkans, of one-time Poland and of the former border states on the Baltic appeared to full advantage.' A Belgian internee counted forty different nationalities 'if the Dutch, Danes, Norwegians, Swedes, later the Italians, an Annamite even, were included'.[2]

It was a curious thing that in spite of the extensive arrests that had taken place, fear of the Fifth Column did not abate. The mental pattern that had arisen under the pressure of fear remained the same: the enemy owed his successes to 'the help of agents'; whenever something went wrong 'treachery had been committed'. When King Leopold of Belgium capitulated in the end of May after a struggle

[1] Lagrou: *Wij verdachten*, p. 141.
[2] A. Mermans: *De parachutisten van Orléans, Het verhaal der Vlaamsche weggevoerden 1940* (Antwerp, 1941), p. 88.

that had lasted almost three weeks, Reynaud spoke of 'a fact without precedent in history'. The Belgians in France called it treachery— Leopold had 'lured' the Allies 'to enter Belgium'. People whispered that he had 'a girl friend' furnished by the Gestapo. Inversely the French said to each other in the streets: 'And that isn't the worst of it. All the refugees probably are spies.' [1] Quite a number of Belgians were molested. There were villages where they were refused admittance—'Fifth Columnists!'

Alexander Werth sat drinking a cup of coffee in Poitiers on his flight to Bordeaux, when a terribly heated argument outside drew his attention:

An N.C.O. of the French Air Force on a motor-cycle has been stopped by a special constable, who has asked him for his papers. The N.C.O. refused to show him any. The special constable, with a blue brassard, flew into a fearful rage. He was an apoplectic elderly man; he screamed and yelled and shook his fists frantically, getting all purple in the face. I thought he'd have a stroke. A large crowd gathered round; some people were shouting that the N.C.O. was a German parachutist. In the end he was taken off to the police station in a car, swearing French obscenities with an unmistakably pure French accent. People are nervous, jumpy and have parachutists on the brain.[2]

The British journalist wrote this down on June 14, 1940, when the issue had already been decided.

Two days later Marshal Pétain formed his cabinet that offered the Germans the subjection of France.

The struggle was at an end.

But the minds of the French people were still awhirl with questions, there was a veritable witches' cauldron in their memory of strange apparitions that had been observed—light signals and false orders, parachutists and saboteurs, schemers and intriguers—and the Fifth Column haunted it all, nowhere proved yet feared everywhere.

With brains tortured by those same questions a handful of refugees crossed over to the island where the flag of freedom still streamed in the western breeze—to England.

[1] Liebling: 'Paris Postscript'. *The New Yorker book of War Pieces*, p. 47.
[2] Werth: *The Last Days of Paris*, p. 185–6.

CHAPTER V

Tension in England

★

IN England, besides indignation, the reports about the Fifth Column in Norway had aroused a vague sense of uneasiness rather than a feeling of being directly menaced. After all, Norway lay on the flank of Europe. But when Hitler attacked the Netherlands, Belgium and France, the general attitude changed: the result of that struggle would have a direct effect on people's own fate. With eagerness they listened to the BBC and read the papers. There was little dependable news from the front in the first week. So much the greater was the susceptibility for the particulars given of Fifth Column activities. The first reports came from the Netherlands.

Official announcements about the way the Germans had used Dutch, even British, uniforms to their own advantage were printed in the English press. On May 12, 1940, the *Observer* published a story from a Dutch source about *Reichsdeutsche* living in the Netherlands who, furnished with special passes, had awaited the parachutists of the German Air Force. British correspondents working in Holland, who with their own eyes had seen the furious struggle that was put up by the Dutch against the supposed internal enemy in Amsterdam, Rotterdam and The Hague, never wearied of telling about the ruses and stratagems of the Fifth Columnists. On May 13 *The Times* and the *Daily Telegraph* reported that in The Hague over a hundred German citizens had been killed in street fighting in one day. On the 14th one might read in the *Daily Express* that 'poisoned chocolates and wine, spies disguised as priests and postmen and housemaids, every kind of trick to sap confidence and cause confusion has been used by the Nazis'.

British citizens who had escaped from the Netherlands in the very nick of time and were eager to tell the story of their shocking experiences were met at the harbours by reporters standing ready with sharpened pencils to note down what 'English people, bombed as they left Holland', had to tell:

On the first day of the invasion parachutists dropped out of the sky like a vast flock of vultures. Most of them were disguised in Allied and Dutch uniforms, others came down in the uniforms of Dutch policemen and began to direct the population in the streets and mislead the army. One 'policeman' told a group of isolated Dutch troops that their friends were round the corner. When the soldiers turned the corner, German troops, barricaded across the road slaughtered them. The 'policeman' was shot by troops following. But, most fantastic of all, the steward of the English ship said that he and some of the crew had watched parachutists descend in women's clothes. They wore blouses and skirts and each carried a sub-machine gun. The steward could not tell if they were women or men disguised as women. Several eye-witnesses in the boat confirmed it and said others had come down disguised as priests, peasants and civilians. . . . As machine guns came out of the sky like unnatural lightning peppering the streets below, the Fifth Column crept out of their homes in German uniforms, heavily armed. Holland had combed out the Fifth Column for weeks before, but as the doors opened at 3 a.m. the men who had been proclaimed anti-Nazis and refugees from Germany, held rifles.[1]

British business-men who had escaped from the Continent told of butcher's and baker's boys in the Dutch towns who had carried hand grenades and other ammunition in their baskets covered with white cloths: they had been parachutists in disguise. 'When they heard women clapping their hands at the windows of houses, they approached and made contact with the spies inside.'[2]

Scores of similar stories were told by the Dutch refugees. And on the strength of what he himself had experienced and of what he had heard from his colleagues who got away a few days later, the Dutch minister of Foreign Affairs warned the British people, just as he had warned the French, against the 'abominable stratagems' of the Germans. The British Minister to Holland, who had escaped from The Hague, spoke over the BBC about the 'dreadful number' of Germans who had been left at large in the Netherlands. They had carried out 'the instructions they had from Germany'.

The struggle in Belgium and France gave rise to whole series of similar reports. Not a journalist, not a refugee, not a soldier landed in England who was not full of tales about the Fifth Column and treachery. German parachutists had landed everywhere, even in the

[1] *Daily Express* (London), May 13, 1940.
[2] *Daily Telegraph* (London), May 15, 1940.

gardens of the Belgian Queen Mother! 'Somehow one never thinks of Quislings in connection with the French,' a BBC employee wrote in his diary when the French premier Reynaud had announced that 'the bridges over the Meuse had been betrayed'. 'But I have no doubt that German thoroughness has succeeded in planting a Fifth Column at vulnerable points.'[1]

The fact in itself of the rapid collapse of four countries in just over a month seemed proof enough of the use of exceptional means. A normal war did not develop like that! It could not possibly have been only a superior force of tanks and aircraft that had enabled Hitler to reach the Channel in ten days, so people felt. The abnormal had here become an essential part of an impetuous method of attack, just as the *Führer* himself had described it in Rauschning's disclosures. He would not even have risked the offensive if he had not been certain of the eager help which tools in the enemy's country would render him in co-operation with parachutists who were to be dropped everywhere.

Different British government departments hastily collected further particulars about the shape this help was taking. Hitler's offensive was hardly a week old when the Ministry of Information announced to the British people that Fifth Columnists were making signals to German planes, for instance 'by setting haystacks on fire or spreading sheets or even newspapers on the ground'. Navigating those planes was thereby made easier 'both by day and by night'.[2]

Beware! How could one prevent England falling a victim to that Fifth Column, as had happened to Denmark, Norway and the Netherlands, and as was threatening to happen to Belgium and France? Had agents been smuggled into England too? Were there Fifth Columnists there as well, who one day would open their doors and rush out to meet Hitler's airborne landing troops 'rifle in hand at three o'clock in the morning'? It seemed hardly credible—but had not states like the Scandinavian ones, or a country like the Netherlands, fallen a victim to their own gullibility? For that matter, had not the BBC on May 12 had to withdraw a call for reservists of the Royal Air Force three hours after it had been announced? The BBC had received the text from the Air Ministry by telephone. After the announcement it appeared, so it was reported, that the Air Ministry did not know anything about the matter. So it had been a false report, sowing confusion! It was the first instance that had been heard of. Would it be the last?

The government took far-reaching precautionary measures all

[1] Anthony Weymouth: *Journal of the War Years and One Year Later* (Worcester, 1948), Vol. I, p. 245.
[2] *The Times* (London), May 20, 1940.

along the line. On May 11 the Home Office urged the public to be on the alert against parachutists—'dangerous pests' whose presence, said *The Times*, should be reported at once.[1] Alarmed by the reports from the Netherlands, farmers and occupants of country houses started forming small work parties in various rural districts as early as Saturday and Sunday, May 11 and 12. Armed with shot-guns and other weapons, they stood on guard. Anthony Eden, Secretary of War in the cabinet that Churchill had started to form on the 10th, made an appeal on the evening of May 14, 1940—the news of the capitulation of the Dutch army had just been received—for the forming of a special civic guard, the Local Defence Volunteers, who were later to be called the Home Guard. Within twenty-four hours a quarter of a million men had reported to the local authorities. The police were commissioned to seize the stores in arms shops. Wherever there were not sufficient guns, pitch-forks and flails were kept ready to hand. England was not going to be given up without a struggle! 'We must expect in any case to be attacked here on the Dutch model before long,' Winston Churchill wrote to President Roosevelt on the 18th.[2]

In the same Whitsun week-end that the Local Defence Volunteers started to look for German parachutists, inspection of traffic began on the main roads. Tens of thousands of cars were stopped and the occupants asked for their identity cards. All the troops had been given the alarm. On May 16 the minister of Information, Duff Cooper, cautioned people against spreading rumours. That same day the protection of government buildings began. The entrances to the departments were closed off with barbed wire, soldiers stood on guard day and night. At vital points in Whitehall machine-guns were brought into position. Barbed wire barricades were erected on the arterial roads leading to London. Police patrols checked the shipping on the Thames. All the owners and proprietors of cars and garages were called upon to see to it that no Fifth Columnists should get hold of any conveyance, either by day or by night.

At the end of May fresh measures were taken, all inspired by the stream of reports from the Continent. Place-name plates and sign-posts were removed. Wireless sets in cars were prohibited. It was also prohibited to make or sell any official uniforms, badges or emblems without having a permit. The police and the military were empowered to enter any dwelling if they expected to find apparatuses there with which 'intentionally or unintentionally' signals could be made to help the enemy. All the warehouses along the Thames and

[1] *The Times* (London), May 11, 1940.
[2] Winston S. Churchill: *The Second World War*, Vol. II: *Their Finest Hour* (London, 1949), p. 50.

all the ships lying in the river were carefully searched for crates containing arms or ammunition: London was not to become a second Rotterdam!

By the beginning of June the police and all military men were given the right to require citizens to show their identity cards. The power to arrest was extended. Instructions were delivered at every house not to take to flight in the case of an invasion and not to allow oneself to be influenced by 'false rumours' and 'false instructions' such as had been circulated by the Germans on the Continent 'in order to create confusion and panic.'[1]

The liberty of groups of people who were not considered completely reliable was restricted. On May 30 it was ordered that all aliens and people without nationality must from then on be in their own houses at night. Before six o'clock in the morning they were not allowed to be in the streets. All foreigners were removed from a zone 20 miles deep along the south-east coast. Foreign refugees, who arrived in large numbers, were tested for reliability in camps before being allowed to look for a house and work. The crews of foreign ships in English harbours were not allowed to go ashore, officers were only allowed to do so at fixed hours. A watch-post was stationed near all the wireless installations on board.

Many of these measures were meant to have the effect of hindering the movements of possible German parachutists, whether in false uniform or not, and of preventing them from entering into contact with helpers in England.

Who were those helpers?

Were the native fascists keeping themselves in readiness, in the same way as the members of the Dutch Nazi party had done in the Netherlands?

Security measures were taken that were heartily applauded by the millions who were convinced that Sir Oswald Mosley was no whit better than Vidkun Quisling or Anton Mussert. Many people were indignant that the British Union of Fascists was still allowed to demonstrate in public. Mosley was routed by furious workmen in Middleton on May 19. Three days later a paragraph was added to Defence Regulation 18b, giving the Home Secretary the right to intern persons whom he had good reason to think were members of an organisation that sympathised with the enemy. A few dozen leaders of fascist organisations, Mosley included, were at once taken into custody. Many other arrests followed, and by the end of the year almost eight thousand people were interned under this Regulation.

Under the influence of the reports from the Continent, the government had also proceeded to intern some tens of thousands of refugees,

[1] 'Official instructions to civilians', *The Times* (London), June 19, 1940.

mostly Jews, who had fled to England as a result of persecution by the Nazi régime in Germany and Austria in the preceding years. Their presence in the belligerent country had formed a problem from the very beginning. Formally the great majority of the refugees were still German citizens. Most of them hated the Nazi régime. Were there perhaps exceptions? Had the Gestapo perhaps got its agents among the refugees as well? And inversely, were there not among the *Reichsdeutschen*—non-refugees, who had sometimes been living in England for years—many who were ready to support the struggle against a régime which they themselves looked upon as a stigma for Germany?

The government very sensibly decided to subject all foreigners of enemy nationality to an enquiry about their political convictions. Persons of whom the police and the security services knew, thought or assumed that they formed part of the German espionage nets or that they were active national socialists, fell outside this closer enquiry: they, to the number of two thousand, had already been rounded up and interned in the first days of September 1939. Serious mistakes had sometimes been made, because in this first group that was robbed of its liberty there were many hundreds of Jewish refugees whose reliability ought never to have been called in doubt.

On the second day of the war, September 4, 1939, it was ordered that all foreigners of enemy nationality were to report to the police and that each case was to be investigated by special tribunals. For the German and Austrian refugees this was very good news: they never doubted that they would get through successfully.

The persons to be investigated had to be classified in three categories: A cases (unreliable); B cases (absolute reliability uncertain); C cases (reliable). The A cases were to be interned, the B cases were to be subjected to certain restrictions, the C cases were allowed to go their various ways and were even permitted employment in the civil defence corps and armament industry. 'There is no case whatever for a policy of general internment,' wrote *The Times*.[1] The *Manchester Guardian* was of the opinion that 'it would be a crime to waste such resources of intelligence, knowledge, high purpose and noble passion'.[2]

Early in October, 1939, a hundred and twenty Aliens Tribunals were set up. When four months later they had finished their work, they had investigated close to 74,000 cases, including 55,000 refugees. Nearly 600 persons (A cases) were interned; 6,800 were considered as B cases; the rest were declared reliable. Of the 55,000 refugees, 51,000 had received this certificate of reliability.

[1] *The Times* (London), Sept. 14, 1939.
[2] *Manchester Guardian*, Sept. 15, 1939.

Taking the refugees as a group, the opinion of the Tribunals therefore was favourable, but it was not endorsed by all the authorities nor by public opinion as a whole. As early as January, 1940, the Home Office and the War Office were 'flooded' with anonymous letters charging German and Austrian refugees with being Gestapo agents.[1] 'Are we getting a bit too lenient? Are we taking too many chances? . . . That is the question you hear people asking,' wrote the *Daily Express*.[2] From an article in the *Daily Telegraph* it appeared that the military security services were 'greatly concerned by the leniency of the Aliens Tribunals'.[3] 'Being a refugee in England is becoming not only a pleasant but a prosperous life,' the *Sunday Express* insinuated.[4] In the beginning of March the same newspaper asserted that 'the nucleus of a Fifth Column' had already been set up among the refugees.[5] More and more voices were raised advocating general internment. On March 18 Colonel Burton, member of the House of Commons for Sudbury, demanded in parliament that aliens—'who undoubtedly give away a great deal of information'—should be forced to leave the neighbourhood of the ports.[6]

In April, 1940, the accounts of the German Fifth Column in Norway helped increase the general anxiety. 'Would it not be far better to intern all the lot and then pick out the good ones?' Colonel Burton asked on April 23.[7] For many people this was no longer a query. Public pressure had become so strong that *The Times* spoke of 'hysterics'. The Home Secretary, Sir John Anderson, was exposed to ever sharper attacks especially from the conservative backbenchers.

The reports from the Netherlands turned the scale.

Late in the evening of May 10 representatives of the military departments called on Sir John,

and represented that, in view of the imminent risk of invasion, it was in their view of the utmost importance that every male enemy alien between sixteen and seventy should be removed forthwith from the coastal strip which in their view was the part of the country likely, if invasion took place, to be affected.[8]

Thus driven into a corner Sir John decided to have all enemy aliens

[1] *Daily Herald* (London), Jan. 24, 1940.
[2] *Daily Express* (London), Jan. 16, 1940.
[3] *Daily Telegraph* (London), Jan. 23, 1940.
[4] *Sunday Express* (London), Jan. 28, 1940.   [5] *Ibid.*, Mar. 3, 1940.
[6] England, *House of Commons, Debates*, 5th series, Vol. 358, column 1739. (358 *H.C. Deb.* 5s, 1739; this source will further be quoted in the abbreviated form as indicated.)
[7] 360 *H.C. Deb.*, 5s, 33.
[8] Sir John Anderson, Aug. 22, 1940. 364 *H.C. Deb.*, 5s, 1543.

interned who were living in the coastal strip (including the B and C cases). The whole press applauded his decision, the liberal papers among the rest, even the *Manchester Guardian*; 'no half measures will do,' it said.[1] In Ipswich, where four Germans were taken to the police station, a crowd collected and 'though there was nothing to indicate that these were anything but innocent enemy aliens, there were loud cries against them from the crowd'.[2] Three thousand persons from the coastal strip, running from the North of Scotland to beyond Southampton, were interned.

The press and the public did not consider this first measure sufficient. The ministerial mail-bag was 'full of letters urging us to go further'.[3]

Churchill, who remembered the anti-German rioting of 1915, was afraid that in case of a crisis the refugees would become the victims of popular fury: 'If parachute landings were attempted and fierce fighting attendant upon them followed these unfortunate people would be far better out of the way, for their own sakes as well as for ours,' he argued early in June.[4]

The cabinet decided to continue on the course they had already chosen to pursue.

On May 16 all the male B cases throughout the country were rounded up, about three thousand in all. In London all the available police-cars were mobilised for this purpose. Those who had been fetched out of their houses left the stations under escort. 'Country saved from Fifth Column stab,' the *Daily Herald* exulted.[5] The *Daily Mail* and the *News Chronicle* insisted on the internment of the female B cases as well. The government proceeded to take this measure in the latter part of May. About 3,500 women were transferred with their children to the Isle of Man, a thousand coming from London. 'Several of the elder women were in tears'.[6] On the way there, 'a little misguided stone-throwing by members of the public' occurred.[7] The B cases between the ages of 60 and 70 were rounded up early in June.

Many people were still not satisfied. The great mass of the refugees, the C cases, were still at large. On June 12 the old cry of 'intern the lot' was raised in the House of Lords by Lord Marchwood.[8]

[1] *Manchester Guardian*, May 13, 1940.
[2] *New York Times*, May 13, 1940.
[3] Sir John Anderson, Aug. 22, 1940. 364 *H.C. Deb.*, 5s, 1544.
[4] Winston Churchill, June 4, 1940. 361 *H.C. Deb.*, 5s, 794.
[5] *Daily Herald* (London), May 17, 1940.
[6] *The Times* (London), May 28, 1940.
[7] *News Chronicle* (London), May 31, 1940.
[8] England, *House of Lords, Debates*, 5th series, Vol. 116, column 548. (116 *H.L. Deb.*, 5s, 548; this source will further be quoted in the abbreviated form as indicated.)

Over a week later, on June 21, three days after the capitulation of France, it was decided to intern the whole C group 'after the fullest and most earnest consideration', as was disclosed by Sir John Anderson in August.[1] Within a period of a few weeks the whole group was 'quietly rounded up'.[2] A few refugees committed suicide. But most of them by far resigned themselves to their fate and spent difficult months, isolated as they were from the outside world, in camps where—especially at first—the conditions left much to be desired. Almost eight thousand of them were transferred to Canada and Australia; one of the transport ships, the *Arandora Star*, was torpedoed early in July and sank. A number of interned German clergymen arrived in Canada on another ship, the *Ettrick*; on their arrival 'it was assumed that they were Nazi parachutists in disguise who had dropped on Rotterdam during the frightful raid which almost destroyed the city; and they were treated as such. They and the others were greeted with jeers of 'How's Hitler?' and comments which were a good deal more thorough going than that.'[3]

Not only in England were measures being taken against the Fifth Column during those two agitated months of May and June, 1940. Almost the whole world watched the collapse of Holland, Belgium and France with horror and fear. And the reverberations of the reports of the press and the radio reached the farthest corners of the globe, telling of the large-scale treachery of the *Reichsdeutschen* in co-operation with the fascists. On all hands people were arming themselves against the internal enemy.

In Sweden the populace was urged to redouble its watchfulness, and a civic guard was formed, numbering five thousand men.

In Switzerland, where there lived 70,000 *Reichsdeutsche*, a German offensive was expected at any moment on Tuesday evening, May 14. A civic guard was set up for the purpose of fighting saboteurs and parachutists. By the end of May the whole population was urged to be on the watch for suspicious-looking persons loitering in the neighbourhood of bridges, railway junctions or power stations. Spreaders of false rumours were arrested.

The Rumanian Government put a number of Germans across the frontier. And in Yugoslavia there was great tension in the areas where the German minorities lived. 'Every German living here, whatever his occupation, is to some extent engaged in espionage; every German of military age living here can be considered a Fifth Columnist,'

[1] Sir John Anderson, Aug. 22, 1940. 364 *H.C. Deb.*, 5s, 1545.
[2] *Manchester Guardian*, July 3, 1940.
[3] Alan Moorehead: *The Traitors* (London, 1952), p. 77.

one might read in a pamphlet that was being circulated by mail and reflected 'what every Yugoslav is thinking'.[1]

In Turkey, too, the public was warned against Germans. 'The older Germans are spies,' the newspaper *Yenisabah* wrote; 'the younger ones belong to the Fifth Column'.[2]

The island of Cyprus prepared for the internment of Fifth Columnists. The use of wireless-sets and cameras was put under supervision.

In Egypt the military governor of Cairo decreed on May 20 that all citizens were to deliver up their arms immediately. Steps were taken in case parachutists should land.

In South Africa about 150 German Nazis had been interned in the autumn of 1939, and well over 100 in the mandated territory of South-West Africa. In May 1940, many more hundreds were interned, some of whom were Jewish refugees. Fascists were also rounded up. 'Profiting from the experience of Norway and Holland, South Africa does not intend to be stabbed in the back by Quislings,' said the minister of the Interior.[3] And Germans were interned in other parts of Africa as well.

In June Australia directed all foreigners to deliver up their arms and ammunition. Many of them, 'mostly Germans', were interned, after federal officials had come to the conclusion 'that it was necessary to take the utmost precautions against Fifth Column activities'.[4]

In the Dutch East Indies on May 10, when the mother country was attacked, several thousand male Germans and members of the Dutch Nazi Party were sent to internment camps. Many of those arrested were badly handled, and the public demonstrated against the Fifth Columnists who had been rounded up. The women were interned later.

All these measures were inspired by the reports from Europe.

That these were true seemed to be beyond doubt. Ministers and ambassadors, experienced businessmen and journalists had pledged their word on it, and what they had said and written was not based on vague hearsay; no, they had been eye-witnesses. Hitler, arch-liar that he was, had called 'talk of the Fifth Column stupid and fantastic' in an interview with the American journalist Karl von Wiegand, and had asserted 'that the whole story was the product of the imagination of propagandists,'[5] but this was taken as even more evidence of the reality of a conspiracy the ramifications of which apparently embraced the entire globe, the Americas included.

[1] *The Times* (London), May 16, 1940.
[2] Quoted by *Le Temps* (Paris), May 19, 1940.
[3] *The Times* (London), June 1, 1940.
[4] *Ibid.*, June 6, 1940.   [5] *Ibid.*, June 17, 1940.

CHAPTER VI

The Americas in alarm

★

Together with the British people the American nation saw many of its illusions vanish into thin air in the weeks following May 10, 1940. Where Dutch, Belgian, British and French troops had stood on guard from the North Sea to the Mediterranean, a great void yawned five weeks later. People were almost inclined to rub their eyes: the turn fate had taken could hardly be grasped. The 'great awakening'[1] was too sudden and too painful. What had happened to the Allied armies? What mysterious forces had undermined the powers of resistance of so many old-established states and made four of them (The Netherlands, Belgium, Luxemburg and France) crumble in as many weeks, while the fifth, England, seemed to be tottering on the brink of the abyss?

Just as in the case of Denmark and Norway it was assumed that in the German offensive in Western Europe the Fifth Column took a prominent, if not the chief part. Only in that way did the collapse of Western Europe seem to be rationally explicable. In the special message which President Roosevelt addressed to Congress on May 16, 1940, he too spoke of 'the treacherous use of the "fifth column" by which persons supposed to be peaceful citizens were actually a part of an enemy unit of occupation'. And ten days later, on May 26, he pointed out to all American listeners in his fireside chat that America's safety was not only menaced by military weapons: 'We know of new methods of attack. The Trojan Horse. The Fifth Column that betrays a nation unprepared for treachery. Spies, saboteurs and traitors are the actors in this new tragedy.'

It was typical of this whole trend of thought that in the series of articles Otto D. Tolischus was writing from Stockholm for the *New York Times Magazine* under the title, 'How Hitler Made Ready', he

[1] Langer and Gleason: *The Challenge to Isolation 1937–1940*, p. 435.

105

devoted the *first* to the Fifth Column. Following on a resumé of the Fifth Column technique [1] came a description of what the Fifth Column had performed in Poland, the Scandinavian states and Western Europe. 'Its work,' Tolischus concluded, 'especially its constant stream of information has been largely responsible for the 'trancelike surety' and deadly accuracy with which Hitler so far has been able to evaluate the situation in each country and for the amazing advance of German armies in sometimes small and isolated columns in defiance of all laws of military tactics.' [2]

It was especially by these new *methods* of agression that the American people felt menaced. Against an orthodox attack an orthodox way of defence was possible, but what defensive method fitted this revolutionary offensive, as sinister as it was intangible?

Hitler's fancy seemed to be inexhaustible, his ambition boundless. What painful surprises had he got in store for America? 'There has suddenly flared up a panic,' wrote John T. Flynn in the *New Republic* on May 27, 'about our defenceless state, as if somebody was on the point of invading us.' To Fiorello La Guardia, mayor of New York, were attributed the words that America would not even be able to defend so much as Coney Island. [3]

A nervous suspicion haunted the country. Numbers of people no longer trusted their neighbours. The Federal Bureau of Investigation that had had to investigate 1,600 cases of reported espionage for the whole year 1939, suddenly got almost 2,900 similar complaints submitted to it 'in one day in May'. [4] The 'Fifth Column' had become 'a phrase on every tongue'. [5] The *New York World Telegram* devoted a series of articles to it, in which full daylight was let in on the whole matter of fascism in America.

Besides suspicion and anxiety the need was also felt for active resistance. In a township in Pennsylvania 'a gun club got ready to pot any Nazi parachutists descending from the sky'. [6] The legislative assembly of that state discussed setting up air-raid precautions for industry. In Bloomington a patriotic American Column was started, and in Albany a First Column. Frank Hague, mayor of Jersey City, threatened that 'he would exterminate all un-American plots and plotters'. In the states of New York and Massachusetts the arsenals of the National Guard were watched day and night. From

[1] Quoted in the Preface, p. vi.
[2] Otto D. Tolischus: 'How Hitler made ready. I. The Fifth Column.' *New York Times Magazine*, June 16, 1940.
[3] *New York Times*, May 14, 1940.
[4] Shepardson and Scroggs: *The United States in World Affairs, 1940* (New York, 1941), p. 327.
[5] *New York World Telegram*, June 6, 1940.
[6] *Time* (New York), May 27, 1940.

106

New York City the National Legion of American Mothers called upon its two million members to arm themselves with rifles; 'enemy parachutists in America will regret the day they first drew breath', they declared.[1] In Buffalo seven thousand men of the National Guard were mobilised 'in order to prevent treasonous activities along the Niagara border'.[2]

The United States had lost their unshakable faith in their absolute safety. The castle of prosperity seemed built on quicksand. But the wish to remain outside the war, notwithstanding everything, was still strong. After the fall of France two-thirds of the population took it for granted that America would be drawn into the struggle sooner or later, and an equally great percentage was convinced that Hitler would try to conquer part of the New World, but only one-seventh was in favour of taking things into their own hands and declaring war on Germany and Italy. Confusion and an inability to decide what stand to take, together formed a fertile soil for rumours about mysterious weapons that were going to be used to harass England. There were also jokes, which in fact were a sign of a dawning faith, but as far as content went were still only a mixture of self-mockery and self-pity. 'The newest Wall Street gag was a tale that Hitler had ordered 10,000 tanks from General Motors and, on being asked where he wanted delivery, replied: "Never mind that. We'll pick them up on our way through Detroit."'[3]

'Those weeks of May and June,' Sumner Welles later wrote in his memoirs,

will represent to some of us as long as we live a nightmare of frustration. For the United States government had no means whatever, short of going to war, to which American public opinion was overwhelmingly opposed, of diverting or checking the world cataclysm and the threat to the very survival of this country. I remember the dismay with which we heard of the crumbling of the fortresses along the Belgian eastern frontier, and our realization for the first time of the extent of the assistance rendered the German armies by its hidden accomplices within countries destined for invasion. Worst of all was the increasing apprehension that the German war machine was so overwhelmingly superior in might, quality, strategy, *matériel* and morale, to the available forces of the Western European powers, that Germany might well become the supreme master of all Europe before the summer had passed.[4]

[1] *Newsweek* (New York), June 10, 1940.
[2] *New York Journal and American*, June 5, 1940.
[3] *Life* (New York), July 1, 1940.
[4] Welles: *The Time for Decision*, p. 118–19.

In point of fact except for a formidable fleet that was mostly tied to the Pacific, the United States were all but unarmed. The army only ran to five serviceable divisions and possessed no more than 52 bombers and 160 fighters. The shortage of guns, according to the Chief of the Army Staff, General George C. Marshall, was 'terrible'. There was no ammunition for the anti-aircraft guns and it would take at least six months to get minimum supplies. The stores of rubber and tin—strategic raw materials for which America was entirely dependent on imports were just sufficient for three months.

These facts and figures tormented President Roosevelt and his closest advisers.

They were especially uneasy about South America.

This uneasiness, as we have already seen, was not new. Since the spring of 1938 Washington had wondered whether the republics of Central and South America possessed enough internal stability and external strength to be a match for the world offensive of the Axis powers. No one for a moment doubted that this offensive would receive the support of millions of South Americans of German and Italian extraction. The war had only stimulated this uneasiness. In Latin American ports eighty German ships lay at anchor which 'might well be used to service Axis submarines or even to supply shock-troops for the seizure of bases along remote stretches of the coast'.[1]

Rumours kept cropping up of suspicious-looking submarines in the Caribbean Sea. In Mexico the tale went that German ships in Mexican ports were in secret wireless communication with Berlin. The American Government took special trouble to replace the German instructors serving in various South American armies by American ones, and to put an end to the German control of part of the South American airlines. That apparently was of especial urgency in Columbia, where a fanatic Nazi was at the head of the *Scadta* company, whose machines were flying a small distance from the Panama Canal on the one side, and the most important refineries in Curaçao and Aruba on the other. Not till the end of February 1940 was an arrangement made to replace the German personnel of the *Scadta* by Americans and Columbians. Likewise, before the beginning of the German May offensive, the American government had found Brazil willing to place at their disposal some airfields along the north-east coast of the republic opposite French Dakar.

On May 16, 1940, after Hitler's assault had started, General Marshall and Admiral Stark, Chief of Naval Operations, drafted a memorandum in which they argued that all the governments of Latin America should be invited without loss of time to confidential

[1] Langer and Gleason: *The Challenge to Isolation, 1937–1940*, p. 207.

consultations about the aid the United States would be able to offer. The recommendation was accepted, a week later the invitations were sent off, and early in June American army and navy officers went to the various capitals in order to carry on technical discussions.

Meanwhile it had been decided to reserve the available military forces for the defence of Latin America.

On May 22, 1940, the head of the War Plans Division of the War Department, Major Matthew B. Ridgway, submitted a note to General Marshall in which he surveyed America's possibilities in a world changing with terrifying speed. Ridgway thought Nazi risings in South America, followed by a German invasion, were by no means impossible. South America must be protected and the European settlements there must, if necessary, be preventively occupied. President Roosevelt, General Marshall, Admiral Stark and Under-Secretary of State Sumner Welles concurred with these conclusions: here at least was a plan that embodied positive suggestions.

Hardly had it been accepted when, on top of the appalling news from Dunkirk, alarming information arrived. The British ambassador presented a sheaf of reports from Uruguay to Cordell Hull, which seemed to point to a Nazi revolution near at hand in this republic. And from London a telegram arrived with the warning 'that 6,000 Nazis loaded aboard merchant ships were possibly headed for Brazil, there to be joined by the crews of other German merchantmen in harbour and employed by Nazi elements in Brazil as a means of seizing the government'.[1]

That must be prevented!

President Roosevelt ordered plans to be drawn up immediately for the preventive occupation of the French, British and Dutch possessions in the West Indies, and for offering aid to Brazil, where at most 100,000 men in troops were to be sent, the first 10,000 by air. The navy received the order, if danger were really threatening, to send four battleships, two aircraft-carriers, nine cruisers and three squadrons of destroyers to the Southern half of the Atlantic Ocean. Sumner Welles was given the task of pronouncing a public warning, declaring in a speech that 'any act of aggression by a non-American power whether it be committed north or south of the equator, is a challenge to the security of all and will be so regarded by them'. The great majority of the American people applauded this vigorous language.

Before the end of May the new military plans had been worked out in Washington. The German economic offensive was clearly starting in South America: in Brazil German firms were willing to

[1] Watson: *Chief of Staff. Prewar Plans and Preparations*, p. 95.

guarantee that they would be able to deliver goods ordered in Germany before the end of September: England would undoubtedly have given up the struggle before that time or be destroyed. Who could say with any certainty that a combined Italo-German military-*cum*-political offensive would not also develop via Spain and French Africa?

Reports from Uruguay resulted in this question being thrust upon the authorities in Washington with oppressive force.

In Uruguay there lived only a small number of Germans, not more than eight thousand, including people of German origin who were still in touch with Germany. That was probably one of the reasons why the government of Uruguay had not taken a prominent part in the general efforts South America made to drive back national socialism during the period 1937–9, and to assimilate the German immigrants to their own Latin culture by coercive measures. This compulsion was strongest in the Argentine and Brazil. Part of the work of the *Auslands-Organisation* (which had been prohibited but had continued its existence under another name) was shifted from these two large states to nearby Uruguay.

This did not fail to provoke various people to counter-action. One of these was a youthful professor of philosophy at Montevideo, Hugo Fernandez Artucio, a socialist, who had attended the World Youth Congress in Washington in 1938. Fernandez Artucio was convinced that the Third *Reich* meant to get hold of the whole of South America. He thought it probable that the offensive would first be directed against the small and weak state of Uruguay where the government, to his mind, showed an inexplicable laxness. For this reason he decided to rouse the Uruguayan people to watchfulness by means of a radio campaign.

In October 1939 he began his appeals against 'the German danger' via a broadcasting station in Montevideo. He spoke every day, month after month. In December the sinking of the *Graf Spee* on the Uruguayan coast caused interest in his appeals to rise quickly, for behold, a German pocket-battleship had penetrated as far as the River Plate! Fernandez Artucio urged his listeners to send him news of suspect Nazi activities they might have observed. In two months time 'tens of thousands of accusations, many with supporting evidence' came pouring in.[1] Fernandez Artucio became more and more convinced that he had got onto the track of a big and dangerous conspiracy. The disclosures about the Fifth Column in Denmark and Norway made him resolve to submit his material to the government, ten days after the occupation of Copenhagen and Oslo.

[1] Fernandez Artucio: *The Nazi Octopus in South America*, p. 95.

110

The government gave no response, which Fernandez Artucio considered highly culpable negligence. But he had more strings on his bow:

I thereupon went to Buenos Aires and conferred with two great democratic newspapers of Argentine—*La Prensa* and *La Vanguardia*, both of Buenos Aires. On May 2, 1940, they published the news of the situation in Uruguay. The British Broadcasting Corporation picked up the accusations from the Argentine newspapers and spread them throughout the world. The Uruguayan newspapers then realized the true import of the situation and took up the campaign. Throughout the country they opened their columns to a discussion of the Nazi peril. Public opinion was reawakened. Montevideo was full of rumours. The public grew aware of the Fifth Column.[1]

Then the reports came in from the Netherlands, Belgium and France; they could hardly fail to convince the greatest sceptic of the actuality of a conspiracy on the part of the *Reichsdeutschen*.

Indignation against everything German increased. A socialist member of Parliament, Dr. José Pedro Cardozo, who had been associated with Fernandez Artucio's 'private investigation', declared the government in default. In the House of Representatives he read the memorandum his friend had submitted to the government in the middle of April and which he was able to supplement with a few new documents. Enormous sensation! 'No political bloc dared refuse its consent to the appointment of an investigation committee.'[2] Dr. Tomas Brena, a member of the Catholic party, became its chairman. Fernandez Artucio, although he was not a member of Parliament, was nevertheless included in the committee. The day it started its investigation (May 17, 1940) stones flew through the windows of the shops of German firms during a great pro-Allied demonstration in Montevideo. The atmosphere was tense.

The government felt that it could not lag behind parliament. So two days after the parliamentary committee had been established, the Ministry of National Defence made it known that Fernandez Artucio's memorandum was convincing and that it seemed desirable to prohibit the *Landesgruppe* of the *Auslands-Organisation*. It was whispered that a Nazi *Putsch* was at hand, to be launched on May 25 or 26. Nothing happened. Had the rising been postponed? Tension continued.

In the middle of this state of affairs the parliamentary committee, led by Dr. Tomas Brena and armed with a search warrant from the district judge, raided the house of a German citizen, one Gero Arnulf

---

[1] *Ibid.*, p. 10.   [2] *Ibid.*

Fuhrmann, in Salto—a place situated 200 miles upstream on the Uruguay river—who was generally believed to be an active Nazi. Fuhrmann proved to be a photographer. Photos were found of 'public buildings, bridges, military barracks and a little local river port'.[1] Thereupon his correspondence was searched. Letters from the *Fichtebund* in Hamburg turned up, but also—and that seemed infinitely more important—a worked-out plan for a military coup, obviously written by Fuhrmann himself on three pages, the first of which, however, was missing. Of the remaining two the interpreter read aloud the following: [2]

The entire so-called military action would be completed within fifteen days. The distribution of the troops of occupation would be as follows: two regiments of artillery and cavalry in Montevideo; two companies in Colonia, Fray Bentos, Paysandú, etc.; a battalion in Salto; another in Bella Union; two companies in Artigas; two in Rivera, and a battalion in Jaguarao. It is to be supposed (only a call to arms being necessary) that within two weeks a thousand combatants from Argentine could be mobilised to join those at Montevideo. The maintenance of order would require only one battalion of sharpshooters. It should be remembered that there are four or five thousand people in the country with detailed knowledge of the key points. Of the two or three million inhabitants, it would be necessary to eliminate immediately all the Jews, the political leaders, and the Free Masons. The lodge files should be searched immediately and a guard put over the establishments of all small organisations. The government employees would be retained in their positions for the time being, but German secretaries would be assigned to all the more important posts. Steps would be taken immediately to convert the country into a German colony of farmers. The directors of the colony would immediately take over the lands belonging to the National Banks (National Mortgage Bank, The Insurance Bank, and the Bank of the Republic). Next would come the taking over of the land of absentee landlords and finally the land of all those unwilling to live under German domination. A financial corporation would be founded for Argentine and Brazil to handle the lands belonging to German settlers in those countries in such manner as to carry out the shifting of colonisation without the loss of capital.

That very same day Fuhrmann was dragged into court and

[1] Fernandez Artucio: *The Nazi Octopus in South America*, p. 10.
[2] According to the English text, published in Fernandez Artucio's book, pp. 91–2. The translation in the *New York Times*, June 19, 1940, shows a few unimportant divergences.

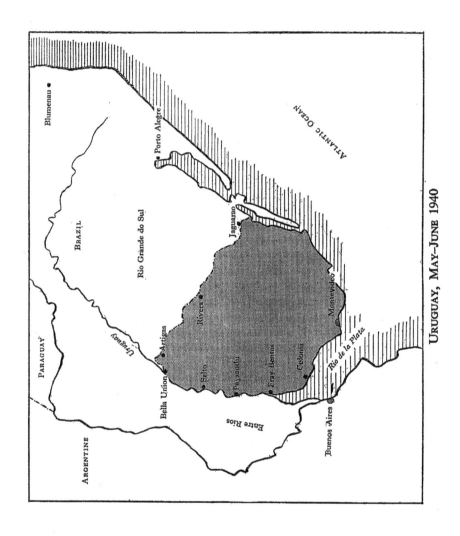

URUGUAY, MAY–JUNE 1940

confessed that he had written the incriminating document, but, he said, 'it was merely a joke that had no importance'.[1] His defence made no impression on the judge. He was locked up and his papers were seized. Dr. Brena and his colleagues rushed back to Montevideo to warn the authorities.

The American ambassador was also warned.

The latter, Edmund C. Wilson, who had been in touch with Fernandez Artucio for a few months, had begun to give credence to his warnings. Wilson knew that public opinion in Uruguay was pro-Allied, but he had also heard that there were politicians and officers who sympathized with the Third *Reich*. In a series of dispatches, dated May 13, 14 and 15, 1940—days brim-full of news about the Fifth Column in the Netherlands—he pointed out to Washington that a handful of determined men could easily occupy Montevideo. If the Nazis were to try anything at *some* spot in South America then it was the most probable that they would do their worst in the 'soft spot'—Uruguay.[2]

After having read these dispatches President Roosevelt instructed Sumner Welles to inform the government of Uruguay that he was uneasy about the situation. From Wilson came one cry of alarm after another. On May 30—the day after the discovery of Fuhrmann's plan—he wired that 'unless the United States acted effectively and without delay there was genuine danger that countries like Uruguay might fall under Nazi domination'.[3] A day later, after a consultation with Norman Armour, the American ambassador in Buenos Aires, he urgently recommended sending a squadron of from forty to fifty men-of-war to the east coast of South America.

Wilson asked much more than the President, as long as there was no dire necessity, dared give. He took a rapid but limited decision: the heavy cruiser *Quincy* which lay at anchor at Guantanamo base, was commissioned to sail at once to Rio de Janeiro and Montevideo, followed a few days later by a second heavy cruiser, the *Wichita*. How Japan would react to Germany's fantastic victories in Europe was not known, but for the time being the President and his naval advisers did not consider themselves justified in weakening the Pacific fleet.

General Marshall, Chief of the Army Staff, saw things in a different light. He thought the Atlantic more important than the Pacific. If the French fleet were to fall into Hitler's hands, the German, Italian and French naval forces combined would be considerably stronger than the British or the American navies. 'We may suddenly find

---

[1] *New York Times*, June 18, 1940.
[2] Quoted by Langer and Gleason: *The Challenge to Isolation 1937–1940*, p. 612.
[3] *Ibid.*

Japan and Russia,' so he argued, 'appear as a team operating to hold our ships in the Pacific. If the French navy goes to Germany and Italy, we will have a very serious situation on the South Atlantic. Germany may rush the South American situation to a head in a few weeks.'[1]

At the time that General Marshall set forth these views the suspense in Uruguay had reached its height.

The committee of Dr. Tomas Brena, who had travelled back to Montevideo with Fuhrmann's documents, had called Parliament together in a secret session in order to announce the sensational find of the *Putsch* plans. All the documents were subjected to a close investigation. They showed that there was a strange organisation in close touch with Germany, with 'leaders' and 'points of support'. The members of Parliament, who had had all the data laid before them in a translation from the German, gained the impression that the Nazis formed a mysterious order, a sort of secret Brownshirt Masonic Lodge, organised under three 'castles'. And it also appeared from the documents 'that in the Nazi mind the world is divided into only two parts, the German *Gau* and the foreign *Gau*. Uruguay like all other countries that the Nazis hope to absorb in their "World Reich" is a "district" of the foreign *Gau*, or "Germany Abroad".'[2]

Yet more evidence was brought to the notice of the committee, which seemed to point to the fact that months earlier, suspect *Reichsdeutsche* had rented or bought property 'close to army barracks, police-stations, bridges, railroad stations and junctions, important cross-roads and repair shops belonging to the railroad and bus companies'.[3]

It happened that in those agitated days the police arrested a *Reichsdeutscher*, a cartographer, who carried a map of the Netherlands, 'showing how the Fifth Column there had prepared gun emplacements for the bombardment of strategic objectives before the Germans invaded the country'.[4] This man also had in his possession a map of Montevideo, on which military details about the town and its surroundings had been marked.

Great excitement seized the authorities. People had the feeling that the German Fifth Column was on the point of taking control.

On June 7 all telegraph stations were put under military guard. The police started carrying out house-searches throughout the whole country. In the neighbourhood of Montevideo 'three German gliders,

---

[1] *Notes on the Conference of June 17, 1940*. Watson: *Chief of Staff. Prewar Plans and Preparations*, p. 108.
[2] *New York Times*, June 19, 1940.
[3] Fernandez Artucio: *The Nazi Octopus in South America*, p. 41.
[4] *New York Times*, June 6, 1940.

one parachute and one dismantled radio-station' were discovered,[1] and from the Argentine came the news that in the province of Entre Rios—near Salto!—arms had been found in the house of a *Reichsdeutscher*. Soldiers were sent to all lighthouses, harbours, frontier custom-houses and stations. Other soldiers patrolled the main roads. On June 13 parliament passed a bill prohibiting all organisations dangerous to the state. 'In order to prevent misunderstanding' [2] the German ambassador disbanded all *reichsdeutsche* associations. Too late! Twelve *Reichsdeutsche* were taken into custody 'amidst tremendous popular excitement'[3] and were interrogated mercilessly, hours on end. On the 17th the German embassy was pelted with stones by two thousand students.

That same day parliament met in private session to listen to the report of the Brena committee, which lasted twenty hours. At the end, the head of the Criminal Investigation Department, who 'had steadily denied that the Nazi plans were of any importance',[4] was arrested. The minister of the Interior, who up to the 15th had contended that people were getting excited about nothing, admitted that he was wrong. The minister of Defence, the third sceptic, now also declared himself satisfied and called upon the whole nation, men and women alike, to form voluntary auxiliary corps.

The shooting-ranges where people could practice without charge were soon crowded to capacity. Over three-fifths of all the men able to bear arms had responded to the ministerial appeal. The American cruiser *Quincy*, which had come to anchor in the roadstead on the 20th, was cheered enthusiastically. An enormous crowd stood waiting in the rain for hours, shouting: 'Long live Roosevelt!', 'Long live the United States!' The statement of the American Minister made at a banquet, saying that Uruguay could count on the support of the United States, was received with enthusiasm. The people only jeered at the letter of the German Ambassador, which was printed in all the newspapers. In it he denied that there was any plot against Uruguay and said that Fuhrmann was completely unknown to him. The masses felt a thrill of great exaltation. They had the feeling of having saved their country's freedom with wonderful dash and in glorious solidarity. These were 'unforgettable days', Fernandez Artucio wrote later.[5] They must never pass into oblivion!

When the crisis was over, a Fifth Column Museum was opened in Montevideo.

In none of the South American states in that summer of 1940

[1] *New York Times*, June 13, 1940.
[2] Quoted by Langer and Gleason: *The Challenge to Isolation 1937–1940*, p. 613.
[3] *Ibid.*   [4] *New York Times*, June 20, 1940.
[5] Fernandez Artucio: *The Nazi Octopus in South America*, p. 11.

was fear for the German Fifth Column so great as in Uruguay. In nearly all the republics, however, measures were taken against the *Reichsdeutschen* living there and against all persons of German origin.

In Brazil the situation remained comparatively quiet. The authorities declared that there was nothing to fear from the Fifth Column; 'dangerous over-confidence', thought the London *Times*.[1]

In the Argentine, as has already been mentioned, arms were found in the house of a *Reichsdeutscher* in June, 1940. The police believed a rising was being planned. In the summer of 1941 anxiety flared up again. In July, parliament appointed a committee of investigation under the chairmanship of Damonte Taborda. In August over thirty *Reichsdeutsche* were arrested. During that autumn the Taborda committee published four reports—a fifth appeared in September, 1942—in which it was proved that, under another name, parts of the *Auslands-Organisation* had continued their existence, keeping up semi-military formations and imbuing the curriculum in German schools with the national socialist spirit.

In Chile, in July, 1940, and June 1941, a native fascist attempt at seizure of power was frustrated, and in August, 1941, it was made known that a conspiracy had been discovered in Southern Chile— the centre of German colonisation. A number of Germans were arrested, twelve rifles and fifty thousand cartridges were seized, and all the Nazi organisations disbanded.

The Bolivian Government ordered an investigation of the German schools in June, 1940. Over a year later, in July, 1941, the German Minister was accused of having prepared a *coup d'état* in co-operation with the military attaché of the Bolivian legation in Berlin, Major Elias Belmonte. The country was under martial law for a short period, and the German diplomat was forced to leave.

In Ecuador it was a staff officer, Colonel Filemon Borjas, who made 'sensational disclosures' in a daily paper in June, 1940, and who later invited the attention of the senate to 'a compilation of rumours which had been circulating in Quito', the capital, 'for some time'.[2] He pointed out that the German pilots of the *Sedta* airways were probably mapping all the strategic points, and that many Germans had leading positions in vital industries.

Columbia, too, where another airways company with German personnel had been closed down, remained vigilant against Germans in 1940 and 1941. Not everyone considered the vigilance great enough. The American journalist Cornelius Vanderbilt was appalled at the number of aerodromes that he saw near German estates

[1] *The Times* (London), June 3, 1940.
[2] Fernandez Artucio: *The Nazi Octopus in South America*, p. 194.

and which he looked upon as 'advance preparations for a Nazi invasion'.[1]

In the Central American republics of Costa Rica, Nicaragua and Guatemala instructions were given at the end of 1940 that in all the flat parts of German landed property, stakes were to be driven into the ground; then the Germans would not be able to land with their aircraft.

Mexico also had bestowed its attention on the Fifth Column in the summer of 1940. One of the biggest weeklies, the *Estampa*, had devoted a special number to it. In it one might read, among other things, that the Netherlands had been undermined by Germans, working as administrators in the postal service, as business men, commercial travellers, hotel keepers, interpreters, taxi drivers, luggage porters, maids and cooks, 'altogether about a hundred thousand'. Besides this, somewhere in the east of Holland there had been a German nudist colony. On May 10 its members had manned bridges and aerodromes, dressed in uniform for this particular occasion.[2]

Rumours to the effect that the Germans in Mexico possessed aerodromes were not infrequent. 'About 5,000 Nazi families' lived there, wrote a widely read American weekly.[3] The press attaché of the German legation was deported in the summer of 1940.

These and similar measures taken by the Central and South American republics were highly welcome to the authorities in Washington. At every Pan-American Conference they urged the necessity of action against the Fifth Column. Congressman Martin Dies, chairman of the Committee to investigate un-American activities, declared at the end of September 1941 that Germany had 'about one million potential soldiers' in South America, 'organised in companies and battalions'. President Roosevelt and his chief advisers, however, gradually came to feel surer of their ground: Hitler had achieved nothing in South America by the summer of 1940—would he succeed any better as time went on? Vigilance remained necessary in any case. It was the price that had to be paid for safety.

This was just as true for the internal affairs of the United States. There, too, from the summer of 1940 onwards, measures were being taken under the influence of the news from Europe, aimed at warding off the danger of an internal Fifth Column. Late in May it was decided to debar Nazis from government service, this with particular reference to the members of the German-American *Bund*.

[1] *Liberty* (New York), Nov. 23, 1940.
[2] *Estampa* (Mexico), July 29, 1940.
[3] *Collier's Weekly* (New York), June 22, 1940.

A month later (June 28, 1940) the President gave his signature to a bill obliging aliens to fill in special registration forms. There appeared to be five million people living in the United States who were not American citizens. In October 1941 they were compelled to declare their incomes. The Department of Justice kept a card index system of all suspect Germans. Besides this a sharp look-out was kept for possible spies and saboteurs.

In September, 1939, the Federal Bureau of Investigation took on 150 new detectives, and in June, 1940, another 250. Over a year later, on June 28, 1941, two large German espionage rings were rounded up, according to the FBI. Forty-nine persons were arrested. The FBI was not easy about the future. In September, 1941, it made known that 'Axis spies and saboteurs' were still working in America in key positions, that they had collected a large amount of military data, and that the German Government had drawn up plans for the launching of a sabotage campaign against 'American defence industries, transport and shipping'.[1]

Three months later Japan struck at Pearl Harbour and Germany declared war on the United States.

The American people accepted this double challenge with the assurance of winning the struggle in the end, however long it might last. As it was clear that Germany's strength was being depleted by the murderous struggle in the Soviet Union, people began to feel less frightened of a large scale Third *Reich* offensive against America, with machinations on the part of a Fifth Column. They went on trying to prevent espionage and sabotage as a matter of course, however. As a precautionary measure the movement of persons of German citizenship was limited. They were not allowed to possess arms, wireless-sets with an ultra-short wave-range, transmitters, codes, cameras and military illustrated works or maps. Of the 264,000 *Reichsdeutschen* about 7,000 were interned. In less than a year about half that number were set at liberty again on the recommendation of special tribunals.

There was great distrust of these *Reichsdeutschen*. They and the non-interned Italian citizens lost their jobs on such a large scale that in July, 1942, President Roosevelt appealed to employers and employees not to make life impossible to persons, who, it is true, were of enemy nationality, but who were well-disposed towards America. In that same month 26 leaders of the German-American *Bund* were indicted. In the previous month, in June, eight German saboteurs, who had been taken to Florida and Long Island in German submarines, had been arrested; two of them were American

[1] Quoted by Michael Sayers and Albert E. Kahn: *Sabotage! The Secret War against America* (New York, 1942), p. 23.

119

citizens, while most of them had been members of the *Bund*. Their outfit of false papers and means of sabotage impressed the general public more than the fact that the Federal Bureau of Investigation had been able immediately to round up these agents.

Much of the news people had read after 1933 had created the impression that, even if things did not go well for Germany at the front, the German secret service anyhow was in admirable working order, and that in America in particular it had built up an espionage system that was 'probably the best-organised, best-financed, most skilful and most efficient' system 'the world has ever seen'.[1] In the two weeks following the arrest of the eight saboteurs over 400 Germans were taken into custody.

In Central and South America too, fear of the German Fifth Column continued to exist after December, 1941, when the second World War started to engulf the entire globe. Following the Pan-American conference held in Rio de Janeiro in January, 1942, all Axis diplomats were forced to leave, except in Chile and the Argentine; the latter was becoming increasingly jealous of the leadership of the United States. But even in those two most southerly Latin American republics measures were taken against the Germans. Persons considered dangerous were interned, and in 1942 in the Argentine there was a big trial of *Reichsdeutsche* accused of espionage. In Chile and Mexico parliamentary committees investigated German intrigues. In 1942 almost the whole German colony in Costa Rica was transferred to Texas and interned there. It was a curious thing that whenever the surge of battle neared Central or South America, signs of Fifth Column activity were immediately to be observed. When in the spring and summer of 1942 ships had been sunk on the Brazilian coast, the view soon spread that *Reichsdeutsche* and persons of German origin had given secret directions to the German U-boats. On August 22, 1942, Brazil declared war on Germany. The following day the police raided a convent in the state of Santa Catharina in South Brazil. The mother superior was arrested. 'Nuns', so the world press reported, 'had communicated from the cemetery by wireless while apparently praying. They were of German origin.'

[1] *New York Post*, Jan. 18, 1942.

CHAPTER VII

1941—Germany attacks again

★

O<small>N</small> April 6, 1941, Yugoslavia and Greece were invaded by Germany and on June 22, the Soviet Union.

Did the peoples of Yugoslavia and Greece and those of the Soviet Union believe, as did the peoples of Northern and Western Europe, that a German Fifth Column constituted an integral part of German aggression?

We may answer in the affirmative as far as Yugoslavia and the Soviet Union are concerned, even if we do so somewhat hesitantly, with insufficient data.

As far as Greece is concerned the data are even more scarce. We shall start there.

In the principal towns of Greece there existed small colonies of German citizens, some of whom had become members of the usual *Landesgruppe* of the *Auslands-Organisation der NSDAP*. In Athens, on April 6, 1941, these people were arrested by the police, together with others who were considered suspect. In the end there were a thousand persons in the police office who had been rounded up, a veritable 'tangle of languages and peoples'.

The leaders of the *reichsdeutsche* colony in the Greek capital, however, had arranged with the police that the *reichsdeutschen* Nazis would not be put behind barbed wire in case of war, but would be lodged in three houses that had been chosen and put into readiness before-hand. The police kept to this arrangement, and after a talk with one of their leaders, let the German aliens in question leave the camp and go to the three houses. There they were left in peace for almost three weeks (except for a small demonstration of young people who shouted 'Down with the Fifth Column!'), until the swastika was planted on the Acropolis (April 27, 1941). All this does not lead one to think that, in Athens at least, the German Fifth Column seemed very important in the minds of the authorities and the citizens. It was otherwise in Yugoslavia.

After the end of the first World War a number of *Reichsdeutsche* settled in the Kingdom of Yugoslavia just as they did elsewhere, mainly as traders. It was of more importance that there were large districts in the north of the country where, altogether, about 600,000 persons of German descent, language and customs lived. In the west, in Slovenia, the German minority were townspeople, a remnant of a formerly larger group, but reduced in numbers after 1800 by the pressure of the Slovenes. There also, at Gottschee, in the midst of the infertile Karst region, was a pocket of impoverished German-speaking people. Further to the east, in the river valleys of the Save, Drave, Danube and Theiss, were large German agricultural colonies, mostly dating from the eighteenth century, and founded there by the Habsburgs as part of a defence-line of fighting settlers whose task it was to protect Central Europe from the Turks. These German groups, *Volksdeutsche*, were in for a difficult time in youthful Yugoslavia. Their schools and organisations were objects of attack. Political rights were denied them. Especially in Slovenia, the pressure brought to bear on them was great.

Under these circumstances the *Volksdeutschen* could not be expected to remain unmoved. The younger generation especially sought support from the Third *Reich*, after 1933, and thus the vicious circle, already sketched in Poland, also came into existence in Yugoslavia: the actions of the oppressors and the reactions of the oppressed influenced and inflamed each other and called hatred and aggressiveness into being that could not be stemmed. Both groups continually found their vindication in the deeds perpetrated by their opponents. The *Anschluss* of Austria caused the tension to increase; the annexation of the Sudeten region and the subsequent establishment of the Protectorate, augmented the Slovenes' and Serbs' hatred of *Deutschtum*, the more so because of their Slav kinship with the Czechs.

Yugoslavia was especially sensitive about the news of the German Fifth Column that came from Denmark and Norway in April, 1940, from the Netherlands, Belgium and France in May and June.

It was noticed by the Yugoslav authorities that *volksdeutsche* recruits frequently did not respond to their call-up for military service, and disappeared instead; it was surmised that they had presented themselves for service in the German army, which foretold no good. Especially during the autumn of 1940 such desertions were numerous. German diplomatic pressure on Yugoslavia increased month by month, and finally Prince Regent Paul and his cabinet decided to join the Tripartite Pact between Germany, Italy and Japan. An agreement to this end was signed by two Yugoslav Ministers in Vienna on March 25, 1941. Serbian patriotism, however, refused to swallow this mortification; in the early hours of March 27 a party of resolute officers led by General Simovitch took power into their own hands, the Council of Regency was dissolved, and the young son of King Alexander was proclaimed as King Peter II.

Tremendous enthusiasm took hold of the Serbs. The contumely of Vienna had been wiped out! Yugoslavia had broken with Hitler and Mussolini! Hatred of the Germans reached an unprecedented pitch. In the capital, Belgrade, the windows of the German Travel Agency were smashed in no time; the office was wrecked, furniture thrown into the street and triumphantly set on fire. The German Air Attaché, driving through the town on the morning of the 27th with a little Swastika flag on the bonnet of his car, refused to stop at the demand of an excited band of demonstrators; he was consequently man-handled in such a way that he had to be taken to a hospital. As the German Ambassador was on his way to the Cathedral on the 28th to attend a religious ceremony in honour of the young king, he was loudly jeered; and a French journalist heard on the same day that people had spat in his face.[1] *Reichsdeutsche* living in Belgrade and elsewhere were molested; many fled the country precipitately.

Two days afterwards the German storm broke.

In the early morning of April 6, large parts of Belgrade were destroyed by air bombardment. German divisions rushed the frontiers. In the south they penetrated into Macedonia from Bulgarian territory, thus cutting off communications with Greece. In the north they surrounded and annihilated the Yugoslav armies, which, inadequately mobile as they were, tried to defend the whole frontier zone.

As in Poland, so here too the struggle was unequal; but German superiority was even more crushing, the speed of their experienced and hardened divisions even greater. The confusion, disorganisation and panic among the Yugoslavs must have been correspondingly greater, especially among those troops awaiting destruction at the hands of the irresistible enemy in the districts inhabited by the unreliable Croats and *Volksdeutsche*. Again fear of treachery pervaded the minds of the people. There were rumours in certain parts of the country that the water-supply had been poisoned.

When, on April 10, the fifth day of the war, the Frenchman cited previously found himself in Sarajevo after an adventurous journey, he heard that the Germans had already bombed the nearby place at which the government had taken up residence after its flight from the capital. His first reaction to the news was one of suspicion.

[1] Jean Hussard: *Vu en Yugoslavie 1939–1944* (Lausanne, 1945), p. 80.

'This precision of action appears surprising. Besides anxiety there is distrust too. Who is informing? Who is the perfidious traitor helping the enemy? The farther from Belgrade, the less trustworthy the country and the people seem to be.'[1]

Naturally the *Volksdeutschen* were the first object of distrust on the part of the Serbs and Slovenes. This is evident from a report compiled by the Yugoslav War Crimes Commission in December, 1945, in which the first paragraph includes the following serious accusation: *The Government of the Third Reich and Hitler's party organised secretly the German Minority in Yugoslavia.* In support of this it was stated:

> Since 1920 they [i.e. the *Volksdeutschen*] had their own national organisation called 'the *Schwaebisch-Deutscher Kulturbund*'. It was this organisation (and through it all the Germans in Yugoslavia) that the Nazi Party secretly transformed into political and military organs for the attack on Yugoslavia.
>
> Nazi *Gaus* were secretly formed in Yugoslavia and *Gauleiters* appointed. Under the guise of various 'gymnastic' and 'sport' societies, para-military Hitlerite organisations were formed. From the *Reich* there came innumerable 'tourists', 'commercial travellers' and 'relatives', who in fact were only Nazi organisers and instructors.[2]

An appendix to this report gave the following picture of the activity of the *Volksdeutschen* during the fighting:

> At the time of the German attack on Yugoslavia, in April, 1941, the well-organised German minority in Yugoslavia rendered the German army notable service. The *volksdeutschen* recruits spread wild rumours amongst the troops and hastened their demoralisation, deserting when their units came in touch with the German army, thus causing confusion among the loyal soldiers. As they surrendered they shouted, *'Heil Hitler'*.
>
> The civilian *Volksdeutschen* attacked the retreating Yugoslav troops in the rear, disarmed small units, captured arms, guarded bridges and other important points and presented themselves at their first opportunity for service under German military command. Furthermore, they took over authority from the Yugoslavs wherever they were able in accordance with a pre-existing plan.[3]

---

[1] Jean Hussard: *Vu en Yugoslavie 1939–1944* (Lausanne, 1945), p. 113.

[2] *Yugoslav War Crimes Commission. Report to the International Military Tribunal, Nürnberg*, Dec. 26, 1945. USSR-036. *Trial of the major war criminals before the International Military Tribunal, Nuremberg*, Vol. XXXIX, p. 273–4. The volumes of this trial published from 1947 to 1949 will henceforth be referred to as: *IMT*.

[3] Appendix to the report quoted in the foregoing note. NG-4630, p. 16.

The struggle did not last long.

A week from the beginning of the campaign the Germans entered a still smoking Belgrade. Another four days, and organised Yugoslav resistance had ceased to be.

Three weeks later, on Sunday June 22, 1941, the shrill whistles for the attack sounded again. From the Baltic to the Black Sea the Germans advanced in force towards the heart of the Soviet Union and their own doom.

Looking back at the development during the years 1933–9, we noted in the Introduction to Part I that fear of the German Fifth Column was pre-eminently an international phenomenon. In the regions treated—the countries surrounding Germany, Northern, Western and Southern Europe, their colonies, the British Commonwealth and North and South America—we might describe the free press and radio as an organic whole. Suspicious activity in one country was immediately reported in all. But as we noted earlier, the Soviet Union stood apart: 'There the press and the radio kept themselves strictly to the directives given by the Kremlin, and how far these reflected public opinion it would be difficult to say.'

In a democracy the relationship between organs of publicity and public opinion is of a very complex nature. Certainly not all readers believe all they are told by press or radio. Inversely it may be doubted whether the deepest desires and fears which move the people ever find adequate expression in what is published by a newspaper or spoken over the wireless. Nevertheless, in every society characterised by relative freedom of thought, public opinion and published news and comments interact in a healthy way.

In a totalitarian society, however, in which there is a systematic attempt to inculcate certain views in the public, at least those people who are in any way conscious of the coercion under which they live will constantly doubt, or even disbelieve on principle, the reports and views handed out by the state and party organs. The deadly uniformity of such publications gives rise to scepticism. Another source of distrust is the abrupt way in which the 'line' followed by the authorities is changed, a shift of direction which is obeyed pre-eminently by the press and the radio. But how widespread the distrust of official news is, and to what *real* opinions it may lead cannot be measured in a totalitarian state; in fact, it can hardly be discovered at all.

It would not have been surprising if the Russians had been apprehensive of Germany when Hitler came to power. The traditional invader of Russia came from the west, and the Germans had shown themselves hard masters in those parts of Russia which they had occupied during the first World War. The peace of Brest-Litovsk had been imposed by a flint-hearted conqueror. In the twenties, however, the Soviet Union, secretly co-operating with the Weimar Republic, had pictured Britain rather than Germany as the symbol of the imperialism supposed to be the last phase of capitalism, and had depicted her as the main opponent of socialism and the Soviet state.

Shortly after the usurpation of power by Hitler a new 'line' was projected, and duly administered to the Russian people. More and more Germany and Japan were painted as the arch-enemies of the Union of Soviet Socialist Republics. Speeches by prominent leaders, articles in the newspapers, films like 'Alexander Nevski' (showing the annihilation of the invading German army in the thirteenth century), all did their bit. It seems more than likely that the trials accompanying the purges of 1936–8 performed the same function, if we note that all Stalin's opponents were supposed to have collaborated with national socialist Germany, and in doing so, found no misdeed and no baseness too outrageous.

It was said and considered proved that Zinoviev and Kamenev (who were tried together with fourteen others before the Military Chamber of the Supreme Court in August, 1936), after the successful assassination of Serge Kirov (December 1, 1934), had made preparations for the murder of Stalin, Voroshilov, Kaganovitch, Zhdanov and other front-rank party functionaries. One of the members of the 'Trotskyist-Zinovievist terrorist centre' had, it was said, taken steps together with a group of German Trotskyists for the murder of Stalin.

Five months later, in January, 1937, came the trial of a second group of 'Trotskyists', including the well-known journalist Karl Radek. Radek confessed that he and his co-suspects had wanted to cede the Ukraine to Germany. Another prisoner, Piatakov, agreed that the Trotskyists had been prepared to grant German firms important concessions, and that they would have acted as saboteurs in case of war, in accordance with plans which, during a conference between Trotsky and 'Hitler's deputy Hess, had been definitely worked out and accepted'.[1]

Again, five months later, in June, 1937, it was announced that the Chief-of-Staff of the Red Army, Marshall Tukachevsky, had been executed after a secret trial, together with four other highly-placed military men. They had committed espionage and treason in favour of a foreign power. Germany again?

The last great trial took place in March, 1938, in the same week

---

[1] *Prozessbericht ueber die Strafsache des Sowjetfeindlichen trotzkistischen Zentrums, verhandelt vor dem Militärkollegium des Obersten Gerichtshofes der UdSSR vom 23.–30. Januar 1937, gegen J. L. Pjatakow, K. B. Radek, G. J. Sokolnikow, L. P. Serebrjakow* [and 13 others] (Moscow, 1937), p. 8.

of the *Anschluss* with Austria. Old Bolsheviks like Bukharin, Rykov and Krestinsky stood in the dock before a military court, together with Yagoda, chief of the secret police. They also confessed, among other things, to having taken steps to cede the Ukraine and White Russia to Germany. Krestinsky stated that he had worked as an agent of the German secret police from 1921 onwards. Another prisoner, Rosengoltz, had started spying for Germany in 1923; a third, Grinko, in 1932.

A fourth, Bessonov, had had conferences with 'the close collaborator of Rosenberg in the *Aussenpolitische Abteilung* of the fascist party'.[1] A fifth suspect, Tchernov, according to his own story a German spy since 1928, had received sabotage assignments from Paul Scheffer, Moscow correspondent of the *Berliner Tageblatt*, and from others as well. In his capacity as People's Commissar for Agriculture, he had effectuated those assignments by slowing down the construction of silos, by spoiling military supplies with the help of 'parasites and larvae', by causing the breeding of horses to miscarry, by infecting the pigs in the Leningrad district 'artificially' with red diarrhœa, and those in the districts of Woronesh and the Black Sea with the plague.[2]

Did all these terrible details impress the Russian masses?

We do not know.

But if such was the case, these masses must have been confused by the pact with the instigators of all those misdeeds into which Stalin entered in August, 1939, and by the obliging attitude of the rulers of the Kremlin towards the Third *Reich* during the following one and a half years—an attitude only offset in 1941 by some warnings directed to the Russian people, clothed in the usual phraseology.

For no other people perhaps did the German attack come so unexpectedly as for the inhabitants of the Soviet Union.

The Russian frontier detachments were taken completely unawares as the Germans sprang upon them in the dawn of June 22, 1941. Tactical surprise was absolute. The Russian armies posted in the districts behind the frontier were surrounded, attacked and annihilated amid utter confusion. Officers and soldiers sometimes fought on doggedly till their ammunition gave out, but for weeks there was nothing which might be called an organised counter-operation. There was fear of German parachutists. It was thought

---

[1] *Prozessbericht über die Strafsache des anti-sowjetischen 'Blocks der Rechten und Trotzkisten', verhandelt vor dem Militärkollegium des Obersten Gerichtshofes der UdSSR, vom 2.–13. März 1938 gegen N. I. Bucharin, A. I. Rykow, G. G. Jagoda, N. N. Krestinski* [and 17 others] (Moscow, 1938), p. 10.

[2] *Ibid.*, p. 111–13.

that suspicious light-signals were being given behind the front. Tales were common that Germans or German agents, dressed in Russian uniforms or as farmers or even as women, were operating dozens of miles ahead of the advancing German troops, cutting the Russian lines of communication, occupying points of tactical importance for the German advance, keeping in touch with the enemy by radio.

Even in Moscow protected by a number of lines of defence, the people were soon in fear of the parachutists. A fortnight after the attack was launched, Alexander Werth, then Moscow correspondent of the London *Sunday Times* and the BBC, heard about the difficulties encountered by three British non-commissioned officers on their way by open truck from the airport to the Russian capital where they were to act as instructors: 'At a street corner they were stopped by the police, and, puzzled by the unfamiliar British uniforms, a crowd had gathered round them, and somebody said "parachutists" and the crowd grew angry and vociferous, and the three NCO's were taken off to a police station. In the end somebody from the Embassy had to come and rescue them.'[1] Werth himself was arrested the following day because someone heard him speaking a foreign language. During a walk in the evening of July 12, while the Germans were still 300 miles from Moscow, he had been asked to show his *dokumenty* 'every two or three minutes'.[2]

It is hardly surprising that the gigantic retreat of the Russian armies, from the frontier to the gates of Moscow, Leningrad and Rostov, during five months and with bloody losses, was accompanied by a feeling of insecurity, by nervousness and local panic, augmented by rumours about the power of the enemy, his superiority and resourcefulness. Moscow suffered such a panic in the middle of October, 1941; people were expecting the entry of the Germans at any moment. Many prominent persons fled helter-skelter eastwards. Stalin remained and ordered that all panic-mongers be shot without quarter. A Russian officer in the capital at that time of confusion was convinced that the chaos was fomented by 'German agents who mingled with the crowds'.[3] Fifth Column!

Reliable documentation for a broader painting of the situation is lacking.

At the time of Hitler's attack there were still many hundreds of

[1] Alexander Werth: *Moscow '41* (London, 1942), p. 30.   [2] *Ibid.*, p. 56.
[3] Michel Koriakoff: *Moscou ne croît pas aux larmes* (Paris, 1951), p. 105. Hardly any information has been published so far on the state of mind of the Russians during those first terrible six months of the war. One of the few books we have is a novel, Theodor Plievier's *Moskau*. Plievier was living in the Soviet Union at that time. Stalin and his successors have not been particularly eager to publish studies on a period during which so many mistakes have been made.

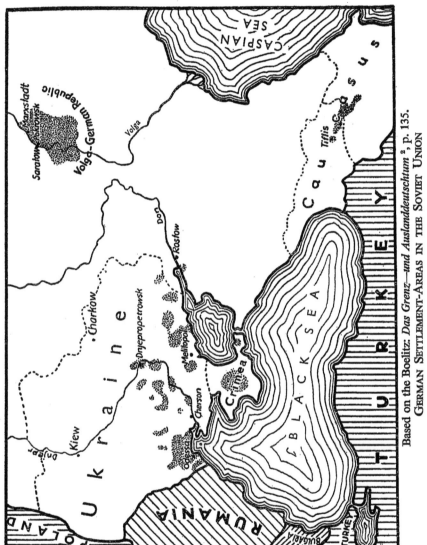

Based on the Boelitz: *Das Grenz—und Auslanddeutschtum*[2], p. 135.
GERMAN SETTLEMENT-AREAS IN THE SOVIET UNION

thousands of people of German origin living in European Russia, partly in communities of their own; through many generations they had retained their German language, and so we shall again refer to them as *Volksdeutsche*. Their ancestors had migrated to Russia in the second half of the eighteenth and the first half of the nineteenth centuries at the instigation of the Romanovs, who had offered them land and privileges. They settled in Volhynia (West Russia), in the Ukraine, near the Black Sea, in the region of the Caucasus and in the districts along the Lower Volga. Many of them became wealthy farmers. Others became professional men or tradesmen in the Russian towns. Others again had had their homesteads in the Baltic provinces for generations.

From 1933 onward the Russian government had introduced severe security measures against many of the *Volksdeutschen* in the rural districts; in the towns there were few left. They were not trusted, and Stalin was hardly a man to accept avoidable risk. Shortly after 1933 missionaries of the German Evangelical Church were expelled from Russia. It was alleged that their religious tracts contained Nazi propaganda, and also that the actors of the travelling theatres performing for the *Volksdeutschen* along the Volga—where there was a separate Soviet Socialist Republic—were really spies. For the time being Stalin let the inhabitants of this republic alone.

From the Caucasus regions, however, people were deported, and from the more westerly parts of the Soviet Union large numbers of *Volksdeutsche* were transferred to North Russia and Siberia during the years 1935 to 1938. The German colonies situated less than sixty miles from the western frontier of the Soviet Union were practically depopulated. From these colonies, according to a German report in 1941,[1] many *Volksdeutschen* fled to the towns of the Ukraine, where they went into hiding. In the period of 1937–38 many men of military age in the colonies of the Ukraine and the Black Sea districts were sent east.

In the autumn of 1939 and the summer of 1940 Moscow approved the migration of the *Volksdeutschen* still remaining in the Baltic states and Volhynia, to the German-occupied part of Poland.

The *Volksdeutschen* in the other parts of the country were in for a hard time after the outbreak of hostilities in 1941.

In the Ukraine an order was issued that all *volksdeutsche* males from 16 to 60 were to be sent east. To the west of the Dnjepr many of them found means to go into hiding or to escape while in transport; to the east of the river deportation was more common.

[1] C. von Kügelgen: 'Von den deutschen Kolonisten in Wolhynien und in der Ukraine westlich des Dnjepr', *Deutsche Post aus dem Osten* (Berlin), XIII, 12 (Dec. 1941), pp. 2–6.

The same can be said of the German colonies in and near the Crimea, and further east along the coast of the Black Sea. People were deported from the region to the north of the Caucasus as well. Altogether, in these districts there had been about 600,000 *Volksdeutsche*; on arrival, the German armies found only about 250,000 of them.[1] The rest had disappeared. In the Crimea there was 'not a single German left'.[2]

With reference to the large group of *Volksdeutsche* in the Volga Republic, totalling about 400,000, a decree was issued by the Kremlin on August 28, 1941, more than two months after Hitler had opened the attack, and published in all the newspapers on September 8:

According to reliable information received by military authorities, there are thousands and tens of thousands of diversionists and spies among the German population of the Volga region, who are prepared to cause disturbances in these regions at a signal from Germany. No Germans (living in the Volga districts) ever reported to Soviet authorities the presence of such great numbers of diversionists and spies. Therefore, the German population of the Volga regions are covering up enemies of the Soviet people and the Soviet power. If diversionist acts were to take place under orders of Germany by German diversionists and spies in the Volga German republic or neighbouring regions and there were bloodshed, the Soviet government would be forced, according to martial law, to adopt measures of reprisal against the entire German population. In order to avoid such undesirable occurrences and to forestall serious bloodshed, the presidium of the Supreme Council of the USSR has found it necessary to resettle the entire German population of the Volga regions under the condition that the resettlers are allotted land and given state aid to settle in new regions. Resettled Germans will be given land in the Novo-Sibirsk and Omsk districts, the Altay region, the Kazakstan Republic and neighbouring localities rich in land. In connection with this, the National Defence Council is instructed to resettle as soon as possible all Volga Germans, who will be given land estates in new regions.

When this decree was published most of the deportations had

---

[1] Joseph B. Schechtman: *European Population Transfers* (New York, 1946), p. 208. Kolarz assumes that of the 480,000 Minority Germans still present in 1941, 'probably about 200,000 were deported' (Walter Kolarz: *Russia and Her Colonies* (London, 1952), p. 75).

[2] Affidavit of A. E. Frauenfeld, Greifelt-24, Trial of the principal officers of the *Rasse- und Siedlungshauptamt* ('Case VIII').

already taken place. A fortnight after the beginning of the German invasion the public buildings in the Volga republic had been seized by the security police. The populace was not allowed to leave the villages; all means of communication between those villages were cut, and all the officials of the republic were arrested. Next, the *volksdeutsche* population were notified that they were to get ready to leave. They had to deliver up their cattle, corn and agricultural implements. More and more disorder set in: the Germans were approaching! When early in August the Russian committees arrived to see to the still surviving and neglected cattle, they found evidence that in many villages the *Volksdeutschen* had had to leave abruptly; in some of the houses bowls with mildewed soup were still on the tables. A large part of the harvest was rotting in the fields, horses and pigs had disappeared, the cattle were lowing in the meadows.

The *Volksdeutschen* who as a group had lived on the Lower Volga for six generations were on their way to Siberia. Werth assumed that this was 'a rather rough affair'.[1] Maurice Edelman saw them on the move: 'A mournful procession of refugees filled the roads leading to the railway stations of the Middle Volga, four hundred thousands of them, carrying bedding, dragging domestic animals, the women weeping, all with the bitterness on their faces of those who have been driven from their homes.'[2]

We do not know how these people, among whom, according to the Kremlin, were 'thousands and tens of thousands of diversionists and spies', were treated in this country engaged in deadly struggle. We do not know how they crossed the Urals, moving against the stream of west-bound military transports, and were set down in inhospitable regions at the onset of an early winter. How these four hundred thousand men, women and children, or what was left of them, built up a new life for themselves during those years of oppression and privation, or, perhaps, forgotten and neglected, gradually went under—we do not know. It is stated of one group of deported *Volksdeutsche* that it took them two whole weeks to cover a railway section that normally took one day, and a few persons had collapsed by that time, in crammed railway vans suffering from thirst. A second report six months later states that some of the *Volksdeutschen* who had been transported to the Altai area had been divided among the collective farms, where they received a great deal of help.[3] According

[1] Werth: *Moscow '41*, p. 173.
[2] Quoted by Schechtman: *European Population Transfers*, p. 385.
[3] W. Wolshanin: 'Das Ende der autonomen Sowjet-Republik der Wolga-Deutschen', *Freiheit* (Munich), I, 4 (July, 1953), p. 24. Wolshanin was a member of one of the committees that had taken over the care of the cattle left behind by the Minority Germans.

to a third report many of the families had been broken up.[1] In 1954
Harrison E. Salisbury, the Moscow correspondent of the *New York
Times*, stumbled upon the remnants of a group of twenty thousand
Volga-Germans who had been settled in Central Asia along the
Afghan frontier, where 'thousands died of disease and hardship.' [2]

For the rest, there is neither word nor sign.

Werth, with earnest sympathy for the heroically fighting Russian
people, could find no word of pity for the fate of these Volga-Germans. His opinion—which found general agreement in most of the
western world—was that these deportations should be viewed as
'a realistic approach to the problem of a German minority; a problem
the essence of which was demonstrated only too clearly in the
Sudetenland and elsewhere'.[3]

And so it happened—it was hardly surprising, it was understandable, even necessary—that the severest measures ever taken against
the Fifth Column anywhere during the second World War were
immediately associated with the treason perpetrated by the Sudeten-
German Konrad Henlein. As people saw it, it had started in 1933,
when Hitler had become Chancellor of the *Reich* which was to have
lasted a thousand years.

---

[1] Helmut Gollwitzer: '*Und führen wohin du nicht willst . . .*' (Munich, 1952),
pp. 300–1.

[2] *New York Times*, Sep. 28, 1954.

[3] Werth: *Moscow '41*, p. 173.

CHAPTER VIII

The fixed image

★

THE time has come for a review of the conceptions of the German Fifth Column which had come into existence after 1933—before the term itself had been coined, that is—but more especially during the years of war in the countries outside Germany. How far these conceptions agree with reality is as yet irrelevant. Our present aim is not to investigate but to sum up.

As we have seen, the actual term only came into general use after the German invasion of Denmark and Norway, and more especially after the invasion of the Low Countries and France. Stress was laid at that time on what might be called the 'military' Fifth Column. The tourists and young hikers who, it was assumed, had spied so thoroughly in Norway; the *reichsdeutschen* civilians who, according to reports, had carried out an armed attack on the centre of government in The Hague; the German agents who had passed on false orders or handed out poisoned sweets in Belgium and France—all such were called 'Fifth Columnists'. 'Fifth Columnists' was also the appellation for the 'traitors' in the countries attacked: in Norway Quisling and his followers, who, it was believed, had been ready to upset the defences and usurp authority; in the Netherlands those numerous members of the Dutch Nazi movement, who, so the public was convinced, had shot at Dutch troops from their houses; in Belgium the Flemish and Walloon fascists of whom it was reported that they had spread rumours to lower morale; in France the politicians who were said to have wilfully sabotaged the country's war effort so as to be able to come to terms with Hitler as quickly as possible.

Once the term Fifth Column had come into general use, it was also projected into the past and used to indicate all those acts which since 1933 had been connected with the great, aggressive national socialist conspiracy. There was no hesitation about using the term 'Fifth Columnist' to denote those *Reichsdeutschen* who had been doing their subversive work abroad, or those *Volksdeutschen* who, although they were citizens of other states, regarded Hitler as their true leader.

The way in which this image of the Fifth Column grew does not lend itself to an exact description. The currents, conscious and unconscious, running through the minds of men cannot be charted accurately. Generally speaking, however, there were actual events which first gave rise to the general conviction that there was such a thing as a Fifth Column. The murder of Dollfuss, the *Anschluss* of Austria, the formation of Henlein's Sudeten German Legion, but also: the demonstrations by national socialist *Reichsdeutsche* abroad, their intrigues, disclosed by house-searches and trials in widely scattered countries from Lithuania to South-West Africa —all these were undeniable facts. During the German invasion the Poles regarded as equally undeniable the mass treason of the *Volksdeutschen*, the Dutch that of the German and Dutch national socialists.

The 'international' image of the Fifth Column evolved from the 'national' ones which had developed more or less independently. The actions of Seyss-Inquart and Henlein made the Fifth Column *international news*, and a theme, as well, which was constantly stressed by newspapers and radios the world over. Again and again it was written and talked about, but naturally never so intensively as during that catastrophic spring of 1940, when, as was thought, the Fifth Columnists went into action from Narvik to Montevideo, from Rotterdam to Batavia. Only then did the image of that Fifth Column really and truly become engraved, sharply and clearly, in the minds of hundreds of millions of people.

What was observed *later* in the way of deeds on the part of Germans and other national socialists only helped to *fix* that image. That the *Reichsdeutschen* and *Volksdeutschen* in the countries occupied by Germany closed their ranks beneath the swastika emblem and that the 'native' national socialists evidently sided with Hitler, was additional proof for the belief that these groups had actively promoted the coming of the Germans in the guise of Fifth Columnists.

An important factor in fixing the image, not to be underestimated, was what might be read about the Fifth Column *after* German aggression had taken place.

As early as October, 1940, Huntington, going back only as far as the outbreak of war, had already collected 121 articles dealing with 'The European "Fifth Column"'. These came from the leading

American periodicals.[1] Hellman, in 1943, was able to compile a bibliography on 'The Nazi Fifth Column' in which only books and the more important articles from American periodicals were included; they totalled 290.[2]

As regards the United States, special significance should be attached to a series of articles on the Fifth Column by Colonel William J. Donovan and Edgar Ansel Mowrer. Donovan, an enterprising and brave man, had seen the fighting in Abyssinia and Spain at first hand, besides having a fine record in the first World War. He was a personal friend of the republican Frank Knox, publisher of the *Chicago Daily News*. With the approval of Roosevelt, who distrusted the pessimistic dispatches of his Ambassador to the Court of St. James, Kennedy, Knox sent Donovan to London with a commission to report on Britain's chances of holding her own against the inevitable blows to be expected from Hitler. He departed on his mission on July 20. Early in August he was back in Washington with strongly favourable impressions.

In London he had at the same time collected data on the work of the Fifth Column on the Continent of Europe. To this end he had associated himself with Mowrer, the author of *Germany puts the Clock Back*, published in 1933. Mowrer was European representative of the *Chicago Daily News*. He had been able to get away from France only with difficulty, reaching England by way of Portugal. The data collected by Donovan and Mowrer were considered to be of such importance that they were released as four articles to the press services, which in turn passed them on to practically all American newspapers. They were published on August 20, 21, 22 and 23, 1940, and deserve to be summarised here as a typical and influential example.

Donovan and Mowrer began with a sketch of Hitler's victories. His armed forces had been superior, they said, but they could never have achieved victory so quickly and decisively were it not for the aid of Germans and other allies within the countries attacked. The Sudeten Germans had brought about the defeat of Czechoslovakia. Poland had been stabbed in the back by its *Volksdeutsche*, led by the Gestapo; tens of thousands of them had been trained as agents and guides for the invasion armies; others had spread false orders and marked military targets with special signals. In Denmark the Germans had furthered demoralisation, while Norway was surprised by

German soldiers who had concealed themselves in ships. In Holland 120,000 *Reichsdeutsche* had fired upon their hosts 'with the fury of dervishes',[1] and in Belgium 60,000 of them had financed the Flemish and Walloon fascists. German agents like Friedrich Sieburg and Otto Abetz had sowed the seed for capitulation in France. England had interned all dangerous elements in time, including the refugees.

There had been no 'native' Fifth Column in Czechoslovakia and Poland, Donovan and Mowrer continued. In Norway, on the other hand, Quisling had made German success possible. In the Netherlands members of the Dutch Nazi party had helped Hitler. Flemish Nazis had betrayed the vital bridges over the Albert Canal. French spies had kept Hitler perfectly posted all the time, and the French upper class and intellectuals had for years been plied with arguments by German propagandists. Perhaps even in England there were defeatists.

The Germans had spent 200 million dollars, according to Donovan and Mowrer, on this organising and propaganda work abroad. Part of it had been put at the disposal of the *Auslands-Organisation der NSDAP*, which numbered 'nearly four million members, all of whom were conscious agents'.[2] *Reichsdeutsche*, naturalised Germans and non-Germans belonged to it. By the side of the *Auslands-Organisation* you had the Gestapo, the Ministry for Propaganda, the Labour Front, the espionage services and the *Auswärtige Amt*, thirty thousand employees in all, five thousand of whom worked for the Gestapo, and all equipped with small transmitters. German students and maids had often acted as agents.

The democracies had been too little alive to all this. This also applied to the United States, where probably 'the finest Nazi-schooled Fifth Column in the world was to be found'.[3] Great vigilance was asked to curb the danger.

After they had appeared in the press, these observations of Donovan's and Mowrer's were also published as a pamphlet, with a preface by Secretary Knox, who warmly recommended this 'careful study made with every official source at [the authors'] disposal'.[4]

Well over two years later, in 1943, the State Department sponsored the appearance of a detailed work which, mainly on the strength of material published in Germany, illustrated absorbingly the development of the relations between Germany and the Germans outside the frontiers. The 'Fifth Column' was also discussed in it, partly on the basis of confidential information. The most important supporting materials were excerpts from 'a confidential, reliable account,

---

[1] William Donovan and Edgar Ansel Mowrer: *Fifth Column Lessons for America* (Washington, 1940), p. 4.
[2] *Ibid.*, p. 11.   [3] *Ibid.*, p. 14.   [4] *Ibid.*, p. 2.

verified by other sources, of the many-sided German fifth-column activity in the Netherlands before the German invasion'.[1]

According to this report, the *Reichsdeutsche Gemeinschaft*, the organisation of German citizens living in the Netherlands, which pretended to be neutral, had in fact been a national socialist body. Its leader, Otto Butting, was 'the uncrowned king of every German national' living in the Netherlands. He possessed a card-index containing particulars about numerous non-Germans and about the 100,000 Germans who had been compelled to join the Nazi *Arbeitsfront*. Many of these acted as spies. With the help of Dutch Nazis he had been able to get 80,000 Dutch unemployed stationed in Germany, who had there been converted into partisans of Hitler. After their return these people had been 'among the Hollanders of every social stratum, high and low, who helped to welcome, shelter and guide the German parachutists'.[2]

This document attracted attention on account of all the particulars it gave which obviously rested on inside information. Many publications based on personal experiences were accepted as equally authentic, written by such authorities as the Speaker of the Norwegian Parliament, Carl J. Hambro,[3] and the Dutch minister of Foreign Affairs, Mr. E. N. van Kleffens,[4] by journalists, or other eye-witnesses who had left the areas occupied by Germany.

Other governments contributed their share to the fixation of the Fifth Column idea. The Poles published a series of reports of military men who had escaped from Poland,[5] and the Czechs a large group of documents about the Henlein movement.[6] All data which had become known since 1933, were in their turn worked up into monographs by many writers, each in his own way.

Especially with regard to the central organisation of the Fifth Column, they often contradicted each other. Some of them saw in Bohle, head of the *Auslands-Organisation der NSDAP*, a most important figure, who 'controlled 99 per cent of the Germans abroad',[7] and who exercised 'direct supervision' over the *Auswärtige Amt*.[8] According to others, Wilhelm Canaris, head of the German

---

[1] Raymond E. Murphy, Francis B. Stevens, Howard Trivers, Joseph M. Roland: *National socialism. Basic principles, their application by the Nazi party's Foreign Organization and the use of Germans abroad for German aims* (Washington, 1943), p. 132.   [2] *Ibid.*, p. 137.

[3] Carl J. Hambro: *I saw it happen in Norway* (London, 1940).

[4] E. N. van Kleffens: *The Rape of the Netherlands* (London, 1940); American edition: *Juggernaut over Holland* (New York, 1940).

[5] *The German Fifth Column in Poland* (London, 1941).

[6] B. Bilek: *Fifth Column at Work* (London, 1945).

[7] Heinz Pol: *AO—Auslandsorganisation. Tatsachen aus Aktenberichten der 5. Kolonne* (Graz, 1945), p. 87.

[8] Fernandez Artucio: *The German Octopus in South America*, p. 24.

espionage service, was the chief culprit; he had 'almost unlimited power'.[1] Again, still others saw in Ribbentrop the man who undermined the states about to be attacked 'by means of bribery, soft words, voluptuous women—aye, and even imported servant girls and hotel porters '.[2] And yet others reported that the *Volksbund für das Deutschtum im Ausland* had sent out 'over ten thousand well-trained agents and confidential persons'.[3]

Only a few expressed any clear doubts of the omnipotence of the Fifth Column. Soon after its arrival in London, the Belgian Government declared that in their country 'the Fifth Column consisted of only a few individuals'.[4] In 1941 Professor David Mitrany published his conclusion that the Nazi action in North and South America had not amounted to much.[5] In 1952 Professor Arnold J. Toynbee showed himself to be of like mind.[6] Professors Langer and Gleason had their doubts about the importance of the Fifth Column in Norway and France,[7] and Dr. T. K. Derry was disposed to admit frankly that the effect of Quisling's action had been seriously overrated. [8]

As against this, we find that in other authoritative works of a high standard the Fifth Column rose again, even if in short passages, in all its fascinating glory. This was done in the paragraphs Churchill devoted to Norway in his stirring memoirs, on the authority of Hambro.[9] Hugh Seton-Watson spoke of the 'exemplary efficiency' of the Fifth Column work of the *Volksdeutschen* in Poland.[10] Louis L. Snyder, in his masterly analysis of German nationalist thought, inserted a passage in which there was mention of the 'spies, saboteurs and assorted conspirators' of the *IG Farben*, the great German chemical trust, whose agents, according to Snyder, had formed 'the core of Nazi intrigue in foreign countries'.[11] And lastly Martin Wight, in a publication of the Royal Institute of International Affairs, called the German minorities in Eastern Europe 'an international fifth

[1] Kurt Singer: *Duel for the Northland. The War of Enemy Agents in Scandinavia* (London, 1945), p. 37.
[2] H. W. Blood-Ryan: *The Great German Conspiracy* (London, undated), p. 167.
[3] Pol: *AO*, p. 44.
[4] *België. Een officieel overzicht van de gebeurtenissen 1939–1940* (London, 1941), p. 37.
[5] In: Toynbee and Boulter: *Survey of International Affairs 1938*, Vol. I (London, 1941), pp. 586–7 and 672–4.
[6] *The World in March 1939* (London, 1952), p. 12.
[7] Langer and Gleason: *The Challenge to Isolation 1937–1940*, pp. 420, 448.
[8] Dr. T. K. Derry: *The Campaign in Norway* (London, 1952), p. 244.
[9] Churchill: *The Second World War*. Vol. I. *The Gathering Storm*, pp. 478–9.
[10] Hugh Seton-Watson: *Eastern Europe between the Wars, 1918–1941* (Cambridge, 1946), p. 283.
[11] Louis L. Snyder: *German Nationalism: the Tragedy of a People* (Harrisburg, 1952), p. 295.

column of unique power',[1] and he gave a description of the *Auslands-Organisation* and the *Volksbund für das Deutschtum im Ausland* in which, among other things, mention was again made of disguised tourists, technicians and commercial travellers.[2]

In Germany on the other hand the national socialists stated categorically that there had never been such a thing as a Nazi Fifth Column at all.

During the Nuremberg trial of the principal German war criminals an affidavit of Bohle's was read, in which he asserted that neither the *Auslands-Organisation* nor its members had ever 'in any way received orders the execution of which might be considered as Fifth Column activity'—either from Rudolf Hess, whose immediate subordinate Bohle was, nor from himself. Nor had Hitler ever given any directives in that respect, Bohle said. He admitted that there had been Germans abroad who had been used for espionage purposes, but that sort of work had been carried out by the French and the British for *their* espionage services as well, and in any case the espionage work done by the Germans in question had had nothing whatsoever to do with their membership in the *Auslands-Organisation*.[3]

A member of the staff for the prosecution then went at him with a few questions that showed how completely he doubted the reliability of Bohle's statement:

LT.-COL. GRIFFITH-JONES: Did it never occur to you that in the event of your army's invading a country where you had a well-organised organisation, that organisation would be of extreme military value?

BOHLE: No, that was not the sense and the purpose of the Auslands-Organisation and no offices ever approached me in this connection.

LT.-COL. GRIFFITH-JONES: Are you telling this Tribunal now that when the various countries of Europe were in fact invaded by the German Army your local organisations did nothing to assist them in a military or semi-military capacity?

BOHLE: Yes, indeed.[4]

An affidavit was read that came from Alfred Hess, brother to Rudolf and deputy leader of the *Auslands-Organisation*, from which the International Military Tribunal could gather that the slogan 'the Fifth Column' was considered in the *Auslands-Organisation* as 'a clever bluff of anti-fascist propaganda, and it caused genuine amusement'.[5]

The arguments used by Hess and Bohle were not printed by the

[1] *The World in March 1939*, p. 332.   [2] *Ibid.*, pp. 314–16.
[3] *IMT*, Vol. X, p. 15.   [4] *Ibid.*, p. 19.   [5] *Ibid.*, p. 76.

world press. It was not thought worth while. If they had appeared they would have been received by readers in most countries with an irritated shrug; two liars the more! People like Goering, Ribbentrop and Seyss-Inquart had also played innocent; they had been sentenced to death notwithstanding. And anyhow, of what value were the most sinister German Fifth Column tales compared to the actuality that had been exposed about concentration camps and gas chambers?

In this way, the idea of the Fifth Column that had sprung up during the years 1933 to 1941 was maintained among most people in the non-German countries; and there was an understandable tendency to hand this idea on to the generations for whom national socialist Germany and its outrages would be mainly or exclusively history, read about in books. It is characteristic, for example, for many of the Anglo-Saxon historical works on the second World War, in the passages devoted to the invasion of the Netherlands to rely heavily on information dating from 1940. In these we again come across Germans living in Rotterdam, who 'set up machine-gun nests and destroyed strategic bridges' [1] or 'who had got into Holland as "tourists", "commercial travellers" or "students" '; [2] we again meet Fifth Columnists who 'disrupted the air-raid siren system and cut what was left of Amsterdam's water supply',[3] or who 'spread confusion and terror behind the lines'; [4] we hear of parachutists who co-operated with 'spies, traitors, Fifth Columnists and German tourists' [5] or who descended from the sky, 'many in Dutch uniform, speaking excellent Dutch, baffling civilians and soldiers alike'.[6] And even in a 'miniature history' of the second World War enough space was found for mentioning that the Germans in Holland 'made skilful use (as in Norway, but on a larger scale) both of parachutists and of treachery'.[7]

Why should one doubt information with such general support, given by votaries of historical learning of such authority? As a matter of fact, the view that a powerful German Fifth Column had been at work during the years of national socialist expansion was, as it

[1] C. Grove Haines and Ross J. S. Hoffman: *The Origins and Background of the Second World War* (New York, 1947), p. 571.
[2] Walter Consuelo Langsam: *The World since 1914* (New York, 1948), p. 764.
[3] Francis Trevelyan Miller: *History of World War II* (Philadelphia, 1945), p. 170.
[4] Henry Steele Commager: *The Story of the Second World War* (Boston, 1945), p. 51.
[5] Frederick L. Schuman: *International Politics. The Western State System in Transition* (New York, 1941), p. 580.
[6] Walter Phelps Hall: *Iron out of Calvary. An interpretative history of the Second World War* (New York, 1946), p. 94.
[7] R. C. K. Ensor: *A Miniature History of the War* (Oxford, 1945), p. 25.

were, embedded in a trend of thought wherein the concept 'Fifth Column' as such had started to play an ever greater part. The western world came more and more under the spell of the communist Fifth Column and vice versa. Shortly after 1945 an era dawned wherein one could hardly read a paper or listen to a news bulletin without coming across that term, weighted with fear.

That it came from a boastful speech of a general in the Spanish Civil War was remembered by only a few.

People could hardly imagine a world in which there was no Fifth Column.

If we now wish to examine the truth behind the notions people had about the German Fifth Column, it seems sensible to state explicitly what was meant by the term.

Exact definitions are seldom wholly satisfactory, especially so when their content is that of a term so worn down by usage that a sharply outlined image can hardly any longer be discerned. 'Fifth Column' has become such a term—a combination of words in which, in daily usage, a certain amount of vagueness formed an essential element from the very beginning.

Let us try and state it thus:

Any group outside national socialist Germany was considered to belong to the German Fifth Column which consciously, and in agreement with secret instructions from German authorities, sponsored activities to further Germany's territorial expansion.

Let us look at this definition more closely.

To start with, 'German Fifth Column' is an ambiguous concept.

It may be used to describe a *pro-German* Fifth Column, or a Fifth Column *made up of Germans*. The first description is of wider application than the second: it includes all non-German groups that carried out pro-German activities. In the Preface we pointed out that the activities of these non-German groups do not yet lend themselves to a scientific description of international scope. Nevertheless they cannot be wholly neglected. The communities that felt menaced by the Third *Reich* looked upon the Fifth Columns consisting of Germans and those made up of 'native' fascists and national socialists as a whole. The question of whether those 'native' Fifth Columns gave military support to German aggression cannot simply be set aside—but the political backgrounds of all those Norwegian, Dutch, French, British, North and South American fascist and national socialist movements we shall leave for what they were.

Let us return to our definition.

Fifth Columnist activity was looked upon as *conscious* activity. Actually others engaged in quite a good deal of activity before and during the war which furthered Germany's territorial expansion, objectively, 'unintentionally'. If one were to apply the term 'Fifth Column' to them, one would debase it into a senseless political term of abuse. It is the *subjective intention* which must be present.

In the case of the German Fifth Column the organising link with German authorities (of the party and of the state) may not be lacking either. The Fifth Column was looked upon as a tool that Germany *manipulated*.

Furthermore, the activity of this Fifth Column had to be directed pre-eminently *in secret*. It was considered a conspiracy. Even in those cases where national socialist institutions (the *Auslands-Organisation der NSDAP*, for instance, or the *Propaganda-Ministerium*) worked in foreign areas, people nevertheless assumed that they did not own up to their *true* aims and that their 'real' work consisted in following secret German instructions.

This work, as people saw it—Tolischus had already put it clearly into words—bore a different character in peace time from in time of war. In peace time it might be summed up in the notion of 'undermining': 'By means of the Fifth Column national socialist Germany undermined other states'. Was not that the general impression that had come into being during the years 1933–1939? War activities on the other hand were considered to be characterised by *the rendering of assistance to military aggression by means of internal attack during that aggression*. In this second case we shall henceforth speak of the *military* Fifth Column in distinction to the *political* one. Between those two Fifth Columns there were, naturally, all sorts of transitions. The military Fifth Column was really considered to be the logical conclusion, the culmination of the political one.

Now, by the side of the picture of what people *thought* this military Fifth Column had to answer for, we wish to give another picture in Part II: what *actually* happened.

Part Two

REALITY

CHAPTER IX

Poland

★

DURING the months between the Munich Agreement (September 29, 1938) and the occupation of Prague (March 15, 1939) Poland was subjected to heavy political pressure by Germany. It was made clear that Germany intended to see the status of Danzig changed, and desired a 'solution' to the problem of the Polish Corridor. Whether Hitler was entirely convinced that the Polish Government would yield, or believed that it would resist to the utmost, is not known. Probably he reckoned with the latter alternative from the first, and in any case, in the latter half of March, with Poland feeling herself more and more threatened and partly mobilising her army as well as obtaining a guarantee from Britain, Hitler decided that the preparations for a decisive military coup must be speeded up. The first sketch-plans for an attack on Poland at that time had already been made. On April 3, 1939, however, General Keitel, chief of the *Oberkommando der Wehrmacht*, (German armed forces high command), informed the Commanders-in-Chief of the Army, the Navy and the Air Force (von Brauchitsch, Raeder, Goering) of Hitler's wish that the plans be worked out at such a rate that their execution would be possible at any time after September 1, 1939.[1]

As regards the Army, the plans were worked out by the Chief-of-Staff, General Halder, under the responsibility of von Brauchitsch. Both men thought strictly along military lines. Knowing Germany's superiority, they intended to destroy the Polish Army by means of a double encirclement, in which operation the German Army would attack Poland on both flanks instead of in the centre.[2] At first it remained a matter of doubt whether the disposition of the Polish

---

[1] C-120, *IMT*, Vol. XXXIV, pp. 380–1.
[2] See for all geographical names and indications the map on p. 41.

147

divisions would favour the execution of that plan or not. Even on June 14 and 28, 1939, the German officers working out the campaign noted that they lacked trustworthy information concerning the Polish mobilisation and operational plans.[1] Later on the Germans assumed that the Polish troops would be concentrated in the west of their country for an offensive in the direction of Berlin.[2]

In the documents concerning the German plan of action, as far as they are known, nothing is said of the existence of military or para-military formations of *Reichs-* or *Volksdeutsche* supporting the German operations.[3] This does not warrant the inference, however, that *Reichs-* and *Volksdeutsche* remained inactive everywhere. Members of these groups definitely aided the preparation and execution of German operations, in some cases considerably. Before illustrating this in detail, a word should be said about the *Reichs-* and *Volksdeutschen* generally.

Of the *Reichsdeutschen* little is known. In 1938 there were about 13,000 of them in Poland.[4] Most of them dwelt in Poland's western provinces, ceded by Germany at the Versailles Treaty, and in Galicia (South Poland). 1800 of them were members of the *Landesgruppe* of the *Auslands-Organisation der NSDAP.* Another 1200 were members of the subsidiary organisations for workmen, office workers and women.[5] In all there were thus 3000 organised Nazis in 1938. The German Embassy in Warsaw attempted to keep in touch with as many *Reichsdeutschen* as possible, and to this end had organised, in 1939, in collaboration with the leader of the *Landesgruppe,* a secret network of picked men each with the care of a number of *Reichsdeutsche.* The idea was to give protection to the latter in case of war. Presuming that this was not a sufficient guarantee of safety, the *reichsdeutschen* men were advised, during the summer of 1939, to send their womenfolk and children to Germany. In the last week of August the Embassy was also to warn the unemployed or 'those of whom it may be assumed that they incur special danger' to repatriate. Those who remained were to try to protect themselves against the persecutions which were regarded as inevitable. Party

[1] PS-2327, No. 6, *IMT,* Vol. XXX, p. 190. Letter, June 28, 1939, from the *Arbeitsstab* Rundstedt, NOKW-215.

[2] According to Professor K. Rheindorf, Hiddesen near Detmold, the Polish mobilisation and operational plans were revealed to the Germans by an officer of the Polish General Staff who was being blackmailed on the grounds of his homosexuality. It is not exactly certain when this happened.

[3] C-120, *IMT,* Vol. XXXIV, pp. 380–422; C-126, *ibid.,* pp. 428–58; C-142, *ibid.,* pp. 493–500; PS-2327, *IMT,* Vol. XXX, pp. 180–200.

[4] *Jahrbuch der Auslands-Organisation der NSDAP, 1940* (Berlin, 1939), p. 278.

[5] *Ibid.,* p. 279.

functionaries and journalists were to seek refuge in the homes of friendly nationals of neutral states.

In the frontier provinces the situation was rather different. There the *Reichsdeutschen* were 'to be covered by the measures to be taken there for the protection of the *Volksdeutschen*'.[1]

On August 24, 1939, the head of the *Auslands-Organisation,* Bohle, telegraphed an order that the officials of the *Landesgruppe* must stay at their posts.[2] The same day the *Reichsdeutschen* in Poland generally were warned by Berlin to leave the country.[3] How many persons availed themselves of this timely warning is not known, so that it also remains uncertain how many *Reichsdeutschen* were actually in Poland at the time of the German attack. Presumably their number was considerably less than the above-mentioned 13,000.

Proof that these *Reichsdeutschen,* or even only the national socialists amongst them, furthered the German military operations in any way, is not available, except for those districts where the *Reichsdeutschen* were 'covered by the measures to be taken for the protection of the Volksdeutschen'.

It is not known how many *Volksdeutschen* there were in Poland. The estimates vary considerably. The Poles usually cited about three quarters of a million; the Germans, over a million. In the introduction to Part I we have seen that they were subjected to continually increasing pressure on the part of the Poles. This is closely bound up with the fact that after 1933 those amongst the *Volksdeutschen* in favour of aggressive action had gained increasing influence. Besides the national socialists, there were also groups of Liberal, Catholic and Socialist *Volksdeutschen.* There was much antagonism among them all, to the annoyance of Berlin. In 1938 a Berlin office of the party, the *Volksdeutsche Mittelstelle,* (Liaison office for Minority Germans), concocted a plan according to which all the *volksdeutschen* organisations in Poland were to be brought together in one main organisation, of which the leader was to be appointed by Berlin.

Towards the end of May, 1938, the proposal was forwarded to the leaders of the more important organisations through the German consuls. These leaders objected to the proposed *Führer.*[4] The union, called the *Bund der Deutschen in Polen* (League of the Germans in Poland) was nevertheless launched in August, 1938. That its leaders

---

[1] Note, Aug. 21, 1939, by Schliep, a member of the German Embassy in Warsaw, intended for the *Auswärtige Amt,* NG-2427.

[2] NG-4154.

[3] Jodl: *Diary,* PS-1780, *IMT,* Vol. XXVIII, p. 390.

[4] *Documents on German Foreign Policy 1918–1945,* series D, Vol. V (Washington, 1953), p. 51. Further to be referred to as: *Doc. Ger. For. Pol.,* D.

kept in close touch with the *Volksdeutsche Mittelstelle* may be taken for granted; further evidence has not yet been published. The Liberal, Catholic and Socialist parties may have been able to retain part of their active members, but on this point again we know nothing for certain.

It may reasonably be assumed that through the influence of Hitler's successes in 1938 and as a result of the increasing pressure exerted by the Poles, a process of radicalisation developed amongst the *Volksdeutschen* in the course of 1939. The German radio fostered their fighting spirit. At the same time secret steps were taken with the aim of further worsening the strained relations between *Volksdeutsche* and Poles.

Agents were for instance sent to Poland before the war by the German *Sicherheitsdienst*, which took its orders from Himmler. Their task was to commit offences which could be laid at the door of the Poles, and would arouse indignation and embitterment amongst the *Volksdeutschen.* The plans which the *Sicherheitsdienst* had carefully worked out for performing such provocations were of considerable extent. They embraced 200 separate actions, which were to be carried out during August, 1939, preferably in the latter half, by twelve *Kommandos* (small units, composed of only a few persons) to be aided by *Volksdeutsche* domiciled in Poland.[1]

Whether and to what extent these provocations were actually carried out has not been established, but it seems hardly likely that the *Sicherheitsdienst* went no further than making plans. *Abwehr* headquarters were aware that a number of *agents provocateurs* of the *Sicherheitsdienst* had succeeded in entering Poland to carry out their assignments [2] and from a report dated August, 1940, it becomes apparent that the *Sicherheitsdienst* was engaged in the 'preparation of the war against Poland' by means of 'special detachments (*Einsatzkräfte*) for carrying out illegal actions'.[3]

One should not, however, be led to think that the tension existing between *Volksdeutsche* and Poles owed its existence to provocations by the *Sicherheitsdienst*; it was only fostered by them. Many *Volksdeutschen* had long been hoping that the day would come on which they would once again find themselves under German rule. However, proof that any *volksdeutsche* organisation of an economic or political nature had, as such, taken steps to lend aid to the military operations of the Germans is not available. It seems likely that the *Volksdeutschen*

[1] Survey in Edmund Jan Osmańczyk: *Dowody Prowokacji. Nieznane Archiwum Himmlera* ['Evidence of provocation. The unknown Himmler Archives'] (Cracow, 1951), pp. 35–48.
[2] Information supplied by General Erwin Lahousen, head of the second (sabotage) section of the *Abwehr*, 1939–43.
[3] Note, Aug. 8, 1940, on the *Einsatz des SD im Ausland*, NG-2316.

POLAND

in some districts took measures to ward off, if need be by force of arms, the attacks they were fearing if it came to war. For this purpose, perhaps in quite a number of places, secret organisations were created, which, especially in the frontier districts, may also have been equipped with arms smuggled in from Germany. Possibly arms had been kept hidden since the fighting in 1918–19. Nothing definite is known about all this. One German author mentions the spontaneous formation of a German defence organisation by the older *Volksdeutschen* in a village in the Polish Corridor, south of Danzig.[1]

There are further indications that in several places *Volksdeutsche*, of their own free will, lent aid to the advancing German troops. The *Luftwaffe* publication, '*Flieger, Funker, Flak*', reported shortly after the campaign had come to an end that the *volksdeutschen* men had become 'the best of comrades with our soldiers':

> They have helped to clear the roads of obstructing trees and stones. They knew or spied out where the Poles had prepared ambushes. They cut down trees to assist in replacing destroyed bridges, to the joy of our engineers. They crept through woods and undergrowth together with our soldiers to help, to the best of their ability, with clearing the woods of Polish brigands.[2]

In Pless (Eastern Upper Silesia) a German tank was repaired by *Volksdeutsche* on the second day of the German offensive.[3] There also a *Volksdeutscher* was used as a guide, to which end he was given a seat in the car of the regimental commander.[4] Near Lemberg an Austrian showed the Germans the way on September 12.[5] It seems very likely that such assistance occurred to a far greater extent. Wherever the German troops appeared they were heartily welcomed by the *Volksdeutschen* and often treated to banquets.[6]

The acts of the *Volksdeutschen* described so far can be explained without resorting to the assumption of organisational contact with any German agency. Besides those mentioned, however, other actions by the *Volksdeutschen*, both before and during the German invasion, and also undermining Polish resistance, were certainly organised from within Germany. There were *reichsdeutsche* organisations which considered war with Poland inevitable and who, partly directly, partly via the connections kept up by some *volksdeutsche* organisations, used to their own advantage the will that inspired part

[1] Hugo Landgraf: *Kampf um Danzig* (Dresden, 1940), p. 62.
[2] Quoted in: *Deutschtum im Ausland, 1939*, p. 528.
[3] *Die polnischen Greueltaten an den Volksdeutschen in Polen*, p. 122.
[4] *Ibid.*, p. 124.
[5] *Kampferlebnisse aus dem Feldzug in Polen* (Berlin, 1941), p. 68.
[6] Examples in Leo Leixner: *Von Hamburg bis Bordeaux* (Munich, 1941), pp. 65, 74–5, 90.

151

of the *volksdeutsche* youth to contribute to the 'liberation' of areas that had been German up to 1918.

The *Volksdeutsche Mittelstelle* might be included among these institutions, and probably the *Hitler-Jugend* as well. Further particulars are lacking. The archives have been destroyed, and the witnesses have remained silent.

We know more about the *Abwehr*.

The willingness among part of the *Volksdeutschen* to render assistance to Germany made it easy for the *Abwehr* (the organisation of the German armed forces responsible for intelligence, counter intelligence and commando operations) to support the offensive against Poland in numerous ways.

Let us consider espionage first.

It has been made known by the Poles that the number of trials for espionage, which amounted to 300 from 1935 to 1938, doubled in number during the six months from March to August 1939.[1] It may properly be assumed that during those last six months before the signal for the attack was given, espionage was zealously practised. As early as October, 1938, an official of the *Auswärtige Amt* had found that the *Volksdeutschen* were regularly appealed to to carry out military espionage. He considered it especially dangerous that the people drawn into that work played a leading part in German life. The *Abwehr* promised to mend their ways and gave the assurance that in future they would make use of as few *Volksdeutschen* as they could. 'It would not be possible, however,' they declared, 'to dispense with their co-operation altogether.'[2] In support of the German offensive a number of secret wireless stations had been set up in Poland, but owing to the rapidity of the German advance 'not one of them was able to contribute anything of importance'.[3]

Before the outbreak of hostilities the *Abwehr* and other bodies of the NSDAP circulated among the young *Volksdeutschen* word not to report for mobilisation in case of war. If it was not possible to avoid this, then they were not to shoot at the German troops but were to go over to them at the first opportunity.[4] This happened in a number of cases.[5] Other *Volksdeutschen* were instructed to carry on

[1] *The German Fifth Column in Poland*, pp. 37–8.
[2] Memorandum, Nov. 15, 1938, by von Heyden-Rynsch, concerning a discussion with the *Abwehr*. *Doc. Ger. For. Pol.*, D, Vol. V, p. 113, note 3.
[3] Paul Leverkuehn: *German Military Intelligence* (London, 1954), p. 82.
[4] Information supplied by General Lahousen.
[5] Kurt Lück's book *Volksdeutsche Soldaten unter Polens Fahnen* gives a striking picture of the wish to desert among the *Volksdeutschen* who had been mobilised. Other examples in: *Der Sieg in Polen*, p. 45, and Leixner: *Von Lemberg bis Bordeaux*, p. 67.

defeatist propaganda in the army. Similar orders were issued to Ukrainians[1]—also representatives of a minority oppressed by Poland.

The *Abwehr* did not stop at that.

Some *Volksdeutschen* and Ukrainians had received training in the Third *Reich* for diversionist work and guerrilla fighting. Probably there were various sorts of training courses. One training camp was in the Dachstein Mountains to the south-east of Salzburg. Ostensibly a course in sports training was given there for farmers from the mountainous regions. In reality, about 250 Ukrainians [2] were schooled there after August 1, 1939, in 'independently carrying out small actions based on ruse and surprise by shock troops'.[3] These Ukrainians were not thrown into the fight. Hitler feared that if he were to use them, the Soviet Union, with whom he had come to terms at the end of August, would be needlessly nettled.[4]

Other detachments for shock tactics *did* go into action.

Generally it was their task to clear up barricades on the roads for the benefit of the approaching Germans, to prevent the Poles from destroying bridges and roads, to carry on guerrilla fighting, and to cut the Polish communications. Some of the members of the detachments were to operate as civilians, in which case they had as insignia a red handkerchief with a large yellow circle in the centre, a light blue band round the arm with a yellow centre or a band with the swastika. Other members were to act in beige overalls with yellow marks on the collar and sleeves or as parachutists in greyish-green overalls also with yellow markings. Special parachutists were to be dropped in civilian clothes.[5]

How extensive the operations of these agents became cannot be said. It is asserted from the German side that because of the swift advance of the German divisions many of the orders for sabotage

[1] Information supplied by General Lahousen.

[2] *Id.*

[3] Order of General Lahousen, Aug. 4, 1939, NOKW-423. The stencilled document is signed 'Lehmann'. That this should be 'Lahousen' appears from the Proceedings of the trial of the German generals before one of the American Military Tribunals, Nuremberg ('Case XII'), p. 1240.

[4] Lahousen's excerpts from the *Kriegstagebuch* of the second department of the *Abwehr*, Aug. 28, Sept. 1, 11 and 17. 1939. This important source will be henceforth referred to as: *KTB-Abwehr*. It covers the period August, 1939–April, 1941.

[5] These particulars are recorded in the *Merkblatt zur Bekanntgabe an die gegen Polen eingesetzten Truppen*, which we mentioned on p. 44. There would be good reason to doubt the trustworthiness of this carelessly typed document, were it not for the fact that in the passages that matter it is identical with a document, dated Aug. 23, 1939, in which General Lahousen gives instructions for the manner in which the German commanders are to receive the persons operating in the enemy's rear, NOKW-083. A letter which I sent to the probable signer of the *Merkblatt* remained unanswered.

and guerrilla warfare were *not* carried out.[1] That is not improbable, but it has definitely been established that a number of them were really carried out, and what we know in general of the preparation for the execution of these orders gives the impression of great activity.

It was the *Abwehr* who saw to it that particular groups of *Volksdeutsche* and Ukrainians were furnished in time with arms and means for performing diversionist work.[2] Part of the arms were smuggled into Poland from Rumania.[3] Furthermore, at special sectors on the front select detachments of the *Abwehr* were sent into Poland, immediately before or together with the launching of the offensive, in order to perform acts of sabotage and to stir up strife, presumably in disguise. This, among other places, was done from East Prussia.[4] In Southern Poland the Jablonka pass, close by the Czechoslovakian frontier, was occupied on the night of August 25 by a detachment of about 360 men, organised by the *Abwehr*. At first Hitler had wanted to attack Poland in the early morning of August 26, and when on the evening of the 25th the order was issued to return to quarters, it was no longer possible to get in touch with the Jablonka detachment. It fought for some days against the Polish frontier troops, and succeeded in removing the dynamite charges the Poles had put in the railway tunnel near the pass.[5]

Nowhere was the activity of the *Abwehr* more marked than in Eastern Upper Silesia. The *Oberkommando der Wehrmacht* was particularly interested in preventing the Poles from executing demolitions in that important industrial area.[6] To this end the great electricity station at Chorzow was put out of action early enough so that the electric detonators of the dynamite charges placed by the Poles did not function.[7] The Breslau office of the *Abwehr* had further formed and trained a detachment of from three to five thousand Sudeten German national socialists, who slipped over the frontier in civilian clothes during the night before the German offensive began—some, 'disguised as coal miners and workers', even a few days earlier —so that they might occupy the most important factories and mines in co-operation with national socialist *Volksdeutschen*. The latter showed the way.[8]

---

[1] Information supplied by General Lahousen.

[2] *KTB-Abwehr*, Aug. 15, 1939.

[3] *Ibid.*, Aug. 16, 1939.

[4] *Ibid.*, Aug. 23, 1939.

[5] *Ibid.*, Aug. 25, 26, 27, 1939.

[6] C-120, No. 13, *IMT*, Vol. XXXIV, p. 408.

[7] Kurt Franz: 'Erste Fahrt in die befreite Heimat', *Deutschtum in Ausland*, 1939, p. 526.

[8] Information supplied by General Lahousen. Leverkuehn: *German Military Intelligence*, p. 45.

Other *Volksdeutsche* displayed even greater activity. The zealous head of the *Abwehrstelle* Breslau had succeeded in establishing secret organisations of *Volksdeutsche* in various towns in Eastern Upper Silesia, who were to co-operate with the Sudeten Germans coming from Germany, and who, if the opportunity should arise, were to rebel against the Poles by force of arms. This *Kriegs-Organisation* of the *Abwehr*, set up in the industrial centre of Eastern Upper Silesia, numbered 1200 members.[1] The town of Kattowitz was conquered from the Poles by 400 of them before the regular German troops had arrived at the spot.[2]

A similar armed rising had been prepared by the *Abwehr* in those parts of Poland that were inhabited by Ukrainians.[3] For this purpose they had got into contact with Lieutenant-Colonel Andrej Melnyk, head of the organisation of Ukrainian Nationalists, OUN.[4] At first Hitler wanted to allow the rebellion of the Ukrainians to occur. The chief of the *Abwehr*, Admiral Canaris, received orders as late as September 12, 1939, to launch an insurrection in the Ukrainian part of Poland, 'directed towards the destruction of the Jews and the Poles'.[5] This rising, however, was not allowed to take place, when, in the south, on September 17 the Russians marched into Eastern Poland where the Ukrainians lived. All preparations were stopped and on September 23, in order to oblige Stalin, Hitler ordered that the Ukrainians should be prevented from fleeing over the German-Russian demarcation line from the area occupied by the Red Army.[6]

A few more German operations that fell outside the 'normal' conduct of war deserve mention.

In the Free State of Danzig the Polish officials and troops were attacked by surprise in the early morning of September 1, 1939, by members of the *Brigade Eberhardt* (so named after its commanding general) which had been secretly formed out of members of the SA, SS and the local police.[7]

To the south of the Free State Hitler had personally paid great attention to plans for attacking by surprise two important bridges in the Polish Corridor—the railway bridges of Dirschau, about 20 kilometres to the south of Danzig on the Vistula, and of Graudenz, 60 kilometres further south. Both were of vital importance for

[1] *KTB-Abwehr*, Sept. 3, 1939.
[2] *Ibid.*, Sept. 5, 1939.
[3] *Ibid.*, Aug. 15, 1939.
[4] Karl Heinz Abshagen: *Canaris* (Stuttgart, 1949), pp. 214–15.
[5] *Canaris' Kriegstagebuchaufzeichnungen über die Konferenz im Führerzug in Illnau am 12. September 1939*, in Abshagen: *Canaris*, pp. 208–9.
[6] *KTB-Abwehr*, Sept. 23, 1939.
[7] Landgraf: *Kampf um Danzig*, p. 10.

155

forming swift lines of communication with East Prussia, from where the German armies were to advance beyond Warsaw. The plan was to surprise the Polish garrisons with parachutists and soldiers dressed as railway employees. In the end the attack on Graudenz was not carried out; the chance of success was considered too slight.[1] The attack on Dirschau did take place, however. It was performed by making use of twelve members of the SS who knew the place well, and of a company of soldiers belonging to the corps of army engineers, who were to approach the railway bridge in a freight train that was to be followed by an armoured train, at the same time that the Polish garrison was being bombed. The attack miscarried, however, and the Poles were able to blow up the bridge in time.

How many *Reichsdeutschen* and *Volksdeutschen* were involved, all told, in the operations described above, is not known. It must have been a few thousands at least. Taking the nature of those operations into consideration, that is a high figure and evidence of extensive activity. No German data, however, have been made known that conflict with the view that the large majority of the *Reichsdeutschen* and *Volksdeutschen* living in Poland played a passive part up to the arrival of the German troops.

Many of the Fifth Column phenomena observed by the Poles, which we sketched in Chapter I, tally with the secret operations which, as has now been proved from German sources, were indeed planned and carried out.

The Polish sources, however, also mention other operations, such as the following:

The *Volksdeutschen* put marks on their roofs, painted chimneys in special colours, placed their hay-ricks in a strange way, mowed their grass 'according to design' and stamped or ploughed figures in the soil—all of which was done with a view to making pre-arranged signals to the German armed forces, more particularly for the air force.

The *Volksdeutschen* showed the German air force the way by leaving on the lights in their houses, by letting light shine up through the chimneys, by striking matches, or by making signals with smoke, mirrors or white material.

The *Volksdeutschen* made themselves known to each other as agents by means of special buttons, sweaters or scarves.

The *Volksdeutschen* carried out espionage while disguised as priests and monks.

[1] Information supplied by General Franz Halder, chief-of-staff of the German army's general staff, 1939–42.

The *Volksdeutschen* kept in touch with the German troops by means of numerous secret transmitters, some of them concealed in hollow trees or graves, others so small that they fitted into a box not much larger than a match-box.

Proof is lacking that these observations, reported by the Poles, actually derived from the actions of *Volksdeutsche* who were in some sort of way connected with German military operations. One can look for such proof in vain in the publication *The German Fifth Column in Poland*, from which we quoted many similar observations. The value of that publication as an historical source is debatable. At least 500 statements were collected for it,[1] only 109 of which were printed, most of them in fragmentary form. The statements in question look reliable, in that the witnesses who give their opinions seem in fact to have stated what they saw with their own eyes or heard with their own ears. But it is a remarkable fact that there is no proven or even clear connection with the German military operations for many of the reported observations.

[1] Statement no. 512 is quoted on p. 58.

CHAPTER X

Denmark and Norway

★

Denmark

THE Germans did not look upon the occupation of Denmark as an independent operation, but only as part of the occupation of Norway. This occupation of Norway, in which airborne troops were to play a prominent part, would be even riskier than it already was if Germany, in case of need, were not able to back up the struggle in Southern Norway from the Danish aerodromes in Northern Jutland. 'Air force demands Denmark. Make forces available!', General Halder noted down in his diary on February 21, 1940.

That very day General von Falkenhorst was charged by Hitler with the detailed working out of a plan for the occupation of Denmark as well as Norway, after preparatory studies had been carried out by a small military staff since the middle of December. Eight days later he was able to submit his plan in outline to Hitler, who approved of it except that where Denmark was concerned he wished to have a 'representative group' in Copenhagen, with apparently more forces than von Falkenhorst first considered necessary.[1] Von Falkenhorst proceeded with his work and chose General von Kaupisch for the conduct of the operations in Denmark. The work was carried into effect with the greatest secrecy.

The German plan of attack was simplicity itself. Denmark was to be taken completely by surprise and the government in Copenhagen was to be coerced to such an extent that it would capitulate immediately. For all this a minimum of troops was to be used, no more than two reinforced divisions and a brigade. More than half of these, i.e. one division and the brigade, was to occupy Jutland to its

---

[1] Jodl: *Diary*, Feb. 29, 1940, PS-1809, *IMT*, Vol. XXVIII, p. 409.

northernmost point in one day's time. The second division was to take by surprise all strategic points on the islands of Seeland, Fünen and Falster.

At the same time as the beginning of the German offensive, the Danish Government was to be required to capitulate. In the early morning of the day on which the operations were to begin the German air force was to execute a demonstrative flight over Copenhagen, and, if that should not be effective enough, was to bomb the town. The German ambassador, von Renthe-Fink, was to deliver the German note at exactly the right hour. He was not going to be instructed long beforehand. Nor was this done with the minister of Foreign Affairs, von Ribbentrop.

It was naturally of essential importance to the military experts to know where and how the landing operations might take place and how much resistance might be expected from the Danish troops. Von Falkenhorst and von Kaupisch found much data already in Berlin. 'The documentation on Denmark and the Danish forces was very useful,' wrote von Kaupisch after the venture had succeeded, 'but on certain points it had to be supplemented.'[1] For this the *Abwehr* was roped in. With the help of agents a special military reconnaissance of Denmark was carried out from the end of February till the end of March. All agents of the *Abwehr* (which possessed a 'whole network of confidential agents' on Danish soil)[2] are not yet known. Some of them were Germans who entered Denmark in order to carry out their allotted task and who returned to Germany immediately afterwards.[3] Others were Danish citizens. After the war Danish authorities were able to collect the names of sixteen of these.[4] Von Kaupisch called the documentation, which the German air attaché, Lieutenant-Colonel Petersen, sent him from Copenhagen, 'extremely valuable'.[5] There were, however, yet other *coups* waiting to be put into effect, but of that more later.

In the early morning of April 9 the offensive was duly launched.

In Northern Schleswig the German columns swiftly crossed the frontier. Here the important thing had been to prevent the Danes from blowing up a few of the principal road and railway bridges. To this end the *Abwehr* sent small detachments, which slipped over

[1] *Bericht über die Besetzung Dänemarks am 9. und 10.4.1940 und die dabei gemachten Erfahrungen*, April 30, 1940 (further to be referred to as von Kaupisch: *Bericht*), *Danish Parl. Enq.*, Vol. XII (docum.), p. 248.

[2] Note of Major Herrlitz's, April 1, 1940, *ibid.*, p. 203.

[3] Leverkuehn: *German Military Intelligence*, pp. 83–4.

[4] Information supplied by Captain C. J. Villumsen of the Intelligence department of the Danish army general staff.

[5] Von Kaupisch: *Bericht, Danish Parl. Enq.*, Vol. XII (docum.), p. 248.

the frontier on the night of April 8, and were able to reach their objectives in time.[1] Altogether, they included one officer and ten men.[2] Their principal object, however, the railway bridge at Padborg, had not been mined; here the action of the *Abwehr* was wholly superfluous.[3]

The *Volksdeutschen* who lived in Northern Schleswig numbered some thirty thousand persons.[4] In 1932 a national socialist organisation had come into being. Many *volksdeutsche* economic and cultural organisations ranged themselves at the end of 1938 under the central organisation, the *Deutsche Volksgruppe* (German minority group), which was politically controlled by the *NSDAP-Nordschleswig*,[5] numbering some 2,000 members.[6] Its development was furthered from Berlin. There the *NSDAP-Nordschleswig* was controlled by the *Volksdeutsche Mittelstelle*—the office we have come across in Poland—but conflicts between this office and the aggressive Dr. Jens Möller, leader of this miniature Nazi party, were frequent.[7]

We have already mentioned that sixteen people became known to the Danes as German espionage agents. Most of these were *Volksdeutsche*,[8] some of them local leaders of the German group.[9] Their co-operation with the *Abwehr* was unknown to Dr. Möller. He did not know the date of the German invasion although, two days earlier, he and others had heard rumours that something was brewing.[10] The fact that special detachments from Germany were sent to prevent one or two demolitions seems to support the view that the *Volksdeutschen* in North Schleswig had not been acquainted with an operation which Hitler above all wished to keep secret. All the same on the day of the invasion acts were committed by these *Volksdeutschen* which deeply wounded the feelings of the Danes. Many of them welcomed the German troops with exuberant enthusiasm.[11] Some appeared with rifles on their shoulder.[12] Others[13] started regulating the traffic and collecting Danish arms, or even guarding Danish prisoners-

[1] *Von Kaupisch: Bericht, Danish Parl. Enq.*, p. 249. Note, April 11, 1940, of Major Herrlitz, *ibid.*, p. 203.
[2] *KTB-Abwehr*, April 9, 1940.
[3] Information supplied by Captain Villumsen.
[4] Holger Andersen: 'Le Danemark et la minorité allemande du Slesvig du Nord', *Le Nord* (Copenhagen), 1938, no. 1–2, p. 69.
[5] *Deutschtum im Ausland*, 1938, p. 694, and 1940, p. 30.
[6] *Danish Parl. Enq.*, Vol. XIV-2, p. 677.
[7] *Ibid.*, pp. 647, 648, 650.
[8] Information supplied by Captain Villumsen.
[9] *Danish Parl. Enq.*, Vol. XIV-1, p. 620, Note 3.
[10] *Ibid.*, pp. 31–2.
[11] Hans Schmidt-Gorsblock: *Der neunte April* (Apenrade, 1943), pp. 29–30.
[12] Photo in *Danmark under Besättelsen*, Vol. I (Copenhagen, 1946), p. 147.
[13] *Danish Parl. Enq.*, Vol. XIV-2, pp. 659–60.

of-war and in one place a man who was suspected of having been an anti-German spy, was arrested by *Volksdeutsche*.

Further north in Jutland, Esbjerg on the west coast was taken in the course of the morning without a struggle by the crews of a few German naval vessels. The same thing happened in the case of the bridge over the Little Belt near Middelfart, where a German battalion landed in the early morning.[1]

Nyborg, the port on the east coast of Fünen, was occupied on April 9 at daybreak by a German detachment consisting of two officers, eighteen petty officers and a hundred and forty men. They had come up to the harbour in a torpedo-boat and two minesweepers. The torpedo-boat was moored by a sleepy watchman from a Danish naval vessel, who had no idea that the vessel that wanted to moor was German. The German commander rushed into the still slumbering town and used as his guide a railway employee who happened to be passing. The Danes were taken completely by surprise.[2]

In the small seaport town of Korsör on the isle of Seeland opposite Nyborg the German plan also succeeded. There two steamships full of German troops put into port. This was made easier by the fact that all the navigation lights and the street lights were burning, which the German commander considered 'a reassuring sign that the isle of Seeland suspected nothing'. The Danish garrison had held manœuvres the day before which actually took the line that the Germans would land in Korsör. When the Germans really stormed ashore the garrison lay asleep.[3]

The attack on Gjedser, the Danish harbour for the ferry-boat from German Warnemünde, had received special attention from the Germans. Local conditions were not very accurately known. For this reason a German officer went there and back by ferry as an ordinary passenger on March 30, 1940, and in this way was able to survey Gjedser with the naked eye and with a telescope. The Danes made 'an unsuspecting, easy-going, almost bored impression', he reported to Berlin on April 1.[4]

On the night of April 8 the employees and customs officials of the Danish ferry-boat from Warnemünde were interned by the military

[1] Prof. Dr. Walther Hubatsch: *Die deutsche Besetzung von Dänemark und Norwegen 1940* (Göttingen, 1952), p. 96. Further to be referred to as Hubatsch: *Besetzung*. A fine study, but Hubatsch fails to keep in mind that Hitler's attack on Scandinavia cannot be dissociated from the general aggressiveness which characterised him and his paladins.

[2] Report of *Hauptmann* Kanzler, April 14, 1940, *Danish Parl. Enq.*, Vol. XII (docum.), pp. 210–12.

[3] Report of *Oberleutnant* Schultz, April 17, 1940, *ibid.*, pp. 225–9.

[4] Report of Erfurth, March 30, 1940, *ibid.*, pp. 111–12.

of the *Abwehr*.[1] A few hours later the telephone communications running from Gjedser northwards were cut by a wrecking party consisting of a German officer and four men, who, coming from Warnemünde, had sailed right up to the Danish coast.[2] At almost the same time the two ordinary German ferry-boats, the *Mecklenburg* and the *Schwerin*, sailed into the harbour of Gjedser as if nothing was wrong, helped by the lighthouses which were alight as usual. They moored, and immediately heavily armed Germans jumped on shore, some of whom drove to the long bridge at Vordingborg in military trucks. There, over an hour later, German parachutists landed. At 5.45 a.m. the bridge was in German hands. The first Danish soldiers had appeared in the streets only a quarter of an hour before. They mounted their bicycles. The German cars were faster.[3]

In the German plan the surprise attack on Copenhagen ranked first. There all the vital points were to be taken so fast and so irrevocably that every wish to resist on the part of the Danish Government would be nipped in the bud. One battalion and some technical troops were to be conveyed by boat to the *Langelinie*, the nearest quay to the town. The Germans had to know exactly where the ship, the *Hansestadt Danzig*, that was to convey the battalion, could moor and how the citadel might be stormed. Moreover, it was of vital importance that they should immediately have a transmitter at their disposal in the citadel where the temporary German headquarters were to be set up. This was necessary for communication with Germany, but also and especially for broadcasting the expected news of the capitulation.

The data provided by the *Abwehr* about the situation near the harbour and the fort were not sufficiently detailed. The commander of the battalion that was to carry out the assault, Major Glein, therefore received an order to perform some intensive reconnoitring. In the late afternoon of April 4, 1940, he flew on the passenger plane of the *Lufthansa* to Copenhagen, where he arrived at 9 o'clock. He was furnished with the papers of a civil servant. It was snowing, and there were not many people in the streets.

That same evening Major Glein accurately surveyed the quay and the approaches to it. A policeman asked him what his business was there. He said he had lost his way. He was conducted to the street car stop, but when the policeman had disappeared, he returned to

---

[1] Order of the *Oberkommando der Wehrmacht*, April 3, 1940, *ibid.*, p. 141.

[2] *KTB-Abwehr*, April 9, 1940.

[3] Lieutenant-Colonel Buck's report, April 10, 1940, *Danish Parl. Enq.*, Vol. XII (docum.), pp. 197–8.

the harbour in order to examine the road to the citadel accurately. At half-past one at night he arrived at his hotel. At eight o'clock the next morning he was back at the harbour. Then he walked past the watch into the fort. We shall follow him:

In order to put them off the scent I first took the road to the church. When I arrived there I found that it was closed. A Danish sergeant who was passing saw this and asked me whether I wanted to see the church. When I assented he told me that the church was only open on Sundays. After some more talk I asked the sergeant if he would not show me the objects of interest in the old citadel and give me an explanation of it all. The sergeant complied with my request in the friendliest manner. To start with, he took me to the corporals' canteen where I drank a glass of beer with him. At the same time he told me something of the citadel, its garrison and its importance. After I had drunk some beers with him he showed me the quarters of the commanders, the military offices, the telephone exchange, the watch-posts and the old gates by the north and south entrances. When I had seen everything that was of interest to me I took my leave of the sergeant.

In the afternoon of April 5 Major Glein flew back to Berlin.[1]

On April 7 two other Germans went to the Danish capital by the ordinary passenger plane. One of them was *Legations-Sekretär* Dr. Schlitter, who acted as diplomatic courier. The sealed papers containing the instructions for ambassador von Renthe-Fink were in his bag. The other was Major-General Himer, chief-of-staff to General von Kaupisch. Himer travelled as a high-ranking civil servant. His uniform was packed into the diplomatic luggage in the charge of Dr. Schlitter.

On the 8th, the day before the landing, General Himer, together with the air attaché, Lieutenant-Colonel Petersen, did some more reconnoitring near the harbour. The ice had disappeared. There were many ships, but Petersen heard that two were going to sail in the course of the 8th so that there would be more room by the quay. They had another look at the citadel and came to the conclusion that it would be easy to enter it from the south-east corner. Their findings were hastily passed on to Berlin in a code telegram.[2]

There was only one problem left: how would it be possible to carry the heavy transmitter from the *Langelinie* to the *Kastellet* in the early morning, a distance of some hundreds of yards? Himer invited a reserve officer, a German national, von Zimmermann,

---

[1] Report of Major Glein, April 15, 1940, *ibid.*, pp. 216–18. Further to be referred to as: Report Glein.
[2] *Ibid.*, pp. 261–2.

who lived in Copenhagen to come to him and informed him that
early the next morning a German ship would come alongside the
Langelinie 'in order to unload some cases.'[1] Was it not possible for
him, together with four reliable party members to be at the harbour
with a van at 4 o'clock in the morning and could not one of them
immediately afterwards dash to the artillery barracks to see if the
alarm was being sounded there? In that case Lieutenant-Colonel
Petersen was to be warned. The affair was a dead secret. If they were
to come across a Danish police patrol, it was to be put out of the
way.

Von Zimmermann accepted the commission. He happened to
have an appointment immediately afterwards with a functionary of
the *Ortsgruppe* Copenhagen of the *Auslands-Organisation*, Werner
Thiele. He asked him whether he could turn up at the harbour and
take upon himself the expedition to the artillery barracks. Thiele
thought it a risky undertaking. If the affair should miscarry it would
mean at the very least the prohibition of the NSDAP in Denmark.
He did not dare decide without the approval of the head of the District Denmark of the *Auslands-Organisation*, Schäfer.[2] Von Zimmermann therefore called on Schäfer, who could not himself take part
in the affair; he had just been ill. Schäfer gave him four names,
Thiele's included.

Von Renthe-Fink was informed at 11 o'clock in the evening. Dr.
Schlitter handed him the envelope with the instructions; General
Himer explained the plans. The Ambassador was 'taken completely
by surprise'[3], but 'in an excellent manner he quickly adapted himself
to his difficult task'.[4]

Of the four party members whom von Zimmermann had chosen,
one appropriated a lorry belonging to the German coal firm where
he worked, without the knowledge of the management, and shortly
before four o'clock he drove to the harbour. Not a policeman was to
be seen. 'Everything slept and everything was quiet in Copenhagen.'[5]
Von Zimmermann and Thiele also turned up. Thiele had seen to it
that there was no party correspondence in his house.[6] What was
about to happen they did not exactly know, but when at 4.20 a vessel
came alongside the *Langelinie* and armed Germans jumped ashore

[1] Report of Major Glein, April 15, 1940, *Danish Parl. Enq.*, Vol. XII
(docum.), pp. 261–2.
[2] Letter, April 12, 1940, from Thiele to Schäfer, *Danish Parl. Enq.*, Vol. III
(docum.), p. 243.
[3] Hubatsch: *Besetzung*, p. 142.
[4] *Danish Parl. Inq.*, Vol. XII (docum.), p. 262.
[5] Letter, April 20, 1940, from Sporns to Thiele. *Danish Parl. Enq.*, Vol. III
(docum.), pp. 254–5.
[6] Letter, April 12, 1940, from Thiele to Schäfer, *ibid.*, p. 244.

'our guesses were realised', one of them wrote later. This German national described himself as 'glad that I was allowed to take active part in the occupation of Copenhagen'.[1]

The ship, the *Hansestadt Danzig*, had been able to steam into the harbour unhindered, preceded by the German ice-breaker *Stettin*. It had been observed from the big fort just in front of the entrance to the harbour and a search-light had played upon it. The Danes had wanted to fire a warning shot but through technical difficulties they had not been able to get the shell into the barrel of the gun.[2]

The police station and the custom house by the harbour were taken by the Germans within five minutes. The north gate of the citadel, nearest to the *Langelinie*, was shut, but it was blown open. The south gate was open. The Germans stormed in through both gates, took the watch by surprise, smashed the telephone exchange and ten minutes after the landing were masters of the *Kastellet*. The surprised Danish soldiers, who had been taken completely off their guard, were disarmed and shut up in a cellar of the citadel. The Chief of the Danish General Staff, the Danish minister of the Interior and the English commercial attaché, who had been arrested in the streets, were also brought there. A weak attack by the guard of the royal palace, Amalienborg, was beaten off.[3]

Von Zimmermann meanwhile had conveyed the transmitter, which was soon put into working order, to the citadel. Thiele rode in a taxi to the artillery barracks, the address of which he had looked up in the directory the evening before, patrolled the streets there till half-past six, but saw nothing of any alarm.[4] As a result of inadvertence on the part of the Danes, General Himer in the meantime had been able to telephone unhindered to the headquarters of von Kaupisch as late as six in the morning.[5] Consequently he was able to give instructions for a squadron of bombers to bring extra pressure to bear on the Danish Government. The latter capitulated shortly after half-past six. Radio Kalundborg was not yet working, but the Germans could broadcast the news of the capitulation immediately via the transmitter in the citadel. German technicians, who had arrived with the battalion, occupied the wireless stations and the main post office;[6] members of the *Propaganda-Staffel* (Propaganda Staff) took the news agencies and the press in hand;[7] a group of

---

[1] Letter, April 20, 1940, from Sporns to Thiele, *ibid.*, p. 254.
[2] Hubatsch: *Besetzung*, p. 98.
[3] Report Glein, *Danish Parl. Enq.*, Vol. XII (docum.), pp. 220–3.
[4] Letter, April 12, 1940, from Thiele to Schäfer. *Danish Parl. Enq.*, Vol. III (docum.), p. 244.
[5] Report Goes, *Danish Parl. Enq.*, Vol. XII (docum.), p. 262.
[6] Report Glein, *ibid.*, p. 223.
[7] Report, April 11, 1940, of the *Propagandastaffel D(änemark)*, *ibid.*, pp. 205–6.

Abwehr men (one officer and five men),[1] who had also sailed to Copenhagen in the *Hansestadt Danzig*, tried to arrest British and French espionage agents [2]—in short, the programme of activities that was to be carried out immediately after the surprise attack, was quickly under way.

On the Danish side thirty-six military men were killed or wounded,[3] on the German side 'about twenty'.[4] Von Kaupisch could truly state after the conclusion of operations that the people and the forces of Denmark had been completely taken by surprise; 'the German pace took their breath away'.[5]

We are not so well-informed on any other German offensive as on that against Denmark. The account given above offers, so it seems to us, a satisfactory, conclusive explanation for the complete surprise which the Germans managed to achieve, and for the overwhelmingly swift success that they obtained. The hypothesis that an extensive Fifth Column was involved in the surprise attack on Denmark is superfluous. It is not supported by any of the numerous documents published by the Danish parliamentary commission of inquiry.

The number of German nationals living in Denmark in 1940 is not known with any certainty. In 1930 they numbered 9400, of whom upwards of 3000 lived in Copenhagen.[6] Schäfer estimated that in April, 1940, the number of German nationals over 15 years of age (possibly he meant only the male population) in Copenhagen and on the isles of Seeland, Falster and Laaland amounted to about 1500. Of these a hundred and twenty were members of the *Auslands-Organisation*.[7] Evidence of any actions undertaken by these people in support of the German operations, except in the surprise attack on Copenhagen, does not exist. Nor is there any evidence to show that the questions Schäfer put to the members of the *Landeskreis* in

---

[1] Order, April 5, 1940, of Major-General Himer, *Danish Parl. Enq.*, Vol. XII (docum.), p. 153.

[2] Information supplied by General Lahousen.

[3] Hubatsch: *Besetzung*, p. 94.

[4] Report Goes, *Danish Parl. Enq.*, Vol. XII (docum.), p. 263.

[5] Von Kaupisch: *Bericht*, *ibid.*, p. 251.

[6] *Handwörterbuch des Grenz- und Auslanddeutschtums*, Vol. II (Breslau, 1936–41), p. 78. This publication will further be quoted as: *HWB*. This is a valuable dictionary. Preparations started in 1925. Almost 850 scholars took part in it. Unfortunately only two volumes had been published (A–Fugger) when the Third *Reich* collapsed.

[7] Appendix 2 to the letter, April 25, 1940, from Schäfer to the *Stabsamtsleiter der Auslands-Organisation der NSDAP*, *Danish Parl. Enq.*, Vol. III (docum.), p. 268.

1935 [1] (such as: 'Do you own a car? Have you a typewriter? Can you write shorthand?') contained a semi-military code connected with some German plan for attack. In a private letter written after the assault Schäfer complained about the foolish conclusions people had come to through his questions. [2]

The supposition expressed by the Danes themselves that General von Kaupisch 'stayed in Denmark under a false name in November–December 1939' [3] nowhere finds confirmation. The same applies to their assertion that the setting-up of German cafeterias in Copenhagen 'to a greater or lesser extent' aimed at making German political, economic and military espionage possible. [4]

As to the poisoning of water supply sources in Northern Schleswig, nothing has been proved.

And finally, the generally circulated and believed rumour that German soldiers had been secreted in the holds of ships which had already been lying some time in the harbours of Copenhagen, has nowhere been confirmed.

If this ruse had been put into effect, then almost certainly mention would have been found of it in the secret military reports; no German, when he wrote them, ever supposed that they would fall into the hands of Germany's opponents.

Let us see now what happened in Norway.

Norway

On the German side the first impulse leading to the attack on Norway came from high naval circles. Some person there, in studying the first World War, came to the conclusion that Germany could have conducted the naval war with a greater chance of success if it had possessed bases on the Norwegian coast, and if it could have prevented the English from laying a mine barrage as far as that coast. The naval commander of the North Sea, Admiral Carls, was especially alert to this idea. He submitted it to the Commander-in-Chief of the German navy, Admiral Raeder, who considered it of sufficient weight to report on it to Hitler. This happened on October 10, 1939. 'The momentousness of the Norway problem was at once clear to the

---

[1] Karl Moeller: *Hinter den Kulissen der dänischen antisemitischen Agitation* (Apenrade [1936 or 1937]), p. 20.

[2] Letter, April 25, 1940, from Schäfer to the *Stabsamtsleiter der Auslands-Organisation der NSDAP, Danish Parl. Enq.*, Vol. III (docum.), p. 264.

[3] Memorandum from the Danish Government to the International Military Tribunal, Nuremberg, D-628, *IMT*, Vol. XXXV, p. 192.

[4] *Ibid.*, pp. 193–4.

Führer; he . . . declared that he would occupy himself with the question.'[1]

But no unanimity prevailed among the German naval experts concerning the desirability of the operation. Raeder held fast. He secured the adherence of the German naval attaché in Oslo, *Korvetten-Kapitän* Schreiber. In this way, and also through the *Aussenpolitische Amt der NSDAP* (an office of the party which was conducted by Alfred Rosenberg), he came into contact with Vidkun Quisling, the leader of the main Norwegian national socialist movement, and with Albert Viljam Hagelin, one of Quisling's nearest fellow-workers [2] and for years his secret representative in Germany.[3]

As early as December, 1930, when he was still Norway's minister of Defence, Quisling requested a German Nazi, who happened to be staying in Oslo, to bring him into secret communication with the leaders of the NSDAP. But the leaders would have nothing to do with him.[4] In 1933 Quisling started his own movement, *Nasjonal Samling*, and there is reason to believe that from about that time on Himmler [5] and the *Abwehr* [6] maintained a certain measure of contact with him. There are no particulars on record with regard to this. We know more of Rosenberg's contact with Quisling.

Rosenberg, who had been born by the Baltic Sea, had early been interested in the Scandinavian states. In 1933 he received Quisling for the first time and had a short talk with him.[7] In 1934 he addressed a memorandum to Hitler in which he drew attention to 'the politico-strategical significance of Norway.'[8] Through his private secretary, he kept in touch with Quisling. In the early summer of 1939 the latter came to Berlin to warn Rosenberg that in case of war Britain would probably attempt to occupy Scandinavia. Rosenberg thought that Goering might be interested in Quisling's statement, and managed to arrange a meeting between the Norwegian and one of Goering's closest collaborators, on which occasion Quisling asked for a subsidy of six million *Reichsmark*.[9] Rosenberg personally warned Hitler,

[1] Memorandum, Jan. 30, 1944, from Admiral Raeder to Admiral Assmann, C-066, *IMT*, Vol. XXXIV, p. 281. Further to be referred to as: Raeder to Assmann.

[2] *Ibid.*

[3] Note, July 22, 1940, from *Reichskommissar* Terboven to Hitler, PS-992.

[4] Letter, Nov. 19, 1932, from Max Pferdekämpfer to Himmler (Collection-Skodvin).

[5] Information supplied by Himmler's physician, Felix Kersten, and General Lahousen.

[6] Information supplied by General Lahousen.

[7] Statement by Rosenberg, Proceedings *IMT*, Vol. XI, p. 455.

[8] Alfred Rosenberg: *Diary*, April 11, 1940.

[9] *Norw. Parl. Enq.*, Vol. I. p. 13.

168

and sent one of the officials of the *Aussenpolitische Amt*, Scheidt, on a 'holiday trip' to Norway; the latter wrote a report on his 'observations' there. Quisling had asked whether a number of his leading party members might take a course at the training centre, the *Schulungshaus*, of the *Aussenpolitische Amt*. Rosenberg granted this request, and so in August, 1939, a course was held for 25 members of *Nasjonal Samling*.[1] 'They were taught how to make more effective propaganda.'[2]

In September, 1939, war broke out. About then, Hagelin, Quisling's liaison officer in Berlin, came to warn Rosenberg that the Allies intended to start action in Scandinavia.[3] When as a result of the outbreak of the Finno-Russian war tension rose in all Scandinavia and public opinion in Britain and even more in France demanded that an expeditionary force be sent to the assistance of the Finns, the readiness in Berlin to pay attention to Quisling and Hagelin increased.

Quisling realised that he needed German military support to gain power in Norway. He believed that a number of high officers would be willing to co-operate with him once he was in power, and even that the King would accept a *fait accompli*. But how was he to obtain power? His plan was to have a number of carefully selected collaborators trained in Germany, and to smuggle them back to Norway together with some experienced German Nazis. They would then capture by surprise all the strategic points in Oslo; he, Quisling, would usurp the office of Prime Minister, and—like Seyss-Inquart in Vienna—call in the aid of Germany. If at that moment a German naval squadron lay ready to sail up the Oslo fjord, with troops on board, the *coup* could succeed before anybody in Norway, Britain or France had realised what was happening.[4]

There are signs that Quisling had already been seeking support for his plans for some time.[5] On December 10, a week and a half after the outbreak of the Finno-Russian war, he travelled to Berlin, where he stayed at Rosenberg's *Schulungshaus*. With an introduction from Rosenberg and in the company of Hagelin he paid a call on Admiral Raeder on the 11th. Raeder was only slightly acquainted

[1] Rosenberg's report, June 17, 1940: *Die politische Vorbereitung der Norwegen-Aktion*, PS-004, *IMT*, Vol. XXV, pp. 26–7. To be cited in future as: Rosenberg: *Nowegen-Aktion*.
[2] Statement by Rosenberg, Proceedings *IMT*, Vol. XI, p. 455.
[3] *Ibid*.
[4] The clearest picture of this plan is to be found in Rosenberg's undated note *Besuch des Staatsrats Quisling-Norwegen*, C-065, *IMT*, Vol. XXXIV, pp. 273–5.
[5] On Dec. 11, 1939, Rosenberg wrote in his *Diary* that Quisling had laid the plan before him 'again', and on the 19th that Quisling had unfolded his plan to 'several people'.

with Rosenberg, and had never even heard of Quisling,[1] but agreed to give him a hearing. Quisling sketched his intentions. The Norwegian Government, according to him, had decided to postpone the elections. The term of the sitting parliament which was to have ended on January 11, 1940, would be extended by a year: it would then be a suitable time for the *coup d'état*. He made much of his following in high offices, for instance in the railways.

Raeder listened to him, but did not altogether trust the Norwegian. Next day he brought the plan to Hitler's notice, observing 'that in the case of such offers you can never know for certain whether those persons only want to promote the interests of their own party, or whether they are really concerned about the interests of Germany. Caution [was] therefore indicated.' A British occupation of Norway must in any case be prevented.[2]

Hitler listened. Pre-occupied by the plans for the great offensive on the western front, he was not immediately in favour of an extension of the theatre of war to Scandinavia. However, he was not insensible to Quisling's statement that prominent Norwegians were positively working towards future British landings. He deemed it good policy to get a hold on Quisling, and meanwhile to have the practicability of the plan gone into. On December 13, he decided in principle to have this done. The *Oberkommando der Wehrmacht* was to examine the matter.[3]

Now the fact should be underlined that the German military experts did not have any faith in Quisling's operation. They considered Rosenberg to be a crank, and Hitler had not ordered them to collaborate with Quisling, but only to study the feasibility of his plan. Serious doubts soon arose. Quisling 'had nobody behind him', said General Halder.[4] The Navy staff remained sceptical. And the main objection was: how could such an operation, dependent in the first place on the discretion of all concerned, be kept secret if so many Norwegians were to participate, with only Quisling to vouch for their integrity?[5] If the project were to fail, it would probably lose Germany the war.

The plan was not further worked out in earnest. The military experts considered the operation too risky.[6]

The decision not to carry out the plan was not communicated to Rosenberg; he and his collaborators were used by Hitler and the

[1] Statement by Raeder, Proceedings *IMT*, Vol. XIV, p. 92.
[2] Note by Raeder on his report to Hitler, Dec. 12, 1939, C-064, *IMT*, Vol. XXXIV, pp. 271–2.
[3] Raeder to Assmann, C-066, *IMT*, Vol. XXXIV, p. 281. Jodl: *Diary*, Dec. 13, 1939, *Die Welt als Geschichte*, XIII, 1, p. 62.
[4] Halder: *Diary*, Jan. 1, 1940.
[5] Raeder to Assmann, C-066, *IMT*, Vol. XXXIV, p. 281.
[6] Hubatsch: *Besetzung*, pp. 25–6.

generals to keep Quisling on the hook. The latter received money. Scheidt visited Oslo again on January 19, 1940 with 'all that was necessary'.[1] Four weeks later Quisling had already received the equivalent of 100,000 *Reichsmark* in British pounds.[2]

Meanwhile the *Oberkommando der Wehrmacht* had started on the preparation of a purely military plan of action. One sketch after another was drawn up. On January 27, 1940, however, Hitler ordered the matter to be dealt with in a quicker way by a small staff responsible directly to headquarters.[3] He had by no means decided whether or not to carry out the plan.

Three weeks later, on the night of February 16, the British destroyer *Cossack* violated Norwegian territorial waters to rescue British prisoners-of-war from the German vessel *Altmark*. This incident was jumped on by Hitler, but even more so by Rosenberg, Quisling and Hagelin, as proof that Britain and France would not hesitate for a moment, if it were to their advantage, to occupy Norway. There were indications that the decision for such an occupation had already been made, and Hagelin informed Scheidt that he knew for certain Norway would not resist. Rosenberg zealously passed this news on to Hitler. Hitler told him, first on the 19th, then on the 29th, that he no longer favoured the 'political plan of the Norwegians'; on the other hand he was prepared to give them more money.[4]

'On behalf of Quisling', Admiral Raeder wrote later, 'Hagelin repeatedly urged that Quisling should be given an assault group in good time, with the aid of which he could at once seize power and install a new government with the consent of the King. This request could unfortunately not be met, since Quisling and Hagelin, according to orders, could not be informed of the imminence and the time of the operation.'[5] It is true that on January 5, 1940, Rosenberg's emissary, Scheidt, reported that Quisling 'is now selecting from his shock-troops a suitable number of reliable men who can be considered for a possible surprise action'.[6] There is no evidence, however, that Quisling did form an assault group of this nature. While in Norway Scheidt did not even meet Quisling whose name was used

---

[1] Rosenberg: *Diary*, Jan. 19, 1940.

[2] Scheidt's report on his stay in Norway, Jan. 20–Feb. 20, 1940, *Doc. Ger. For. Pol.*, D, VIII, p. 797.

[3] *Kriegstagebuch der Seekriegsleitung*, Jan. 29, 1940, doc.-Wörmann no. 24.

[4] Rosenberg: *Diary*, Feb. 19 and 29, 1940.

[5] *Beitrag zum Kriegstagebuch des Oberbefehlshabers der Kriegsmarine*, April 22, 1940, *Führer Conferences on Naval Affairs*, *1940* (London, 1947), p. 39 (further to be quoted as: *Führer Conferences*). Paragraph 1 of this piece is document C-071.

[6] *Doc. Ger. For. Pol.*, D, Vol. VIII, p. 626.

by Hagelin to foster his own ambitious plans. Every detail suggested by him was embellished by Scheidt in his reports to Berlin the contents of which should be treated with great caution.[1]

Hitler forced the pace. On February 21, 1940, General von Falkenhorst, who had fought in Finland towards the end of the first World War, was summoned before him. This was five days after the *Altmark* incident. Hitler told him that he considered it possible that Germany would have to occupy Norway shortly. How was such an operation to be carried out? Von Falkenhorst was to come back in the afternoon with definite proposals. He could reckon with having five divisions at his disposal. The German general left the *Reichskanzlei* and, as he confessed after the war: 'I went to town and bought a *Baedeker*, a travel guide, in order to find out just what Norway was like. I didn't have any idea, and I had to find out what all the harbours were, how many inhabitants there were, and just what kind of a country it was. I had no idea about the whole thing.'[2]

With the *Baedeker*—according to another, plausible version von Falkenhorst bought *Baedekers* of a number of different countries at the same time so as not to arouse the suspicion of the bookseller[3]— he went to his hotel, examined the maps, studied and pondered, and at five o'clock that afternoon was able to lay a plan before Hitler, based on a simultaneous surprise attack of all the more important ports.

The outline of the plan was as follows.

Narvik, Trondhjem, Bergen, Stavanger, Kristiansand and Oslo were to be occupied in the early hours of some future day. In Oslo von Falkenhorst was to march to the Royal Palace with a military band in front, to render a musical homage to the King.[4] Airborne troops were to land at the airports of Oslo and Stavanger. All the ports were to be forced by German men-of-war carrying troops. Heavy arms and stores would not be taken along by the already crowded naval vessels, but, covered by coal, they were to be sent ahead on board seven freighters disguised as neutrals, and intended to arrive at their destination the night before: one at Stavanger, three at Narvik, three at Trondhjem; an eighth ship, the tanker *Jan Wellem*, would be sent to Narvik from *Basis Nord*, a German naval base near Murmansk. The ports and airports captured, troops held in reserve could be poured into the country.

[1] Information supplied by Magne Skodvin, member of the staff of the Institute of Norwegian Historical Research, Oslo, and by Sverre Hartmann, Oslo.
[2] Interrogation of von Falkenhorst, Oct. 24, 1945. *Danish Parl. Enq.*, Vol. XII (docum.), p. 284.
[3] Bernhard von Lossberg: *Im Wehrmachtführungsstab* (Hamburg, 1949), p. 60.
[4] Statement by Schreiber. *Norw. Parl. Enq.*, Vol. I, p. 25.

The operation would be very risky. All the ports in question were defended by forts. A large part of the German fleet—of far inferior strength than the British fleet—would twice have to run the gauntlet, there and back. Strict secrecy was therefore essential. The troops' commanders could only be instructed at the last moment.

It is not known whether Hitler expressly gave orders to keep the *Auslands-Organisation* as uninformed of these plans as Quisling and Hagelin. It is a fact, however, that none of the numerous military documents concerned with the preparation or execution of the plan even so much as mention the Norwegian national socialists or the *reichsdeutschen* Nazis living in Norway.[1] Amongst the papers of von Falkenhorst's staff was found a note about Quisling, stating, 'Friend of Germany, of no importance, held to be a dreamer of phantasy'[2]. Von Falkenhorst was confident that he could come to terms with the Norwegian minister of Foreign Affairs, Prof. Koht.[3]

The detailed working-out of the plans in Berlin was hindered by lack of sufficient documentation on Norway. Operational and military-geographical studies did not exist, little was known about the position and strength of the Norwegian troops and coastal fortifications 'there wasn't even a usable map'.[4] Maps and travel-guides were bought unobtrusively in the Berlin bookshops.[5] With the aid of such materials new maps were produced by the end of February.[6] One must assume—although proofs are not available—that the *Abwehr* was instructed to fill in the gaps by observation locally. This was not, in any case, very successful. Some Norwegian coastal batteries remained unknown to the Germans, the strength of others was under-estimated, and in other instances batteries were pre-supposed which were non-existent.[7] A part of such faulty information was supplied by Quisling. When on April 2, 1940, Hitler—for one reason, as a result of signs that the Allies were preparing a landing—selected the night of April 8 as the time for the German squadrons to put into the Norwegian fjords under cover of the new moon, vital information had still not been obtained. By way of Hagelin, Quisling was invited to meet Colonel Pieckenbrock, head of the espionage department of the *Abwehr*, in Copenhagen.[8] They

---

[1] Hubatsch: *Besetzung*, pp. 404–47.   [2] *Ibid.*, p. 158.

[3] *Beitrag zum Kriegstagebuch des Oberbefehlshabers der Kriegsmarine*, April 22, 1940, *Führer Conferences*, Vol. *1940*, p. 41.   [4] Hubatsch: *Besetzung*, p. 35.

[5] Affidavit, Nov. 19, 1945, by the Generals von Brauchitsch, von Manstein, Halder, Warlimont and Westphal, PS-3798.

[6] Statement, March 28, 1948, by Admiral Krancke, Wörmann-25.

[7] Hubatsch: *Besetzung*, p. 35.

[8] Rosenberg: *Norwegen-Aktion*, *IMT*, Vol. XXV, p. 33. Details on the fortifications of the Oslo-fjord were passed on to the Germans by Hagelin (Annexe 18 to Rosenberg: *Norwegen-Aktion*).

met on April 4, when the ships destined for Narvik were already under way. Quisling's answers to Pieckenbrock's precise questions were 'generally evasive'; he did give some useful tips about 'strength of the troops, situation of the airports, the time in which the fighters would be ready for action, etc.' He did not believe that the coastal batteries would open fire without first getting into touch with the government.[1] Hitler later said that Quisling had given a wrong impression of the batteries at Narvik at that talk.[2] Proofs that Quisling was told the time of the landing at the last minute have not been found.[3] One may take it for granted, however, that he could at least conclude from the questions asked, that the hour at which his dearest wish was to be fulfilled was coming near.

In this he was right.

At Narvik, where a few lighthouses were still working, the German squadron was able to enter the port after a sharp clash with a gunboat stationed there. The three freighters under way from Germany all missed their objective. The same, incidentally, applies to the other four, whose destinations had been Trondhjem and Stavanger. Only the *Jan Wellem* made its arrival on time at Narvik.[4] Nine other German ships rode at anchor there.[5] The crews were completely unaware of what was really happening, and one of the ships was run ashore from the conviction that British men-of-war were approaching.[6]

The battle for the town was quickly over. The garrison's commander, Colonel Sundlo, soon capitulated, but some of the troops withdrew, still fighting, from Narvik. Sundlo knew nothing of a coming German attack. After the war the court-martial which examined his conduct found that however pro-Nazi Sundlo undoubtedly was, there was no evidence of conscious sabotage of the military preparations or of insufficient readiness to fend off the German attack.[7]

[1] *Kriegstagebuch Seekriegsleitung*, April 4, 1940.

[2] *Adolf Hitler, Libres propos sut la guerre et la paix recueillis sur l'ordre de Martin Bormann* (Paris, 1952), Feb. 9, 1942, p. 298.

[3] *Straffesak mot Vidkun Abraham Jonssön Quisling* (Oslo, 1946), p. 373.

[4] Hubatsch: *Besetzung*, p. 130.

[5] Jacques Mordal: *La campagne de Norvège* (Paris, 1949), p. 221.

[6] Hubatsch: *Besetzung*, p. 72.

[7] Judgment against Sundlo, May 13, 1947. Scheidt reported on Jan. 5, 1940, that Quisling had received 'another message from Colonel Sundlo' in which Sundlo repeatedly stated 'that on his own initiative he has made all preparations at Narvik and now only waits Quisling's order to attack' (*Doc. Ger. For. Pol.*, D, VIII, p. 627). There is no evidence to support this statement which should be seen as another effort on the part of Scheidt and Hagelin to exaggerate the importance of their intrigues (information supplied by Magne Skodvin).

At the Trondhjem fjord the forts had been alarmed at 1 a.m. The German heavy cruiser *Hipper* had tried to pass unmolested by signalling: 'Have order of the government to proceed to Trondhjem. No hostile intentions.' The trick itself was not successful, but the Norwegian batteries were dazzled by the glare of the German searchlights, and a chance hit by a German shell destroyed the electric cable feeding their own searchlights. Just at 4.30 a.m. the German ships moored in the harbour; the local command capitulated.[1]

At Bergen one of the approaching German cruisers was requested to disclose its identity, and professed to be the British man-of-war H.M.S. *Cairo*. A passing destroyer was told in English: 'are going to Bergen for short stay'. The forts nevertheless gave fire, despite a third misleading signal: 'Stop firing! We are friends!', but were unable to halt the German squadron. In the early hours of the morning, Bergen was occupied before people realised what was happening. A few hours later a vessel of the German navy, disguised as a timber-carrying freighter, put in with a cargo of mines which were immediately used by the Germans to lay a minefield.[2]

At Stavanger the Norwegian airfield, defended by only two machine-gun emplacements, was quickly captured by airborne troops. The port was occupied from the land side.[3]

At Kristiansand it nearly went awry for the Germans. Fog and the forts kept the German squadron from entering for several hours. At 11 a.m. it was at last able to put in, when the Norwegians mistook the flag of the cruiser *Karlsruhe* for the French naval ensign, and ceased fire.[4]

In the Oslo fjord, as well, the Germans ran into serious obstacles. The forts had been alarmed. The two outer ones could not fire accurately because of the fog; the minefield which should have lain in between them had in fact never been laid 'for one reason because of the hope that the British fleet would bring assistance'. The naval base behind the outer forts was captured by German landing-forces. At 4.20 a.m. the inner forts sank the heavy German cruiser *Blücher* by gunfire, and the squadron was trapped.[5]

In the capital only a few Germans knew the hour of the attack; the German naval attaché Schreiber and the air attaché Spiller had been informed nine days beforehand, and Scheidt (Alfred Rosenberg's collaborator in Norway), who was only to be told on the 8th, managed

[1] Hubatsch: *Besetzung*, p. 75, 77. Dr. T. K. Derry: *The Campaign in Norway* (London, 1952), p. 40. Further to be quoted as Derry: *Norway*.
[2] *Ibid.*, pp. 81–2 and p. 40 respectively.   [3] *Ibid.*, p. 83 and p. 40 respectively.
[4] *Ibid.*, pp. 83–5 and p. 39 respectively.
[5] *Ibid.*, pp. 87–91 and pp. 35–6 respectively.

to obtain detailed information about the secret previously.[1] The German Minister, Bräuer, knew of nothing. Like his colleague von Renthe-Fink at Copenhagen he was to be instructed by a special confidential courier about the plan of attack and the role that had been assigned to himself. To this end one of the closest collaborators of von Falkenhorst, *Oberstleurnant* Pohlman, had flown to Oslo in mufti on April 7, accompanied by a courier of the *Auswärtige Amt* carrying the envelope holding the instructions to Bräuer.[2] Pohlman conferred with Schreiber on Friday, April 8; Schreiber was of the opinion that the Norwegian Government was not likely to show fight, but Pohlman was less optimistic and instructed Spiller, the air attaché, to send someone to the airfield of Fornebu, where German parachute troops were to land in the early hours of the 9th.[3] Spiller sent the Oslo representative of the *Lufthansa*, who was connected with the *Abwehr*, on this job. Because of the fog, however, the German parachute troops were at first unable to land; when Spiller realised that nevertheless the attack was to go forward, he scaled the gates of the airfield, together with the man of the *Lufthansa*, and while the Norwegian soldiers were still wondering whether or not to shoot, the first German planes landed. The two Germans on the airfield could now guide their compatriots to the town.[4]

There Pohlman had informed the German Minister, Dr. Bräuer, about things to come at 11 p.m. on April 8. 'Seldom', the former wrote afterwards, 'have I seen anybody so surprised.'[5] Bräuer was instructed to hand the German ultimatum to the Norwegian Government at 4.20 a.m. The answer was (as we know) that Norway would accept battle.

Naval attaché Schreiber was at his post by the harbour in the early morning, at four o'clock, to meet the Germans there. He had sent an assistant out on a German ship down the fjord to act as pilot, but to no avail, for the squadron did not appear. Schreiber went back to his office. There pistols were already being handed out for the defence of the house. They were not needed, however. That afternoon the airborne troops from Fornebu arrived at Oslo. Schreiber assisted them 'by giving them plans of the town, and so on'.[6]

The same afternoon Bräuer and Pohlman were in for a big surprise. They heard that Vidkun Quisling was carrying out a *coup d'état*. What were they to do? They had no instructions in this matter. 'Then a young man entered the room', as Pohlman wrote later on,

[1] *Norw. Parl. Enq.*, Vol. I, p. 24. Letter, May 26, 1940, from Scheidt to Rosenberg, Annexe 29 to Rosenberg: *Norwegen-Aktion*.
[2] Hubatsch: *Besetzung*, pp. 55–6. [3] *Ibid.*, p. 156.
[4] Information supplied by Magne Skodvin.
[5] Pohlman report, Hubatsch: *Besetzung*, p. 157.
[6] *Kriegstagebuch* Schreiber, *Führer Conferences*, Vol. *1940*, p. 29.

'and introduced himself as *SA-Standartenführer* from Rosenberg's office'—Scheidt!

He announces that he has just conferred with Mr. Quisling, who will become Prime Minister and appoint the other ministers. I turn amazed to the German Minister: 'Who determines German foreign policy, I should like to know, the minister of Foreign Affairs or *Reichsleiter* Rosenberg?' The Minister merely shrugs. 'How did you get here? When did you arrive?' The *Standartenführer* ignores the question. 'If you please, my credentials are in order, *Herr Oberstleutnant*, my instructions have been signed by *Reichsleiter* Rosenberg; that should be sufficient for you.'

General Engelbrecht [Commander of the division that has just occupied Oslo] telephones: 'What is the matter here? In Hotel Continental, where I am setting up headquarters, a Mr. Quisling has just made his appearance with an armed bodyguard, and declares that he is the new Prime Minister and occupies the third floor. We are to let his guards post the hotel, next to our sentinels. I've never heard of the fellow. Can I arrest him?'

'Quarter of an hour ago I should have said throw the man out, General, but there's a representative of Rosenberg in the next room who says Quisling is his protégé and intermediary. So we can do nothing about it. We had better wait till the Commander-in-Chief comes, perhaps he knows more about the matter.'

That afternoon Pohlman rang up von Falkenhorst at his headquarters in Hamburg. The reply was: Hands off![1] Bräuer warned Berlin that no Norwegian was willing to collaborate with Quisling, and that his bid for power would seriously increase the will to resist. For more than half an hour he battled over the telephone, to no avail.[2] Hitler had decided to make use of Quisling; and the confusion in the Norwegian capital was so great, the population so absolutely unable to do anything organised, since the departure of the government, that Quisling was able, later in the day, to launch his first proclamation without hindrance.

The role of the *Auslands-Organisation* in this whole matter is not completely clear.

In 1930 there were about 4500 German nationals domiciled in Norway.[3] The figure for 1940 is not known.[4] Bohle thought, after the war, 'that only about eighty' of them had been members of the

[1] Pohlman report, Hubatsch: *Besetzung*, p. 159.
[2] *Norw. Parl. Enq.*, Vol. II (Oslo, 1947), p. 270.
[3] Dr. Paul Lévy: *Le Germanisme à l'Etranger* (Strasbourg, 1933), p. 75.
[4] Information supplied by *Sentralpasskontoret*, Oslo.

Landeskreis of the *Auslands-Organisation*,[1] which after January, 1940, was led by a certain Carl Spanaus.[2] During the war Spanaus wrote an article in which he stated that from September, 1939, 'large numbers of party-members' were given 'new and often dangerous assignments'. After the *Altmark* incident he took 'secret organisational precautions'. When it became known on April 8 that Britain and France were going to lay mines in Norwegian territorial waters he warned his party members, and 'all took up their posts', but 'the impression was, then, that Britain would strike first'. On the evening of April 8 Spanaus sent out an extra warning. At 3 a.m. on the 9th, he himself was summoned to the German chancellery, and was told: 'The time has come.' Just after 4 a.m. he ordered the 'highest state of alarm'. A messenger service became operative. Spanaus remained at the chancellery for a while, and then went to review the situation at Fornebu. He was the first to be back with the joyful tidings that the airfield had been captured. After that he arranged for a number of party members to act as guides and interpreters.[3]

What did those 'new and often dangerous assignments' and the various 'states of alarm' really mean? Spanaus obviously expected a crisis and acted accordingly. It is probable that he gave orders for espionage; the extent and importance of such assignments are, however, unknown. It would seem unlikely that he and his underlings knew about the actual German plan of attack. Nothing is known to the Norwegians of any direct support to the German operations on April 9th.[4] Quisling's coup took Spanaus completely by surprise. 'Everything has been arranged over our heads,' he complained in a telephone call to Berlin on April 16, tapped by the Swedes in Stockholm. One should not neglect the possibility that Spanaus, in the year 1941, wanted to bring himself before the public by his article, and so exaggerated his military exploits.

We should realise, however, that more may have taken place than can be gleaned from the documentary evidence now available. The *Oberkommando der Wehrmacht* had carried on political talks with Quisling towards the end of March[5]—Admiral Canaris, chief of the *Abwehr*, visited the Norwegian capital at that time[6]—about which we only know that it seems to be certain that there was no personal meeting between Canaris and Quisling;[7] neither is anything

[1] Statement by Bohle, Proceedings *IMT*, Vol. X, p. 23.

[2] *Mitteilungsblatt der AO der NSDAP*, 1940, no. 1.

[3] 'Die Arbeit des Landeskreises Norwegen der AO der NSDAP im Kriege', *Jahrbuch der Auslands-Organisation der NSDAP 1942*, Vol. I, pp. 37–43.

[4] Information supplied by Magne Skodvin.

[5] Rosenberg: *Diary*, April 9, 1940.

[6] *Norw. Parl. Enq.*, Vol. I, p. 23.

[7] Information supplied by General Lahousen.

known of the espionage work of the *Abwehr*, of which Berthold Bennecke, the assistant commercial attaché of the German chancellery in Oslo, was the chief representative, beyond the fact that in the principal western ports of Norway 'experienced observers' had been installed, 'who were in daily touch with their command post in Germany', thus assuring 'an almost complete coverage of all shipping movements'.[1]

As regards direct action: in March, the sabotage department of the *Abwehr* had worked out plans for the prevention of railway traffic to and from Narvik, and for the wrecking of the Norwegian copper and iron-ore mines in the case of Allied landings in Norway, by the use of secret agents. General Lahousen, head of this department, had carried on talks in Germany with a Norwegian Nazi, Herman Harris Aall, on March 11; Aall furnished him with useful information and even promised that he would get into contact with Quisling in order to build up a defence organisation that would probably consist of active members of *Nasjonal Samling*.[2]

It is not certain whether this *Schutzorganisation* ever came into being. On March 19 Lahousen sent Aall an adviser, a captain in the *Abwehr*.[3] The explosives the saboteurs were to use, however, still lay in the German embassy in Stockholm on the day of the German invasion three weeks later.[4]

A Norwegian enquiry concerning the question whether any prominent member of *Nasjonal Samling* had played an active part in the German invasion, gave a negative result: there are no proofs, and Quisling, Hagelin and Aall did not know the date of the invasion.[5] Hitler and the generals wished to keep their plans completely secret, and this precluded making full use of any military fifth column. There was, we can be sure, enough willingness on the part of Quisling, Spanaus and their followers, to do their bit.[6] All the same, one must realise that the German forces in Narvik, Trondhjem, Bergen and Stavanger were master of the situation in a few hours, and that at

[1] Leverkuehn: *German Military Intelligence*, p. 82.
[2] *KTB-Abwehr*, March 11, 16, 1940.
[3] *Ibid.*, March 19, 1940.
[4] *Ibid.*, April 9, 1940.
[5] Information supplied by Magne Skodvin.
[6] On Feb. 21, 1940, Scheidt reported that at his suggestion 'and at the request of the German naval attaché, Quisling is now organising an intelligence network along the Norwegian coast with the help of the members of his party. . . . Wherever possible, an effort is made to have an agent on every vessel, who will duly report to Quisling. The questions of interest to us will then be transmitted by Quisling to the German naval attaché through me' (*Doc. Ger. For. Pol.*, D, VIII, p. 797). There is no evidence that this network was set up. (Information supplied by Magne Skodvin.)

Oslo, despite the chaos there, they had little difficulty in holding their own, in a situation which for a short while might have been called critical. In view of the facts as they are now known, the success of the German invasion, taking into account the too unsuspecting attitude of the Norwegians, must undoubtedly be mainly ascribed to the purely military aspect of the German operations.

Let us now review the opinions circulating amongst Germany's opponents during and after April, 1940, concerning the German attack.

There is nothing to prove that for years German attachés, consuls travellers, tourists, crews or hikers had been carrying out intensive espionage in Norway.

There is no evidence that in all the captured ports German troops and arms had been previously smuggled through to their hiding places; only the tanker *Jan Wellem* was able to reach Narvik according to plan.

Neither has anything turned up to show the truth of the rumour that large numbers of Germans went to Norway as 'commerical travellers' and 'tourists' to support the attack. That the German Nazis in Oslo were in the plot is not certain, and seems unlikely.

The Norwegians have not been able to demonstrate actual sabotage by German or Norwegian Fifth Columnists.[1] The minefield in the Oslo fjord, of which the electric wiring system was reported to have been cut, had, as we know, not even been laid. Hambro pointed this out as early as 1940.[2] In not a single case has it been proved that the Norwegian military received false orders by letter or telegram.[3] Neither has it been shown that, during the fighting immediately after the landings, German spies in Norwegian uniforms were among the Norwegian troops.

It is true that in May in Central and Northern Norway a few treacherous surprise attacks on Norwegian troops and on objects of importance to them in their operations, were carried out by military detachments of the *Abwehr*. They probably dressed themselves in Norwegian uniform, or disguised themselves in some other way. About 100 men were used by the Germans to this end; they

---

[1] Information supplied by Colonel Johannes Schiötz, former head of the war historical department of the Norwegian army general staff.

[2] Hambro: *I saw it happen in Norway*, p. 180.

[3] There are only two 'authentic cases' known. In one, a Norwegian fighter-squadron received telegraphic orders not to bomb a number of German ships, on April 9. Most probably this message was from the German ships themselves. In the second, the commander of the fort at Bergen received orders to cease fire. The origin of this message remains unknown. (Information supplied by Colonel Schiötz.)

belonged to a special unit that had been trained by the *Abwehr* in Germany.[1]

It is out of the question that there was large-scale treason among the Norwegian officers; 'hardly half a dozen' laid down their arms, and even in these cases misunderstanding, as a result of Quisling's counter-mobilisation order, may well have been responsible.[2]

It is not true that the German divisions were composed of Viennese men, who had been kindly cared for in Norway as boys after the first World War: of the seven divisions five were German, and the two Austrian divisions were recruited from the rural provinces of Tyrol, Carinthia and Styria.[3]

The opinion—expressed by none more clearly than by the American journalist Leland Stowe—that the German invasion succeeded thanks to 'bribery and extraordinary infiltration by Nazi agents and treason on the part of a few higher Norwegian civil and military personages', is quite beside the truth. Stowe, a good reporter and prophetic antagonist of national socialism (a book of his, published in 1934, carried the title *Nazi Germany means war*), nobly admitted before the end of the war that his reports from Stockholm had not given a true picture of the real situation.[4] Meanwhile his story had been swallowed whole by tens of millions of readers; his self-refutation, however, received scant notice.

[1] *KTB-Abwehr*, April 13, 24, 29, May 1, 9, June 17, 1940.
[2] Information supplied by Colonel Schiötz.
[3] Hubatsch: *Besetzung*, pp. 412–13.
[4] Information supplied by Magne Skodvin.

CHAPTER XI

Holland, Belgium, Luxemburg and France

★

Holland

WHEN the German armies invaded Holland, Belgium, Luxemburg and France on May 10, 1940, almost six months had elapsed since Hitler had exposed his political and military strategy in a secret address to the commanders of the army, navy and air force. 'I hesitated a long while,' he said on that occasion, 'whether I should attack first in the east and then in the west. After all I did not build up the *Wehrmacht not* to attack. The resolution to attack had always burned in me. . . . It was force of circumstance that entailed my first sallying out to the east.'[1]

When Hitler thus expressed himself on November 23, 1939, he had already annihilated Poland. These words of his bespoke the unbridled aggressiveness of a man who was firmly resolved from the very beginning that he would be the one to attack; and they also evinced the long uncertainty he had been in as to where to begin. As far as is known, it is indeed a fact that before 1938 not a single concrete plan of attack had been drawn up by the German military staffs. In 1938 Hitler's attention, insofar as foreign countries were concerned, had been entirely engrossed in Austria, and later in Czechoslovakia.

However, from the beginning of his political career he had looked upon revenge on France as inevitable. Holland and Belgium did not crop up in his remarks until the die was cast for the attack on Poland, when he foresaw that it might well result in a conflict with France and England. He then said, on May 23, 1939, in a discussion in which Goering, Raeder, von Brauchitsch and Keitel, to name but

[1] PS-789, *IMT*, Vol. XXVI, p. 30.

a few, took part, that in case of war key-points for the air force would have to be taken by force in the Low Countries.

By about the middle of October he ordered the working-out of a plan of attack whereby the German army in Holland would at first not break through the Grebbe Line, the fortified zone in the centre of the country covering the western, most densely-populated provinces.[1] Further south, in order to reach the Dutch lines that lay beyond the Meuse it appeared desirable to prevent the blowing up of the bridges. Hitler, who felt that his generals did not possess enough imagination, thought he knew of a good enough plan: a number of daring volunteers should be put into the uniforms of the Dutch military police or of railway personnel, and these people were to take the bridges by surprise.[2] The head of the *Abwehr*, Admiral Canaris, was commissioned to get models of the uniforms in question. His representative in The Hague had to carry out this task.[3] In doing so one of the transports, as we saw in Part I, was discovered in early November, 1939.

At about that time Hitler toyed with other ideas as well. Besides the airborne division that had already taken part in the fight in Poland, a parachutist division was got ready. Late in November he thought of occupying the isle of Walcheren with it.[4] Six weeks later another plan: the parachutists would perhaps land in the very heart of the Fortress of Holland, near Amsterdam,[5] in which case the German army would have to pass the Grebbe Line as soon as they could.[6] On January 17, 1940 the *Führer* went even further: 'the whole of Holland' was to become the objective of the attack.[7] Two weeks later he knew still more accurately what he wanted: the parachutist division was to occupy the government centre of The Hague and at the same time a special envoy (for which office the choice fell on a mobilised German diplomat, Werner Kiewitz) was to hand a letter to Queen Wilhelmina that would contain the usual mixture of threats and blandishments.[8]

On the eve of the German offensive Kiewitz's mission went wrong. The request for a visa was mistrusted by the Dutch Legation in

[1] L-079, *IMT*, Vol. XXXVII, p. 550–1; C-062, *IMT*, Vol. XXXIV, p. 268–9.

[2] In *KTB-Abwehr* this plan for a surprise attack is first mentioned on Oct. 26, 1939.

[3] Abshagen: *Canaris*, p. 238.

[4] Letter, Nov. 28, 1939, from the *Oberkommando der Wehrmacht* to the staffs of army, navy and air force, C-010, *IMT*, Vol. XXXIV, pp. 161–2.

[5] *KTB-Abwehr*, Jan. 10, 1940.

[6] Letter, Jan. 11, 1940, from the *Oberkommando der Wehrmacht* to the staffs of army, navy and air force, C-072, *IMT*, Vol. XXXIV, pp. 294–5.

[7] Halder: *Diary*, Jan. 17, 1940.

[8] Jodl: *Diary*, Feb. 1, 1940, PS-1809, *IMT*, Vol. XXVIII, pp. 397–8. The printed text has 'Kieritz'.

Berlin as well as by the Ministry of Foreign Affairs in The Hague, on account of the signs that a German offensive was at hand. Kiewitz was first to have gone by train, later by air. Permission to land was refused by the Dutch authorities and it was made clear to the Germans that a guest announced in such strange circumstances would be most thoroughly watched.[1] On May 9, 1940, he had to return to his military post without having accomplished his object.[2]

Meanwhile the staffs of the German *Wehrmacht* had worked out their plans during the early months of 1940. Parachutists and airborne troops were to conquer the three airfields—Valkenburg, Ypenburg and Ockenburg—all situated near The Hague, and were then to march from there to the government centre in order to capture the Queen, her ministers and the Dutch high command. Starting from the idea that this plan might fail, or that even if it did succeed the Dutch army might fight on, a powerful offensive was set on foot. In order to prepare the way a detachment from the *Abwehr* was to try and conquer the bridge over the Yssel, near Arnhem, while other detachments were to try and get into their hands the bridges across the Maas-Waal Canal, the Juliana Canal in South Limburg and those across the Maas from Mook to Maastricht. In order to conquer the bridges at Nijmegen, barges with a company of infantry concealed in them were to try to be close to their objectives at the hour of attack.[3] A powerful army aided by four armoured trains would cross those bridges for the launching of the attack. At one go the Germans would try to break through the Grebbe Line north of the big rivers, and with one more action they would try to reach The Hague in the south, via the bridges of the Moerdijk, Dordrecht and Rotterdam.

The special units recruited by the *Abwehr* for conquering the bridges by the frontier numbered altogether a full thousand men. In the main they were people from Upper Silesia;[4] and there were also about a hundred or two hundred Dutch citizens. In order to recruit the latter, officers of the *Abwehr* stationed in West Germany had sought contact with a certain Julius Herdtmann, a *Reichsdeutscher* by birth, who had obtained Dutch citizenship in 1924. Herdtmann, who had left for Germany again in the thirties, had there become the leader of a camouflaged continuation of the principal Dutch Nazi

---

[1] Statement by J. G. de Beus. *Neth. Parl. Enq.*, Vol. Ic, p. 628.

[2] Interrogation of Werner Kiewitz by Fred Rodell, *ibid.*, Vol. IIb, p. 130.

[3] Halder: *Diary*, March 13, and May 10, 1940, and further information from him and from General V. E. Nierstrass, member of the staff of the war historical department of the Netherlands army general staff.

[4] Information supplied by General Lahousen.

party, the NSB, the *Nationaal-socialistische Bond van Nederlanders in Duitsland* (National Socialist Association of Dutchmen in Germany). Most of the members, although formally Dutch, had been born and bred in Germany. Ordinary NSB members who had gone to look for work in the Third *Reich* were also members of the *Bond* however. The *Bond* had a sort of SA under the designation 'Sports and Games'.

For the so-called performance of police services and for acting as interpreters and guides, members of 'Sports and Games' were recruited with the help of Herdtmann. Amid the deepest secrecy they were given military training in four camps situated between the Rhine and the Dutch frontier. On May 9, 1940, the detachments who were to slip over the frontier—disguised as military police with so-called prisoners-of-war, or as railway personnel and even as Dutch soldiers —in order to approach and take their objectives, left these camps wrapped in the darkness of the night.[1]

Most of these surprise attacks failed; the one on the bridge near Arnhem collapsed because among other reasons, the *Abwehr* detachment of 25 men was rigged out in an outlandish sort of Dutch uniform with cardboard helmets.[2] With some other bridges the *Abwehr* was successful; especially the taking of the railway bridge at Gennep was of importance. A German armoured train rode over it into Holland, followed by a transport train, both of which added to the swift collapse of the first line of fortifications. A number of Dutch soldiers were treacherously shot down in all these attacks.

The attempt to conquer the bridges at Nijmegen—an operation that had received the code name 'Trojan Horse'—failed. The Dutch appeared to be watching the Rhine so closely that the Germans did not dare drop down the river in their barges with the concealed troops.[3]

With regard to the bridges in Western Holland the German plans succeeded.

Those near Moerdijk and Dordrecht were overwhelmed by parachutists. The defensive forces were unable to wreck their objectives. Dutch headquarters had not foreseen these German parachutist landings; moreover, they wanted to keep open the route via Moerdijk and Dordrecht for the coming of the expected French auxiliary army. For this reason no explosive charges had been placed on the

[1] Trial of J. Herdtmann and H. Köhler. *Nederland in oorlogstijd* (Amsterdam), 1950, No. 3, pp. 22–32.
[2] *De krijgsverrichtingen ten Oosten van de IJssel en in de IJssellinie, Mei 1940* (The Hague, 1952), p. 13.
[3] Information supplied by General Nierstrass and General Halder.

bridges.[1] Near Dordrecht the Germans dropped dummies in order to bring about confusion in the defence, and with success: 'false reports came in from all sides.'[2]

The same diversion manœvres were applied near Rotterdam, where dummies attached to parachutes descended near the airfield.[3] There the bridges across the Maas were conquered with little difficulty by a company which alighted on the river in seaplanes. The soldiers clambered up the banks with their arms. The bridges were unguarded.

We saw in Part I that the surprise attack on The Hague with parachutists and airborne troops failed. The Germans were able to overwhelm the airfields in a short space of time, but on account of the swift counter-movement of the Dutch reserve troops they were not able to consolidate their position, let alone get the chance to march into the royal capital. The assault on the heart of the country had this advantage for the Germans, however, that the Dutch high command was unable to send strong reserves to the eastern lines of fortifications. The opposite happened. Those fortifications had to be given up after fierce German attacks on the fourth day of the offensive. That day the first German tanks reached the southern bank of the Maas in Rotterdam. On Tuesday, May 14, 1940, the centre of the great port was bombed by the *Luftwaffe*. With the menace of similar bombings of towns before him, and realising that help from the Allies was out of the question, General Winkelman, Commander-in-Chief of the Dutch armed forces, decided to capitulate.

The better trained, better equipped and better led German *Wehrmacht* had gained a swift and decisive victory in a campaign of only five days. There are no indications that *reichsdeutsche* guests living in Holland or Dutch national socialists rendered active support in that campaign in any organised relation to the military or to any considerable extent.

To start with it is worthy of note that in not one of the German documents bearing on the preparations for the offensive is there so much as a single passage referring to such a Fifth Column.[4] That the

---

[1] *Beknopt overzicht van de krijgsverrichtingen der Koninklijke Landmacht, 10–19 Mei 1940* (Leyden, 1947), p. 29. Henceforth to be referred to as: *Beknopt Overzicht*.

[2] Interrogation of Colonel M. R. H. Calmeijer, *Neth. Parl. Enq.*, Vol. Ic, p. 309.

[3] Nierstrass: *Rotterdam*, p. 20.

[4] To the already mentioned documents may be added: (*a*) The papers of the *Oberkommando des Heeres*, '*Fall Gelb*', Oct. 7–Nov. 19, 1939, PS-2329, *IMT*, Vol. XXX, pp. 200–36. (*b*) The orders of the *Oberkommando der Wehrmacht* concerning '*Fall Gelb*', Nov. 7, 1939–May 7, 1940, C-072, *IMT*, Vol. XXXIV, pp. 284–98. (*c*) The order, Nov. 17, 1939, for the *Luftwaffe*, TC-058(a), *IMT*, Vol. XXXIX, pp. 61–7. General Jodl speaks in his diary of the possible putting into action of

Germans had to let *Abwehr* detachments come sneaking out of Germany for the capture of the bridges near the frontier proves that they were not in possession of such squads on the spot.

We stated that in those operations directed at the bridges use was made of bogus Dutch uniforms. It has never been proved that the Germans made use of Dutch uniforms in other places than those near the frontier. In not a single case has it been definitely established that they dressed their forces in the western part of the country in Dutch, British, Belgian or French uniforms. Nor is there any case on record in which their parachutists, airborne troops or accomplices operated in the disguise of farmers, policemen, postmen, conductors, delivery boys, priests, nuns, maid-servants or nurses.[1] Moreover there is no concrete proof that German parachutists descended anywhere else than near Moerdijk, Dordrecht and Rotterdam and near the three airfields in the vicinity of The Hague. It *is* possible that provisions were dropped by parachute at other places for the use of the advancing German troops.

In almost every part of the country taken so unawares, and more especially in big towns like Amsterdam, The Hague and Rotterdam, it was taken for granted that numerous helpers of the enemy had shot at the Dutch troops. No proof has been found for this either. 'Possibly a bit of firing may have occurred here or there,' the head of the historical department of the Dutch Army General Staff declared after the war, 'but we have no proof. We have no proven case anywhere that soldiers forced their way into houses, where people were caught red-handed with arms or the like.'[2] A few observations were made leading to the idea that projectiles were dropped from German airplanes which, exploding against the paving in the streets or the bricks of houses gave the impression of rifle fire.[3] The confusion on the Dutch side was greatly increased by such means.

For the fairly widely distributed tales of poisoned water or meat or that the Germans and their accomplices had handed round poisoned chocolates and cigarettes, no proof has been found. Nor is there any indication that similar stories were circulated by enemy agents spontaneously or in co-operation, or that light signals were made systematically, or that 'large figures in the shape of a swastika' were burnt or dug out 'at special points that were apparently about

special agents in The Hague (Mar. 7, 1940, PS-1809, *IMT*, Vol. XXVIII, p. 410). Other notes of that sort were not jotted down either by him or by General Halder.
[1] *Beknopt Overzicht*, p. xiii. 'Notities van lt.-gen. van Voorst tot Voorst over de mobilisatie 1939–1940 en de Meidagen 1940', *Neth. Parl. Enq.*, Vol. Ib, p. 107.
[2] Interrogation of Major-General D. A. van Hilten, *Neth. Parl. Enq.*, Vol. Ic, p. 320.
[3] *Ibid.*, pp. 320–1.

to be attacked by the Germans', as was reported from various parts of the country.[1]

And finally, as regards the reports about German refugees having given support to the German offensive—reports which led to many tens of thousands of refugees being interned, or being interned afresh in France and England—again no grounds can be found for such conclusions.[2]

Let us now, after these prefatory remarks, consider the situation in the large towns in greater detail. These were looked upon as centres of Fifth Column activity during those May days of 1940.

It is certain that in their advance from the airfield (Waalhaven) in the south of Rotterdam, the Germans were shown the way by *reichsdeutsche* citizens living there,[3] but from this one should not infer that this form of co-operation was organised beforehand. It is characteristic that on the vital Maas bridges it was a Dutch policeman who simply happened to be there who '[had to] give information with the help of a map they showed him'.[4] There is no convincing evidence of the truth of the tales that arms had been deposited beforehand near the Maas in German ships or ships of other nationalities or in the sheds of German firms.[5]

Nor is there anything to suggest that Fifth Columnists came into play during the fighting in the contested town. 'Nobody [was] found who could be caught on account of a rifle or a revolver.'[6]

As regards The Hague there is no evidence that on the first day of the war Fifth Columnists really tried to take the central police

---

[1] Poort and Hoogvliet: *Slagschaduwen over Nederland*, p. 283.

[2] Nationwide publicity was given to these negative conclusions in the Dutch daily and weekly press at the time this book first appeared, in the middle of November, 1953. This led to a number of letters to the author in which examples were cited of the action of German military men disguised as priests (Amsterdam) or in Dutch uniforms (The Hague) and of the distribution of poisoned chocolates (The Hague) which, according to the writers of the letters, had actually happened. None of these reports proved to hold good upon further detailed investigation.

[3] *Deutsche Schulpost* (Rotterdam), July, 1940.

[4] *Historisch Overzicht PTT-1940*, p. 625.

[5] The only positive report that a Swedish ship had discharged military supplies came from a Dutch officer who '[drove] at top speed in a requisitioned limousine across the Maas bridges that had already been occupied by the Germans' (Nierstrass: *Rotterdam*, p. 30)—circumstances that can hardly be called ideal for making accurate observations. This report was investigated by the Rotterdam police together with other similar ones, after the capitulation. It was not borne out in any way. (H. de Jong: *De Rotterdamse politie gedurende de oorlogsjaren 1939–1945* (MS.), p. 94.)

[6] Interrogation of Lt.-Col. J. D. Backer, *Neth. Parl. Enq.*, Vol. Ic, p. 368.

station by surprise; from a military point of view it was of small importance anyway. The big block of flats in the centre of the town from which there was said to have been shooting was thoroughly searched: nothing suspicious-looking was found there however.[1] There is as little to suggest that, as was reported on the second day of the war by general headquarters, 'Germans living in The Hague' had tried to march on the centre of the town, and had fled back to a house on the Suezkade which was then fired upon. 'Next day', writes the then burgomaster, 'there was not a single house on the whole of the Suezkade that was at all seriously damaged!' [2]

There *is* evidence of a number of German agents present in The Hague on May 10, before the offensive began.

It may be recalled that during those May days a few German documents were found that seemed to point to the existence of such agents: a battalion order in which amongst other things it said that in the area of attack 'German citizens' with 'special instructions' had been sent in, who were to be 'given every support they ask for', and also a specimen form of such a pass, duly provided with the German divisional commander's signature and bearing the number 206.

How are we to account for these papers?

The data derived from German documents[3] and other sources may be combined into the following picture.

It was Hitler's intention to eliminate those who had to lead Dutch armed resistance at the same time that he launched his offensive. The Queen, the Premier, *Jonkheer* de Geer, the Defence Minister, Dijxhoorn, and the Commander-in-Chief of the army and navy, General Winkelman, were to be isolated and the headquarters in The Hague were to be seized forthwith. Where these persons and institutions would probably be on the day of the surprise attack was being investigated as accurately as possible by the German espionage. The German troops that were going to land at the airfields near The Hague were to send a few small vanguard units to the residences of the Queen, the principal ministers and the Commander-in-Chief of the army and navy, as well as to the buildings where the various headquarters had been stationed. This was a case for swift action. Every moment's delay might prove fatal.

The *Abwehr* saw to it that some agents were sent to The Hague from Germany who would be able to take the vanguard units straight

---

[1] Information supplied by B. Rugers, head of section VI headquarters Fortress Holland.   [2] De Monchy: *Twee ambtsketens*, p. 230.

[3] Papers of the 5th company (IInd battalion) of the 65th regiment of infantry, found in The Hague on May 10, and of the intelligence officer of the 22nd airborne division, found on the body of a German soldier near the airfield Valkenburg on May 12 (the so-called Sponeck-papers). Further: parts of the *Kriegstagebuch* of the 22nd airborne division.

to their objectives. The agents in question, dressed in civilian clothes, were to act as guides.[1] They were not armed.

The surprise parties were to come thundering into The Hague on their way to their objectives on the motor cycles they had brought along with them.[2] The units following them up, in order to move quickly had to commandeer cars on the roads or in garages. The Germans had collected the addresses of 77 garages on the outskirts of the town out of local telephone books or directories.

The total number of agents amounted to no more than a few dozen. It is possible that they received help from the *Reichsdeutschen* living in The Hague for instance in the form of housing accommodation. Evidence, however, is lacking.

As regards the active part this Fifth Column took we are still groping in the dark. Their specific task was to assist in the great plan for a surprise attack. That plan failed. The Germans had the greatest difficulty in holding their ground at the airfields near The Hague, let alone get to the place of residence of the Queen and to the centre of government. Did the agents then quietly remain where they were or did they act individually or in small groups? We do not know.

In Amsterdam, so far as is known, not one Fifth Columnist working for the enemy was caught in the act. No magnesium bombs were concealed in the *Hôtel de l'Europe*[3] and there is nothing to prove that the chalk lines that were hastily scrubbed off the streets and walls during the last days of the war were of any military significance. Nobody tampered with the air-raid sirens, and the water supply was never interrupted for an instant. For the reports to the contrary, suspecting Fifth Column activity, not a trace of evidence is to be found.

Not counting the Jewish and other refugees from Germany, there were 52,000 *Reichsdeutsche* living in Holland on May 10, 1940.[4] Only

---

[1] Information supplied by General Lahousen and General Werner Ehrig, chief-of-staff of the German division that landed near The Hague.

[2] After the capitulation according to a communication of General D. A. van Hilten who was present when the talk took place, a German officer said to the commander of the first Netherlands Army Corps, General Carstens, whose headquarters were at The Hague: 'Yes, general, things did not look well for you, because if we had succeeded then you and your headquarters would have been among the first to have been made prisoner, because it was our intention to enter The Hague on motor-cycles that were conveyed in airplanes that had landed at Ockenburg together with a shock troop, and among other things take general headquarters by surprise and certainly the headquarters of the first Army Corps' (*Neth. Parl. Inq.*, Vol. IIc, p. 382).

[3] Information supplied by the management.

[4] Data supplied by the *Rijksvreemdelingendienst*, The Hague, and contained in an annex to a letter, Mar. 23, 1941, from the *Generalkommissar für Verwaltung und Justiz* to several German authorities.

a minority was at all in touch with national socialist organisations. Two months before the German invasion, in 38 places 6348 persons, men, women and children, shared in the national socialist common meals (*Eintopfessen*), for which a great deal of propaganda had been made.[1] On May 24, 1940, Bohle claimed he had 3000 party members in Holland.[2] The number is probably too high, but in the correct neighbourhood.[3] Dr. Otto Butting, who had taken upon himself the leadership of the *Reichsdeutsche Gemeinschaft*, was not very enthusiastic about the combativeness of his relatively small number of party members in Holland. In February, 1938, he called them 'for the most part very timorous and fearful'.[4]

In the light of these figures alone the views expressed after the invasion that 'tens of thousands of *Reichsdeutsche*' had suddenly come out as an attacking unit, and had shot at their hosts 'with the fury of dervishes', seem rather improbable. The action as guerrilla fighters or saboteurs of *Reichsdeutsche* living in Holland has not been proved in one single case. Nothing has been found to show that there was any armed resistance on their part against their internment. On the other hand it is certainly a fact that the German troops marching into Holland were heartily cheered by many *Reichsdeutschen* and that there were some among them who immediately after the struggle offered their services as guides or interpreters or to prepare refreshments.[5]

However improbable it may be that the great majority of the *Reichsdeutschen* gave their support to the German operations, a number of them were not insensible to the impulses in that direction coming from the leader of the *Reichsdeutsche Gemeinschaft*, Otto Butting.

Butting was a keen party man who was consumed by a desire to further the expansion of national socialist Germany. In the Netherlands he did not regard himself as guest but as conqueror. He actively encouraged espionage by *Reichsdeutsche*.

Towards the end of 1938 Berlin decided to recall the German servant girls working abroad because of the shortage of workers in Germany. There were about 3500 such girls in the Netherlands.

[1] *Rechenschaftsbericht über das Kriegswinterhilfswerk 1939/40*, April 7, 1940.

[2] Report May 24, 1940, of his talks with Rudolf and Alfred Hess, NG-4314.

[3] From papers of the *Reichsschatzmeister der NSDAP* Franz Xaver Schwarz, it appears that on February 1, 1941, 2,341 *reichsdeutsche* Nazis were living in the Netherlands.

[4] Letter, Feb. 11, 1938, to the *Chef der Auslands-Organisation*.

[5] Nierstrass: *Rotterdam*, p. 194. *Jahresbericht-1940 der national-sozialistischen Frauenschaft der NSDAP in den Niederlanden*.

They ought to have reported any change of address to their legation, but a third had neglected to do so. They could thus not be called upon to return to Germany as soon as desired; of those who did receive the call-up, a quarter ignored it, and many of those who did appear moved heaven and earth to be allowed to remain in the Netherlands where life suited them. Such an attitude on the part of these girls, a considerable number of whom were Roman Catholic, was more than Butting could understand. In February, 1939, he made a proposal to the Minister, Count Zech von Burkersroda, gradually to 'prevail upon all German girls to repatriate, unless they are employed by *Reichsdeutschen* or would have to live on the dole in Germany on account of old age, or are employed by political personages who are of special importance to Germany'.[1] Butting's intention to use the last-mentioned girls for espionage purposes is obvious. Whether he obtained any results in this respect is not certain.

A similar intention on Butting's part is betrayed directly after the outbreak of war, by his offer to the *Abwehr* to spy on shipping in the Netherlands with an organisation of his own. The liaison-officer of the *Abwehr* for the *Auslands-Organisation*, Heinz Cohrs, informed him that the *Abwehr* did not require his services: shipping espionage in the Netherlands had already been arranged for. Butting was requested to put his organisation at the disposal of the German naval attaché.[2] Whether he acceded to this request is not known.

It is certain, seeing what an ambitious fanatic he was, that in any case he also took his own line of action. He demanded of the leading local functionaries of the *Reichsdeutsche Gemeinschaft* that they should let him have all data that might be of military importance. These he worked up into reports for Cohrs. Making use of his diplomatic immunity, he took them across the frontier to the German town of Cleves, where he posted them to Berlin. Butting had his own private letter box in Cleves. Schulze Bernett, The Hague representative of the *Abwehr*, received copies of his reports to Berlin. It was one of these envelopes addressed to Cohrs that was found in the streets near The Hague early in April, 1940—as we have stated. The contents of this envelope lead us to think that the number of persons whom Butting had been able to prevail upon to perform acts of espionage was no more than a few dozen, perhaps not more than twenty. It further deserves mention that Butting made himself greatly hated among the members of the legation, and particularly by Schulze Bernett, the *Abwehr* man. The result was that when Butting turned up in The Hague shortly after the capitulation, without leave of the

---

[1] Letter, Feb. 2, 1939, from Butting to the *Chef Auslands-Organisation*.
[2] Letter, Sept. 19, 1939, from Cohrs to Butting.

German military and under a fictitious name, they seized the opportunity of ordering him out of the country.

Our general impression that only a relatively small number of the *Reichsdeutschen* living in Holland took part in espionage or sabotage against their host country is confirmed by what is known about the *Abwehr*.

Routine military espionage against the Netherlands was conducted from Germany, by various offices of the *Abwehr* in Western Germany. After the Dutch mobilisation, the Germans tried to recruit agents among the Dutch citizens resident in Germany who had to join the Dutch army. In a few cases their efforts met with success,[1] after which the Dutch military authorities, who wanted to put a stop to this obvious leak, proceeded to send back to Germany all the mobilised men in question, during the early months of 1940.[2]

The espionage reports about The Hague and its environs were naturally of the very greatest importance to the airborne division that was to conquer the town. The intelligence officer of this division kept them in a portfolio that fell into the hands of the Dutch. One comes across a number of agents in these reports. This number is not specified, but one gets the impression that it was a few dozen at most. Moreover, one comes across abundant evidence showing that a great deal of espionage work was carried out by the German military attaché in The Hague, by his deputy and by the air attaché. On maps—ordinary commercial maps that could be bought in any bookshop—these people marked the houses of the two ministers, de Geer and Dijxhoorn, the air-raid shelter and the residence of the Queen in Scheveningen, the chief public utility services and the military headquarters. It was the deputy military attaché Otzen who reported on April 9, 1940, that the heiress to the throne and her husband usually resided at Soestdijk and that he had not yet succeeded in finding out exactly where the dwelling was of the Commander-in-Chief of the army and navy, General Winkelman. It was Otzen and Wenninger, the air attaché, who reported in special cables, the last of which was received in Berlin on May 9, what they had been able to observe driving round in a car in The Hague and Leyden, as far as the Moerdijk bridges and even Schiphol airfield. Meanwhile it has not been established as a fact that any member of the German embassy knew of the date and hour of the German invasion.

---

[1] The memoirs of one of those agents were published in the *Aachener Nachrichten* between Oct. 6 and Nov. 6, 1951. Among other things he had been involved in the smuggling of uniforms and had taken part in the surprise attack on one of the bridges in south-east Holland.

[2] Information supplied by General Nierstrass.

Besides this, it is of importance that the Dutch did not always take steps, perhaps could not do so, to prevent the Germans from carrying out their reconnaissance. The main fortifications, because no state of siege had been proclaimed, were viewed by 'whole parties, sometimes conducted round by the commandant',[1] and 'various Germans' lived in the fortification area or 'came to visit it'.[2] And finally, numerous reconnaissance flights were carried out by the Germans over Dutch soil till just before the attack, in fact right up to May 8, 1940.[3]

Thus, roughly speaking, one may explain the Germans' knowledge of the locality during the offensive without having recourse to the hypothesis that hundreds of *Reichsdeutsche* living in Holland must have formed a spying Fifth Column—an hypothesis which as a matter of fact is nowhere confirmed by the original German documents that have been found.[4]

As to sabotage carried out by the *Abwehr* or other German services nothing has been established with any certainty. When on May 7, 1940, it was discovered that a lock near the main Dutch fortifications had been destroyed, it was at first thought that it was due to sabotage. An investigation by experts lent no confirmation to this supposition.[5]

Regarding the Dutch national socialists we earlier mentioned that some hundred or two hundred members of the NSB—the principal Dutch Nazi party—who lived in Germany and who had for the most part been born and bred there, took part in the treacherous surprise attacks on the bridges along the southern part of the Dutch frontier. When the leader of the NSB, Anton Mussert, later heard of this he was greatly dismayed. Repeatedly he spoke of 'a black page in the history of the movement'. *Such* treason, he felt, went too far.

The leader of the NSB did, however, hope to get into power after

[1] *Neth. Parl. Enq.*, Vol. Ia, p. 25.

[2] *Ibid.*, Vol. Ib, p. 22.

[3] Halder: *Diary*, May 8, 1940.

[4] The 'reliable report' quoted on pp. 137–8, published by the State Department in 1943, consists of excerpts from a longer report. This latter had been written by an American publicist on the strength of statements made by Wolfgang zu Putlitz, first secretary to the German legation at The Hague, who fled to England on Sept. 14, 1939. In the witness-box at Nuremberg zu Putlitz was only able to name one unspecified case in which the *Abwehr* had gained military information via Butting. (Proceedings, Trial against Weizsäcker *et al.*, p. 3681). His report is a mingling of facts and phantasy. The final impression left on the reader on the points that are of importance for our enquiry is not in agreement with the facts. Zu Putlitz, who followed the struggle in Holland, like anyone else, only from the papers, admitted this in a talk with the present writer on Nov. 7, 1951.

[5] Information supplied by General Nierstrass. The Netherlands Parliamentary commission of enquiry confirmed the hypothesis of sabotage on insufficient grounds. *Neth. Parl. Enq.*, Vol. Ia, p. 27.

a military struggle in Western Europe. He foresaw the German offensive. In January 1940, two agents of that section of the *Abwehr* which kept in touch with malcontent minorities had sounded him about what the NSB would do if the Germans crossed the frontier. Mussert had replied that the NSB would not stab Holland in the back.[1] That implied the possibility of a passive attitude—a possibility that was publicly suggested by Mussert in the notorious interview that took place late in April: when he was asked how his members would behave in case of a German invasion, he answered by crossing his arms over his chest and leaning back in his chair. Privately the leader of the NSB went further. To yet another representative of the *Abwehr* who visited him during the last week of April, Dr. Scheuermann, he answered 'that he would most like to fight on the German side with force of arms. . . . In case of a German entry into Holland one should take into account the experiences Kunsinen and Quisling had had, that is to say the new government should be able to pose as "saviour in time of need". He had at his command a sound organisation of 50,000 men.'[2]

Meanwhile there is no indication whatsoever that any German official body drew Mussert into the German military plans in any way. Butting thought him weak and uncertain and called the bulk of the members of his movement 'middle-class people who do not sacrifice their quiet repose because economically things are still going fairly well with them'.[3]

Mr. M.M. Rost van Tonningen, Mussert's liaison man with Germany, was a keener figure. Since the middle of the thirties he had been in constant touch with Himmler. There is no proof that he was involved in the German military plans. Rost feared that a German invasion would thoroughly spoil the chance for national socialism in Holland. There are various similar statements to show that he personally pointed out these views to Himmler early in March, 1940.[4]

It is by no means inconceivable that there were some persons in the NSB who, in case of warlike operations, wanted to play a more active part than Mussert and Rost van Tonningen considered desirable. There is an occasional indication that similar figures were to be found among the extremists of the smaller national socialist movements. All this did not amount to much. As has already been noted,

---

[1] Letter, Nov. 25, 1940, from Mussert to *Generalkommissar* Schmidt, *Nederland in Oorlogstijd*, 1951, No. 3, pp. 36–7.

[2] *KTB-Abwehr*, May 9, 1940.

[3] Letter, Jan. 2, 1939, from Butting to the *Gauleiter der Auslands-Organisation*.

[4] Information supplied by Mrs. E. Fraenkel-Verkade, who is editing Rost van Tonningen's correspondence on behalf of the Netherlands State Institute for War Documentation.

no sort of proof has ever been found for the supposition that Dutch national socialists shot at the Dutch troops in large numbers and in organised groups. As regards the members of the NSB who had been mobilised into the army it deserves mention that 'no actual data have become known of treason committed by officers, non-commissioned officers and soldiers in the Dutch army'.[1] As to the NSB members having acted as guides to the German troops, apart from 'the black page' at the frontier only a few examples are mentioned in the literature of the time.[2]

Belgium

In the ideas people had about the great German offensive in Belgium and France in 1940, the Fifth Column played a less central part than in their notions about the German operations in Norway and the Netherlands. In the Western world Norway in particular was looked upon as the victim of a wily, carefully prepared conspiracy, which opened the gates wide for the German forces simply to march in. In the Netherlands too, so people thought, treason, espionage and sabotage had played a vital part; but however confused the news from Belgium and France may have been in May and June, 1940, the stress did not lie on the intangible Fifth Column so much as on military operations in the proper sense. Many people realised that the Germans, although it was thought they received important aid from helpers, owed their victory to their military superiority. 'The Fifth Column consisted of but a few individuals', the Belgian Government declared shortly after its arrival in London, alluding to the Belgian fascists. 'Their operations were not able to make themselves felt.'[3] And as early as June 1, 1940, an article appeared in the London *Times* based on the personal experiences of various Belgian officers who agreed that 'in general Fifth Column activity was negligible'.[4]

As to France it is striking that in the serious studies of the struggle in 1940 one no longer comes across the Fifth Column, about which the radio and the press had made daily mention in May and June 1940. As early as May 24, 1940, when a French staff officer, in reporting to the French war cabinet on his impressions, had to repeat his words, because Marshal Pétain owing to his deafness had not been able to follow it all, he said, to sum up the matter: '*Monsieur le*

---

[1] *Beknopt Overzicht*, p. xiv.
[2] In Goes. Nic. J. Karhof: *Bezet, verzet, ontzet. Goes en omgeving in de bewogen jaren 1940–1944* (Goes [undated]), p. 20. In Workum. Leixner: *Von Lemberg bis Bordeaux*, p. 142.
[3] *België. Officieel overzicht van de gebeurtenissen 1939–1940*, p. 29.
[4] *The Times* (London), June 1, 1940.

Maréchal, the German army of 1939 has defeated the French army of 1920.'[1]

In the chief post-war writing about the struggle that view has been increasingly voiced. The more the French people pondered on the defeat, the more they realised it had its roots in France's history in the twentieth century—an inevitable outcome, as it were, of a number of general defects that had started to attach themselves to the whole national system. 'It is my conviction', said Raoul Dautry, Reynaud's energetic minister of Supply, before the French parliamentary commission of enquiry, 'that there are but few Frenchmen who in a greater or lesser degree are not guilty of the defeat and the armistice.'[2]

How France's energy was internally sapped by many factors and how the Germans, attacking with better equipped troops in accordance with a daring strategic plan, were able to gain a victory in Western Europe in five weeks time—all that we do not wish to treat fully here. It would lead us too far. But however plausible it may already seem, that public opinion in 1940 and later greatly over-estimated the importance of the Fifth Column in the German offensive in Western Europe, we yet do not consider ourselves absolved from the task of reviewing in detail the body of evidence for the notions about the Fifth Column that were rampant in 1940 as regards Belgium, Luxemburg and France.

We shall begin with Belgium.

After the first World War Germany had to cede to Belgium the frontier districts of Eupen and Malmédy, where the majority of the population spoke German. In the course of the twenties a pro-German movement developed here which, after Hitler's coming to power, set itself up as the *Heimattreue Front,* and which gained above half the total votes cast in different elections, the last ones in the summer of 1939. Within the *Heimattreue Front* was a nucleus of active young national socialists. As camouflage they had founded a glider-club. It was members of this organisation who deserted to Germany after the outbreak of the second World War, where they were received by the *Abwehr.* They operated as guides to the German troops and moreover set up their own attack detachments, which saw some fierce fighting against the Belgians. Furthermore, in Eupen a group of about 80 German ex-servicemen from the first World War tried to seize the chief

---

[1] Jacques Mordal: *La bataille de Dunkerque* (Paris, 1948), pp. 102–3.
[2] *Les événements survenus en France de 1933 à 1945. Témoignages et documents recueillis par la commission d'enquête parlementaire* [henceforth to be cited as *Fr. Parl. Enq.*], Interrogations, Vol. VII (Paris, 1952), p. 2036. The publications of the French parliamentary commission of enquiry are somewhat disappointing: too little enquiry, too much diffuse apology.

government buildings in the early morning of May 10. Members of the *Segelflugverein* took the Town Hall.[1]

Nothing has been reported of such activities in other Belgian districts, lying near Luxemburg, where lived a *volksdeutsche* minority, just as in Eupen and Malmédy.

No more are there any reliable data about treacherous behaviour of national socialists among the ten-thousand-odd *Reichsdeutschen* living in Belgium. No definite indications have been found after the war of their operations as agents 'dressed in light brown uniforms with buttons bearing the swastika and insignia with the letters DAP' —as the official description ran. It seems improbable that the members of a secret organisation, if it existed, would have made themselves so easily recognisable.

A number of agents operating in the rear of the Belgian, French and British armies were sent out by the *Abwehr* after the beginning of the offensive. They were disguised as refugees and had mingled with the civilians journeying westward. Beneath their disguise they carried machine-guns along in prams and trucks or under mattresses. They numbered one to two hundred. They were split up into bands whose task it was to take by surprise objectives that were of importance to the German divisions—main bridges, the Scheldt tunnel near Antwerp—and prevent their destruction. In the last phase of the struggle in Belgium the same detachments were used to prevent inundation in the Yser river districts.[2] Several of these operations were successful.

Nothing is known for certain of any co-operation of German parachutists with *reichsdeutsche* Nazis or agents of the *Abwehr*. There are no concrete indications that such parachutists disguised as labourers, priests, Belgian soldiers, policemen or women, whether or not equipped with small wireless transmitters, did actually operate in the hinterland. They did, however, drop imitation machine-guns that imitated the sound of shooting[3] and according to the testimony of General Student, commander of the German parachutists, a large number of dummies were also dropped (as had also been the

[1] *Organisations secrètes du pangermanisme et du nazisme dans les cantons rédimés avant le 10 mai 1940 (Auditorat-général, service central de documentation, doc. No. 370)*. This report contains the notes taken down about the examination of Dr. Peter Dehottay in July, August and September, 1946. Dehottay was the son of Joseph Dehottay, who for a long time had been the leader of the pro-German movement in Eupen and Malmédy.

[2] Information supplied by General Lahousen. *KTB-Abwehr*, May 31, 1940.

[3] Lt.-General Oscar Michiels: *Dix-huit jours de guerre en Belgique* (Paris, 1947), p. 58.

case in some districts in the Netherlands).[1] This occurred especially in the Ardennes.[2] The impression that parachutists descended everywhere, even in the palace gardens of Queen Elizabeth, was greatly strengthened by this. As regards this last case, the gardens in question were thoroughly searched but nothing suspicious was found. The nervousness of the guards was so great, however, that one shot down another, thinking he was a German parachutist.[3]

Regarding the possible co-operation of Germans with Belgian fascists and national socialists, it should first be noted that Léon Degrelle's Rex Movement, whose supporters were to be found especially in the French-speaking parts of Belgium, was oriented more towards Mussolini than Hitler. Degrelle received considerable subsidies from Rome.[4] He admitted as much after the war.[5] Moreover, at the end of January, 1940, he approached the German ambassador in Brussels in order to obtain a regular subsidy of nearly 13,000 *Reichsmark* a month which would enable him to publish a camouflaged evening paper.[6] So far no evidence has been published to show that his request was granted. On the other hand the Germans did keep up contact with Flemish national socialists, mainly as a result of the ties they had made during the German occupation of Belgium in the first World War. The leader of the *Vlaams Nationaal Verbond* (Flemish National League), Staf de Clercq, was in constant touch with officers of the *Abwehr*. He received subsidies from them (his weekly paper received 800 *Reichsmark* per month from Berlin in 1939),[7] and after the war had broken out, in consultation with them he built up an organisation in the Belgian army for carrying on defeatist propaganda. Part of the propaganda material was printed in Germany. The first such material sent, in which there were also ingredients for acts of sabotage, was smuggled into Belgium in the middle of January, 1940, by an officer of the *Abwehr* and taken to Brussels.[8]

In March and April de Clercq had a talk with Dr. Scheuermann,

[1] B. H. Liddell Hart: *The Other Side of the Hill* (London, 1951), p. 163.
[2] Information supplied by Colonel R. Lutens of the war historical department of the Belgian army general staff.
[3] Henri de Man: *Cavalier seul* (Geneva, 1948), pp. 221–2.
[4] On Sept. 8, 1937, Count Ciano wrote in his diary: 'I have decided to give the Rexists their subsidy once again (250,000 [lire] per month).' At pre-war rates this was about $9200 (Galeazzo Ciano: *Journal politique 1937–1938* (Paris, 1949), p. 28).
[5] Léon Degrelle: *La cohue de 1940* (Lausanne, 1950), p. 34.
[6] Telegram, Feb. 1, 1940, from the German ambassador, Brussels, to the *Auswärtige Amt. Doc. Ger. For. Pol.*, D. Vol. VIII, pp. 724–5.
[7] *Doc. Ger. For. Pol.*, D, Vol. V, p. 644 (note 1).
[8] Information supplied by General Lahousen and *KTB-Abwehr*, Jan. 10, 16, 1940.

whom we have already met as a visitor of the leader of the Dutch national socialists.[1] The Germans were of the opinion that the demoralising propaganda of the so-called regimental clubs of the VNV had had its effect. That the VNV had 'achieved certain merits' was acknowledged in an official German document in the summer of 1940.[2]

The vital bridges over the Albert Canal were not lost due to activities on the part of the Flemish Nazis, as was asserted at the time; it was the result of the surprise attack and of an unfortunate coincidence. The officer who had to give the order for blowing up the bridges was killed at the very moment that the German gliders descended near them. The messengers sent out by his deputy were unable to get to the bridges and the guards, who had been attacked by surprise, did not succeed in getting the charges to explode: the Germans had immediately cut the wires. 'There has been no treachery.'[3]

There is no evidence, either, of the co-operation of Belgian railway employees with the Germans. The French suspected treachery especially in connection with the disorder at the railway-embankments at Soignies on May 16, 1940, as a result of which it was said that French tanks were not unloaded in time. A close investigation on the part of the Belgian railways revealed that the section in question was hit by bombs on the 15th; on the 16th, however, the rails were clear again. That same day the French tanks were unloaded in the usual way. There was no question of sabotage.[4]

It is hardly necessary to say that King Leopold's decision to capitulate was not caused by the Gestapo acting as intermediary, as was said in June, 1940. This accusation was not repeated afterwards.

As regards the organised spreading of rumours it is conceivable that members of the *Vlaams Nationaal Verbond*, in so far as they were not arrested, carried out the same defeatist propaganda among the civilian population as they had done among the soldiers.

And finally in May, 1940, it was maintained that on the backs of the posters for *Pascha* chicory, secret signs had been put to help the German parachutists. That by moving curtains to and fro, by hanging up curtains of different colours or by making light signals,

---

[1] *KTB-Abwehr*, March 14, 17, May 9, 1940.

[2] Report, July 31, 1940, from General von Falkenhausen, *Militärbefehlshaber in Belgien und Nordfrankreich*, to the *Oberkommando des Heeres* about the political situation in Belgium, NG-2381.

[3] Michiels: *Dix-huit jours de guerre en Belgique*, p. 86.

[4] *Rapport aan de secretaris-generaal van de Nationale Maatschappij der Belgische Spoorwegen*. Information supplied by C. Pierard, head of the press and documentation services of the Belgian National Railway Company.

indications of some sort were given to the German air force. That accomplices of the enemy laid down strange shafts, for instance 'with three gramophone records at the back', in order to indicate the place where the military headquarters were to be found, or that they gave indications to the Germans by setting fire to specified haystacks or by spreading out maps or papers on the ground in accordance with special designs.

No evidence can be found that these observations reported by the Belgians, the French or the British should be looked upon as activities on the part of German agents or tools standing in some sort of connection with the German military operations. It is a significant phenomenon that in the official British military history of the war in Flanders [1] the term 'Fifth Column' does not even occur, nor are any activities mentioned therein which were ascribed in 1940 to those sinister bodies of enemy agents.

Luxemburg

With regard to Luxemburg, a swift passage through the territory of the Grand Duchy was of primary importance to the German supreme command: the German tanks had to go to the Meuse between Namur and Sedan via the Ardennes as quickly as they could. With this end in view a number of *Abwehr* agents dressed in civilian clothes were put over the frontier with motor-cycles. The task of these agents was to dislocate telephone communications, and to prevent the destruction of some important objectives for German military traffic. They also had to see to it that the main electricity station was not blown up. [2] A Luxemburg source says that the agents were recognisable by an orange handkerchief by day—we also came across such handkerchiefs in Poland—and by a green light signal by night, which they had to make with a pocket flashlight. [3] There are indications that similar activities, like dislocating telephone communications with the frontier posts, raiding those posts and preventing the placing of street barricades, were performed by other persons than the *Abwehr* agents.

A national socialist group had come into existence in Luxemburg in 1936, the *Luxemburger Volksjugend* (Luxemburg National Youth). In January, 1940, they received a request from Germany to stop the propaganda 'since ... other tasks, not further specified, were more

[1] Major L. F. Ellis: *The War in France and Flanders 1939–1940* (London, 1953).
[2] Information supplied by General Lahousen. *KTB-Abwehr*, Mar. 23, 1940.
[3] Paul Weber: *Geschichte Luxemburgs im zweiten Weltkrieg* (Luxemburg, 1946), p. 17. Weber reports that these activities were organised by the Gestapo.

urgent'.[1] Some pro-German Luxemburgers therefore probably played an active part in these matters. Others were found in their houses in the morning of May 10. They were arrested and transported to France.[2]

The struggle in Luxemburg lasted only a very short time and was not very intensive: only 75 of the Luxemburg military forces were made prisoner, six gendarmes and one soldier were wounded and no-one was killed.[3]

Only a minority of the *Reichsdeutschen* living in Luxemburg (in 1936 they numbered 17,000) were national socialists. Over 2000 of them were members of the *Auslands-Organisation der NSDAP* and its sub-sections; 3700 took the small trouble of taking part in the elections in Germany on March 29, 1936, which Hitler had decreed after the occupation of the Rhineland.[4]

No confirmation has been found for the reports that a few thousand German agents were smuggled into Luxemburg under the guise of tourists or of the personnel of a German circus. Nor that women had shot at the French troops from windows or that children had made signals to German soldiers. On this subject nothing is known in Luxemburg either.[5]

France

When, in regard to France, we again start with the work of the *Abwehr* we have to admit the data are lacking which might give an adequate idea of the reconnaissance and espionage carried out in France before and after the outbreak of war. That it was intensive, however, may be deduced from the fact that the German supreme command as early as the autumn of 1938 was able to put the necessary documentary material at the disposal of the German air force for possible bombing raids. These documents contained specifications of the French airfields, refineries, munition works, arms depots, electricity stations and the aircraft-engine factories that were situated

---

[1] Report, *Die bisherige Arbeit und die zukünftige Zielsetzung der Luxemburger Volksjugend*, inserted in Prof. R. Csaki's report, July 12, 1940: *Volkspolitische Grenzfahrt durch die deutschbesiedelten Teile der besetzten Gebiete im Westen*, enclosed in the letter of Aug. 7, 1940, from the *Abwehrstelle* Münster to the *Amt Ausland-Abwehr*, Berlin.

[2] Hermann Bickler: *Widerstand. Zehn Jahre Volkstumskampf der Elzass-Lothringischen Jungmannschaft* [Strassburg, 1943], p. 255.

[3] *Livre d'or de la résistance luxembourgeoise de 1940–1945* (Esch s. Alzette, 1952), p. 480.

[4] *Wir Deutsche in der Welt, 1937* (Berlin, 1936), pp. 93–5.

[5] Information supplied by Prof. Paul Weber, Luxemburg.

in the neighbourhood of Paris.[1] Another reason for believing that the German espionage must have been intensive lies in the fact that the German supreme command was fully informed as to the French mobilisation system.[2] A number of German spies were arrested and sentenced. The names of about thirty of them were published in the French press between September, 1939 and June, 1940.

In that same period acts of sabotage were committed in France on some occasions before the beginning of the German offensive; these had been organised by the *Abwehr*. One of those operations aimed at setting fire to the cotton warehouses in Marseilles; the preparations for this had been made in Italy.[3]

Just as in Belgium and Luxemburg, small squads of agents of the *Abwehr*, dressed in civilian clothes, were sent through the lines in France after the German offensive had started, to try and get to the hinterland on their own or amidst refugees, in order to prevent the French from carrying out demolitions which might be a hindrance to the German advance, or to commit acts of sabotage. From German instructions found by the French it appeared that these agents were to identify themselves by sporting a yellow handkerchief by day and by displaying a green light at night.[4]

Besides this, a small number of agents were dropped by parachute by the *Abwehr*. They were equipped with the means for committing arson.[5]

Further, it deserves mention that the *Abwehr* in France kept in touch with a small group of Breton nationalists who had been in rebellion against the French central government since the beginning of the twenties, just as they had done with the Flemish extremists in Belgium. These Bretons were of importance to the German intelligence service because many sailors in the French navy came from Breton fishing-towns. But the results were disappointing.[6] There is no evidence from which it appears that these extremists were active in any way during the German offensive.

The same applies to the pro-German autonomists in the Alsace, who had been in touch with Germany ever since the Treaty of Versailles. After the aggressive nature of national socialism showed more

[1] Letter, Aug. 25, 1938, from the *Generalstab* to the *Chef Luftwaffe-Führungsstab*, PS-375, *IMT*, Vol. XXV, pp. 386–7.
[2] Peter Bor: *Gespräche mit Halder* (Wiesbaden, 1950), p. 144.
[3] *KTB-Abwehr*, Mar. 29, 1940.
[4] *Le Temps* (Paris), June 6, 1940.
[5] *Ibid.*, May 25, 1940, affirmed by General Lahousen.
[6] Information supplied by General Lahousen. That there were German agents in Brest in April, 1940, appears from the *Meldungen der Wehrmacht über Lage am 13.4. abends*. Hubatsch: *Besetzung*, pp. 284–5.

clearly, however, their movement shrank into a sect of fanatics. As early as April and May, 1939, the French authorities started arresting the leaders of the autonomy movement. Three hundred fresh arrests followed after the war had broken out.[1] Nothing has appeared of anything like considerable support given to the German armies by the Alsatian autonomists. One should remember in this connection that a large part of the population of Alsace had been evacuated in the autumn of 1939, and that the Germans marched into the country when the struggle was decided. In that last phase just before the fate of their country was decided, persons suspected of pro-German sympathies were arrested and transported to the centre of France. A number of innocent people met with the same fate. It may be that in a few cases autonomists who were then still at liberty showed German troops the way. A concrete example of this is mentioned about Colmar.[2] In the same town the German Security Police appeared to have at its disposal a list with the addresses of the chief Jewish families.[3] The *Abwehr* too had maintained friendly relations with certain autonomists,[4] but no particulars are known.

Apart from all this nothing is known for certain about the activities of the German military Fifth Column in France.

It was not within the power of the *Reichsdeutschen* living in France to be detrimentally active. Those who on the eve of war had not responded to the appeal of their government to leave France at the earliest opportunity were interned. The total number of *Reichsdeutsche* is not known. In 1931 there were as many as 30,000 but later on that figure had dropped.[5] In 1937 hardly 3000 persons in the whole of France were members of the *Deutsche Gemeinschaft* (German Alliance), the general league set up by the *Auslands-Organisation der NSDAP* for Germans who kept up some sort of touch with the Third *Reich*.[6] In that same year about 130 people—men, women and children—joined in the demonstrative *Eintopf* meals in Paris, where over half of all the *Reichsdeutschen* lived.[7]

Nothing has emerged about Fifth Column activities carried out by refugees from Germany and Austria.

The impression that had arisen in May 1940 that the loss of the vital bridges across the Meuse between Sedan and Namur should be imputed to treason on the part of Fifth Columnists in the French army is incorrect. According to Doumenc, the historian of the

---

[1] M. J. Bopp: *l'Alsace sous l'occupation allemande, 1940–1945* (Le Puy, 1946), p. 42.   [2] *Ibid.*, p. 47.   [3] *Ibid.*, p. 50.
[4] *KTB-Abwehr*, July 4, 5, 17, Aug. 30, 1940.
[5] *HWB*, Vol. II, p. 551.   [6] *Ibid.*, p. 552.
[7] *Deutsche Zeitung in Frankreich* (Paris), April 15, 1937.

French Ninth Army, all the bridges across the Meuse were blown up in time.[1] Just to the north of Dinant the Germans were able to reach the western bank by means of a lock.[2] Everywhere else they had to cross the river in ordinary vessels or rubber boats, on pallets or by swimming across,[3] and after the war Reynaud frankly admitted that he had erroneously mentioned the name of General Corap, the commander of the Ninth Army, in connection with the report that bridges had not been destroyed;[4] as early as 1940 an official French enquiry led to the conclusion that Corap could not be reproached with anything.[5]

Nowhere has it appeared that false instructions were circulated by the Fifth Column. People connected those instructions especially with the precipitate evacuation of large parts of the French civil population. In actual fact the French civil and military authorities did really order those evacuations to take place. They wanted to spare the population of Northern France a repetition of the suffering they had undergone during the German occupation of 1914–18. The evacuation of a considerable part of this area was commanded on the night of May 10, 1940, by the French supreme command.[6] In not a single concrete case have we any evidence that the flight of the population was furthered by false orders circulated by enemy agents. An extensive post-war enquiry brought no more to light than that in one place in Central France—Chaumont, on the Loire—the hairdresser there who repeatedly urged the population to fly, did indeed get into touch with the Germans immediately after their arrival.[7] Perhaps there were other persons who tried to increase the general confusion, either on their own initiative or as part of a German plan; but proof we have none.[8]

And then finally it was thought that during the weeks of war in France a large number of traitors in the hinterland helped the Germans—that enemy agents who were already in France or had been smuggled in as Belgian refugees lent the Germans a helping hand, preferably disguised as priests, monks, or nuns, by shooting at the

---

[1] A. Doumenc: *Histoire de la neuvième armée* (Grenoble, 1945), p. 60.

[2] *Ibid.*, p. 83.

[3] *Ibid.*, pp. 99, 102–3, 116.

[4] Reynaud: *La France a sauvé l'Europe* (Paris, 1947), Vol. II, p. 80.

[5] Statements by General Georges, *French Parl. Enq.*, Vol. III (Paris, 1952), p. 717, by General Lacaille, *ibid.*, Vol. IV (Paris, 1952), pp. 937–8 and by General Véron, *ibid.*, Vol. V (Paris, 1952), pp. 1289–90, 1293–4 and 1307.

[6] M. Lerecouvreux: *Huit mois d'attente, un mois de guerre* (Paris, 1946), p. 144.

[7] Prof. Jean Vidalenc: 'l'Exode de 1940. Méthodes et premiers résultats d'une enquête', *Revue d'histoire de la deuxième guerre mondiale* (Paris), I, 3 (June, 1951), pp. 51–55, supplemented by statements by the author.

[8] Information supplied by Prof. Vidalenc.

French troops, by extensive spying, by purposely circulating alarming rumours, by making special signals to the German air force—the 'morse signals all over Paris' that had been noticed by an English novelist—or by handing out poisoned sweets.

For none of these ideas has any confirmation been found. In the French military literature on the struggle of 1940 there is not one single truly convincing Fifth Column case of this nature described. It is typical that those officers who remained free from the all-pervading panicky atmosphere did not notice anything suspicious. The quiet Cheynel, who described the retreat of his unit from the Belgian frontier into Central France in his diary,[1] personally noticed no more of the Fifth Column than that he and his troops were branded as Fifth Columnists in the neighbourhood of Nancy by a lunatic whom he promptly had placed in custody.[2]

[1] Henri Cheynel: *Carnet de route d'un médecin de l'avant* (Paris, 1946).
[2] *Ibid.*, p. 133.

CHAPTER XII

England and America

★

England

IN so far as they have become known, not one of the documents about the German plans for a landing in England lead to a presumption that Hitler expected to find any considerable number of people on the spot to help him in his fight. On July 21, 1940, he said: 'We cannot count upon any supplies whatsoever being available for us in England.'[1] It is characteristic that during the weeks in which he was seriously thinking of invading England he had no idea what he would have to do with his parachutists and landing troops, who after all would have to co-operate with a Fifth Column if any existed. Twice, on July 16 and August 26, 1940, he asked the component parts of the *Wehrmacht* for 'suggestions' for the operations of these specialised units.[2] Whether such suggestions were given is not known.

Even if the big attack on England was not to take place, the German military had nevertheless taken great pains before the war to collect information about the island empire that might stand them in good stead in case of an armed conflict. In August, 1938, most of the British airfields, in so far as the Germans knew, had been mapped out, and the German general staff had collected maps (and air and land photos) of the harbours, docks, chief warehouses and oil tanks near London and Hull. It was then thought that the whole of the districts of London and Hull would be mapped out before the end of September, 1938.[3]

The collection of data was continued. In June, 1939, the German

---

[1] *Führer Conferences*, Vol. *1940*, p. 72.
[2] *Ibid.*, pp. 68, 86.
[3] Letter, Aug. 25, 1938, from the *Generalstab des Heeres* to the *Luftwaffe-Führungsstab*, PS-375, *IMT*, Vol. XXV, pp. 387–8.

Government was requested to recall the consul-general in Liverpool: he had acted as intermediary in espionage for Germany that had been carried out by a workman in a munitions factory who had come in contact with a German cook in Manchester. Furthermore, still before the war, three workmen in the great arsenal works at Woolwich were sentenced for giving information to the Germans. It may be assumed that other spies remained at liberty. When the great struggle started the British security services had a list with the names and addresses of 350 persons who were considered suspect. In so far as they were still in England, they were all interned in the early days of September, 1939.[1]

There are no indications that before the war started German espionage in England made large-scale use of German tourists, visitors of Youth Hostels or maids. It is conceivable that in a few cases they did indeed try to collect information with the help of such people; detailed evidence is lacking, and the writers who are prodigal of their accusations in this field, contradict each other. One of them asserts that 'more than a thousand German girls' had been lodged with English families as maid-servant spies,[2] while another confines himself to the statement that the British counter-espionage office knew 'that at least four hundred of the thousands of Germans who were employed as domestic servants in Britain before the war were listed as potential spies of the German *Nachrichtendienst*' [3]—he means the *Abwehr*. Who listed these girls is not clear, and that these potential agents developed into real agents is only certain, so far as we know, in the one case cited above of the cook in Manchester.[4]

One does not gain the impression from the data at hand, which, it is true, are incomplete, that the German espionage in England *during* the war was very extensive.

As far as is known the *Abwehr's* chief success involved the activity of the American diplomatic official, Tyler Kent. This man was a fanatical fascist attached to the American Embassy in London, who from the autumn of 1939 up to his arrest on May 18, 1940, put no less than 1500 micro-filmed code messages into the hands of the *Abwehr* via the Italian Embassy. They were notes that had been exchanged

[1] F. Lafitte: *The Internment of Aliens* (London, 1940), p. 65.
[2] Stanley Firmin: *They Came to Spy* (London, 1947), p. 16. Mr. Firmin did not feel entitled to give me further information.
[3] E. H. Cookridge: *Secrets of the British Secret Service*, p. 84.
[4] After the outbreak of the war a certain Mrs. Ingram was arrested, a German woman by birth, who had lived in England since 1922 and who fervently admired Sir Oswald Mosley. It was her plan to aid the German troops. She was employed as housekeeper in the house of a naval officer. This impulsive lady told everyone who cared to listen that the Jews had started the war and that Churchill was a calamity for England. *Ibid.*, pp. 83–5.

between Whitehall and Washington as well as reports from the American ambassador, Kennedy.[1] For the rest, up to the end of the war 'the number of German agents in Britain was small, their information unreliable and most of their communications under observation'.[2] A number of agents were smuggled into England in various ways. Eighteen of them were arrested, most of them soon, and hung.[3] In the documents that have been published about the preparations for a German landing one only comes across one piece of espionage news, with the partly incorrect visual observations of 'a secret agent'.[4] The quality of information received from another agent, that came to Goebbels' notice in September, 1940, was no higher. According to this man there was such a state of emergency in London that titled ladies had to relieve themselves in Hyde Park.[5]

Some of the above-mentioned agents, all of them sent out by the *Abwehr*, were commissioned to carry out acts of sabotage. It was not only Germans who tried to get into Britain. In the autumn of 1940 a Spanish Falangist was trained for action via Ireland,[6] and a short while later a trawler with three Cuban agents aboard tried to reach England from Brest.[7]

As concerns England, the efforts of the *Abwehr* were particularly directed at spurring on the active nuclei of nationalist movements that were rebelling against the British state authority to perform diversionist work. In the spring of 1940 a group of Welsh nationalists lent themselves for this purpose. Six months later (November 14) it was noted in Berlin that they developed 'busy activity along the lines of the tasks set by *Abwehr II*'.[8] The *Abwehr* also tried to get into touch with Scottish nationalists.[9] Whether they succeeded is not known. The Germans did meet with success in contacting the leaders and members of the Irish Republican Army. Some of these had committed bomb outrages in the period preceding the outbreak of war. In January, 1940, an explosion occurred in an electricity power station in Lancashire. It was an act of sabotage which—so it

[1] E. H. Cookridge: *Secrets of the British Secret Service*, pp. 122–5.
[2] Ian Colvin: *Chief of Intelligence* (London, 1951), p. 75.
[3] Cookridge: *Secrets of the British Secret Service*, p. 104.
[4] *Führer Conferences*, Vol. *1940*, p. 89. 'It seems incredible, but we do not have a single informant in Great Britain', Count Ciano wrote in his diary on Sept. 11, 1940. 'On the other hand, the Germans have many. In London itself there is a German agent who makes radio transmissions up to twenty-nine times in one day. At least it is so stated by Admiral Canaris' (*Ciano Diaries*, p. 291).
[5] Wilfred von Oven: *Mit Goebbels bis zum Ende*, Vol. II (Buenos Aires, 1950), p. 43.
[6] *KTB-Abwehr*, Sept. 11, 1940.   [7] *Ibid.*, Nov. 6, 1940.
[8] *Ibid.*, Feb. 17, April 27, Aug. 15, Nov. 11 and 14, 1940.
[9] *Ibid.*, Nov. 11, 1940.

was recorded in Berlin— 'was performed by Irish activists who have been charged with such orders'.[1] A year later the *Abwehr* heard via Spain that members of the IRA had blown up a munitions train in the county of Leicester.[2]

In 1940 the *Abwehr* took a great deal of trouble to increase the activities of the IRA in Eire. It was there, after all, that the Irish agents had to be recruited who were intended for operations in England and Northern Ireland. The relations Berlin kept up with the Irish extremists were cut off shortly after the outbreak of the war. Late in October, 1939, they were restored again.[3] The Germans had a radio transmitter sent to the extremists from America. When, after a time, these also started using it for propaganda it was soon traced and seized.[4] A certain Jim O'Donovan is mentioned as the leader of those extremists in the War Diary of the *Abwehr*.[5] Early in May the Germans sent him a liaison officer, one Lieutenant Goertz, who brought a new transmitter with him and a sum of money. All this was soon discovered in the house of his host by the Irish police.[6] In the middle of January, 1941, Lieutenant Goertz reported that his work was going well but he urged that more help should be sent him.[7] Some time later the difficulties he encountered reduced him 'to a state of nervous prostration' and he was soon arrested.[8]

Meanwhile the leaders of the *Abwehr* had tried hard to improve their co-operation with Ireland. In January, 1940, Sean Russell, the adjutant of the former leader of the Irish Republican Army (he had escaped to America), suggested to the *Abwehr* via the German consulate-general in Genoa that they bring him to Germany so that he would be able to prepare his operations in Ireland there.[9] Russell had used a steward on an American ship as intermediary.[10] The *Abwehr* accepted his offer, Russell received news to that effect, and late in April, 1940, he was able to get to Genoa as a stowaway.[11] In Berlin he was given emergency training in sabotage work.[12] The plan was that he should be taken to the Irish coast in a submarine. Another Irish extremist, Frank Ryan, was to accompany him. This man had already acted for some time as an *Abwehr* agent.[13] They were to have a few followers whom they had found among the Irish

[1] *KTB-Abwehr*, Jan. 27, 1940.   [2] *Ibid.*, Jan. 7, 1941.
[3] *Ibid.*, Oct. 22, 1939.   [4] *Ibid.*, Feb. 4, 1940.
[5] *Ibid.*, March 30, April 20, 1940.
[6] *Ibid.*, May 25, 1940.   [7] *Ibid.*, Jan. 14, 1941.
[8] Leverkuehn: *German Military Intelligence*, pp. 102–3.
[9] *KTB-Abwehr*, Jan. 30, 1940.
[10] *Ibid.*, Feb. 22, March 19, March 30, 1940.
[11] *Ibid.*, April 26, May 1, 1940.   [12] *Ibid.*, May 20, 1940.
[13] *Ibid.*, July 13 and 17, 1940, Witness Kurt Haller, Proceedings 'Case XI', pp. 20,442–3.

prisoners-of-war of the British Expeditionary Force, and a trans-mitter and material for sabotage would also be given them.[1] Russell was not given any concrete tasks. He was to judge for himself what it was best for him to do, but he was especially to try to make his plan for action co-ordinate with a possible German invasion of England. He was to be informed when this was to happen at the last moment 'by a signal still to be agreed upon (for instance a bunch of red flowers in front of a particular window in the German embassy in Dublin').[2] Russell's operation was financed by the *Auswärtige Amt*, which was hoping to be able to reduce the *Abwehr* into an institution that rendered technical co-operation only.[3]

On August 8, 1940, the submarine sailed with Russell and Ryan on board. The operation failed pitiably. Before they had reached Ireland Ryan died of a heart attack, whereupon the expedition was called off.[4]

It is not impossible that besides all this the Germans made plans for attempts on Churchill's life and that of General de Gaulle and President Benes.[5] Detailed evidence to this effect has, however, never been made known.

Regarding the actual extent of the operations here outlined—the work of German agents and of extremists from Wales, Scotland and Ireland—nothing is certain. Moreover, our chief source, the War Diary of *Abwehr II*, unfortunately comes to an end in April, 1941. One gets the impression from the available data that before that time mention has only been made of the activities of relatively small parties of fanatics. In 1940, however, three large groups were con-sidered potential or real Fifth Columnists in England, namely the *Reichsdeutschen*, the German refugees and the British fascists. We shall have to consider the activities and the dispositions of these groups a little more closely.

No figures have been made public with regard to the influence which the *Auslands-Organisation der NSDAP* exercised on the *Reichs-deutschen*. In 1931 they numbered 15,500 in England, Scotland and Wales. Almost two-thirds of them lived in London.[6] In 1934 the Germans admitted that most of the *Reichsdeutschen* who had lived in England a long time would have nothing to do with national

---

[1] *KTB-Abwehr*, May 25, 1940.
[2] *Ibid.*, Aug. 3, 1940.
[3] *Ibid.*, May 23, Aug. 3, 1940.
[4] *Ibid.*, Aug. 8 and 15, 1940. Abshagen: *Canaris*, pp. 275–8.
[5] Cookridge: *Secrets of the British Secret Service*, p. 185.
[6] Figures supplied by the Central Office of Information, London.

socialism.[1] If we keep the general conditions in Western Europe in mind it seems reasonable to assume that the number of *Reichsdeutsche* who had anything to do with the *Auslands-Organisation* and its by-organisations was perhaps one thousand. An estimate of no less than 'twenty thousand organised German Nazis' in England on the eve of the war seems much too high.[2] After the outbreak of the war, at any rate, only 7400 persons of German nationality were considered not absolutely reliable by the Aliens Tribunals, and almost 4300 of them claimed to be genuine refugees.[3] Among the remaining 3100 were the *Reichsdeutschen* resident in England, of whom it was assumed that they sympathised with national socialism. 350 of them—those known or suspected to be espionage agents—had, as was shown, been taken into custody at the outbreak of the war. It is altogether probable that there were members of the *Auslands-Organisation* among them.

As concerns the refugees from Germany, it is not impossible that there may have been a few among them who, like Dr. Hans Wesemann (who, as we saw in the Introduction to Part I, kidnapped the anti-fascist writer, Dr. Berthold Jacob, from Basle) were willing to help the Gestapo in various ways, for instance by collecting information about foreign exchange smuggled out of Germany. It is a fact, however, that when thirty thousand refugees were interned, no more had been learned in their disfavour than 'one or two petty isolated instances, such as the undergraduate Mr. Solf, who had photographed a burning aeroplane' (this had not been an act of espionage but reprehensible photographic zeal) 'and one or two black-out offences'.[4] During a debate on August 22, 1940, in the House of Commons the Under-Secretary of State for the Home Department again admitted that 'no serious act of a hostile character' had come to his notice among the refugees. In a few cases, however, he suggested Germans disguised as refugees had tried to get into England, and it was therefore 'not impossible' that a few *bona fide* refugees were also really German agents.[5]

There is no evidence that this was in fact the case.

Most of the refugees enthusiastically took part in the great war effort, as they were gradually set free. Many joined the Auxiliary

[1] C. R. Hennings: 'Vom Deutschtum in England', *Der Auslandsdeutsche* (Stuttgart), 1934, p. 508.
[2] Churchill: *The Second World War*, Vol. I, *The Gathering Storm* (London, 1948), p. 313.
[3] Lafitte: *The Internment of Aliens*, p. 63.
[4] Statement by O. Peake, Under-Secretary of State for the Home Department, July 10, 1940, 362 *H.C. Deb.*, 5s., 1236.
[5] 364 *H.C. Deb.*, 5s., 1579.

Military Pioneer Corps, and over a thousand joined the Commandos and the airborne troops. After the war something like 34,000 were naturalised in quick succession as British citizens.[1]

Regarding the British fascists, who were united in such organisations as the British Union of Fascists, the Link and the Right Club, it may be assumed that several of them would have been willing to introduce England into Hitler's 'New Order'. There are no indications, however, that the chief fascist leader, Sir Oswald Mosley, had any very close touch with Berlin. In October, 1936, he visited Goebbels.[2] After the outbreak of war fascist propaganda was circulated by members of his organisation and by similar groups, but 'with a few exceptions there is little evidence that any of them ever really attempted to spy for the Nazis or endeavoured to get useful military or other information out of the country for the German Secret Service'.[3]

Perhaps the reader will remember that in Part I, mention was made of the fact that the BBC broadcast an erroneous order for mobilisation on May 12, 1940. At the time it was looked upon as one of those 'false reports' passed on by enemy agents—the sort of reports, so it was thought, with which the Germans had been so successful in Holland, Belgium and France. Where the order in question came from has never been discovered. An enquiry that was set on foot brought to light that there was lack of co-ordination within the BBC.[4] It is not impossible that it was simply a mistake.

America

At the time of his great conquests in Western Europe Hitler had not a single plan of attack against England at his command. The same applies *a fortiori* in connection with America—*a fortiori* because the *Führer*, separated as he was from England by the Channel, would first have to defeat that country and cross the Atlantic if he wanted to carry out military operations in the Americas or aid a Fifth Column carrying on a campaign on his behalf. Not that an offensive against the New World was considered impossible by Hitler! In the autumn of 1940 he paid attention to the problem of the occupation of the Azores and the Canaries 'in view of a later

[1] *The Refugee in the Post-war World* (Geneva, 1951), p. 352.
[2] Frederic Mullaly: *Fascism inside England* (London, 1946), p. 75.
[3] Firmin: *They Came to Spy*, p. 30.
[4] Information supplied by the Head of the Air Historical Branch, Air Ministry, London, and the British Broadcasting Corporation, London.

waging of war against America'.[1] '*Amerika, wenn überhaupt, nicht vor '42*' ('America, if at all, not before 1942') the chief-of-staff of the German army noted down in his Diary on November 4, 1940.[2]

A month before the attack on Russia began Hitler was still toying with the plan of occupying the Azores—again for use as a base for bombing the United States. 'The occasion for this may arise before autumn,' he said hopefully to Raeder.[3] The struggle in Russia had hardly been going on for three weeks when Hitler indicated to his chief military assistants that after the complete overthrow of the Soviet Union the German army could conveniently be decreased. At that point the arming of the Navy was to be confined to measures 'which are of direct importance for waging war against England and, if the occasion should arise, against America'.[4]

When the occasion did indeed arise, and when Hitler declared war on the United States after the Japanese attack on Pearl Harbour, Germany's powers had been taken up to such an extent in the deadly struggle in the east that there was nothing left for conducting an offensive war on a large scale against America. The idea of bombing the big cities on the east coast of America was reluctantly dropped by Hitler in the summer of 1943.[5] Only by throwing saboteurs into the fight would he be able to strike at his industrially strongest opponents in their own country.

Shortly after the outbreak of the second World War the *Abwehr* had drafted plans for sabotage in America by means of agents, and for conducting defeatist propaganda in the army. The *Abwehr* also debated whether it would not be possible to smuggle explosives into British ships lying in American harbours. Hitler was opposed to carrying out these and similar plans. He was rightly of the opinion that the material advantage to be gained would not outweigh the political disadvantage. In April, 1940, he ordered Admiral Canaris to leave the United States alone.[6] The order was repeated in June, when at the same time instructions were given to recall from America 'the only agent deserving consideration'.[7]

When in the autumn of 1940 the United States started lending

---

[1] Letter, Oct. 29, 1940, from the *Major des Generalstabs Freiherr* von Falkenstein to an unknown general, PS-376, *IMT*, Vol. XXV, p. 393.

[2] Halder: *Diary*, Nov. 4, 1940.

[3] *Conference of the Commander-in-Chief, Navy, with the Führer*, May 22, 1941, *Führer Conferences*, Vol. *1941*, p. 57.

[4] Letter, July 14, 1941, from Hitler to the staffs of army, navy and air force, C-074, *IMT*, Vol. XXXIV, p. 299.

[5] *Minutes of the conference of the Commander-in-Chief, Navy, with the Führer*, July 8, 1943, *Führer Conferences*, Vol. *1943*, p. 54.

[6] *KTB-Abwehr*, April 25, 1940.   [7] *Ibid.*, June 4, 1940.

military aid to England in ever increasing measure, fresh sabotage plans were set on foot and this time carried out as well. Whether this was done with Hitler's consent is not known. A certain Rekowski, a German agent who posed as a merchant and who happened to be in Mexico at the time, had got in touch with a group of Irish extremists in the United States.[1] His instructions were to have acts of sabotage committed 'in munitions factories and aboard ships '.[2] The embargo on operations in the United States itself remained in force. German agents like Rekowski had to make their preparations in Canada or Mexico,[3] and, as we have already said, Rekowski chose the latter country as his base. He was able to inform Berlin that he had blown up a few ships by means of high connections he had and that he had set fire to a rubber dump near Cleveland, Ohio.[4] In Mexico he was supposed to have set up real sabotage depots.[5] Rekowski was not trusted in Berlin, however; at the offices of the *Abwehr* people had the impression that his 'successes' grew largely out of his efforts to get as much money out of the *Abwehr* as he could.[6] Moreover, late in April he got into trouble in Mexico, Mexican and American authorities were on his track and he fled the country. A certain Carlos Vogt, a German by birth who had been naturalised in Mexico in 1934 succeeded him.[7]

Meanwhile the telegrams that arrived at the *Auswärtige Amt* about the Rekowski affair had alarmed Ribbentrop. Fearing that continued sabotage would bring America to the verge of war, he requested the head of the *Abwehr*, Admiral Canaris, to end that form of activity. The latter, if we are to believe his fellow-worker and biographer Abshagen, entered into this request with alacrity; if party fanatics were to reproach him in the future that he had left the United States too much in peace, then he would be able to refer to the arguments which the minister of Foreign Affairs had himself employed.[8]

When America entered the war Hitler demanded the renewal of acts of sabotage. In January, 1942, Canaris received instructions to cripple American aluminium production. There was no longer a German sabotage organisation in the United States, so agents were to be sent from Germany. Canaris and the head of the sabotage department of the *Abwehr*, Lahousen, had small faith in the undertaking but were not able to countermand Hitler's instructions. The

---

[1] *Ibid.*, Sept. 5, 1940.
[2] Telegram, April 23, 1941, from the German legation, Mexico City, to the *Auswärtige Amt*, NG-4398.   [3] *KTB-Abwer*, Sept. 20, 1940.
[4] Witness Kurt Haller, Proceedings of the trial against Weizsäcker, *et al.*, pp. 20,432–42.
[5] *KTB-Abwehr*, Jan. 14, 1941.   [6] Abshagen: *Canaris*, pp. 278–9.
[7] Telegram, May 2, 1941, from 'Richard' [Rekowski] to Haller, NG-4398.
[8] Abshagen: *Canaris*, p. 280.

order was given to examine the indexes of the *Amerikadeutschen* at the *Deutsche Ausland-Institut* in Stuttgart as well as the maps and photographs of American factories, railways, canals and harbours filed there; moreover, agents had to be found. The last problem was solved when an officer of the *Abwehr*, Walter Kappe, who had for long lived in America where he had played a prominent part in the German-American *Bund* and its precursors, came and said that a number of members of the *Bund* who had returned to Germany were prepared to undertake the venture. Admiral Doenitz was willing to furnish submarines for this purpose so that the saboteurs could be put ashore on America's east coast.[1]

Nine volunteers were given very thorough training. Late in May, 1942, eight of them set out from Bordeaux. They were divided into two groups, one of which was to land on Long Island and the other in Florida. One of the members of the Long Island group, a one-time socialist, had only taken part in the proceedings with the idea in mind of warning the authorities as soon as he set foot in the United States. This intention he carried out. Within two weeks all the saboteurs were clapped under lock and key. All but two (who were sentenced to lengthy terms of imprisonment) lost their lives in the electric chair, dragging along in their downfall some dozen relatives and friends with whom they had got into touch.[2]

This was 'the only effort in the way of active sabotage the *Amt Ausland-Abwehr* undertook after the outbreak of war in the United States '.[3] 'It was the biggest failure', sighed General Lahousen after the war, 'that ever occurred in my section.'

Regarding German espionage in the United States we earlier mentioned the fact that in 1938 the espionage organisation of Dr. Ignaz T. Griebl (who had especially aimed at collecting data about the American navy) was put out of action. It is probable that the *Abwehr* continued to collect information regarding the navy. Particulars are lacking.

As regards the American air force, we know that the head of the air section of the *Abwehrstelle* Hamburg, Nikolaus Ritter, who had been employed as an engineer in America for a long time, had started building up a network of agents in the United States in 1937. The *Auswärtige Amt* had forbidden any form of espionage, but Admiral Canaris yielded to the pressure brought to bear on him by the general staff of the *Luftwaffe*. Ritter first sent 'investigators' to

[1] General Lahousen, quoted in: *Der Stern* (Hamburg), VI, 12 (March 22, 1953), pp. 12–14.
[2] Jürgen Thorwald: *Der Fall Pastorius* (Stuttgart, 1953).
[3] Abshagen: *Canaris*, p. 283.

America; 'they were ordinary travellers who, without any special espionage instructions, had to find out where people were to be found with whom I might work up connections'. Late in 1937 Ritter visited America personally. He acquired drawings there, among others, from a German workman in the Norden factory who wanted to render his country a service. They were drawings of the secret Norden bomb-sight.[1]

A certain William G. Sebold was roped into Ritter's network of agents in 1939. Sebold, a technician of the Consolidated Aircraft Corporation in San Diego, California, was staying in Germany on a holiday. The *Abwehr* got into touch with him. He declared himself willing to act as agent but at the same time warned the American consul in Cologne. The Federal Bureau of Investigation requested him via the consul to pretend to accept all the instructions the Germans would give him. Sebold was trained as an agent in Hamburg and afterwards travelled back to America. He was to install a secret transmitter on Long Island, and from the day he started operating, this transmitter was worked by functionaries of the FBI. This was not known in Germany where they neglected to notice whether the transmitting was done in Sebold's code 'handwriting' or not. All the callers at Sebold's office were photographed, from a room next door to his. Every word they spoke was recorded. Among the callers was Ritter's liaison man, who had been able to get through the British blockade in the guise of a butcher on board the American passenger ship *America*. Sebold was the only German agent who was in radio contact with Germany. As a result, the central figures of all the other German espionage systems in America were instructed to get in touch with him for transmitting their reports.[2]

All of them were arrested by the FBI during the last four days of June, 1941.

The *Auswärtige Amt* protested energetically, and the *Abwehr* recalled its 'only non-arrested agent' from the United States. A few communications reached Germany from Canada and Mexico 'but signified next to nothing'.[3] Two agents were employed in Mexico. The one who palmed himself off as a merchant worked for Japan at the same time. The other, a 'bank clerk', had been seen drinking himself under the table in a café that was under observation by American counter-espionage agents.[4]

[1] Nikolaus Ritter, quoted in: *Der Stern* (Hamburg), VI, 11 (March 15, 1953), pp. 11–12.
[2] *Ibid.*,p.16.
[3] General Lahousen, quoted *ibid.*, 12 (March 22, 1953), p. 12.
[4] Telegram, April 23, 1941, from the German legation, Mexico City, to the *Auswärtige Amt*, NG-4398.

The *Sicherheitsdienst* also had espionage agents in the United States.[1] In 1941 a few of them called in the help of the German consulate in Los Angeles. One of them who was instructed to return to Germany preferred to leave for Mexico with a girl friend. He 'spoke poor English and had not the slightest notion about general conditions in Los Angeles'. The German consulate was able to collect better data! The German air attaché in Washington received daily what was to be found about American re-armament in the Californian press. And from 1941 onwards an official from the consulate came to have a look at the aircraft factories in question twice a week, to see how many specimens of each type of airplane were in construction. This could easily be observed from the public highway. Similar data were collected for the naval attaché in Washington, although he was also furnished with one agent in Southern California, according to a notation of the *Auswärtige Amt* on November 4, 1941.[2]

A month later the United States was at war.

There is no data about German war-time espionage. Not a trace is to be found about it in the published German documents. It does not seem likely that it was very extensive, let alone that the German espionage system was 'probably the best organised, the best financed, the most ingenious and most efficient that the world has ever seen', as one of the New York newspapers wrote early in 1942.

Our impression that German espionage in America was relatively insignificant tallies with what we know about the measure in which national socialism found a response among the *Reichsdeutschen* living in the United States and among the persons of German origin.

The number of *Reichsdeutsche* before the war is not known. At the *Auswärtige Amt* in Berlin they did not know whether they numbered 100,000 or 200,000.[3] During the war the Americans put the figure at 264,000.[4]

The uncertainty regarding the number of American citizens of German origin was never removed. In Germany people revelled in calculations to the effect that German blood flowed exclusively or largely in the veins of a few dozen million Americans. Estimates of 25 million were not uncommon.[5]

[1] Telex message, July 11, 1941, from Sonnleithner to *Legationsrat* Kramarz, PS-4053, *IMT*, Vol. XXXIV, p. 114.

[2] PS-4054, *ibid.*, pp. 115–16.

[3] Memorandum, Nov. 20, 1939, of Wörmann, *Doc. Ger. For. Pol.*, D, Vol. IV (Washington, 1951), p. 646.

[4] Ernest Puttkammer: *Alien Enemies and Alien Friends in the United States* (Chicago, 1943), p. 15.

[5] See for instance Hugo Grothe: *Die Deutschen in Übersee* (Berlin, 1930), map 1.

The vital question as to how many of them had any inner tie with Germany was made light of by German chauvinism. When that question was posed much lower figures were at once the result. The number of German-Americans, 'who still really speak German, read and write German, think in German, and are fully cognizant of their German origin', was estimated at 4 or 5 million at most by the German ambassador, Dieckhoff, in 1938.[1] A German writer, H. Kloss, who had crossed the United States, estimated a figure of about 2 million.[2] Only a few per cent of them were interested in such organisations as the German-American *Bund*. In 1938, for instance, roughly 700,000 persons of German origin lived in Chicago. 40,000 of them were members of some German association. Only 450 had joined the *Bund*.[3] The U.S. Department of Justice estimated the number of members of the *Bund* in 1938, taking the country as a whole, at 6500.[4] The highest estimate of sympathisers came to well over 90,000.[5] In 1942 about 7000 members and followers of the *Bund* were considered dangerous to the state and were interned. Within a year, half their number were set at liberty again on the basis of further investigations.[6]

It would be going too far to contend that the *Bund* did not constitute any potential danger at all. Here it is only important to record that it was never able to develop into an active Fifth Column of any importance. In this connection the fact deserves mention that, just as in England, the refugees from Germany with very few exceptions distinguished themselves in the United States by their absolute loyalty,[7] and that co-operation between the Third *Reich* and the American isolationists was 'very limited', as appeared from German documents.[8]

From the figures and facts mentioned in this chapter the conclusion

[1] Letter, Jan. 7, 1938, from ambassador Dieckhoff to the *Auswärtige Amt*, *Doc. Ger. For. Pol.*, D, Vol. I (Washington, 1949), p. 667.
[2] H. Kloss: 'Gegenwart und Zukunft des Deutschtums der Vereinigten Staaten', *Deutschtum im Ausland* (Stuttgart), 1938, p. 490.
[3] Letter, Jan. 7, 1938, from ambassador Dieckhoff to the *Auswärtige Amt*, *Doc. Ger. For. Pol.*, D, Vol. I, p. 670.
[4] *Investigation of Un-American activities and propaganda (76th Congress, 1st session, House of Representatives, House Report No. 2)* (Washington, 1939), p. 92. In future to be quoted as: Dies report 1939.
[5] *Investigation of Un-American propaganda activities in the United States (76th Congress, 3rd session, House of Representatives, House Report No. 1476)* (Washington, 1940), *Appendix, Vol. IV: German-American Bund* (Washington, 1941), p. 1446. In future to be quoted as: Dies report 1940.   [6] See p. 119.
[7] George L. Warren: 'The Refugee and the War', *Annals of the American Academy of Political and Social Sciences* (Philadelphia), Sept. 1942, p. 96.
[8] H. L. Trefousse: *Germany and American Neutrality 1939–1941* (New York, 1951), p. 133.

may be drawn that national socialist Germany did not succeed in launching Fifth Column activities on any very great scale in Britain and the United States.

This conclusion gains emphasis from the fact that all through the war the German military leaders were very badly posted on the operations of the Allies. In the western countries, however, people had been so convinced of the excellence of German espionage that after Germany's capitulation they perceived almost with a shock how greatly they had over-estimated the *Abwehr* and the *Sicherheitsdienst*. But the German documents and the German military men told the same tale: Hitler and his generals had on the whole remained in ignorance of decisions taken in Washington and London.

Continually perturbed by incorrect messages that British and American troops were going to land in the South of France or Norway or in Holland or Denmark, they were again and again taken by surprise by the *real* landing operations. The convoys which were on their way to Morocco and Algiers at the end of October and the beginning of November, 1942, were thought by the *Abwehr* to be going to Malta.[1] The landings in North Africa came 'as a complete surprise' to the leaders of the Third *Reich*.[2] In May, 1943, Hitler and his military assistants had been made by skilful British forgeries to think that, now that Tunisia was conquered, Sardinia and the Peloponnesus had become the target of the next Allied attack.[3] Actually it was directed against Sicily. In Berlin, Goebbels heard of Italy's capitulation (September 8, 1943) over the British wireless,[4] and four months later the Allied landing at Anzio to the south of Rome came 'as a great surprise to us', in the words of the chief of staff of Air Marshal Kesselring.[5]

Just as surprising to the Germans were the landings of the Allies in Normandy (June 6, 1944). 'We were completely blind', General Blumentritt admitted; 'we had no proper insight as to what happened in England, what the situation was there, where the ports for shipping the troops were.' Blumentritt, it is true, had seen photos of landing manœuvres in England as well as blueprints and pictures of new landing-craft, but not a single piece of news had reached the Germans about the building of the artificial harbours which the Allies used to such striking effect. When the landings were to take place was unknown to them. 'We knew every week that it might start any

[1] Colvin: *Chief of Intelligence*, p. 157.
[2] Witness General Walter Warlimont, Proceedings of the trial against the German generals, p. 6403.
[3] Ewen Montagu: *The Man who never was* (London, 1953).
[4] *The Goebbels Diaries*, p. 342.
[5] Witness General Siegfried Westphal, Proceedings of the trial against the German generals, p. 8866.

day, but the very night when it happened—that was a certain surprise.' [1]

No wonder that the *Führer* repeatedly expressed his displeasure that, regarding the intentions of his western opponents and the balance of parties in their internal politics, he was utterly in the dark. 'We have an organisation that goes by the name of *Auswärtige Amt*', he said bitterly late in October, 1941, 'one of whose functions it is to keep us posted as to what happens abroad—and we do not know a thing. We are divided from England by a ditch 37 kilometres wide and we are not even able to get to know what is happening there!' [2] Four months later he sighed that he would like to have more data about the anti-Churchill opposition in England: 'well then, what I know about it I have had to gather from the newspapers!' [3] It should be admitted that on certain occasions the Germans *were* able to get hold of important information, as a rule through treachery on the part of malcontents in the camps of their opponents. We should like to recall the case of Tyler Kent, and similarly the notorious Operation Cicero—the treachery committed by the Albanian valet of the British ambassador in Ankara.[4] It is immaterial here that in those cases where the facts were thrown into the Germans' laps, they made hardly any or no proper use of them. Suffice it to say that what has become known about German espionage in Britain and America —the same holds good for the few attempts at sabotage—clashes with the view that there was a powerful and active military Fifth Column in these two countries during the war.

This brings us to South America.

There is not one single indication that Hitler ever entertained concrete plans for a military attack on South America, let alone that he had worked them out. His concrete plans—and even they could not be realised—went no further than the Azores. Only with his submarines did he attack such countries as Brazil, after August, 1942, because it had ranged itself on the side of his enemies.[5] As far as is known, no evidence has appeared out of any of the German archives to show that a German minority prepared themselves for a *coup*, either independently or with the support of the Third *Reich*, in any of the South or Central American states. It is probable that Hitler, if he had been able to subdue the Soviet Union and Britain, would have stimulated such attempts.

[1] Witness General Günther Blumentritt, *ibid.*, p. 8851–2.
[2] *Adolf Hitler. Libres propos sur la guerre et la paix*, p. 100 (Oct. 30, 1941).
[3] *Ibid.*, p. 270 (Feb. 2, 1942).
[4] L. C. Moyzisch: *Operation Cicero* (London [1950]).
[5] *Führer Conferences*, Vol. 1942, pp. 45–6.

Thus it is necessary, in the case of Uruguay, to remark that there are no indications that the people there were rightly anxious about the safety of their republic in May and June, 1940. About 8000 *Reichsdeutsche* lived there. How many of them were members of the *Auslands-Organisation der NSDAP* is not known. If the ratio in Uruguay was similar to that in the Argentine, Brazil and Chile there were not more than a few hundred. The document in which Gero Arnulf Fuhrmann unfolded his plan for the military occupation of the whole of Uruguay and for transforming it into an agricultural colony (to which the Germans who had set up colonies in Brazil were also to be brought) [1] may be looked upon as a sign of the aggressive disposition of its slightly pathological author, *not* as proof of a real conspiracy. Fuhrmann was not a Nazi of long standing; not until 1937 had he become a member of the NSDAP. [2] Of the only other two documents 'used by Germany's "Fifth Column" in Uruguay', published in June, 1940, [3] one was a receipt dated January 28, 1939, of a donation to the *Winterhilfswerk* 1938–9, for the sum of half a dollar, and the other a receipt for a membership subscription paid in April, 1939, to the German *Arbeitsfront*, for the sum of one dollar and ten cents.

But this is not the whole story.

It does not seem unlikely that some of the *Reichsdeutschen* living in Uruguay *did* eagerly look forward to the day on which they might venture to grasp at supreme power. The *Auslands-Organisation* in general cultivated an aggressive mentality whereby para-military drill was given in sports clubs and glider clubs. Associations and clubs of a like nature also existed in Uruguay. Without further evidence, however, one should not deduce from that fact that a *coup d'état* was in prospect in May and June, 1940. That evidence is lacking. [4] What the Uruguayan parliamentary committee reported regarding the matter is not convincing.

It is typical of the limited insight the committee had into the true structure of the *Auslands-Organisation der NSDAP* that they gave the impression that the national socialists outside Germany formed a mysterious Free Masons' Lodge organised under three 'castles'. [5]

[1] See pp. 112–3.

[2] Information based on the register of members of the NSDAP supplied by the *US 7771 Document Center*, Berlin.

[3] Facsimile in the *New York Times*, June 19, 1940.

[4] It should be noted that nothing appeared of any such Fifth Column activity in the Netherlands in spite of the news report (*New York Times*, June 6, 1940) that in Montevideo a *reichsdeutsche* cartographer was arrested who had not only a map of this city on which military details had been marked, but who proved to be in possession of a map of Holland as well, showing how the Fifth Column there had prepared artillery positions beforehand for shelling strategic objectives.

[5] See p. 115.

It further seems of importance that in all the reports of the house-to-house searches in the neighbourhood of Montevideo, only three German gliders were found, together with one parachute, and one dismantled radio transmitter.[1] Besides this, the authority who was best informed as to the goings-on of the *Reichsdeutschen* and other Nazis—i.e. the chief of the security police—emphatically denied the existence of any acute internal danger.[2] And finally the *reichsdeutschen* Nazis who had been arrested in the middle of June 'amidst tremendous popular excitement' were set at liberty again a few weeks later.[3] It does not seem likely that this would have happened if the authorities had got on to the track of a genuine conspiracy.[4]

As has already been said, there is no convincing proof that *Reichsdeutsche* or German immigrants had made preparations for getting into power in any other republic of South or Central America during the second World War. There was spying on behalf of Germany and against England and America in various states, it is true, and a great deal of intrigue went on. Other acts were performed by Germans that were hardly consistent with the obligations arising out of the hospitality and citizenship that had been granted them.

In Brazil they secretly collected data about Allied shipping. It seems probable that it was also from this country that messages were sent on various occasions to German submarines operating in the southern part of the Atlantic Ocean.[5] Functionaries of the *Auslands-Organisation* saw to it that officers of the *Graf Spee* who had been interned in Uruguay but who had managed to escape were furnished with false passports in Rio de Janeiro.[6]

In the Argentine, in spite of all the prohibitions to the contrary, the *Landesgruppe* of the *Auslands-Organisation* continued its work. The *Abwehr* and *Sicherheitsdienst* carried out a considerable amount of espionage. This was connected with the fact that German agents who had found things too hot for them in other parts of South America had drifted to the Argentine. The Germans had secret transmitters there, and part of the news was sent to Germany via Spain. Military, political and economic intelligence was collected,

[1] See pp. 115–16.   [2] See p. 116.
[3] Langer and Gleason: *The Challenge to Isolation 1937–1940*, pp. 613–14.
[4] I have addressed the question whether they knew of any evidence other than that published in 1940 which might throw light on the 'conspiracy' in Uruguay both to the then American ambassador in Montevideo, Edwin C. Wilson, and to the publicist Prof. Hugo Fernandez Artucio, author of 'The Nazi Octopus in South America'. It appeared from Mr. Wilson's answer that this was not the case. Prof. Fernandez Artucio did not reply.
[5] *New York Times*, June 27, 1940. Samuel Guy Inman: *Latin America. Its Place in World Life* (New York, 1942), p. 217.
[6] Telegram, Sept. 24, 1940, from the German embassy, Rio de Janeiro, to the *Auswärtige Amt*, NG-2244.

for instance 'through listening in to the broadcasts from the countries at war, through an analysis of the American press (newspapers, illustrated technical magazines and trade journals), through personal observation and through espionage in the United States embassy'.[1] Further, various Argentine papers were heavily subsidised by the German embassy partly with funds put at its disposal by German firms working in the Argentine.[2] And finally a few Germans tried systematically to reinforce the anti-American forces in the Argentine government. In the summer of 1943 they organised a camouflaged petition for peace in favour of the Axis,[3] and they tried to get President Castillo to ally himself with Germany and Italy and to extend the Argentine territory at the expense of republics working in close co-operation with the United States. Castillo asked for German arms. Berlin could not spare them, and nothing came of the co-operation. Moreover, in the autumn of 1943 the German intermediary, an agent of Himmler's *Sicherheitsdienst*, was arrested and interned by the Allies.[4] Ribbentrop had protested fiercely against these and similar practices of the *Sicherheitsdienst*, but without success.[5]

In Chile too, according to the then German Minister, there existed a German espionage organisation, for which purpose members of the *Auslands-Organisation* had been roped in. The Minister was not allowed to know anything of all this.[6] As a matter of fact he himself was often the object of this espionage.[7] He was convinced that the *Auslands-Organisation* in Chile had been guilty of 'incredible foolishness', but considered it most unlikely that *reichsdeutsche* Nazis or Chileans had ever thought of undertaking a *coup d'état*.[8]

It is not impossible that the *Abwehr* made use of the operations of German airlines to make aerial photos of certain objectives in a few other Latin American states. Documentary evidence is lacking. The scale on which this happened has probably been over-estimated. It was reported from Columbia, a few Central American states and Mexico that airfields or flat territory were already being prepared for the use of the Germans in the case of landing operations.[9] There is no evidence to prove that this was indeed so. It is a fact, however, that the *Abwehr* did succeed in setting up two organisations in the

[1] Undated report of the Argentine police. Annex to the letter of the American embassy, Buenos Aires, of Feb. 21, 1944 to the Department of State, NI-10922.
[2] *Consultation among the American Republics with respect to the Argentine situation. Memorandum of the United States Government (Department of State)* (Washington, 1946), pp. 36-7, 49, 51. In future to be quoted as: *Consultation.*
[3] *Ibid.*, p. 35.   [4] *Ibid.*, pp. 6-7.   [5] *Ibid.*, p. 16.
[6] Affidavit of Wilhelm von Schoen, NG-3402.
[7] Witness von Schoen, Proceedings of the trial against Weizsäcker *et al.* p. 3212.
[8] *Ibid.*, p. 3204.   [9] See pp. 117-18,

south of South America which were to pave the way for acts of sabotage. British ships and vessels sailing for the British would probably form the chief objectives. One of those organisations had its centre in Valparaiso, Chile, and the other in Rio de Janeiro, Brazil.[1] In August, 1940, the German instructions were still not to irritate South America. On the 13th of that month Canaris ordered that in the field of sabotage 'nothing was to be undertaken in South America or with South America as base'.[2] It is not certain that, later, other instructions were issued and carried out, especially in 1942 and the years following, but this seems plausible.

In contrast to what Germany's opponents took for granted before. and during the war, the influence of national socialism in Central and South America on the *Reichsdeutschen* living there and on the citizens who were of German origin was relatively small in most of the republics. The anti-German press often paraded figures for membership that ran into the tens of thousands—'43,626 Nazis' in the Argentine alone, '30,000' in Buenos Aires of whom 20,000 were said to belong to the Stormtroops. In the autumn of 1941 Congressman Martin Dies spoke of 'about one million potential soldiers organised in companies and battalions', on whom the Third *Reich* would be able to count in South America.

It is not easy to reduce these figures to their true proportions. Our data are incomplete. If one wishes to express the influence of national socialism in figures, then one of the first difficulties is that the statistical returns usually give widely different answers to the question of how many people of German origin lived in a given state.

For the Argentine the estimates vary for the number of *Volksdeutsche* from 80,000 to 240,000.[3] The number of *Reichsdeutsche* was estimated at 50,000 by the then German ambassador.[4] 2000 of these were members of the NSDAP.[5] As a rule less than 2000 people took part in the national socialist demonstrations,[6] on one occasion (May 1, 1934) over 12,000,[7] and two years later about 16,000.[8] The membership roll of the trade union of the *Auslands-Organisation* was listed as 11,000 by the Taborda committee in 1941,[9] taking the

[1] *KTB-Abwehr*, Feb. 10, June 10 and 17, Nov. 23, 1940.

[2] *Ibid.*, Aug. 13, 1940.

[3] *HWB*, Vol. I, p. 125.

[4] Affidavit, Oct. 22, 1947, of Edmund *Freiherr* von Thermann.

[5] *Ibid.*

[6] *Der Auslandsdeutsche*, 1938, p. 37.

[7] Dr. Wilhelm Lütge: 'Deutsche Kulturarbeit in Argentinien'. *Wir Deutsche in der Welt, 1935* (Berlin, 1934), p. 119.

[8] See p. 28.

[9] *The Times* (London), Nov. 26, 1941.

Reichsdeutschen and *Volksdeutschen* together. National socialist elements had made themselves masters of the *Deutscher Volksbund für Argentinien* (German People's League for the Argentine) that had been founded in 1916, for the purpose of roping in these 80,000 to 240,000 *Volksdeutschen*. They used it for spreading Nazi propaganda among persons of German origin, who were to be found throughout the country. Local groups were founded and they published their own periodical. At the end of the twenties the *Volksbund* had numbered almost 5000 members,[1] in 1935 nearly 2800,[2] and in 1938 under 4000.[3]

In Brazil, of the 80,000 *Reichsdeutschen* about 1700 were members of the NSDAP.[4] The *Verband Deutscher Vereine* (Union of German Associations), which counted *Reichsdeutsche* and *Volksdeutsche* among its members, had about 15,000 members in all in 1935.[5] The total number of *Volksdeutsche* was usually estimated at 600,000.

In Chile there lived round about 7000 *Reichsdeutsche* during the war. The number of Chilean citizens of German origin was estimated at from 15,000 to 50,000. The then German Minister believed that 30,000 was a reliable figure. About 600 of the *Reichsdeutschen* were members of the NSDAP.[6] In 1940 2600 of the 30,000 *Deutsch-Chilenen* had joined the *Deutsch-Chilenische Bund* (German-Chilean League), comparable to the *Deutsche Volksbund für Argentinien*.[7]

In Paraguay where there lived approximately 9000 persons of German origin,[8] 1700 were members of the *Deutsche Volksbund für Paraguay* in 1937.[9]

These figures show that as a rule only a small minority of the *Reichsdeutschen* in the South American states were members of the NSDAP, and that of the large groups of *Volksdeutsche* only a small minority had joined the national socialist organisations. (Argentine 1¾ per cent to 5 per cent., Brazil 2½ per cent at the most, Chile 9 per cent.) The German 'Fifth Column' in South America consisted of relatively small groups and individuals, who, in order to gain success for their toiling and moiling, were very much more dependent on the international and national contrasts in that part of the world than on the support and sympathy that came to them from the circles

[1] Otto Boelitz: *Das Grenz- und Auslanddeutschtum. Seine Geschichte und seine Bedeutung* (Munich, 1930), p. 228.
[2] *Der Auslandsdeutsche*, 1936, p. 860.
[3] *Deutschtum im Ausland*, 1938, p. 605.
[4] Affidavit of Hans Harnisch, NG-2548.
[5] *Das Braune Netz*, p. 297.
[6] Witness von Schoen, Proceedings of the trial against Weizsäcker *et al.*, p. 3203.
[7] *Deutschtum im Ausland*, 1941, p. 134.
[8] Grothe: *Die Deutschen in Übersee*, map 1.
[9] *Der Auslandsdeutsche*, 1938, p. 39.

of the *Reichsdeutschen* and *Volksdeutschen*. This could be most clearly observed in the Argentine where during the war the German diplomatic representatives and the agents of the *Abwehr* and *Sicherheitsdienst* were able to make use of the envy felt towards the United States and the fear for Brazil, both of which impulses played an important part in Argentine government circles. It does not appear from the documents published so far that they succeeded in interesting the large 'German' minority in the Argentine in their aims. The Third *Reich* got no more organisational hold on the large mass of the hundreds of thousands of 'Germans' living in South America than on the few million living in the United States.

CHAPTER XIII

Yugoslavia, Greece, the Soviet Union

★

Yugoslavia

IN 1945, it was contended by the Yugoslavs, that when Hitler visited Graz in the middle of March, 1938, a few of the leading figures in the *Kulturbund* (Cultural League), an organization of *Volksdeutsche* in Slovenia, had been to see him and had proposed to deport the whole Slovene population from Slovenia in case of war between Germany and Yugoslavia.[1] The document pertaining to this meeting, belonging to the Gestapo archives in Breslau, has never been published.

The statement is not improbable; at least it is in accordance with a letter dated August, 1941, from the *Steierischer Heimatbund*, an organisation of *Volksdeutsche* founded soon after the occupation of Slovenia. In this letter it is reported that deportations of Slovenes from the territory in question, which began soon after the entry of the Germans, mainly took place with the help of 'lists of names, compiled long before the occupation, by *volksdeutsche* agents and other confidential sources in Lower Styria, on the basis of years of observation and political experience.'[2] Part of those lists were kept up to date by the *Südostdeutsche Institut* at Graz. After the war lists were found there, dating from the years 1938–41, on which notes were to be found after the Slovene names, as for instance: 'must be immediately arrested', 'enemy to Germany', 'must be watched'.[3] In Graz and Klagenfurt there furthermore existed so-called *Gaugrenzland-ämter* (Frontier District offices), which among other things saw to

---

[1] Abstract of the report of the official Yugoslav War Crimes Commission, NG-4557.
[2] Quoted in: *Report on the crimes of Austria and the Austrians against Yugoslavia and her peoples* (Belgrade, 1947), p. 21.
[3] *Ibid.*, p. 16.

the collection of data with the help of *Volksdeutsche* living in Yugoslavia. The *Reichssicherheitshauptamt*, Berlin, received from Graz a list with the names and addresses of about 4000 Yugoslav citizens who were to be arrested at once in case of a German occupation.[1] Besides this, taking Graz as their centre, the *Sicherheitsdienst* kept in touch with Croatian fascists, the so-called Ustashi movement of Ante Pavelitch.[2]

Seeing all this, there is sufficient reason to suppose that the compilation of lists with the names of Slovenes who were to be deported, did indeed start in 1938. The year 1939 witnessed the beginning of a second new development. Young *Volksdeutsche*, who had received their summons to serve in the Yugoslav army, slipped across the frontier and reported themselves as volunteers 'for various units in the German *Wehrmacht*'.[3] Neither in 1939 nor in 1940 was the *Wehrmacht* any too eager to have those foreign volunteers; so many special regulations had to be made for them, and the *Wehrmacht* had soldiers enough.

Not so the SS! In the course of 1940, Himmler, the *Reichsführer-SS*, and his closest fellow-workers, decided to set up their own army by the side of the *Wehrmacht*: the *Waffen-SS*, which very well knew how to use those foreign volunteers, who only met with opposition at the hands of the district offices of the *Wehrmacht* in Germany. In the autumn of 1940 'a whole party of volunteers' left by stealth for the *Waffen-SS* and for the *Leibstandarte-SS 'Adolf Hitler'*.[4] Among them were youthful *Volksdeutsche* who had to join up for service in the Yugoslav army in 1941.

Besides the SS agencies, the *Abwehr* had also been active in Yugoslavia in 1939 and the first half of 1940. In the spring of 1940 a secret organisation was set up which was to protect the Danube shipping, so vital for Germany in case of war. As a cover, the organiser, Major Friedrich, was given the position of an employee in the German consulate in Zagreb.[5] In March, 1940, the *Abwehr* officer posted in Belgrade took a hundred revolvers with him 'as the sealed luggage of a courier in his own car'. Those weapons were to be used for the 'protection of transport' in time of need.[6] Late in May representatives of the *volksdeutschen* organisations, fearing that a war would be accompanied by bloody excesses, requested Berlin via the *Abwehr* to

---

[1] *Ibid.*, p. 19. The original of this list has been submitted to the International Military Tribunal, Nuremberg. The document, as far as is known, has not been published.

[2] *Ibid.*, p. 20.

[3] *Deutschtum im Ausland*, 1944, p. 33.

[4] *Ibid.*

[5] *KTB-Abwehr*, Dec. 28, 1939, Feb. 29, 1940.   [6] *Ibid.*, March 13, 1940.

supply them with arms. In view of the political situation at that moment this request was not complied with.[1]

In the autumn of 1940 and the winter of 1940–41 increasing pressure was brought to bear by Germany on Yugoslavia for more close political co-operation, for instance by entry into the anti-Comintern Pact. Tension rose. In December, 1940, and January, 1941, the *Volksdeutschen* proceeded to form para-military organisations modelled after the SA, in order to protect their villages in case of a conflict.[2]

The end of March brought on the crisis.

On the 25th of that month Prince Regent Paul and his cabinet in Vienna signed the treaty whereby Yugoslavia joined the Berlin-Rome-Tokyo Axis. Two days later, in the early morning of the 27th, the Prince Regent *and* his cabinet were overthrown.

Hitler was furious.

That same day he called together his chief political and military advisers and informed them that, without waiting for possible declarations of loyalty on the part of the Simovitch government, he had decided 'to make all the necessary preparations for annihilating Yugoslavia for what it was worth in a military sense and as a political entity', all this 'with relentless severity', and 'in a lightning operation'.[3]

More than five months previously, in the middle of October, the chief planner in the *Oberkommando des Heeres*, General Halder had received instructions to work out an offensive against Yugoslavia.[4] After that, however, German military ideas had taken a quite different turn: all their preparations were concentrated on the invasion of the Soviet Union that was to be preceded by a swift attack on Greece via Bulgaria. Since October, 1940, Mussolini had tried in vain to overpower Greece; he would have to be given help. For Yugoslavia nothing was ready yet. There were not even enough military maps and there was no plan of operation. On March 27, 1941, Halder outlined an improvised plan in the *Reichskanzlei*, for entering Yugoslavia from Austria and Bulgaria, thus getting the Yugoslav army on both flanks. Hitler approved the plan,[5] but all the movements flowing from this plan (the concentration of troops in Austria, Hungary and Bulgaria) had to be 'completely improvised', as General Keitel said.[6] It was also hampered by

---

[1] *KTB-Abwehr*, May 30, 1940.

[2] Telegram, Jan. 15, 1941, from Heeren, the German Minister, to *Staatssekretär* Weizsäcker, NG-3375.

[3] Report, March 27, 1941, *Besprechung über Lage Jugoslawien*, PS-1746, *IMT*, Vol. XXVIII, pp. 21–3.

[4] Halder: *Diary*, Oct. 18, 1940.

[5] Peter Bor: *Gespräche mit Halder* (Wiesbaden, 1950), p. 180.

[6] Witness Keitel, Proceedings *IMT*, Vol. X, p. 524.

the fact that the knowledge the German military had been able to collect about the Yugoslav army was incomplete. They had no clear notion of the mobilisation plans and greatly over-estimated the army's numerical strength.[1]

In Croatia things had remained quiet on March 27. The Croatian members of the government were advocates of a settlement with Hitler. In their view there was no point in resisting Germany. That was also the opinion of Dr. Matchek, the Croatian peasant leader. A *Reichsdeutscher*, a certain Dorffler, had a talk with him on March 28, 1941. What did Germany think, Dr. Matchek asked, of a Croatian movement of independence? Might he hope for support? Dorffler was unable to answer him, but travelled by train to Vienna and from there flew to Berlin, where he arrived in the evening of the 29th. That same evening he received the news via an official of the *Auswärtige Amt*: 'There were no instructions for his friend.' This he had to report to Dr. Matchek, adding, however, that he thought there were further communications coming. Dr. Matchek, who realised that Germany only wanted to keep him on tenterhooks, had 'a complete breakdown' on hearing the negative answer. After all, he could not launch a rebellion with only his weak bodyguard, for which Germany had in the past refused to deliver weapons! Moreover, Belgrade had just started to occupy Croatia with reliable Serbian troops.[2]

In this way the Germans missed the chance of setting loose a rebellion in Croatia. They tried to keep a hold on Dr. Matchek. Both Rosenberg and Ribbentrop sent special envoys, Malletke and Veesenmeyer, to Yugoslavia on April 1 in order to try to persuade Dr. Matchek, in co-operation with the German consul at Zagreb, not to work together with the Simovitch government.[3] Dr. Matchek turned a deaf ear to Malletke's arguments,[4] travelled to Belgrade and called on the Croatian reservists to obey the order for mobilisation.[5]

But Germany proved to have more strings to her bow. Veesenmeyer immediately got into touch with Pavelitch.[6] In consultation

---

[1] Helmuth Greiner: *Die Oberste Wehrmachtführung 1939–1943* (Wiesbaden, 1951), p. 278.

[2] Report (undated) from *Parteigenosse* Malletke concerning his journey to Zagreb. Appended to Rosenberg's report, April 23, 1941, to the *Chef der Reichskanzlei*, Dr. Lammers, NG-2449.

[3] Telegram, April 1, 1941, from the *Auswärtige Amt* to the German consulate, Zagreb, NG-2360. Telegram April 1, 1941, from the *Auswärtige Amt* to the German legation, Belgrade, NG-3260.

[4] Report Malletke, NG-2449.

[5] Constantin Fotitch: *The War We Lost* (New York, 1948), p. 98.

[6] *KTB-Abwehr*, April 6, 1941.

with him the independence of Croatia was to be proclaimed after the German attack had started.[1]

Meanwhile Ribbentrop gave the order 'to organise cries for help in Yugoslavia, which were to come from the *Volksdeutschen*, the Croats, the Macedonians and the Slovenes'. This was to happen without the knowledge of the *Sicherheitsdienst* as well as of the *Volksdeutsche Mittelstelle*, although the last-mentioned bureau had 'offered to organise those cries for help' in the latter days of March.[2]

Regarding the *Volksdeutschen*, Hitler in answering a question that came from Yugoslavia, gave his decision that those who had been called up for mobilisation should go into hiding 'as they might otherwise be attacked or shot'. The *Volksdeutsche Mittelstelle* took upon itself to bring these '*Führer* Instructions' to the notice of the *Volksdeutschen*,[3] without success. Their communications had been cut off. It was the *Abwehr* that stepped into the breach. Its secret organisation in Yugoslavia, operated under the name of 'Jupiter', had a wireless receiver and transmitting station at Zagreb. Hitler's instruction was radioed by these means to Zagreb, where it was brought to the notice of the German consul and the *Volksdeutschen*.[4]

The *Abwehr* especially developed considerable activity during the Yugoslav crisis. General Lahousen flew to Budapest on March 28 in order to organise the smuggling of arms across the Hungarian–Yugoslav frontier.[5] In three days' time he had managed the whole thing. At the same time there were measures in preparation in Yugoslavia that were to retard the Yugoslav mobilisation.[6] Espionage was carried out on a considerable scale. Field Marshal Goering had given an order to sabotage the modern *Messerschmitt* fighters which Germany had delivered to Yugoslavia a short time earlier. These had to be traced.[7] Some of the fighters were stationed on the airfield near Zagreb but appeared to have vanished. Others were on the Semlin airfield, immediately north of the capital, Belgrade.[8] Careful enquiries were also made to find out where the Danube flotilla of the Yugoslav navy was. The relevant messages were radioed to Germany via the 'Jupiter' transmitter in Belgrade.[9] And finally measures were taken to occupy the Yugoslav side of the Iron Gate on the Danube by surprise with part of the detachment the *Abwehr* had built up in Rumania for protecting the oil territory against Allied sabotage.

[1] *KTB-Abwehr.*, April 10, 1941.
[2] Letter, April 3, 1941, from Gottlob Berger to Himmler, NO-5615.
[3] Memorandum, March 28, 1941, to *Staatssekretär* Weizsäcker, NG-3243.
[4] *KTB-Abwehr*, April 2, 1941.   [5] *Ibid.*, March 28, 1941.
[6] *Ibid.*, March 29, 1941.   [7] *Ibid.*, March 31, 1941.
[8] *Ibid.*, April 3, 1941.   [9] *Ibid.*, April 1, 1941.

This was with a view to the fact that the Yugoslavs could easily interrupt the Danube shipping there.[1] 'Orders poured in,' said General Lahousen after the war.

When Germany proceeded to attack without warning on April 6, 1941, some of the Croatian troops refused to fight. 'Several Croat units simply went home or, even worse, led by their officers, attacked the Serbian units engaged in fighting the Germans.'[2] The headquarters of the Northern Yugoslav Army Group was even stormed and occupied by Croatian soldiers. Elsewhere communist pamphlets made an appeal 'to revolt against the Serbian chauvinists'.[3] And yet in other places the *Volksdeutschen* took action. Before the coming of the German troops they made themselves masters of the most important points in several of the towns in the Slovene frontier area by force of arms.[4] In Marburg (the Slovene Maribor), the *Volksdeutschen* thought they could take over power on the morning of the second day of the war. At the early hour of half past three they proceeded to seize the public buildings. Fighting ensued with Yugoslav troops that came flowing back from the nearby frontier. The German main force, soon arriving on the spot, was able to settle the fight. Elsewhere in Slovenia the Yugoslav detachments that had been ordered to blow up the bridges in time, had been taken by surprise by *volksdeutsche* shock troops and put out of the way.

Further east, in the eighteenth-century settlement areas the 'political body of picked men of the *Volksgruppe*' was 'everywhere at its post'.[5] On April 6 Dr. Janko, leader of the Minority Germans, had subordinated 'the whole of the *Volksgruppe*, from a military point of view, to the Organisation "Jupiter"'. *Volksdeutsche* men were mobilised and 'forcible attacks were undertaken for sabotage purposes and for creating unrest'.[6] On April 7 other members of the 'Jupiter' Organisation entered the area from Hungary, distributed arms among the *Volksdeutschen* and committed diversionist acts. '*Volksdeutsche* who were already partly armed, joined them'.[7] They fought against Serbian troops.[8] Two large bridges across the river Drau were taken and held until the first regular German troops arrived, and the airfield of Semlin with its valuable *Messerschmitts* was attacked by *Volksdeutsche* and conquered.[9]

It is not certain that the *Reichsdeutschen* living in Yugoslavia—

[1] *Ibid.*   [2] Fotitch: *The War We Lost*, p. 100.   [3] *Ibid.*
[4] *Report on the crimes of Austria and the Austrians against Yugoslavia and her peoples*, p. 120.
[5] *Deutschtum im Ausland*, 1944, p. 33.   [6] *KTB-Abwehr*, April 6, 1941.
[7] *Ibid.*, April 7, 1941.   [8] *Ibid.*, April 9, 1941.
[9] *Deutschtum im Ausland*, 1944, p. 33.

their number is not known—contributed to the swift collapse of the Kingdom. In Belgrade, of the legation personnel only the military attaché remained behind. He was given orders to go into hiding.[1] When the first German soldiers reached the heavily bombed town he acted as town mayor and was able to effect the surrender.[2]

Many *Reichsdeutsche* had left Yugoslavia [3] just before the 'lightning operation' took place as ordered by Hitler on March 27, 1941.

Greece

As regards Greece, which was also attacked by the German *Wehrmacht* on April 6, 1941, we can be brief.

The *Abwehr* had an organisation there for placing explosives in Allied vessels calling at Greek ports.[4] Moreover, in 1940 two *Abwehr* officers were sent to Greece, 'who, disguised as business-men, spent several weeks in a leading Athens hotel. Their task was to gather such information as they would and to make contacts with potential agents.' [5] Three days before the German offensive started, three sabotage detachments of the *Abwehr*, numbering sixteen men in all, were smuggled into Greece from Bulgaria. They were to commit arson in the frontier area and destroy telegraph communications.[6]

Because he saw the approach of the offensive—as who did not?—the German Minister had taken measures for continuing the work of his embassy in his private house in the case of war. He had also brought the military attaché's wireless transmitter there. The *reichsdeutschen* citizens living in Athens were to take up their quarters in three German buildings.[7]

After the entry of the German troops all the members of the *Auslands-Organisation der NSDAP* were at first roped in to render assistance to the *Wehrmacht*, as guides and interpreters, for instance. The boys and girls of the *Hitler-Jugend*, 'proud and radiant' were given rides on the German military motor-cycles and trucks.[8]

---

[1] Information supplied by General Halder.

[2] Telex message, April 13, 1941, from *SS-Gruppenführer* Heydrich to the *Auswärtige Amt*, NG-2315.

[3] Hussard: *Vu en Yougoslavie*, p. 84.

[4] *KTB-Abwehr*, Dec. 9, 1939. Statement by General Lahousen.

[5] Leverkuehn: *German Military Intelligence*, p. 140.

[6] *KTB-Abwehr*, April 4, 1941.

[7] Telegram, March 11, 1941, from the German Minister Erbach to the *Auswärtige Amt*, NG-3519.

[8] Wrede: 'Unser Kriegstagebuch'. *Jahrbuch der Auslands-Organisation der NSDAP*, 1942, Vol. I, p. 66.

Soviet Union

In February, 1938, the last German consulates had to close down in the Soviet Union. It was quite a disaster for the military attaché at Moscow, whose task it was to form an idea of Russia's military potential. With them, he said, disappeared 'one of his last sources of information'. What the diplomatic courier, who travelled once a month to and fro between Berlin and Tokyo 'saw on the way and would then report to him was in the present situation actually the last remaining source of information outside of Moscow'.[1] The military and naval attachés of course continued to use their eyes to good purpose themselves. In September, 1940, the naval attaché was able to report on 'valuable observations' that he had made on the wharves near Leningrad.[2] The Germans also tried to collect data about the Soviet Union in the neutral states on Russia's frontiers,[3] especially in Finland and Turkey.[4] In the spring of 1941 they had a few agents in the Baltic republics [5] and the eastern part of Poland [6] that had been occupied by the Soviet Union. In the same period their representative in Teheran managed to collect valuable information about the Baku oilfields by establishing contacts with opponents of the Soviet régime in Armenia and Azerbaijan. In his journeys through the Soviet Union this same representative had been able to make valuable visual observations.[7]

And finally the Germans tried to make aerial photos in swift planes that flew into the Soviet Union at a great height; these were of important military objectives, of the communications system and the frontier fortifications. These planes were part of the Rowehl squadron that was stationed on the airfields near Budapest.[8] Von Brauchitsch and Halder wanted to start with these photos in September, 1940. Hitler refused: in doing so, the Russians might see through his plans too soon.[9] Not till 1941 did they start with the Rowehl planes. The results were of some importance. In March Halder

[1] Note, Feb. 22, 1938, of *Staatssekretär* Mackensen, *Doc. Ger. For. Pol.*, D, Vol. I, p. 916.

[2] Admiral Assmann: *Die Seekriegsleitung und die Vorgeschichte des Feldzuges gegen Russland* [Aug. 1943], C-170, *IMT*, Vol. XXXIV, p. 690. Further to be referred to as Assmann: *Seekriegsleitung*.

[3] *Ibid.*, p. 680.

[4] Witness Halder, Proceedings, trial against Weizsäcker *et al.* ('Case XI'), p. 20,718.

[5] Assmann: *Seekriegsleitung*, C-170, *IMT*, Vol. XXXIV, p. 700.

[6] Information supplied by General Lahousen.

[7] Schultze-Holthus: *Frührot in Iran. Abenteuer im deutschen Geheimdienst* (Esslingen, 1952), pp. 9–10, 20–22, 27–31, 42–47.

[8] Witness Lahousen, Proceedings *IMT*, Vol. II, p. 467.

[9] Greiner: *Die Oberste Wehrmachtführung*, pp. 312–13.

noted down that it appeared from the photos that the Russian system of communications was much better than the Germans had supposed.[1] The Rowehl squadron at first did not venture very far into Russia. A fortnight before the invasion they started long distance flights.[2]

Generally speaking, the Germans were surprisingly badly informed as to the military power the Soviet Union possessed or would be able to develop. In 1941 the Germans reckoned with 200 Russian divisions. Six weeks after the beginning of the conflict they had already come across 360.[3] They also 'considerably under-estimated' the Russian air force.[4] And as to the strength of the Russian tank arm Hitler simply had no idea. 'When we marched into Russia', he said later to a German diplomat, 'I expected something like four thousand tanks but found twelve thousand.'[5] It is true that as early as 1937 Guderian, Germany's tank expert, had put the number of Russian tanks down at ten thousand but nobody had believed him.[6] There is ground to suppose that in 1941 the German *Abwehr* had a reasonable idea of the magnitude of Russian tank production,[7] but Hitler attached no more value to its reports than to the warnings of the German ambassador in Moscow, Count von der Schulenburg, and of the military attaché, General Koestring—two of the few Germans who knew the Soviet Union from their own observation and had a true idea of her military power.

Not only Hitler, but the majority of his most prominent generals felt a deep contempt for the Slavs. Presumably the most abundant data had not been capable of shaking Hitler's bias. As regards people like von Brauchitsch and Halder, military technicians *par excellence*, cool, even cold arithmeticians, it is impossible to avoid the impression that their absolutely incorrect views on the Soviet Union were connected with the relative paucity of reliable, factual information the Germans had been able to gather.

There are no data that would justify the conclusion that German espionage in the Soviet Union before the outbreak of war was intensive and efficient.

When the Germans marched into the Soviet Union it became of great importance to Hitler and his generals to know in detail what was going on behind the Russian front. To this end several so-called

[1] Halder: *Diary*, March 11, 1941.
[2] *Ibid.*, June 7, 1941. [3] *Ibid.*, Aug. 11, 1941.
[4] *Ibid.*, July 1, 1941.
[5] Rudolf Rahn: *Ruheloses Leben* (Düsseldorf, 1949), p. 190.
[6] Heinz Guderian: *Erinnerungen eines Soldaten* (Heidelberg, 1949), pp. 171–2.
[7] *The Goebbels Diaries*, p. 246.

V-Mann-Kolonnen were added to the headquarters of the German army groups. They numbered 25 or more, and consisted 'of the native population (i.e. Russians, Poles, Ukrainians, Grusinians, Cossacks, Finns, Esthonians etc.)'. Each of these *Kolonnen* was officered by a German. The officers and men were clothed in Russian uniforms. They made use of captured Russian military trucks and motor-cycles, and it was their task to force their way into the Soviet Union fifty to three hundred kilometres in front of the German armies in order to radio their observations, particularly concerning the Russian reserves, the railways, the road-system and 'all the measures taken by the enemy'.[1]

During the first phase of the war, when there was no question of a coherent Russian front, these *V-Mann-Kolonnen* were indeed able to reach points far beyond the fighting zone and to gather valuable data. The trucks were sometimes made to look like cars for transporting the wounded. The members who did not speak Russian or who only spoke it badly lay there bandaged up and groaning: in this way they did not have to answer the questions put them. The non-commissioned officers among them were mostly Ukrainians from Galicia (Poland) and Ruthenia (Czechoslovakia) and emigrants from the Caucasian highlands. To train these people a camp had been set up in Bavaria as early as 1938. There were about fifty people there. This preparatory work was formally prohibited by Hitler after the German-Russian non-aggression pact had been signed. However it was then taken in hand by the Japanese, with German money to back them.[2]

By the side of these spying *V-Mann-Kolonnen* the second (sabotage) department of the *Abwehr* set up small fighting units, belonging to the *Lehrregiment Brandenburg*, who, once more in Russian uniform and a long way in front of the German troops, were to try to seize bridges, tunnels and military depots. They consisted mainly of Germans.[3] Late in October, 1941, the chief of staff of the German *Heeresgruppe Nord* spoke with the highest commendation of the work of this *Lehrregiment*.[4] In Latvia it had been able to save the important bridge across the river Dwina.[5]

It was also the second department of the *Abwehr* which established contacts with nationalists from the Baltic republics and from

[1] *Vortragsnotiz*, July 4, 1941, of Admiral Canaris, PS-882.

[2] Information supplied by General Lahousen, and *KTB-Abwehr*, Oct. 25, and Dec. 31, 1939.

[3] Affidavit, Dec. 25, 1945, by Colonel Erwin Stolze, USSR-231, Proceedings *IMT*, Vol. VII, p. 273.

[4] Report by General Lahousen about his official journey to the Eastern front, Oct. 24–30, 1941, NOKW-3146 (Oct. 26, 1941).

[5] Leverkuehn: *German Military Intelligence*, p. 163.

the Ukraine to sow rebellion in the rear of the Russian armies.[1] In the Baltic states the *Abwehr* got into touch in the spring of 1941 with people like the former Latvian Minister in Berlin and his military attaché, and with the one-time head of the intelligence service of the Esthonian general staff.[2] As to the Ukraine, the Germans co-operated with such figures as Andrej Melnyk and Stepan Bandera —'a positive martyrdom', General Lahousen remarked after the war. His lamentation is understandable. All the attempts of the Germans to bring about a reconciliation between the two nationalist leaders in the months before the invasion came to nothing.[3] Hardly had Lemberg (Lvov) been conquered by the Germans than Bandera set up a Ukrainian government on his own authority, trying to form his own armed forces at the same time. Melnyk did the same thing with Kiev as centre. The activities of both parties, who tried to murder each other's leaders, was forbidden by the Germans after a short time.[4] The latter continued to recruit agents from the ranks of the Ukrainian nationalists, but many of these, and other agents as well as a matter of fact, went over to the Russians. This held good especially for the Russian prisoners-of-war who in a later phase of the war were trained by the *Abwehr* and the *Sicherheitsdienst* for activities in the Soviet Union.[5]

In German sources one now and again finds mention of the fact that 'agents' from Russia reported things worth knowing. Halder's successor, General Zeitzler, was able to inform Hitler on November 7, 1942—a week before the great Russian counter-offensive near Stalingrad—that 'according to messages from agents' it was said that the Kremlin had decided on November 4 to attack before the end of 1942, either on the Don front or in the centre.[6] Late in November, 1943, Goebbels had 'news from agents in Moscow' giving an idea of the difficult talks between Cordell Hull, Eden and Molotov, which had an 'electrifying effect' on him.[7] One gains the impression that such pieces of news were rare, and this is confirmed by the fact that during the whole of the second quarter of 1942 there was only *one*

[1] Halder: *Diary*, Feb. 21 and May 17, 1941. Affidavit, Dec. 25, 1945, by Colonel Erwin Stolze, USSR-231, Proceedings *IMT*, Vol. VII, pp. 272–3.
[2] *KTB-Abwehr*, Feb. 15 and March 12, 1941.
[3] *KTB-Abwehr*, Oct. 18, Nov. 3 and 7, 1940.
[4] *Tätigkeits- und Lagebericht No. 2 der Einsatzgruppen der Sicherheitspolizei und des SD in der UdSSR* (*Berichtszeit vom 1.1.–31.1.1942*), PS-3876.
[5] Information supplied by General Lahousen. Witness Walter Schellenberg, Proceedings of the trial against Weizsäcker *et al.*, pp. 5147–54.
[6] Greiner: *Die Oberste Wehrmachtführung*, p. 417.
[7] Von Oven: *Mit Goebbels bis zum Ende*, Vol. I (Buenos Aires, 1949), pp. 153–5. The two volumes with von Oven's diary notes deserve mention as giving a clear picture of relations at the top of the Third *Reich*.

place in the War Diary of the *Oberkommando der Wehrmacht* in which mention was made with any certainty of news that reached Hitler from behind the front. This particular item mentioned 'reports from Kuibyshev, according to which the Russians are planning to counter our planned offensive by proceeding to the attack themselves along the entire front'.[1]

The information was incorrect.

It is a striking fact that in none of the operations organized by the *Abwehr*, described in some detail, did they secure the adherence of *Volksdeutsche*. These lived so far in the depths of Russia that it would have been impossible to get into communication with them. Moreover, some of them, especially the young ones, were favourably disposed towards communism.[2] The data they had in Berlin about the *Volksdeutschen* were very imperfect: they did not even know with absolute certainty in which villages they lived.[3] Three weeks after the beginning of the war, it is true, Himmler ordered the *Volksdeutsche Mittelstelle* 'to take all possible measures for registering *das Volksdeutschtum* in the occupied Soviet Union and, by bringing forward non-Bolshevist representatives, to lay the foundations for German rule'.[4] In practice very little came of this, however.

At first nobody so much as paid any attention to the *Volksdeutschen* in the Ukraine. *Gauleiter* Koch, who wielded the sceptre there, brooked no interference. In August, 1942, the situation of the *Volksdeutschen* in the Ukraine was described as follows: 'They were starving. They had to pay double taxes. The schools they had opened were closed down. All trace of national life has vanished.'[5]

The condition of the *Volksdeutschen* was slightly more favourable in the eastern part of Volhynia (Western Russia) and in Transnistria, the area on the Black Sea that Rumania had annexed in 1941. New schools were opened, part of the men able to bear arms united in a *volksdeutsche Mannschaft* so as to protect their villages against assaults from guerrillas.[6] In Transnistria a German traveller, a national socialist, saw that the *volksdeutschen* farmers shortly after the arrival of the German and Rumanian armies had 'everywhere' made swastika-flags out of the Russian flag, and flew them from

---

[1] PS-1807 (May 12, 1942).

[2] Information supplied by General Lahousen.

[3] *Die deutschen Siedlungen in der Sowjetunion. Ausgearbeitet und herausgegeben von der Sammlung Georg Leibbrandt* (Berlin, 1941), p. 4.

[4] Letter, July 11, 1941, from Himmler to *SS-Gruppenführer* Lorenz and *SS-Gruppenführer* Heydrich, NO-4274.

[5] *Aktenvermerk*, Aug. 17, 1942, concerning talks in Hitler's headquarters, NO-2703.

[6] *Ibid.*

their dwellings.[1] Apparently they liked things better under the new system of government than under the old one. One should not see an indication in this that there had been any previous contact with an official body in the Third *Reich*. In October, 1941, there was an official report from this same area to the effect that the *Volksdeutschen*, even when they were not communists, had 'a completely erroneous idea of the relationships in the *Reich* and of the national socialist leaders; a large number of them do not even know the name of the *Führer*, for instance'. The members of the intelligentsia—teachers, technicians, public servants—were said to have no political consciousness or discrimination. They were 'generally indifferent' to the Jews. 'Typical of this attitude is the fact', so it was regretfully remarked, 'that after the entry of the German troops no measures whatever were taken against the Jews by the *Volksdeutschen*; on the contrary they pointed to them as harmless people, from whom one had nothing to fear'.[2]

There are no data from which it would appear that *Volksdeutsche* had attacked the Russian armies in the rear, either in the Ukraine or in the Volga area, or that they had made secret preparations to that end. Nor has any evidence ever been published supporting the accusation that there really were 'thousands and tens of thousands of diversionists and spies' among the Germans on the Volga. The Soviet Union has kept silent and no documents from any German archives have so far been made public from which it might be concluded that there existed some sort of conspiratorial contact between the Third *Reich* and the *Volksdeutschen* living on the Dnieper, the Black Sea, the Don or the Volga.

[1] C. von Kügelgen: 'Von den deutschen Kolonisten in Wolhynien und in der Ukraine westlich des Dnjepr.' *Deutsche Post aus dem Osten*, Dec. 1941, p. 5. The article contains a record of the travels of Dr. Karl Stumpp.

[2] *Tätigkeits- und Lagebericht No. 6 der Einsatzgruppen der Sicherheitspolizei und des SD in der UdSSR (Berichtszeit 1–31.10.1941)*, R-102, *IMT*, Vol. XXXVIII, p. 301.

CHAPTER XIV

The military Fifth Column

★

Tʜᴇ facts collected here which, as we said, might throw light on the question as to whether a military German Fifth Column existed and if it did, how powerful and of what importance it was—these facts are not complete. They cannot be so. Only part of the German archives have been found again, and thus far, only fragments have been published from them. There have not been sufficient reports and reliable preliminary studies in all countries to make it possible to draw final conclusions. There are witnesses who have vanished from the scene for ever—and there are others who envelop themselves in impenetrable silence. Nevertheless, it seems to us that out of the entire body of factual material that has been outlined, a picture emerges which, however incomplete, is very far from arbitrary in its salient features. The curious fact arises that those data—drawn from the most diverse sources, nowhere going back to complete archives, but almost always only to scattered bits and pieces of documentary material, sometimes no more than mere chips—that those data nevertheless show a certain inner harmony and are in agreement with each other when each country is considered separately. They give us a *rough* impression of what happened.

Before we start considering this for each country separately, it may be useful to look at what has appeared to us regarding the essential characteristics of the original picture of the German military Fifth Column, as this was seen by large parts of the population in *all* countries.

This Fifth Column has been looked upon as a gigantic conspiracy conducted by the leaders of the Third Reich according to a fixed plan. It was thought that almost all the establishments of the party and the state in Germany made up an active part of it, standing in close co-operation with each other. And it was also supposed that outside

Germany it embraced, if not all, then at least very many Reichsdeut-schen, Volksdeutschen and native national socialists and fascists. (These last two groups for the sake of convenience we shall allude to in this chapter as 'fascists'.) *This conspiratorial machine would proceed to the large-scale attack-from-within, so it was thought, at the same time with the aggression-from-without, in fact forming a component part of it.*

That *this* conception of the German Fifth Column tallied with reality did not appear from our enquiry.

What *did* appear is that Hitler personally made straight for war from the very outset. ('The resolution to attack had always burned in me.') It did *not* appear that he followed any fixed plan in carrying out this aim. He hesitated for a long time whether to begin in the east or the west. His strategies were unsystematic, often rash and head-strong on account of his impulsiveness. For the preparation of an offensive against Poland he allowed himself five months; immediately afterwards he demanded an offensive for the occupation of France, Belgium and part of the Netherlands; next he allowed his attention to be diverted by a hastily prepared offensive against Denmark and Norway. For an invasion of England he had nothing in readiness at the decisive moment. North and South America lay beyond his grasp. He attacked Greece to relieve his ally Italy. The attack on Yugoslavia had to be improvised in one and a half weeks' time. The offensive against the Soviet Union was thoroughly prepared but with so little knowledge of his opponent and so little understanding of the difficulties in wait for him that four months after it had begun Hitler admitted that if he had known what was in store he might never had started at all.[1]

It *did* appear that in Germany several departments of the party and the state were involved in undermining the military resistance of other countries. It did *not* appear that this applied to most such departments. Besides two fairly orthodox institutions—the *Amt Ausland-Abwehr* of the *Oberkommando der Wehrmacht* and the *Auswärtige Amt* (including the German foreign service)—we more particularly came across four institutions of an essentially political nature: the *Auslands-Organisation der NSDAP*, the *Aussenpolitische Amt der NSDAP*, the *Volksdeutsche Mittelstelle* and the *Sicherheits-dienst*. These four institutions were especially characteristic of national socialist Germany. Ministries of Foreign Affairs and military services for espionage, counter-espionage and for carrying out sabo-tage existed in all the other belligerent powers as well.

It did *not* appear that there was any close, harmonious co-operation

[1] Report of talk, Oct. 25, 1941, between Hitler and Ciano. *Ciano's Diplomatic Papers* (London, 1948), p. 455.

between the six German institutions we have just mentioned, with specific tasks arising from joint consultations. There was tension in their mutual relationships; they often worked counter to each other; they grudged each other every success. Nor was harmonious co-operation furthered by Hitler.

It *did* appear in several cases that *Reichsdeutsche* living abroad, mostly members of the *Auslands-Organisation der NSDAP*, helped prepare or supported the German aggression. It did *not* appear that they were proportionately very numerous. Only a small percentage of those *Reichsdeutschen* were members of the *Auslands-Organisation*: 2 per cent in Brazil, 3 per cent in Switzerland, 4 per cent in Norway and the Argentine, 6 per cent in the Netherlands, 9 per cent in Chile, 12 per cent in Luxemburg and 15 per cent in Poland.

The total number of *Reichsdeutschen* living outside of Germany was not known with any certainty before the war. In 1937 the German estimates varied from 2 to 3 million.[1] A lower, probably more accurate estimate dating from 1929, gives $1\frac{1}{2}$ to 2 million.[2] However this may be, at the beginning of 1933 only 3300 of the *Reichsdeutschen* living abroad were members of the *Auslands-Organisation*.[3] On June 30, 1937, 30,203, on June 30, 1938, 30,289, on March 31, 1939 (five months before the outbreak of the war) 30,273.[4] Later figures are not available.

It *did* appear that in several cases members of *volksdeutsche* minorities actively supported German aggression. It did *not* appear, with the exception of Poland and Yugoslavia, that their activities were at all extensive. In the two countries just mentioned the communal life of the *Volksdeutschen* was dominated after 1938 by national socialist elements. In North and South America national socialism had gained little or no hold on citizens of German descent. With the *Volksdeutschen* in the Soviet Union no contact occurred at all.

It *did* appear that in several cases 'fascists' lent themselves as instruments to German aggression. It did *not* appear that they were very numerous. Sometimes it was only the leaders or some of the people at the top (Norwegian, Flemish, Breton, Irish, Croatian, Ukrainian 'fascists') who with that end in view kept up regular contact with institutions of the German state or of the NSDAP. Sometimes those institutions had got into touch with special members without this being known to the leaders (Denmark, the Netherlands).

[1] Ehrich: *Die Auslands-Organisation der NSDAP*, p. 7.
[2] Dr. H. W. Herold: 'Die deutschen Kolonien im Auslande und das Einwanderungsdeutschtum.' *Jahrbuch des Bundes der Auslandsdeutschen* (Berlin, 1929), p. 42.
[3] Bohle's affidavit, included in Proceedings *IMT*, Vol. X, p. 12.
[4] Figures taken from miscellaneous statistics of the *Reichsschatzmeister der NSDAP*.

It did *not* appear that these *Reichsdeutschen, Volksdeutschen* and 'fascists', in so far as they gave their active support to the German aggression, acted in systematic, close mutual co-operation. One need but call Norway to mind, where neither Quisling nor the leader of the *Landesgruppe* of the *Auslands-Organisation* knew exactly what was going to happen.

It therefore appears that the German military Fifth Column was considerably less extensive and important than was thought outside Germany during and after the war. But it has *also* appeared that this Fifth Column did most certainly exist. No value at all should be attached to the denials of leading figures in national-socialist Germany on this point. *It even appears to us as a remarkable fact that the Third Reich succeeded in building up such a Fifth Column in no more than six or seven years.* Treason and taking undue advantage of hospitality were both furthered by the Third *Reich* to a notable extent. *Before* the German aggressions *Reichsdeutsche, Volksdeutsche* and 'fascists', as has appeared, lent themselves to the armed struggle on the aggressor's side, and to espionage and sabotage, to help undermine the resistance of the army and the nation being attacked, and to direct assistance of the aggressor during and after the fighting.

These forms of military Fifth Column activities, however, appeared, as we have seen, in various degrees and in various forms in the different countries. The way in which the Fifth Column was operating did not always happen to be the same. It made no difference to the people attacked whether the blowing up of a bridge that was important to the Germans was prevented by *Volksdeutsche* who *before the aggression started* had already been in the state about to become the victim of that aggression, or whether it was prevented by members of the *Abwehr* who crossed through the fighting zone from the German camp, dressed in civilian dress but furnished with distinguishing marks and organised as a separate unit, reaching their objectives unnoticed. In both cases the raided nations spoke of 'Fifth Columnists'.

We wish to remark here that the concept of this Fifth Column apparently included two sorts of things. One might speak of an *internal* and an *external* Fifth Column. *The internal one was already present at the moment of the aggression in the country about to be attacked, whereas the external one entered the country in question together with or after the beginning of the aggression.* The internal one betrayed the state whose citizens or guests they were; that was the 'real' Fifth Column, agreeing with the historical origin of the concept.

In the external Fifth Column the treasonable element was lacking, at least if it was made up of Germans, *not* of citizens of the power

244

that was to be attacked. It is true that this external Fifth Column often encroached upon the general laws and usages of war, but this was more akin to impermissible strategem or impermissible modes of warfare. Indeed, many authors in the field of international law are of opinion that up to the moment the real fighting starts it is permissible to make use of the symbols and uniforms of one's adversaries by way of strategem.[1] This repeatedly occurred on the German side, but such ruses were also applied by other powers than Germany in the second World War. The British and American Commando operations had elements akin to the external Fifth Column. Attempts at sabotage by sending out agents were undertaken on both sides.

It is not surprising, however, that the victim nations made no distinction between the internal and the external Fifth Column, nor that they did not trouble themselves about the question as to what was or was not permissible under international law; and that they did not do so was in a certain sense justifiable. Both internal and external Fifth Columns, after all, were treacherous manifestations of an undeniably aggressive Germany. During the war, however, the internal and external Fifth Columns were frequently lumped together, and acts of the second put to the account of the first, the 'real' Fifth Column.

It seems doubtful that one should reckon the Fifth Column activities carried out by *reichsdeutsche* officials abroad, who had normal diplomatic status, as 'real' Fifth Column actions. We met with cases in Denmark (the air attaché), Norway (the naval attaché, he air attaché, the assistant commercial attaché), the Netherlands (the military attaché, the deputy military attaché, the air attaché), Great Britain (the consul-general in Liverpool), the United States (the naval attaché, the consul-general in San Francisco), Yugoslavia (an employee of the consulate at Zagreb, the consul at Zagreb), and the Soviet Union (the consulates, the military attaché, the naval attaché). It is very probable that espionage through the foreign service was much more widespread than can be demonstrated from available documents, but in our opinion we should regard it, however unlawful and intolerable, as a normal phenomenon.

There remains to be considered the internal Fifth Column, consisting of 'ordinary' *Reichsdeutsche, Volksdeutsche* and 'fascists'.

The chief criterion for the existence of an internal Fifth Column of some size was participation in the struggle by force of arms, the formation of fighting parties that harassed the army of the victim country in the rear. We have only been able to find indications that

[1] L. Oppenheim: *International law. A treatise* (7th edition, edited by H. Lauterpacht), Vol. II: *Disputes, war and neutrality* (London, 1952), p. 429.

this actually happened for Poland and Yugoslavia. Besides this, national socialism, as we saw, gained a strong hold over the *volksdeutschen* organisations in both countries. And further, in Poland the percentage of *Reichsdeutsche* that belonged to the *Auslands-Organisation der NSDAP* (15 per cent) was higher, as far as is known, than in any other country. On the other hand there is no evidence that the internal military Fifth Column amounted to very much as regards size in Denmark, Norway, the Netherlands, Belgium (with the exception of Eupen-Malmédy), Luxemburg, France, England, the United States, Latin America, Greece and the Soviet Union.

It is a remarkable contrast.

Evidently the position of the *Volksdeutschen*, even of the Germans in general, was very different in Poland and Yugoslavia from what it was in countries like Norway, the Netherlands, Uruguay and the Soviet Union. The facts we set forth about Fifth Column activities in time of war we wish to place in their historical connection, making possible a better understanding. It will also be necessary to consider more closely the organisational institutions we came across in regard to the external as well as the internal Fifth Column.

For two different reasons it would be incorrect to ignore the political Fifth Column in our closer investigation.

In the first place it is natural to conclude that the *reichsdeutschen* and *volksdeutschen* groups and parties that lent themselves to supporting Germany's military aggression did this only as a consequence, possibly as an extreme consequence, of their *political* development.

In the second place the visible activities of the political Fifth Column before the war were an important stimulus to the fear of the military Fifth Column that gripped tens of millions of people during the war.

This touches on another problem that forces itself on our attention.

There is a striking difference between the ideas about the German Fifth Column which we outlined in the first part of our book and the actual activities of that Fifth Column as we have tried to approximate them in this second part. Those ideas proved to contain elements that tallied with reality. It has also appeared, however, that they contained many other elements for which we were unable to find a vestige of evidence in our enquiry, or of which we have already been able to point out the erroneousness. Generally speaking, in almost all countries the size of the German military Fifth Column was grossly over-estimated.

Why?

Part Three

ANALYSIS

CHAPTER XV

The imaginary Fifth Column

★

Every time Germany started fresh aggressions during the years 1939–41, the following leading theme came to the top in the emotional life and thoughts of the peoples actually attacked or feeling themselves acutely menaced:

'There are large numbers of enemy agents in our own country, some of whom have already been living amongst us for a long time so that they might pave the way unobtrusively, by means of espionage and seemingly harmless measures, for the attack whose victims we have become. Another part consists of enemy soldiers who, now that the attack has started, have put on our uniform, or civilian clothes, or have disguised themselves as clerics or as women. Both these groups of agents are spying; and moreover they are trying to disorganize our defensive system in numerous ways, among others by poisoning our foodstuffs. And finally, they try to get into contact with the invading enemy by performing special, seemingly harmless actions that contain some signal or message for him.'

The curious fact is to be observed that in quite different historical situations, where there was no question of a national socialist German Fifth Column, our *Leitmotiv* yet recurs in the emotional life and thoughts of the community actually being attacked or that felt itself acutely menaced.

Thus the American Secretary of the Navy contended after the attack at Pearl Harbour (December 7, 1941) that 'the most effective Fifth Column work of the entire war was done at Hawaii with the possible exception of Norway' by the something like 160,000 Japanese living on the Hawaian islands (most of whom were American citizens).[1] They had fired on American soldiers, so it was reported. They had

[1] Quoted by Major-General J. F. C. Fuller: *The Second World War 1939–1945* (London, 1948), p. 124.

249

thrown up barricades in the roads, and they had cut big arrows in the fields of sugar cane which pointed in the direction of military installations. Their vegetable merchants had carefully registered the purchases of the American navy in order to deduce its movements.[1] Congressman Rankin shouted 'Damn them!' in Washington in the House of Representatives.[2]

Shortly after Japan had attacked America similar accusations were uttered against the something like 110,000 American citizens of Japanese descent, the so-called *Nisei*, who lived in California. It was said of them that night after night they made hundreds of light signals to Japanese submarines lying in wait in front of the harbours; that they were in touch with those submarines by means of secret transmitters; that they had made flower-beds, or had planted tomatoes or placed hay on racks, in the shape of signals pointing in the direction of airfields and airplane factories; that they had poisoned the vegetables which they sold to the American housewives.[3] The animosity against them grew to such a pitch that in the spring of 1942 the authorities deprived all of them of their liberty and interned them in camps in the western inland areas.[4]

If we seek periods of tension or conflict preceding the second World War we come across similar notions.

When in 1938 Czechoslovakia considered war probable with Germany, the tale was current in Prague that the Germans in their clinic there had prepared thousands of cultures of typhoid germs in order to poison the drinking water after the outbreak of war. And it was further said that members of the Henlein movement had painted the name of the capital in luminous paint on the roof of the German University as a guide to the German bombers.[5] In the Spanish Civil War a foreign visitor saw that light signals were made to the enemy near Saragossa behind the front of the government troops. That happened 'every night', so he heard.[6] Shortly before the outbreak of the war hundreds of women in Madrid were thrown into a panic when they heard the rumour 'that nuns had been distributing poisoned sweets to the children of Madrid, and that the city hospitals were at that moment overcrowded with the little victims'.[7]

How had it been during the first World War?

[1] This was reported in almost the whole of the American press on the authority of United Press on December 30 and 31, 1941. Morton Grodzins: *Americans Betrayed. Politics and the Japanese Evacuation* (Chicago, 1949), p. 399.
[2] Feb. 19, 1942. *Ibid.*, p. 86.
[3] *Ibid.*, pp. 193, 290, 402–3.
[4] *Ibid.*, p. 139.
[5] Alexander Henderson: *Eyewitness in Czechoslovakia* (London, 1939), p. 102.
[6] Franz Borkenau: *The Spanish Cockpit* (London, 1937), p. 99.
[7] John Langdon-Davies: *Fifth Column* (London, 1940), p. 5.

Our *Leitmotiv* cropped up everywhere.

In August, 1914, the first month of the war, it was rumoured in France that numerous German officers in French uniform were *in Paris and its environs* in order to destroy bridges.

A special campaign was directed against the Swiss firm 'Maggi' that worked partially with German capital and which was charged with delivering poisoned milk.[1] When in the autumn of 1914 the strong fortress of Maubeuge on the Belgian frontier fell, an explanation was sought in the fact that the German guns with which the shelling had been done had been brought into position on concrete foundations which Germans living in the neighbourhood had had laid out unobtrusively in the shape of tennis courts or garage floors long before the war.[2]

The tale of the concrete foundations at Maubeuge was also readily believed in England. There people on every hand thought that they saw similar preparations of a seemingly harmless character which in reality were extremely dangerous: concrete approaches, concrete tennis courts, concrete court yards.[3] The news from France about the 'Maggi' advertisement signs led to 'screwdriver parties' being formed in London for inspecting the backs of all the enamelled advertisement-plates.[4] And then also many people were convinced that the Germans had systematically committed espionage on a large scale in England for years. In the same way it was thought that a reconnaissance had been made of the system of water mains 'by a band of itinerant musicians, who, though they played mournful airs in the streets, were really a group of very wide-awake German officers'.[5] German hairdressers and jewellers had opened shops all over the country, even there where, so it was supposed, they could never earn a living. The number of German waiters was alarmingly high: Spies![6] It was generally assumed that all these people would continue their crafty trade after the outbreak of war. Light signals had been observed in hundreds of places. A secret car, so people said, drove through the country transmitting wireless messages.[7] In the Scottish Highlands Germans were supposed to have set up petrol supplies in order to provide their Zeppelins with fresh fuel. The authorities offered a reward to anyone who could furnish information leading to the detection of such supplies.[8] Numbers of people were suspected of being enemy agents during that first phase of the war

---

[1] Dr. Vincent Barnes-Deltour: *Pariser Selbsterlebnisse während des Krieges* (Munich, [1917]), pp. 46–7.

[2] *Ibid.*, pp. 47–8.

[3] William Le Queux: *German Spies in England* (London, 1915), p. 89.

[4] Arthur Ponsonby: *Falsehood in War-time* (London, 1928), p. 153.

[5] William Le Queux: *German Spies in England* (London, 1915), p. 58.

[6] *Ibid.*, p. 60.   [7] *Ibid.*, p. 129.   [8] *Ibid.*, p. 86,

including ordinary Englishmen, 'merely because they looked odd', because they were heard 'whispering', because they had 'voices like Germans'.

In Germany it was supposed early in August, 1914, that many French and Russian agents were in the country, some in German uniform, others disguised as priests or nuns, to do spying work or to carry out raids. 'Many German officers and men were molested and arrested because they were taken to be spies who had disguised themselves.'[1] In Berlin and elsewhere priests and nuns were molested in the streets, and chased by the crowd. Reports that large contingents of gold from France were on their way to Russia clean across Germany led to cars being held up and searched on all hands. The whole military traffic threatened to come to a complete standstill.[2] A few officers and citizens who refused to stop their cars or who failed to do so, were shot or wounded. 'The most harmless people are taken to be spies if they differ somewhat in their outward appearance from their fellow-men,' wrote the English wife of a German nobleman.[3]

The hunt for French agents conveying gold to Russia in inconspicuous cars spread to Austria.

In Russia it was the *Volksdeutschen* who were suspected of being in touch with the enemy. The impression that the *Volksdeutschen* who had been mobilised were committing treason was so strong that in 1915 they were withdrawn from the Russian Western front and were sent to the Caucasus for performing heavy and dangerous labour in the high mountains. Each fresh Russian defeat was supposed to be the result of their extensive espionage.[4]

In the United States during the first World War many of the tales that made mention of the sinister activities of Germans abroad were believed in wide circles. When war with Germany had become a fact (April, 1917) the public gradually became convinced 'that any Germans who had stayed in America from 1914 to 1917 had occupied themselves with plots, nothing but plots'.[5] And as regards Latin America, people talked there of the German danger as far as the Brazilian jungle and beyond. 'The German settlers were looked upon as soldiers in disguise, who, as a well-organised unit, would one day be able to conquer their new fatherland and subject it to the German

[1] Wilhelm Mühlon: *Die Verheerung Europas. Aufzeichnungen aus den ersten Kriegsmonaten* (Zurich, 1918), p. 21.
[2] W. Nicolai: *Nachrichtendienst, Presse und Volksstimmung im Weltkrieg* (Berlin, 1920), p. 31.
[3] Evelyn Blücher von Wahlstatt: *Tagebuch* (Munich, 1924), p. 13.
[4] Adolf Eichler: *Die Deutschen in Kongresspolen* (Berlin, 1919), p. 9.
[5] Captain von Rintelen: *The Dark Invader* (London, 1933), p. 204. The Penguin edition of Feb., 1940, is being quoted.

Reich.[1] In Uruguay all the Germans working in meat-preserving factories were discharged; it was feared that they would poison the meat intended for England.[2]

But the general *Leitmotiv*, sounding so clearly in the first World War ('The enemy has traitors and disguised agents in our midst!') is not a phenomenon of the twentieth century only. It is also to be found earlier.

During the Franco-Prussian war of 1870–71 a veritable hunting-down of Prussian spies went on in Paris, whom people thought they saw 'just about everywhere'. Houses were stormed whence, so it was asserted, light signals were being made to the enemy.[3] The *Figaro* reported that a consignment of French uniforms, addressed to the King of Prussia and intended for the use of his agents, had been detected and held up at the last moment.[4] Cab-drivers and coal-men were suspected of being spies—'the one was recognised as being a German by the fact that he held the reins in his left hand, and the other by his hands being too black'.[5]

Two generations before, on the eve of the September massacres of 1792, Paris was said to be full of aristocrats disguised as ecclesiastics and soldiers disguised as citizens.[6] And the day before the Bastille was stormed (July 14, 1789) the Carthusian Monastery was captured; the monks were supposed to have weapons concealed beneath their cowls!

Nothing was found, however.[7]

Just as in Part I we outlined the notions people had about the *supposed* activities of the German military Fifth Column, while placing the facts about the *actual* activities of that Fifth Column in Part II, so we might now start examining carefully the more or less similar accusations directed at entirely different groups during the second World War and during a few earlier wars.

We will be brief.

No single deed of espionage, sabotage or of any other sort that might be called Fifth Column work has been established about the

---

[1] Walter von Hauff: *Auslandsdeutschtum* (Karlsruhe, 1925), p. 4. Quoted by Dr. Georg Schreiber: *Das Auslandsdeutschtum als Kulturfrage* (Munster, 1929), p. 106.

[2] W. Nelke: *Das Deutschtum in Uruguay* (Stuttgart, 1921), p. 142.

[3] *Le siège de Paris*, Sept. 19, 1871, quoted by Dr. Lucien Graux: *Les fausses nouvelles de la grande guerre*, Vol. I (Paris, 1918), p. 170.

[4] *Ibid.*, p. 169.

[5] Diary of Francisque Sarcey, quoted by Baracs-Deltour: *Pariser Selbsterleb-nisse während des Krieges*, p. 86.

[6] Graux: *Les fausses nouvelles de la grande guerre*, Vol. I, p. 90.

[7] *Ibid.*, p. 72.

Japanese citizens living on the Hawaii Islands, either before, during, or after the raid on Pearl Harbour. Spying was only carried out by the consulates.[1] Nor has anything come to light about the *Nisei* living in California having undertaken any espionage and sabotage or having made any attempts to form resistance groups. All the persons in whose homes the Federal Bureau of Investigation had seized 'arms' (often only shot-guns) or explosives were able to give satisfactory reasons for having them. It further appeared on investigation that the rumours concerning light signals and secret radio transmitters were 'without exception' baseless. And finally it did not appear anywhere that Japanese-American farmers had made 'signs' on their estates for the benefit of the Japanese air force. It was ascertained of one 'sign' that it was the work of a non-Japanese farmer who 'was so happy that he had had a good harvest that he ploughed the letters 'J O E' [probably his own name] in the field to celebrate.'[2]

The tales dating from the first World War, may be said to have been equally baseless. The Germans as well as the Allies at the beginning of the hostilities greatly over-estimated the extent and the effectiveness of the espionage directed against them. Before the outbreak of war the German intelligence service only had at its disposal half a million *Reichsmark* per year at most. Even with these modest means, it was possible to find out the course of the Russian and French mobilisations. Facts about the British navy were also secretly collected.[3] The German espionage organisation in England, which had been carefully watched by the English for some years, was liquidated, however, on the day war was declared (August 4, 1914). Nothing was proved about acts of sabotage performed by *Reichsdeutsche* living in England or by any other persons of German descent.[4]

'The currents, conscious and unconscious, running through the minds of men cannot be charted accurately,' we wrote earlier in this book.

Perhaps it would be a good thing to remind the reader of this now that we wish to ask ourselves how the idea of an omnipresent, universally active Fifth Column can spring up in people's minds, and how it could come about that this idea takes on similar aspects in different countries and different times.

[1] Grodzins: *Americans Betrayed*, pp. 130–2.   [2] *Ibid.*, pp. 134–7, 291–2.
[3] Nicolai: *Nachrichtendienst, Presse und Volksstimmung im Weltkrieg*, p. 6.
[4] Statement of the Home Office, quoted by Le Queux: *German Spies in England*, pp. 100, 174–5, 183. Churchill: *The World Crisis 1911–1918*, pp. 170–1. The edition in two volumes is being quoted, which appeared in London in 1939.

One might picture it to oneself thus:

The outbreak of war causes a feeling of great fear to spring up in the minds of most people. Nobody knows exactly what the war has in store for him. Life itself is at stake. Perhaps one will be killed in battle or be seriously wounded in an air attack. Perhaps one will lose relatives and friends. Ordinary everyday existence, running in regular channels, is suddenly and radically cut off. A tremendous revolution, an unfathomable catastrophe is at hand. What weapons will the enemy use? Whatever one has read or heard from one's youth upwards about the horrors of war, all the reports, suppositions, and whatever one has envisioned about it in the years previous to the war, gathered from newspapers or books—fighting with flame-projectors, bacteria, 'deadly rays'—all these and similar memories come surging upwards and threaten to flood the consciousness. Not only is it difficult mentally to digest the quantity, but also the quality of that intense fear: the relatively vague, undefined character of it. No one knows what *concrete* disaster is threatening, or what concrete calamity is going to befall.

From the outset there is aggressiveness as well as fear.

It is the *enemy* who attacks. *He* started the war. It is *his* fault that peaceful existence of everyday life has been shattered. *He* it is who spreads ruin and destruction. Hatred keeps mounting up. All the feelings of aggressiveness prevailing within the group are directed against him. How gladly people would set on him, crush him, smash him, annihilate him!

Besides fear and aggressiveness there is also a feeling of helplessness. In a war a gigantic mechanism is set working that sets plain people at nought. To continue with the work one did in times of peace seems useless, but what can one do that is of use? And there is also uncertainty: nobody knows what is happening at the fronts or what perhaps has already happened; the news is scanty and of little significance.

The inner tension aroused by the violent yet vague feeling of fear, by the aggressiveness that has no immediate target, and by the feelings of helplessness and uncertainty, would be able to find an outlet as soon as an individual could be discovered *in one's own midst* who might be stamped as 'hostile'. Then fear would lose its mysterious and vague character; the undefined aggressiveness would find an object, and helplessness and uncertainty would be extinguished in a direct task: an attack upon the enemy within one's own ranks. In carrying out such an assault one would 'be doing something', 'helping to win the war'.

The strong *inclination* to find an outlet, to release the inner tension by accepting the idea out of hand that there are enemies in one's own midst is present in very many people in such a situation. It need be but a few who first 'name' the 'enemy'. A cry uttered by one individual is taken up by thousands and hastily passed on to tens of thousands. The press and the wireless see to it that millions hear of it, There is a linear element in this process of dissemination: the releasing spark jumps from one person to another. It is. of much greater importance, however, that most people are so tense that they are, as it were, waiting for that spark. Consequently the sparks spring up in many places at once, their spread is tremendously rapid, and what one person only suspects is passed on as a dead certainty by the next. When once it has been printed or broadcast, then it has acquired the finality of a dogma.[1] Most people feel no need to weigh critically and calmly the things they hear. Moreover, verification is impossible: communications have been interrupted, and consequently no one has a reliable idea in his mind of the fighting.

The 'naming', the 'creating' of 'enemies in one's own midst' is a form of satisfying inner needs, according to the train of thought here set forth. It is an irrational but natural process, in fact an understandable way of assimilating a part of reality felt to be unbearable, a process which is almost inevitable in times of high tension. It seems as if the community that is being attacked is making things more difficult for itself by assuming that there are enemies in its midst;- actually the contrary is the case at the moment that those enemies are being created.

What content the charges display—the rumours, statements, communiqués, which remove the inner tension and by means of which the enemies in one's own midst are singled out—is of secondary importance. That content, up to a certain point, will bear its own peculiar character in each historical situation. Taking for granted that people wish to be convinced that they have accomplices of the enemy in their midst, what more natural than to assume that these tools were committing espionage and sabotage, firing at the troops of the country in which they are residing? This view is shifted to the past: those spies must of course have been there for years, only they were invisible; just as invisible as the enemy agents become once the attack has started. This they can hardly do in any other way than by putting on civilian clothes or the uniforms of the forces being attacked.

---

[1] The emotions causing the process here described need by no means only be emotions such as fear, aggressiveness and helplessness. Intense longing, intensely joyful expectation can awaken the same mechanism. One need but recall 'Mad Tuesday' (Sept. 5, 1944) where Holland is concerned, when in almost all the towns occupied by the Germans the rumour arose based on the report that in the south Breda had been liberated, 'that the liberating armies were close at hand'.

All the charges of this sort are immediately plausible; and this is connected with the fact that the number of possibilities offered by reality is limited. Sometimes old, forgotten charges come surging upwards. This was to be observed in Belgium, where people inspected the 'Maggi' advertisement signs in the first World War and the 'Pascha' posters in the second, in quest of geographical indications marked on them by the enemies in their midst. More often still people bring in elements from recent impressions which add considerably to the plausibility of the charges or even make them look absolutely self-evident. In Holland the view that members of the Dutch Nazi party everywhere shot at their own troops was considerably fortified by the announcement made two weeks previously by their leader that his followers in the case of a German invasion would not offer any resistance.

Why it is that attempts at poisoning are so often ascribed to the enemy in one's own midst we shall leave an open question. Many different factors probably come into play in this matter. If we wish to sort them out in detail, psychological, ethnological and historical investigations would be required. To a certain extent this perhaps also applies to the equally striking fact that people have often thought they saw the enemy in their midst in the guise of priests, monks and nuns. These all wear habits that are eminently suited for concealing arms. Probably the fact that in the eyes of many people ministers of the church are already enveloped in a veil of mystery, arousing fear and awe, plays its part.[1]

This connection with the past is not essential, however.

An absolutely unimportant, topical trifle is enough to be considered an enemy in their midst. Anyone who is in any way conspicuous is suspect to some people. More suspicion is then at once focused on him. In 1914, quite ordinary people were thought to be spies in Germany, 'when they differ a bit in appearance from their fellowmen'. In England the same thing happened to individuals who looked odd, who were whispering or who had voices like Germans. In 1940 many people were arrested who, as far as can be made out, were only seized because there was something conspicuous, something varying from the ordinary run of people, something strange in their appearance—and strange had become identical with hostile. Late in May, 1940, a French lieutenant was manhandled by citizens 'because he had somewhat reddish hair and that seemed suspicious to them'.[2] When in those May days of 1940 a number of prisoners were being

---

[1] Princess Marie Bonaparte speaks in her study in which she treats of some aspects of the Fifth Column, of the 'anti-clericalism always latent in the masses'. Cf. her *Myths of War* (London, 1947), pp. 84–7.

[2] R. Lefèvre: *Raz de marée* (Paris, 1944), p. 90.

taken to the station by tram under an escort of three soldiers and a lieutenant in Brussels, the latter saw

a man walking along the street with his wife who was pregnant. The complexions of both were dark. Foreigners! The tram has to stop and the man is brought to the lieutenant. Sure enough they were foreigners. Order: the man was to be taken along with the rest of the prisoners. Protest: 'I have been living here so long and here are my papers. Everything is in order.'—'Papers?' The lieutenant laughs. 'Ah, and my wife is near her time!'—'You must explain all that at the place where you arrive!'[1]

Suspicion therefore *may* focus itself on comparatively accidental individuals. It happens more often (understandably so) that suspicion centres on individuals or groups of individuals who have already aroused a certain amount of fear and aggressiveness in the time preceding the enemy's attack. These earlier fears and aggressiveness may have different motives, working independently of each other or in unison. Sometimes they are of a social-economic nature but more often of a political one. When a community is being attacked by national-socialist Germany and there is an urge to assume that there are spies and saboteurs in one's own midst—what is then more natural than the assumption that espionage and sabotage are being committed by those who for years have indeed ranged themselves on the side of national socialist Germany: *Reichsdeutsche, Volksdeutsche,* 'fascists', all of whom have systematically been undermining the existing state of things? Now that the war has come some *know* and many others suddenly *assume* that those who aided the political enemy in peacetime will now also aid him in military fashion. It is the political Fifth Column whose members are indicted, interned, sentenced and as often as not executed. 'Traitors all!' The terms of abuse that are poured over them, the blows that rain down on them are the channels that relieve people of their own fear, aggressiveness and uncertainty.

Not every member of the community that is being attacked is involved in equal measure; this depends on numerous individual factors. Notwithstanding the generally prevailing tension that is also alive in their own minds some are yet able to reckon with the promptings of rational insight and common sense and with the dictates of conscience: in Poland the shooting of *Volksdeutsche* as Fifth Columnists was prevented on various occasions by Polish officers. Their courage deserves admiration: whoever jumps into the breach for a 'traitor' at such a moment of supreme tension runs the risk of himself being considered and treated as a 'traitor'. Experience in holding

---

[1] This was to be a French concentration camp at the foot of the Pyrenees. Lagrou: *Wij verdachten,* p. 51.

office and a sense of duty also play their part: it is often the police who defend the arrested Fifth Columnists with great difficulty, at their own peril, against the excited crowd. In that crowd, however, there are often people who, as it were, offer themselves as intruments to the collective fear and aggressiveness. They start stabbing and murdering—actions that at that moment are tolerated by many members of the community that feels menaced; by some, they are even admired and applauded.

Moreover, as soon as the attacked community has to cope with reverses, the scapegoat mechanism is set working, by means of which fresh 'enemies within our midst' are created. The realisation that they, the members of the community themselves, are also responsible for the shortcomings and mistakes whence the reverses arise is not allowed to reach their consciousness: special individuals are charged with the collective guilt. The enemy is victorious through *their* negligence. Is it not probable that it was intentional? In less than no time the imputation becomes graver: they have 'committed treason'. Pointing out the scapegoats—which, once again, *primarily* is done by a few individuals, though hundreds of thousands, quick as lightning, catch up the 'accusations'—has yet another advantage, namely that the reverses need not be looked upon as the result of deeper-lying, comparatively permanent factors of an economic, political and military nature. No, they may then be looked upon as having been caused solely by the temporary functioning of a limited set of individuals who, now that they have been detected, can easily be put out of the way. The names of leading public men—politicians, distinguished generals, important figures in industry—are everywhere in the air: *they* are the traitors. Once they are known, ever fresh charges are added to the old.

In this way in May, 1940, in France, after the collapse in the north, where the bridges across the Meuse were supposed to have been captured by the Germans as a result of the wicked negligence—the treachery—of a few French officers, it was said of the only general whose name Reynaud had mentioned, of Corap (commander-in-chief of the Ninth Army) 'that at the critical moment [he] had withdrawn to the luxurious villa of an immensely wealthy industrialist, and that he had installed his mistress there to make things pleasant for himself'.[1]

No animal has a broader back than the scapegoat.

We should like to return for a moment to the point of time when the enemy within our midst is first named.

[1] Quoted by the former minister, Landry, *French Parl. Enq.*, Interrogations, Vol. VIII, p. 2433.

Rational thinking plays a very minor part in the inner process that leads to that naming. It acts, one might say, like the prosecutor who has received orders from the judge to produce evidence that will warrant the severest sentence. And that evidence is produced at the vital moment. For this no more happens than that comparatively indiscriminate observations made by the senses are stamped as suspicious. All the signals made to the enemy that we so often came across in the course of our enquiry: the signs on the roofs, the painted chimneys, the fields of grain sown or mown according to design or in the shape of an arrow, the signals with light, smoke, mirrors, white material, curtains, chalk lines, maps and newspapers, the indications on the backs of advertisement signs and posters—they were all observations which, looked upon objectively, had no connection whatever with enemy operations, but which, subjectively, were stamped with elemental force as suspect by the individual making the observations. They were the phantom evidence that the emotions needed.[1]

Many normal sensory perceptions are suddenly looked upon as suspect in time of war, or whenever any great danger is threatening. 'A car getting into gear is a siren, a door that bangs is a bomb.'[2] How much more suspect are the observations made with relation to people against whom a certain animosity already exists, or when they are made under circumstances in which the enemy may suddenly make his appearance at any moment! Every shot then heard has been fired by him, and if he is not anywhere in the vicinity then it must be his accomplices. The impression of being fired at by those accomplices from all sides is particularly strong when there is fighting in the streets of a town where the bullets ricochet on every side. Officers and men excite each other; they shoot to rid themselves of their fear. As a rule they shoot at each other, which often happens in the field, too, at the beginning of a war. Each shot that one hears is a new piece of evidence that a Fifth Columnist is lurking in the immediate neighbourhood.

[1] It appeared that nine-tenths of the light signals observed on a large scale in the Netherlands in February and March, 1940, could be accounted for as having absolutely normal causes: headlights shining at an upward slant for a moment because of a slope in the road, induction in light advertisements, etc. In a few cases half-grown youths occupied themselves with alarming the neighbourhood by making light signals, in some other cases the same was done by neurotic people who wanted to draw attention to themselves. For a very small remainder of the signals no explanation has been found. It is not impossible that people who were interested in increasing the nervousness in the Netherlands had a hand in this. It is further a curious fact that during the first period of the German occupation German authorities required the Dutch military commanders immediately to cease making light signals on a large scale to the benefit of the English.

[2] Fabre-Luce: *Journal de la France*, p. 319.

In this situation enormous confusion resulted during the German invasion in May, 1940, notably in the big towns of Western Holland. This confusion was increased by the report that the enemy was misusing Dutch uniforms (a report that turned out to be correct only for a certain sector of the front). There were military men in The Hague who as a result of this removed the insignia from their uniforms. The Germans would surely not be prepared for that!—But the consequence was that they were thought to be Germans in disguise by other military men who had not done so. Order did not return until the troops were withdrawn from the streets on the fourth day of the war. No wonder: that ended mutual shooting.

It need be but very few who first name the enemy within their midst. That also holds good for the putting into words of the evidence. One formulates it—all catch it up. This process may take place in a small group ('Here is a German paper! Therefore this *Volksdeutscher* must be a spy!') It can also be at work on a national scale. Reports that are emotionally determined, insufficiently checked, or that have been added to with partly or wholly incorrect conclusions, and which reach military and civil authorities from below, in the general atmosphere of nervousness are turned into public announcements, communiqués and army reports, all teeming with frightening inaccuracies, which in their turn increase the inclination to detect fresh 'outrages'. Once it is suspected that the water has been poisoned, then it at once tastes strange; and once it tastes strange it *is* poisoned. The general fear produces ever fresh evidence. In this way during the fighting in Rotterdam a gas officer of troops moving into a school building smelled gas: 'Others thought they had already smelled it before. Those who had picked up shell splinters immediately felt their fingers itching: mustard gas! The word gas caused a terrific reaction, gas masks were at once in evidence. The people whose fingers itched got big bandages of chlorate of potash round their hands.'[1] The alarm proved groundless.[2]

During the fighting in The Hague a high government official made a present of a hundred cigarettes, marked with his monogram, to the military guard. The latter were to defend the Department building (where the ministers were tensely awaiting the turn of events) against

---

[1] The memoirs of the army chaplain R. Verhoeven in B. Mol: *Vrij!* (Utrecht, 1945), p. 89. We are inclined to ascribe the case of the Polish lieutenant Kowalski, mentioned in this book on p. 47, to fancy also. He received water from a *volksdeutsche* woman 'with mustard gas, fortunately in a diluted form'.

[2] The day they occupied Rotterdam the German military were so convinced that the drinking water had been purposely poisoned that an inspector of police had to make a written declaration that that was not the case. Fear was alive in them too! De Jong: *De Rotterdamse politie gedurende de oorlogsjaren 1939–1945*, p. 155.

Fifth Columnists: 'A few hours later the cigarettes came back accompanied by the rumour: there are poisoned cigarettes. I then said: I should like to see them. I was thereupon shown cigarettes with my own monogram!' [1] The absolute absurdity of the evidence can sometimes be demonstrated in this way. Light signals on further enquiry prove to be the result of a flickering candle, a curtain that is blown by the wind, a lamp that for quite harmless reasons has been switched on and off a few times in succession, or perhaps the reflection of sunlight in a window that is standing ajar and moving. And again, a house is entered, and what was thought to be a machine-gun is actually a flag staff. 'Strips of material for warning airplanes' are ordinary covers.

It often happens, however, that persons who have ascertained the absurdity of a special piece of evidence are nevertheless not at once willing to concede that other pieces of evidence are equally absurd. The critical thinking faculty of most individuals is swept along on the current of emotions and convictions. And it very often happens (especially among civilians and soldiers, much less so among the officials of justice and police) that every critical verification of the evidence is dismissed out of hand. No appeal can be lodged against the inner verdict passed by the emotions on the basis of a few scattered observations. Often no defence against them is possible. Worse still: all the arguments used by the person under suspicion as proof of his innocence, are converted into fresh pieces of evidence for the indictment. One need but recall the case of the correspondent of the *New York Times* who was almost shot in France (he had been arrested on account of his blue eyes and fair hair!): 'When he pointed out that he had the red ribbon of the Legion of Honour, they were aghast that even a German should have such affrontery; when he showed them his papers carefully supplied by General Gamelin's headquarters with numerous official stamps, they said that he was clearly suspect because he had too many papers.' It required a great deal of effort on the part of the accusers to give up their fictitious evidence.

In Belgium, where fear of parachutists was great in May, 1940, a young German tourist from Antwerp was interrogated by French officers. The German was unfortunate enough to have a sleeping-bag with him:

Now they had one! There lay his parachute! Every shred of the bag was scrutinized, and it was taken to bits to convert it into a parachute again. Some forgotten bits of chocolate were then found in a crease or some far corner of the bag. Believing their own reports, namely that German parachutists enticed children with

[1] Interrogation of Dr. H. M. Hirschfeld, *Neth. Parl. Enq.*, Vol. IIc, p. 367.

poisoned chocolate, the *deuxième bureau* people ordered the camper to eat it. With painfully intent faces they looked at him, in the conviction and expectation that he would fall down dead any minute. The boy did not fall down dead, however, and greedily devoured the forgotten sweetmeat—he was punished with blows for his pains.[1]

At about the same time the war correspondent of the *Figaro*, Maurice Noël, was detained in France somewhere to the north of Paris. He was tall and fair, and was riding a bicycle while passing through a village where shortly before some German bombs had dropped. In less than no time a crowd had gathered about him; he was the 'Fifth Columnist' who had made signals to the Germans—who, as it were, had caused the bombing! Amid the derisive hooting of the populace he was taken to the police station:

> The police carried out a thorough search while the crowd shouted that he should be killed. Noël had taken off his top-boots as it was so hot and had hung them on the handlebars of the bicycle. In them was found a box of white powder which he took against indigestion. 'There it is!' they shouted. 'There is the explosive!'—'Nonsense'! he yelled. 'I will prove that it isn't explosive.' He lighted a match to make his demonstration, but before he could put the flame to the powder, three police officers, ten men and a number of women had flung themselves on him in a desperate attempt to save the police station from total destruction.[2]

Noël did in the end succeed in establishing his innocence.

It would often happen, however, especially at and behind the front, that much shorter work was made of persons suspected of belonging to the Fifth Column.

Accusing an imaginary Fifth Column is by no means a phenomenon that we only come across in time of war. It is then most particularly virulent and general. The formulation of such fictitious accusations by a few individuals and the ready acceptance of them by many others, also occurs in peacetime. Similar mechanisms may be observed in all excessive persecutions of people and groups in any period of international tension. One need but recall the witch trials and Jewish pogroms. They are primitive forms of behaviour which cannot truly be fathomed if one merely points out the absurdity of the accusations that are then uttered. At the actual moment those accusations seem the cause of the persecution, but the true causes lie very much deeper.

[1] Lagrou: *Wij verdachten*, p. 119.
[2] Gordon Waterfield: *What happened to France* (London, 1940), p. 50.

Most of the victims cannot grasp those underlying causes. They feel the blows; they do not ask themselves what is it that moves their persecutors to act in the way they do. Often they are entirely innocent. One need but recall the California *Nisei* in the second World War. Things were different in regard to the 'fascists' who were rounded up and often harshly treated in Western Europe—to take but one example. Would they not have to admit on reflection 'that they had asked for it'? They did not allow that question to enter their consciousness because they could not bear the answer. They had not been shooting from houses, nor did they intend to do so: *therefore* they considered themselves innocent. They did not understand the persecutions they were made to suffer.

Nor were the Germans alive to the psychological process lying at the root of the accusations which pointed to an extensive German military Fifth Column. It escaped their notice that people honestly believed in it. They looked upon the reports mentioning such a Fifth Column as the diabolically astute, consciously thought-out plan of their opponents, a 'weapon in the Franco-British conduct of war'.[1] Or as 'a propandistic proposition', as a German official in the Netherlands expressed it,' which the British Ministry of Information throws out at critical moments during the course of the war, cleverly speculating on the ever present fear for espionage and foreigners'.[2]

As we have already said, the fact that the true causes of the naming and persecution of such an imaginary Fifth Column lie in emotional life is a primary reason why it was difficult to get the persecutors even to consider whether many of those accusations were not perhaps imaginary. Another, to our mind, secondary reason, is that it is not always possible to prove the objective incorrectness of these accusations or to make this rationally plausible. When it is a question of showing that it is not true that 'the witch does not weigh anything' a good pair of scales are sufficient. The accusations, however, that were uttered in connection with the German military Fifth Column were embedded in an endlessly confused and complicated whole of facts and events in the political, military, economic, social and cultural field, that were reported in the human mind in the form of rumours, tales, news-items, articles, books—a veritable tangle of outer and inner factors that influenced each other in all manner of ways, together forming 'human history' that cannot be adequately overlooked in peacetime, let alone in time of war.

Meanwhile those accusations are not always maintained. They

[1] Hans Gracht: *Die fünfte Kolonne* (Berlin, 1941), p. 44.
[2] Introduction by the *Rundfunkreferat, Vertreter des Auswärtigen Amtes im Stabe des Reichskommissars*, to the translation of extracts from F. Lafitte: *The Internment of Aliens*.

often vanish together with the feelings whose expression they are. Man is able to adapt himself to war. He finds out that the chance of becoming its victim is relatively small. The fighting at the front takes a clearer course. A large part of everyday life continues in a comparatively normal way. As a result his fear diminishes and loses its vagueness. His aggressiveness finds a definite aim: the enemy whose power proves to be by no means unlimited. Everyone receives a useful task. In this way the community gradually regains its equanimity, which of course does not alter the fact that later in the course of the war situations may arise in which the general instability of everyday life again becomes unbearably great.

How quickly the restoration of normal conditions occurs depends on a whole train of factors. It may come about fairly soon. A fine example of this is to be found in England, where some of the German refugees, who had been interned as imaginary Fifth Columnists in the summer of 1940, were set at liberty after but a few months had elapsed. The rest were able to leave the camps in batches, later. Much depends in such cases on the power of the civil authorities, which as experience has shown in various countries are much better able to recognise the real Fifth Column danger than the military authorities. In Britain and the United States the civil departments were forced by the military authorities (who temporarily had public opinion behind them), really against their better judgment, to co-operate in the internment of the refugees and *Nisei*.

The general exaggerated notion of the German Fifth Column in the second World War maintained its hold on people's minds in the later phases of that war, and after.

How can this be explained?

Besides the factors we have already mentioned, we should like to draw attention to two others.

In the first World War the reports about the imaginary Fifth Column were lost fairly soon in the overwhelming news of a bloody struggle that was to last for four years, and in which victory or defeat obviously were determined by quite other forces than by spying maid-servants, sabotaging monks and cars 'full of gold and swift as an arrow'. The course of the war itself demonstrated the foolishness of the reports about the Fifth Column, which had figured on the front pages of all the newspapers during the first days and weeks.

In the second World War it was different. In Poland, Scandinavia and Western Europe there was no time to recognise the incorrectness of most of the reports. The German campaigns coincided there with the formation in the minds of the attacked nations of the exaggerated Fifth Column idea. Before any correction had been possible the

Germans had been victorious and the time of occupation set in. Then it became doubly difficult to correct the picture in people's minds. Quisling, Mussert and Degrelle, who co-operated with the German oppressor—had they not probably rendered him military aid? Fool, nay worse, 'traitor', the man who did not believe that!

A second factor was of perhaps even greater importance.

However exaggerated the general idea of the German military Fifth Column had been, it was partly correct. *Volksdeutsche* in Poland had shot at Polish troops, in Denmark there had been German national socialists who had helped the invasion troops, in Holland the Germans had used Dutch uniforms to their own advantage, in Belgium Germans had operated in the disguise of refugees, saboteurs had landed in America. That people did not see these and similar real Fifth Column actions in their true proportions but, in so far as they were observed, looked upon them as the visible part of a no doubt much larger whole, would not surprise us.

The group that is being persecuted as imaginary Fifth Column need not actually have done anything to become the victim of popular fury. The power and persistence, however, of belief in an exaggerated German military Fifth Column to our mind cannot be dissociated from the real actions we have minutely examined. However limited the activities of that German military Fifth Column may have been proportionately, they exercised an extremely powerful stimulating influence on the perpetuation of the original Fifth Column image. The power and persistence of that image should be an indication to us how greatly millions of people felt menaced by national socialist Germany, how diabolically the figure of Hitler affected them, how disquieted they were by the intrigues carried out, for instance by the *Auslands-Organisation der NSDAP*. In the history of some nations they were emotions of recent date, but in that of others only a new expression of deep-seated feelings that formed an accompaniment to a struggle against the Germans that had been going on for generations, even centuries. The fear people had of the Fifth Column was in a considerable part founded on actual fact. This we can only approach in its historical perspective, and the most natural inference is to assume that only in that special perspective can any explanation be found for the fact that the evidences of a German military Fifth Column of any considerable magnitude were confined to Poland and Yugoslavia.

CHAPTER XVI

Historical Summary

★

I<small>T</small> is one of the charms but also one of the dangers of history that one can go as far back as one likes. Most people are not aware to what extent their behaviour is being determined by the past of the community to which they belong. The past of the German communities which we met in the course of our story, forms a fascinating subject, full of variety. The Volga Germans who, in 1941, were deported by order of Stalin, had a history of their own. So have the Sudeten Germans, the majority of whom lent their support to Konrad Henlein in 1935. It would lead us too far, however, to give here a survey, however brief, of the ups and downs in the history of those millions of Germans who left Germany[1] in the course of the centuries. In order to do so we would have to go back to the early Middle Ages.

It is, however, of importance to point out that we must distinguish two principal types among these colonisations extending down the centuries: that in which the Germans settled down in communities which on the whole had the same economic and cultural level they themselves had had, social surroundings therefore in which they did not take up any higher, more privileged position on account of their being Germans than the rest of the community, and in which they as a rule quickly assimilated themselves to their new environment,

[1] Wherever colonisation in foreign parts took place from regions now reckoned to Germany there were often members of related 'peoples' among the 'Germans': 'Dutch', 'Belgians', 'Alsatians', 'Swiss'. In this brief survey we cannot do otherwise than represent matters more simply than they actually were. Thus we leave out of account the fact that the dividing line between 'German' and 'non-German' groups was never absolute. 'On the borders' there was a continuous shifting from one group to another. The real division was not anthropological but social and cultural. In Eastern Europe there have been several 'Slav' groups who counted themselves as belonging to the 'German' social and cultural milieu.

267

and lost their German character in one or two generations; and on the other hand the colonisation wherein the Germans settled in communities representing a much lower economic and cultural level. They then took up a higher, more privileged position on account of their being Germans, which they naturally tried to maintain.

In between these two types of colonisation, the assimilatory and non-assimilatory type, there of course existed many betwixt and between types. The German colonisation in the United States and in parts of the world like Australia and New Zealand formed a striking example of the assimilatory type. The non-assimilatory one has, generally speaking, been characteristic of the position of the Germans in Eastern Europe. Wherever they settled on their own initiative, as conquerors—one need but recall the Teutonic Order in the Middle Ages—or at the invitation of local princes, in that wide stretch of country inhabited by Slavs that stretches from the Finnish Gulf in a large arc to the Adriatic, they usually came as the bearers of a superior civilisation. Their weapons were better. They knew how to mine ore. They had agricultural implements made of iron. They knew where and how to build villages, and how to plan towns. They occupied privileged positions as a matter of course—either as a privileged group that did not oppress other groups of the population (Poland, Volga area, Southern Russia, Rumania) or as harsh rulers (Estonia, Latvia, Slovenia). In both cases they considered themselves far above the native population. A feeling of haughtiness grew in them that was passed on from one generation to the next: they were cleverer, abler, more capable, they were 'born rulers' in fact.

Inversely, a deeply rancorous feeling arose among the Slav masses of the population, who had first been *pressed* down and later *kept* down, against the alien 'intruders' and rulers who took up a privileged position in the community as propertied farmers and burghers, as big landowners and high civil servants.

Generally speaking until about the beginning of this century the colonising German groups maintained but few contacts with Germany itself and on the whole the Germans living in Germany did not have any strong interest in the fate of their sons and daughters who had migrated abroad, and less even in their offspring. All this was changed during the first World War and as a result of it, and it would be impossible to understand the events after 1933, especially the fact that some German groups allowed themselves to become Hitler's political or even military tools unless it is indicated with a few details how after the end of that great struggle the situation developed in the various countries and areas in which groups of Germans lived. We shall only briefly sum up and stress the general disposition of the groups in question.

268

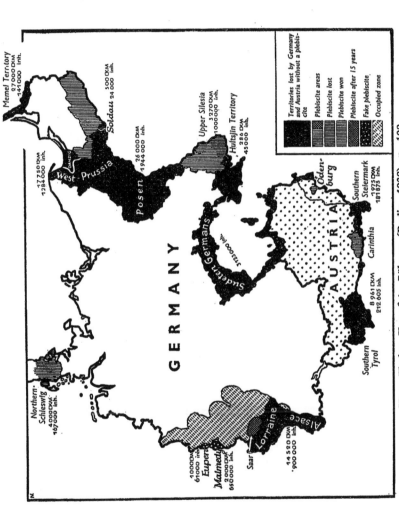

Hans Krebs: *Kampf in Böhman* (Berlin, 1938), p. 108.
GERMANY'S TERRITORIAL LOSSES AFTER THE FIRST WORLD WAR

There were four frontier areas that were mainly or solely German which Germany had to cede at the Peace of Versailles: the Saar, Eupen-Malmédy, Danzig, Memel. In the case of free elections the Saar (with about 800,000 Germans),[1] Danzig (with 350,000 Germans) and Memel (with 60,000 Germans) would have joined Germany with an overwhelming majority as early as the twenties. In the frontier districts of Eupen-Malmédy that had been annexed by Belgium, the *volksdeutsche* group (50,000 persons), which at first had been in the majority, had become a minority owing to the great number of Belgian 'immigrants'.

In Alsace the population was largely German in origin and also spoke German; yet they felt French. It was with joy that they had seen the backs of the 'Prussians' in 1918. Their joy did not remain unalloyed. The French Government, encouraged by the ultra-French party among the Alsatians, furthered teaching in French with all their might. Protestations were not long in coming. From about 1925 onwards a fairly strong movement came up that demanded cultural autonomy.

Germany, after losing the war, had also had to cede territory to two countries where German minorities had lived in 1918: Northern Schleswig to Denmark, West Prussia (the Polish Corridor), Posen and Eastern Upper Silesia to Poland. The Danes treated the *volksdeutsche* minority (30,000 persons) decently. It consisted of Germans who, if it had been left to them, would rather have lived under German rule; so a certain amount of discontent was inevitable, but it was not of a violent brand. It was otherwise in Poland! There the *volksdeutsche* minority had resisted the establishment of Polish rule tooth and nail. In Posen alone a thousand German volunteers had been killed, and six hundred in Upper Silesia. The Poles had won the struggle and at once launched an attack on the Germans. In rather more than ten years, over three-fifths of the German town population had gone back to Germany. Four-fifths of the German landed estates were nationalised. That the *Volksdeutschen* who remained in Poland in spite of all the oppression became possessed of a spirit of recalcitrance and exasperation stands to reason.

Yet another group of Germans had lost their connection with the German *Reich* as a result of the Peace of Versailles: the *Kolonialdeutschen* in South-West Africa (12,000 persons). They too were discontented because they had to share their privileged position as colonists with white immigrants from South Africa, to whom in many respects they were subordinated. They considered that South Africa was reaping what Germany had sown.

[1] Here and henceforth we shall always give the actual or estimated population figures for 1930 or thereabouts.

270

In all these cases, even before Hitler came to power, the German part of the population had but one cherished wish, and that was the restoration of German rule.

What was the state of mind like in the German areas that had made up part of the old Austro-Hungarian Monarchy, i.e. Austria itself, the Sudeten area and South Tyrol?

Anschluss with Germany had been strictly forbidden to Austria. Yet all the big parties continued to express the desirability of this in their programmes. In the course of the twenties, however, the *Anschluss* idea fell into the background because the increasing tension between socialist Vienna and the clerical countryside demanded more and more attention.

The Sudeten German population was not able to stomach the 'treachery' of the Czechs in the first World War and their own failure to attain independence. Here too a considerable part of the German landed estates were liquidated, although in return for adequate pecuniary compensation. It irritated the Sudeten Germans that the Czechs continued in their attempts to penetrate with groups from their own population into the frontier area, so important from an economic and military point of view, for the young republic. In many towns and villages the embittered struggle between Sudeten Germans and Czechs continued. In the Prague parliament the Sudeten Germans had their own parties. More than half of their representatives did not understand a word of Czech. This large contingent of well over three million German-speaking people, whose sympathies were all on the side of the Germans, felt there was nothing for it but to resign themselves to their fate, but they did so with a bad grace.

And finally the German population in South Tyrol (they were concentrated in the northern valleys, the southern half was Italian) had been undergoing Italianisation by means of coercion and force since the establishment of the fascist government. The Germans (280,000 persons), according to Mussolini 'did not form a minority but an ethnical relic—the remainder of barbaric invasions in earlier campaigns'.[1] Their treatment was in keeping with this utterance.

Next, as we have indicated, large groups of Germans had settled among numerous Slav races and in Hungary in the Middle Ages and in the eighteenth and nineteenth centuries. After the first World War all those Germans, seen from their own point of view, had a hard time of it.

In Estonia (18,000 Germans) and Latvia (65,000 Germans) their social and political privileges were abolished. In Latvia something

[1] Speech delivered on Feb. 6, 1926, quoted in: *Die Nationalitäten in den Staaten Europas* (Vienna, 1931), p. 512.

like 1000 big German land-owners had owned half the soil. The young republic started to liquidate estates on a large scale, dividing the land among Latvian agricultural labourers. German 'barons' who had had a thousand or ten thousand hectares, might think themselves lucky if they were able to go on living in their coach-houses as owners of 50 hectares. The German bourgeoisie in the towns also lost their privileges. Many Germans went away, and those who remained behind adapted themselves, resignedly but dejectedly, to the new situation.

In Hungary the *Volksdeutschen* (550,000 persons) suffered from the cultural pressure brought to bear on them. Minority rights were not allowed them. They had a few elementary schools of their own, but secondary schools they had none. Separate political representation was not granted them.

In Rumania too the *Volksdeutschen* (750,000 persons) had to make sacrifices. Part of their landed estates were taken away from them, and teaching in German was discouraged.

In Yugoslavia the pressure brought to bear on the *Volksdeutschen* (600,000 persons) was even stronger. There were still elementary schools where the teaching was done in German, but there were no German secondary schools or training colleges. The *Volksdeutschen* did not throw up the sponge. They fought for 'every form, every teacher, every child, every teach-book and every hour of German'.[1] The struggle in Slovenia was especially intense, where the Slovenes who had been so long oppressed by the Germans, tried to abolish all German institutions, indignant as they were about the Slovene minority in Austria, just across the border, not being allowed any cultural independency.

In the Soviet Union after the revolution and as a result of it most of the German middle-class people had vanished from the towns. Many of them fled to Germany. In the Ukraine, on the Baltic and in the Volga area the well-to-do German farming communities were driven into a corner. As a rule they would have nothing to do with bolshevism. In the civil war many Germans fought against the Red Army. The communists remained victorious. After the civil war the *Volksdeutschen* were stricken with famine, after the famine came collectivisation of farming and after that again famine. Of the 1,100,000 *Volksdeutsche* living on the Volga, Don, Dnjepr and Black Sea there were 760,000 left in 1926. In the German Volga republic there were proportionately almost seven times more communists among the Russians than among the *Volksdeutschen*. That was before the struggle against the 'Kulaks' began, during which numberless *Volksdeutsche* were banished to Siberia, according to an English

[1] Richard Bahr: *Volk vor den Grenzen* (Hamburg, 1933), p. 444.

272

traveller who was visiting the area in 1936, one-fifth of the whole group.[1]

Let us now consider what happened to the relative positions of the various groups in those areas where the Germans did as a rule assimilate themselves to their new surroundings.

In the United States the number of Germans who still spoke German was rapidly decreasing. In the majority of German associations English became the language employed. In 1890 there had still been 1000 German daily papers and periodicals, in 1926 there were only 275. Ten years later a German traveller went in quest of *Deutschtum* in Philadelphia—a town where German immigrants and groups had played a prominent part in the nineteenth century:

> At last one finds a German paper that can hardly hold its own, or a library that has nearly been forgotten, and if one is in luck and goes far enough away from the more important streets and squares, to the districts where the unimportant people live, then on a Sunday one may happen upon the soft notes of a German hymn rising from a brick church, but the vigorous and clear voices of the younger generation are missing. And if one makes enquiries long enough one may get to know where the men from a certain German district meet, and where to find the hall of a German men's choir.[2]

After the first World War there were already Germans who disconsolately prognosticated that in America in a century's time only the gravestones would still speak German. The Germans who had settled there before 1914 had indeed largely become Americanised. The Americanisation of the 'fresh' German immigrants was still to start, however: those who had not been able to find a living under the Weimar republic.

In South America the assimilating process was more gradual.

The German nation had shown scant interest in the fate of the Germans outside Germany's frontiers before the first World War. All that was to change after 1918.

In various frontier districts there was heavy fighting, with the Poles in Upper Silesia, and with the Slovenes in Southern Austria. Thousands of German volunteers, mostly youthful nationalists, journeyed thither and joined the loose military formations, the so-called *Freikorps*. Many people were intensely interested in the outcome of the plebiscites held in certain contested areas in the years

---

[1] *The Times* (London), Nov. 25, 1936.
[2] Karl Götz: *Deutsche Leistung in Amerika* (Berlin, 1940), p. 53.

1920–22. Hundreds of crowded trains would then chug through the country in order to take the voters to the frontier districts where the outcome would be decided; as a rule those who had been born in the contested areas before a given date were allowed to take part in the plebiscite whether they still lived there or not. Millions of Germans felt profoundly bound up with the *Grenzdeutschen* (Frontier Germans). They deplored their fate; they regretted their loss. More even: the struggle along the frontiers awakened a lively interest in the Germans living still further away from home. The feeling of having been wronged by world history, of their turn at 'dividing up the world' having come too late, all tended to their considering the German groups living in foreign parts to be remainders of a glorious past, not yet entirely ended.

Those who had been driven out of the frontier districts stimulated that feeling. They got into touch again with like-minded brethren in the areas that had been lost, and gave them financial aid and advised them to urge that autonomy be granted them, which with time would form a basis for further demands. Scientific data were diligently collected that might 'prove' the 'historical rights' of the Germans. At about a dozen different Universities special institutes were established that were to specialise in the history of certain German groups abroad. The *Deutsche Ausland-Institut* (German Institute of Foreign Countries) in Stuttgart, founded in 1917, was the most active with its staff of sixty people, and had already printed something like fifty publications by 1932. The *Verein für das Deutschtum in Ausland* (League of Germandom Abroad), which was founded in 1881, also flourished in an unprecedented way. It spent 2·5 million *Reichsmark* a year. The number of books and brochures devoted to the fortunes of the *Auslandsdeutschen* ran into thousands. A fairly generally accepted conviction arose that was only rejected in communist and some socialist circles, to the effect that there were 100 million Germans on earth: 65 million in Germany and 35 million outside her frontiers.

But how scornfully, how unfairly millions of members of that proud *Hundertmillionenvolk* were treated abroad! In regions which they, and they alone, had made prosperous, they were persecuted and hunted—dung ('*Kulturdünger*') that was ploughed under by thankless Slavs and Hungarians.

In all this interest that was shown there was some genuine feeling for the fate of the minorities, some real indignation about the indolence with which the League of Nations, which had guaranteed the decent treatment of those minorities, investigated their complaints and protests—an investigation that almost always came to nothing on account of the recalcitrant attitude of the government in question.

How can Germans ever be chauvinists, the historian Oncken wondered in 1926. 'Over against the caricatures of a narrow-minded
nationalism it is our calling to represent . . . the undying cause of
justice, of cultural autonomy and of the right of minorities, and
by so doing to perform a moral mission among the peoples of the
world.' [1]

There were Germans who thought differently. 'Undying cause of
justice?' Nonsense! History was a matter of survival of the fittest. In
order to increase the feeling of guilt among the victors public opinion
abroad was to be shown the bad treatment the minorities were
undergoing. With that as basis the whole system of post-war peace
treaties might be convulsed.

This idea of revenge was strongest in the German Nazi party. It
was often denied, but whoever saw Stormtroops marching knew the
truth. It was by no means accidental that from the very first the
figures who played a prominent part in this party had received a
great deal of their shaping as members of German groups that had
got to be oppressed. Hitler was a typical German nationalist and
anti-semite from Austria. Rudolf Hess, his deputy, had grown up in
Egypt as the son of a German merchant who had lost all his possessions in the first World War. Hermann Goering had spent half his
youth in Austria; his father had been governor of German South-
West Africa. Alfred Rosenberg, editor of the *Völkische Beobachter*,
came originally from Reval in Estonia. Richard Walter Darré, who
planned the national socialist agricultural programme, had been
born in the Argentine. His rival, Herbert Backe, saw the light of day
in the Caucasus.

However much national socialism in Germany was an outcome,
or rather a coming together of different ideological currents, some of
which had already become noticeable in the beginning of the nineteenth century, nevertheless, as a *synthesis* of anti-capitalism, anti-
semitism and chauvinism determined by resentment, it had first
shown its face in the old Austro-Hungarian Monarchy in Vienna,
especially in the Sudeten area.[2] There it was the fanatic fighting
ideology of a minority that felt itself spurned. It was an ideology
that started to get millions of German citizens under its spell, when
the emotional situation in which they found themselves was comparable to that of the Austrian and Sudeten artisans and tradesmen

[1] Hermann Oncken: 'Geistige und sittliche Bedeutung des Auslanddeutschtums', *Nation und Geschichte, Reden und Aufsätze, 1919–1935* (Berlin, 1935),
p. 303.
[2] This was already pointed out by Elizabeth Wiskemann in 1939: *Undeclared
War* (London, 1939), pp. 220–1, 311.

round about the turn of the century. At the beginning of the twenties national socialism was stronger in both Austria and the Sudeten area than in Germany. When Hitler's NSDAP had been broken up after the failure of the Munich *Putsch* in November, 1923, it was the leaders of the Sudeten Nazi party who furnished the first funds for its reconstruction.

But national socialism had also struck root in other German groups before the coming to power of Hitler.

In the Saar the NSDAP members formed a small but active nucleus. In Eupen-Malmédy it was the same. In the Free State of Danzig the NSDAP had acquired one-sixth of all votes in the autumn of 1932. In 1928 a national socialist movement had sprung up in Memel, which, however, on the instruction of the leaders of the NSDAP, only worked in secret. In Alsace the youthful leaders of the autonomist movement were in touch with the German NSDAP from as early as 1925. In South-West Africa a few *Ortsgruppen* of the NSDAP had also been formed. In Austria the NSDAP (Hitler Movement), which received its instructions from Munich, had expanded enormously. By the end of 1932 it is probable that they had one-fifth of the population to back them. In South Tyrol no activities were carried out by the NSDAP. From the outset Hitler took the view that for the sake of alliance with fascist Italy that area would have to be relinquished.

In the Slav frontier areas and in Hungary but little had appeared of any penetration of national socialism among the German minorities there. Estonia and Rumania formed the only exceptions. In Estonia a national socialist grouping had come into existence in 1932. And from Rumania a discredited leader of the old German group, Dr. Karl Wolff, had sent one of his followers, Captain Fritz Fabritius, to Germany in order, he said, 'to look for people who still believed in a future for Germany'.[1] Fabritius had already been the leader of an anti-semitic youth group before the first World War. He returned to Rumania as an enthusiastic follower of Hitler. *Mein Kampf* became Dr. Wolff's 'daily reading matter'.[2]

Among the half million *Reichsdeutsche* who had emigrated to the United States after Germany's defeat, were many younger men who had not been able, or who had not wished to get a normal place in society. Several of them had been members of the extremist *Freikorps*. The large group of pre-war German immigrants had shown no interest in their attempts at arousing sympathy for movements like the NSDAP. The post-war extreme right-wing immigrants therefore set

[1] Otto Fritz Jickeli: 'Karl Wolff. Der Wirtschaftsführer der Siebenbürger Sachsen', *Grosse Deutsche im Ausland* (Stuttgart, 1939), p. 298.
[2] *Ibid.*

up their own organisation, in 1924 in Chicago, for instance, the 'Teutonia' which carried out national socialist propaganda in a small circle. Its leader, Fritz Gissibl, a follower of Julius Streicher, became a member of the NSDAP in 1926. This action met with a certain amount of response in other towns. When at the elections in the autumn of 1930 Hitler suddenly appeared to be the leader of the party that was the strongest but one in Germany, the movement expanded still further. In September, 1932, Hitler appointed a certain Heinz Spanknoebel to be the leader of the Nazi movement in the United States. It was still small at this time. *Reichsdeutsche* and persons who had obtained American citizenship were members. It bore the character of a fanatic sect.

Round about 1930 groups of national socialists had also been formed in South America, where a large part of the German immigrants had failed socially, in Brazil as much as three-quarters even. In 1928 twelve *Reichsdeutsche* set up an *Ortsgruppe* of the NSDAP in Paraguay. In 1931 various *Ortsgruppen* united in a *Landesgruppe*; the first of its kind in the whole world.

Such *Ortsgruppen* were also established in other countries: in Switzerland, Spain, Belgium, and probably elsewhere as well. They were usually small groups. The large mass of the *Reichsdeutschen* living abroad felt no interest in Hitler. There were figures in the NSDAP, however, who realised that their political friends in foreign parts would be able to render them important services. In the autumn of 1930 a *Reichsdeutscher*, Willy Grothe, had set up a bureau in Hamburg that had the aim of keeping in contact with all those foreign *reichsdeutschen* Nazis. Grothe had lived in Africa for twenty years and had been interned there by the British in the first World War. The bureau was recognised by the party leaders on May 1, 1931, and received the title: *Auslandsabteilung der Reichsleitung der NSDAP* (Foreign Department of the Reich Directorate of the NSDAP). At the time of Hitler's coming into power its small staff administered about three thousand members of the NSDAP living abroad. It did not signify much. The party leaders were not very clear of what use the members abroad could be. Hitler was not at that moment interested in the matter: all his attention was concentrated on the consolidation of power within Germany. The liquidation of the *Auslandsabteilung* was even considered by the party directorate in Munich, but a young functionary of the *Abteilung*, Ernst Wilhelm Bohle, was able to forestall this outcome.

Bohle was the English-born son of a German teacher and later professor of electro-technology who went to Cape Town as professor in 1906; the son thus grew up in South Africa. Bohle senior was an ardent nationalist: his five children were not allowed to speak a word of English at home. During the first World War Bohle junior was the only German boy at his school, and for that reason frequently received thrashings from his schoolmates. After the Peace of Versailles he was given the offer of a partnership in a family concern in England promising a good living. He declined the offer and went to Germany instead, where he studied economics; from 1924 onwards he worked for several firms. In 1931 an advertisement caught his eye, in which the *Auslandsabteilung* asked for a collaborator for the Africa section. This was attractive! If only the *Reichsdeutschen* abroad could be imbued with the sentiments of national solidarity and natural superiority for which he so admired and envied the British! He applied for the job and was accepted. On March 1, 1932, he became a member of the NSDAP. It was he who managed to convince the party chiefs of the potentialities of the *Auslandsabteilung*. There were already 160 *Ortsgruppen* at the time, and there were, he wrote in April, 1933, 'great opportunities for extension': the organisation was 'undoubtedly in a position to supply the offices of the party with valuable materials', 'especially political information and espionage reports'.[1]

Perhaps Bohle would never have achieved anything, if he had not been able to get into touch with Hitler's deputy for party affairs, the influential Rudolf Hess, through the intermediary of the latter's brother Alfred. There followed a conference in the Party's Headquarters and the decision was made: the *Auslandsabteilung* was to be maintained and even extended. All party agencies abroad, with the exception of those in Austria, Danzig and Memel, would be subordinated to it. In March, 1934, the membership administration of German seafarers was also transferred to it.

The *Auslands-Organisation der NSDAP*, or AO as it was usually called after 1935, rapidly grew: from 3300 members at the beginning of 1933 to 28,000 four years later, to which were added the 23,000 members of the *Abteilung Seefahrt*. In 1937 there were *Stützpunkte* with at least six, or *Ortsgruppen* with at least twelve members in over five hundred places abroad. The central office in Berlin had a staff of seven hundred persons: one functionary for every 75 members. A large staff indeed! But then there was more than enough work to be done.

Since 1933 the AO had sought systematically to get a hold on the political leadership of the *Reichsdeutschen* abroad. Those *Reichsdeutschen* whose attitude towards the Third *Reich* was reserved or hostile were forced to resign from office in German organisations. Frequently a whole German colony was compelled to re-organise, and a new 'national' agency would be founded in which the AO

[1] Letter, April 4, 1933, from Bohle to Schmeer, NG-5557.

members would be the real leaders behind the scenes. It was necessary, according to Bohle, to act tactfully. Nevertheless in many a
German colony troubles resulted; not a few Germans who had for
years been board members of German schools, hospitals, or clubs,
refused to resign in favour of the fanatics of the AO, who were often
social failures who now endeavoured to climb their way up in
society. In a few years, however, the AO nearly everywhere had
reached its object.

The aim of the AO was to imbue the German colonies abroad
with the spirit of national socialism. All German citizens living
abroad must be brought to stand united behind the *Führer*. Much of
the activity of the AO thus consisted of training and propaganda.
The AO was pre-eminently a political organisation.

An important section of its work was of a secret nature. Functionaries of the AO kept a check on the convictions and actions of
members of the German foreign service and on German journalists.
They spied on German refugees, collected their publications and
attempted to find out whether they were involved in currency smuggling. They drew up reports on German or other persons intending
to visit Germany or to seek employment there. They forwarded
names of German refugees agitating against the Nazi system in order
that they be deprived of their status of German citizen. They reported
on all the utterances unfavourable to Hitler or the Third *Reich* on the
part of Germans abroad. In other words: they were an extension of
the *Geheime Staatspolizei*, the Gestapo. The central office of the AO
had a special section working on Gestapo commissions. These were
acted on abroad either by the highest functionaries of the AO there,
or by special officials, frequently the same as were responsible for
keeping in touch with the groups formed amongst the crews of
German ships. For the latter purpose a separate service was created
within the AO, the *Hafendienst* (Harbour Service). The functionaries
of this service smuggled prohibited propaganda material past the
customs, kept in touch with the Gestapo and in certain cases helped
to bring politically active German refugees or other opponents of the
Nazi régime on board of home-bound ships by force, and so helped
them on their way to the concentration camps.

The central office of the AO had another section, the *Aussen-
handelsamt* (Office for Foreign Commerce), which collected information about the foreign representatives of German firms, with the aid
of local functionaries. Were such representatives sufficiently active?
Did they advertise enough in German newspapers, or too much in
anti-German ones? Did they employ Jews? In 1939 there were files
on 110,000 commercial representatives abroad. Another section had
done the same for foreign legal offices, so that German persons or

bodies needing legal assistance abroad should only use the 'World file of Aryan lawyers'. Finally, in 1937 the central office of the AO was extended with a liaison section of the *Abwehr*, headed by Heinz Cohrs, so that use might be made of the many ramifications of the AO for the collection of military espionage data.

All such and similar data were collected secretly. Protests on the part of foreign governments were ignored. If a *Landesgruppe* were prohibited, it was continued under another name. This occurred in the Netherlands as well as in South-West Africa, in Hungary as well as in Venezuela. Members of the German foreign service were appointed as AO functionaries and other AO functionaries were appointed on the staffs of German legations or consulates to give them diplomatic status. Compromising archives were preferably hidden in such diplomatically safeguarded offices as well.

It is not surprising that before the second World War many countries felt themselves menaced by the actions of the AO. In practically all the *reichsdeutschen* colonies in foreign countries unification had been put through within a couple of years. After that the colonies appeared to all to be an extension of the Third *Reich*. The indifference of many was not observed by outsiders; neither was it noticed that for example many large German firms, though supporting the AO, were not anxious for party interest in their affairs: some of them permitted their Jewish representatives to continue to work for them even when the war had been on for years. By repeatedly announcing that it and it alone could speak for the German citizens domiciled abroad, the AO, however, was able to screen the real inner circumstances from the outside world. In point of fact the AO had relatively few members. Only the actual functionaries were really dangerous, and on the whole their work was directed more against their own compatriots than against foreign states. The AO could do little harm to homogeneous, well-balanced communities; only where the situation was confused and tense was it able to exploit and increase the tension. This was notably the case in Spain where some AO functionaries performed an important intermediary role between Franco and Hitler and presumably were also involved in the smuggle of arms to the generals preparing their revolt. There are furthermore indications that other AO functionaries in collaboration with some national socialist *Volksdeutschen* aided and abetted the *coups* by the fascist Integralist movement in Brazil (1937–8). Otherwise the AO, as far as is known, did little to shake the world. Bohle, its leader, had only a restricted amount of influence within Germany. His appointment as State Secretary meant very little; Baron von Neurath had hoped to have less trouble from the inquisitors of the AO by taking Bohle into the *Auswärtige Amt*. His successor Ribbentrop would have nothing to do with Bohle. In no time they were like a couple of fighting-cocks. Ribbentrop put Bohle on 'diplomatic starvation rations': he was not permitted to set eyes on any diplomatic document of importance. The *Gauleiter*, old party swashbucklers, had no liking for Bohle: his way of speaking was too intellectual for them; he was considered to be too refined. With Hitler he never even had a private talk. The *Führer* was not interested in him nor in his organisation.

The *Aussenpolitische Amt der NSDAP*, which we also came across in our description of the military Fifth Column, was a quite different sort of organisation from the AO. The AO was a mass-organisation with 50,000 members and a central office as busy as a beehive. The *Aussenpolitische Amt*, directed by Alfred Rosenberg, was a relatively small institute with a yearly budget of half a million *Reichsmark*. It had been founded on April 1, 1933. Rosenberg had aspired after the position of minister of Foreign Affairs, permission to found the *Aussenpolitische Amt* had been Hitler's consolation prize for him. The German industrialist Krupp von Bohlen und Halbach had provided the first funds for the new office; in 1933 the German captains of industry freely parted with large donations, as they had done during the Weimar republic: those who gave subsidies right and left were safe. Rosenberg had collected half a million in a few weeks' time.

He set to work.

An office was installed. He took on linguists to read and make abstracts from three hundred foreign newspapers. He collected data on the more important foreign journalists. He organised *soirées*. He took on assistants to draw up reports on the promotion of foreign trade. He founded a training centre. He started sections to observe political life in given parts carefully: first only England, Scandinavia, the Balkans and the Middle East—later on the rest of the world as well. He tried to get influential foreigners to come to Berlin and sent his close fellow-workers (many of them *Volksdeutsche* from Russia) from Berlin to foreign parts in order to make known there the blessings of the Third *Reich*, and to get into touch with fascist elements ranging from England to Afghanistan.

This work, however nasty its purpose, had as a rule but little effect. Only in the case of Quisling did it become of any real importance, and then only because of a curious combination of accidents. On the whole Rosenberg enjoyed too little influence for him to pass on important impulses or even to receive them. He himself thought he was a second Bismarck, a statesman of unique knowledge and intuition, and blessed with a gift for skilful intrigue that would be hard to equal. The top men in the party and the state regarded him as a

281

muddle-headed fuss-box, the writer of books and reports that every-body praised profusely but that nobody read. The military men con-sidered him a dreamer, Ribbentrop hated his pretentiousness (this hatred was mutual), while Hitler did not mind listening to him now and again for half an hour or so. Rosenberg would then enumerate his merits, criticize the *Auswärtige Amt*, and prove that *he*, Rosen-berg, would have done everything much better—and then he would be allowed to take his leave.

The importance of the *Volksdeutsche Mittelstelle* was greater.

From 1918 onwards the German Government had secretly granted subsidies to German institutions and associations in the frontier dis-tricts which Germany had had to cede at the Treaty of Versailles. The government had done this partly openly and partly via the *Deutsche Stiftung* (German Foundation) and some bogus firms. Characteristically enough this work was co-ordinated by the ministry of the Interior: Germany continued to look upon those parts as German. Besides these channels there were also associations like the *Verein für das Deutschtum im Ausland*, the VDA, which let money flow abroad freely.

In 1936 Hitler decided to centralise the supervision over the sub-sidies for the *volksdeutschen* institutions and organisations. The party founded a separate office for this purpose, the *Volksdeutsche Mittelstelle*, that was at first directed by a high official of the Ministry of the Interior. Formally it was subordinated to Rudolf Hess. In 1937 Himmler succeeded in adding it as an additional province to his growing domain. From January 1 of that year a highly placed SS officer, Werner Lorenz, was put in charge.

Lorenz had an imposing figure, his representative powers were thought much of. He knew nothing about the *Volksdeutschen*, how-ever, but that was no bar, because at his request Himmler arranged for another SS officer, Dr. Hermann Behrends, a lawyer by training, a man of experience in official matters and an expert in *Volkstum* questions, to become his deputy and to do all the real work.

Behrends had about thirty men under him. He received the lines of the policy he was to follow from Hitler personally. It devolved on him to see that among all the *volksdeutschen* minorities in Eastern and South-Eastern Europe the national socialist elements got in control. For this purpose supervision over the subsidies was an important weapon. Those subsidies partly came from German big business, the fact being that the largest firms were expected to furnish the *Adolf-Hitler-Spende* (Adolf Hitler Fund) with liberal donations 'voluntarily' every year. In the financial year of 1937–8 this fund amounted to well nigh 46 million *Reichsmark*. Hitler received over two-thirds of this. The *Volksdeutsche Mittelstelle* had over 1·5 million at its disposal from this source during the above-mentioned period. Other receipts came from the two million members of the VDA.

The *Volksdeutsche Mittelstelle* exercised considerable influence outside Germany's frontiers, often after consulting with the *Auswärtige Amt*. In such countries as Poland, Hungary, Rumania and Yugoslavia it took steps to ensure that the leadership in the *volksdeutschen* groups would get into the hands of the national socialists. About the way in which this happened (often Hitler was obliged to interfere personally) unfortunately but little has become known.

Now that we have entered Himmler's sphere of authority through the *Volksdeutsche Mittelstelle* it becomes incumbent to consider in what perspective the *Sicherheitsdienst* should be seen, which we also came across in our enquiry concerning the military Fifth Column.

The *Sicherheitsdienst des Reichsführers-SS* had grown up out of small espionage groups which the SS had already had in the twenties, for keeping abreast of the activities of the opponents of the NSDAP, the communists chiefly. In 1931 Himmler had detached those groups from their regional relationships with the SS and had built them up into a central service: the *Sicherheitsdienst*. Its leader was Reinhard Heydrich, a naval officer who had been discharged from military service. At the time that Hitler came to power the *Sicherheitsdienst* only numbered a few dozen members, but it quickly increased. In June, 1934, Hitler laid down that all the other home information services of the NSDAP—Rosenberg's *Aussenpolitische Amt* for instance owned such an internal espionage centre—were to be merged into the *Sicherheitsdienst*. Round about 1937 it counted something like three to four thousand agents.

Within the framework of this *Sicherheitsdienst* Himmler and Heydrich had small operational groups, that were used for carrying out strictly secret instructions, mostly of a provocative nature. We have already seen examples of this in Poland. These *Einsatzgruppen* were also active in Czechoslovakia. They murdered Sudeten Germans there and left bits of Czech uniforms near the corpses, thereby enabling the press of Henlein and Goebbels to make a great outcry about the violent measures President Benes and his associates resorted to. On the eve of Hitler's offensive in Poland an *Einsatzgruppe* carried out a sham attack on the German transmitter at Gleiwitz. Again another group organized a feigned violation of the frontier whereby some dozen prisoners from concentration camps, dressed in Polish garb, all complete with tram tickets from Polish Upper Silesia in their pockets, were left behind on the 'field of battle'. These 'preserves'—they were thus indicated in the official

283

German documents [1]—had been done to death by means of injections. The corpses were then suitably riddled with bullets.

Himmler and Heydrich, however, had yet other machinery at their disposal.

During the Weimar republic political sections had existed among the police force in the different *Länder* like Prussia, Bavaria, Würtemberg—they were home secret services of the German Government. In his capacity of prime minister of Prussia the political police of Prussia came under Goering's control. In April, 1933, he centralised them in a separate office. First he wanted to call it *Geheimes Polizei-Amt*, but the abbreviation GPA reminded him too much of the Russian GPU. It therefore became: *Geheimes Staatspolizeiamt*. The abbreviation 'Gestapo' was first used by the post office. Not for long did this priceless plaything remain Goering's property. What *he* had done in Prussia, Himmler and Heydrich had done in the remaining parts of Germany. In April, 1934, Himmler succeeded in getting Goering to appoint him as deputy head of the Prussian *Geheime Staatspolizei*. Two years later, in June, 1936, Himmler had gained his end: Hitler made him chief of the German police. The whole police service was centralized. The *Geheime Staatspolizei* and the *Kriminalpolizei* (police for the investigation of normal crimes) were united under the name of *Sicherheitspolizei* (Security Police). Heydrich became chief of the *Sicherheitspolizei*. The *Sicherheitsdienst* (Security Service) with its central office had already come under his control, as we have seen. Late in September, 1939, the centralisation was carried a step further. The offices of all the above-mentioned institutions were united into the *Reichssicherheitshauptamt*.

Now and again every one of these institutions extended its activities to foreign countries, either directly or via organisations like the AO. Data are lacking, however, for giving an adequate survey here. But we do know that lists drawn up by Heydrich's officials accompanied all the German offensives. These lists contained the names of persons who were to be taken into custody at once. We also know that Heydrich had had a card system made with the names and particulars of twenty thousand Swiss who, in the case of a German occupation of Switzerland, were to be shadowed or arrested; and that Heydrich had supported the Woldemaras fascists in Lithuania from the beginning of 1938, amongst other instances when they asked for money in order to 'stage Jewish pogroms'.[2] But much more than this happened. The *Geheime Staatspolizei* which was made the fourth department of the

[1] See the affidavit of Alfred Helmut Naujocks, PS-2751, *IMT*, Vol. XXXI, pp. 90–2.
[2] Letter, June 29, 1939, from Heydrich to Ribbentrop, PS-2953, *ibid.*, p. 387, and Note, July 19, 1939, of the *Auswärtige Amt*, PS-2952, *ibid.*, p. 385.

Reichssicherheitshauptamt, in the end numbered some tens of thousands of functionaries. In 1937 its budget amounted to 40 million *Reichsmark*. As to its foreign intrigues little, too little, is known.

We must also be brief about the *Auswärtige Amt*.

At the moment Hitler came to power there were only a few national socialists among the German diplomats. By far the most of them had watched the rapid growth of the NSDAP with alarm. Of the 600 members of the foreign service who worked under Baron von Neurath at the *Auswärtige Amt*, less than a dozen were members of the NSDAP. What were they to do when Hitler became Chancellor? Almost all of them remained on, following the example of von Neurath, and assuring each other that 'those boys would soon enough settle down'. One after another they became members of the NSDAP, many of them not till 1937 or 1938. As regards Switzerland, as late as 1936 Bohle ascertained 'absence of any absolutely reliable party member' [1] among the Germans belonging to the embassy or the consular offices. At first the diplomats watched Hitler's aggressive foreign policy with trepidation. When he achieved one success after another many of them started wondering whether their uneasiness had not been undue timidity. Several of them furthered Hitler's expansionist policy zealously and enthusiastically. Fear once more came to the top when his bold game threatened to end in war.

All the right-feeling Nazis entertained a heartfelt contempt for the members of the German foreign service: 'they did not dare a thing!' Hitler looked upon the *Auswärtige Amt* before the coming of von Ribbentrop as 'a veritable rubbish heap of the intelligentsia'; [2] nowhere had he come across such a 'jumble of queer creatures'. [3] He rarely read their diplomatic reports. The idea of asking the opinion of his Ambassadors and Ministers never entered his head. As long as Germany was weak he gladly availed himself of von Neurath's respectable outward appearance. When he felt stronger he sent von Neurath packing and Joachim von Ribbentrop made his entry in the great ministerial building in the *Wilhelmstrasse*.

His wife's fortune had enabled von Ribbentrop to belong in the twenties to the international *clique* which spent the summer at Deauville and the winter at Cannes. Problems of high policy attracted him. He sought contact with the Nazis, gave money to the SA, and in 1932 joined the NSDAP. Hitler made clever use of von Ribbentrop's society contacts with von Papen and the son of president Hindenburg in the scheming that led to his appointment as Chancellor. Von

[1] Telex report, June 6, 1936, from Bohle to Hitler, NG-1901.
[2] *Hitlers Tischgespräche im Führerhauptquartier 1941–1942*, p. 106.
[3] *Ibid.*, p. 365.

Ribbentrop's reward was not long in coming. He too was allowed to set up his own office with funds from the NSDAP. It was called the *Büro Ribbentrop*—a second *Aussenpolitische Amt*—where, in less than no time, from two to three hundred young Nazis were diligently reading foreign newspapers, writing reports, preparing receptions, and organising distant official journeys. In the highest circles of the French and British bourgeoisie von Ribbentrop sang Hitler's praises. In 1935, by-passing the German ambassador in London, he was able to conclude the German-British naval agreement, whereby he was able to gain his ends without swerving so much as an inch from his original proposals. A man after Hitler's own heart! In February, 1938, he was Germany's minister of Foreign Affairs.

This personage too—queer mixture of mannerisms and conceitedness, floating across an abyss of ignorance—did not dream of co-ordinating affairs in his foreign service either. The reports sent in by Ambassadors and Ministers he usually left unread. If he did bring himself to receive them, then at most to give them a fitting idea of his own excellence. A large part of his energies went to puffing out the *Auswärtige Amt* into a gigantic organism. In this way he too created his own foreign propaganda section in the spring of 1939 to the annoyance of Goebbels, 'and soon day and night over six hundred people were feverishly making pamphlets and leaflets, radio broadcasts and translations in twenty languages and more'.[1]

All the foregoing does not alter the fact, that the German foreign service on the whole lent itself to being one of the channels by means of which Hitler was able to bring political pressure to bear on foreign countries. The diplomats were in the same boat and helped it forward. The popular idea, however, that made sinister plotters of them all, astute and knowing members of an enormous gang of conspirators, is far removed from the complicated and in part differently constituted reality.

We must now also say some more about the *Amt Ausland-Abwehr* of the *Oberkommando der Wehrmacht*.

In Part II we several times pointed it out as the espionage and sabotage department of the German military high command. This department had evolved out of the military espionage service, which had already been started in the early years of the Weimar republic. After 1933 this service expanded together with the increase in German rearmament. Its management was entrusted to a naval officer, Wilhelm Canaris, on January 1, 1935. In 1938 his headquarters were

---

[1] Rudolf Rahn: *Ruheloses Leben. Aufzeichnungen und Erinnerungen eines deutschen Diplomaten* (Düsseldorf, 1949), p. 136.

made subservient to the recently established *Oberkommando der Wehrmacht*. It had a section *Ausland* for keeping in touch with the *Auswärtige Amt*, the German military attachés in other countries and the foreign military attachés in Germany. And then it had three *Abwehr* sections: (I) espionage, (II) sabotage (i.e. the demoralisation of possible enemy armies, entering into relations with the representatives of discontented minorities, and the preparation of special actions), (III) counter-espionage. In Germany every military district had its *Abwehr* office. Outside Germany the *Abwehr* had representatives in most of the German embassies and legations. At the outbreak of the war the whole organisation numbered three to four thousand officers. The espionage it carried out had a bearing on military, economic and political data. It is true that Canaris had arranged with Heydrich, head of the *Sicherheitsdienst*, that he would confine himself to military espionage, but he did not keep to this arrangement. Boundaries of competency in the Third *Reich* only existed on paper.

The head of section I of the *Abwehr* was Colonel Pieckenbrock, whom we came across as the man who tried to get all sorts of facts out of Quisling at the last moment when Germany was preparing to invade Norway.

The then Colonel Erwin Lahousen became head of section II early in 1939. Lahousen, who before that had been head of the Austrian espionage service, had worked with Canaris against the Czechs. In the Sudeten German area *Abwehr* II had recruited numerous volunteers who were going to support a German offensive against Czechoslovakia by sabotage on a considerable scale. It turned out that they did not have to be used. Lahousen retained them and formed the *Kampf- und Sabotage Trupps* from them, which acted as 'external' Fifth Columnists in Poland. They were rough customers and complaints about their behaviour poured in during the first phase of the German occupation of Poland. For this reason *Abwehr* II decided to incorporate them into a permanent military body. To that end the so called *Bau- und Lehrkompanie Brandenburg* was set up in the autumn of 1939. It was called after its garrison town, Brandenburg, on the river Havel. The company developed into a regiment, and into a division even in 1942. It was members of this formation that we came across as prominent representatives in numerous countries of the 'external' Fifth Column. Most of them were *Volksdeutsche*.

As a rule the *Abwehr* was not in political contact with the *volksdeutschen* groups, the other discontented minorities (Ukrainians, Caucasians, Bretons) and the national socialist and fascist movements in other countries. Usually its endeavours were confined to building up its *own* network of agents, by making use of the connections of those groups and movements.

287

It is difficult to give a definite judgment about Canaris and the personnel of the *Abwehr*. In general they furthered German aggression, but they also put a check on it. They too were in the same boat and had to go whither it went, but there were some among them— one need but recall Colonel Oster who warned Norway and Holland of the coming invasion—who tried to make leaks in the boat at great personal risk.

It is of importance to point out that the espionage services we have so far come across were not the only, and perhaps not even the most important means by which Hitler and his political and military experts received the information from abroad that they needed.

When during some German invasion soldiers or citizens of the country attacked noticed that the German enemy knew all about the positions of their reinforcements, the concentration of their troops, and where headquarters were, they usually assumed that the German had found out those facts by making use of what we may call 'old-fashioned' spies.

This conception needs correction.

Since the beginning of the first World War the collection of secret military information has become in large part a mechanical process. Every big power has services which in time of peace tap the telephone calls of foreign representatives, intercept their telegrams, and which in time of war do the same thing with the political and military wireless traffic of the enemy. What they get hold of they try to decode. Sometimes they fail, but often they succeed. The Weimar republic had already a separate institution for this sort of thing, and the Third *Reich* had as many as five, which all thwarted each other where they could. The largest belonged to Goering. This was the *Forschungsamt* (Research Office). It had been founded in 1933 and it ultimately had over three thousand people for its personnel; during the fighting in Russia, for instance, it succeeded in decoding 20,000 a day of the 100,000 wireless telegrams that were exchanged between the Russian high command and army groups, armies, divisions and lower units. Hitler had no need of a single spy in the Soviet Union in order to know exactly what units were attacking or were about to attack him. The value of this decoding of intercepted messages was extremely high for the whole German conduct of the war, according to General Halder. Nearly all the enemy codes had been 'broken' by the Germans. 'Military information about the enemy was in large part, in some periods even predominantly, based on observing the enemy wireless traffic.' [1]

For collecting data air reconnaissance was also of importance.

[1] Information supplied by General Halder.

Other data of a geographical and historical or of a military or economic nature, were collected by getting into touch with foundations like the *Deutsche Ausland-Institut*, or with big German firms like the *I.G. Farben, Krupp, Zeiss* and *Rheinmetall-Borsig*. Sometimes these firms were prepared seemingly to take agents of the *Abwehr* into their service so as to enable these people to do their work abroad. As a rule, however, they did not do this willingly, it was considered too risky. It happened more often that the political and economic reports which these firms made for their own commercial ends, were put at the disposal of the *Abwehr*, or that the trained staffs that drew up these reports made special reports for the use of the *Abwehr*, by means of data, however, that were published in scientific periodicals or technical journals. This should not be called spying. The directors of *I.G. Farben* were acquitted of the charge brought against them concerning this point.[1]

Hitler did not dream of making any of these institutes or firms privy to his plans.

It should also be mentioned that the form of collecting data, which we have outlined in the foregoing paragraphs, was by no means typically German. At most there was a difference in quantity between Germany and the other powers, not in quality. Public opinion, however, was unaware of all that 'mechanised' and 'open' intelligence work. It saw 'German spies' where in reality as often as not facts had been collected by means of radio-receivers and swift fighters, stock-exchange reports and technical journals yellow with age.

The effect of the individual activities of functionaries of the *Auslands-Organisation*, of diplomats of the *Auswärtige Amt*, and of agents of the *Aussenpolitische Amt, Geheime Staatspolizei* and *Abwehr*, cannot, so it seems to us, be expressed concretely. That it was favourable to Hitler's ends in the years leading up to 1939 goes without saying. The German political Fifth Column certainly was no myth.

Many 'native' national socialist and fascist groupings and movements of malcontented, non-German minorities also furthered Hitler's policy. As a rule, they carried on their agitations largely independently. Their relations with Germany were less intimate than has often been supposed. Hitler preserved a certain aloofness towards his foreign imitators: too close co-operation could only cause foreign governments and peoples to take fright. Moreover, it would engender obligations towards these imitators, whereas he would rather be a free agent and dominate Europe and the world as he felt prompted. And anyhow—what were they worth, people like Clausen,

[1] Judgment of the trial against the directors of *I.G. Farben*, pp. 59–60.

289

Quisling, Mussert, Degrelle, de la Rocque, Pavelitch, Codreanu, Mosley, Kuhn? Novices who did not even succeed in coming to power in their own countries!

We must say some more about the political activities of the German and *volksdeutschen* groups of the population living outside of Germany at the time Hitler came to power.

We have seen that the position and nature of those groups exhibited great diversity as a result of their historical development. *Now, the factors that existed from before 1933 were responsible in the first place for determining in how far the Fifth Column impulses, emanating from national socialist Germany, and briefly described in the preceding pages, were able to turn those groups into an effective Fifth Column.*

The following factors may be distinguished:

Relative size of the group. If the group is to form a mass movement that has a noticeably dislocating effect then it should be of considerable extent compared to the rest of the population of the state in which it finds itself.

Its situation with regard to Germany. The nearer to Germany the more closely allied to Germany the group will feel, and the greater too will be the possibilities for intensive contact between the two.

Geographical concentration. The political activities developed by the group will be greater in proportion as it lives in adjoining areas where it may even be in the majority.

Economic development. In modern societies political activities more often originate in towns than in the countryside. The less the group consists of farmers living scattered about, the quicker they will develop.

Social situation. If the group is socially necessitous, then its discontent can express itself in political activity. People who are contented do not start revolutions.

Historical ties with Germany. If the group was once part of Germany, or has been separated from Germany against its will, or both, then it will be inclined to support any movement for reintegration or integration with Germany.

The feeling of being oppressed as a minority. If the group feels oppressed, then the discontent thus engendered will be able to find an outlet in political activities.

Historical feeling of superiority. This discontent will be the stronger in proportion as the group had the ingrained feeling that their members are the 'true rulers' in the country in question. If they are then oppressed they will wish to 'take revenge' with a vengeance.

Existence of a national socialist cadre. If a national socialist nucleus of any permanency has already been formed, then the possibilities

SURVEY OF FACTORS THAT CAN FURTHER THE RISE OF A POLITICAL FIFTH COLUMN AMONG *VOLKSDEUTSCHE* GROUPS (1933)

THE GERMAN GROUP

The factor is applicable

- (crosshatch) To a large degree
- (diagonal hatch) To a small degree
- (blank) Not or hardly at all

Legend used in table below: **L** = to a large degree, **s** = to a small degree, blank = not or hardly at all.

	Is proportionately of considerable size	Lives near Germany	Lives in strong geographical concentration	Is highly developed economically	Is in a position of social distress	Has been separated from Germany against its will	Feels oppressed as minority	Has a historical feeling of superiority	Possesses a national socialist cadre
Saar (99%)	L	L	L	L	L	L			
Eupen-Malmédy (½%)		L	L	L		L			
Danzig (98%)	L	L	L		L	L		L	L
Memel (4%)	s	L	L	s	L	L	L	L	s
Alsace (2%)	L	L	L	s			s		
Northern Schleswig (1%)	L	s	s	s		L			
Corridor, Posen, Eastern Upper Silesia (3%)	s	L	L		L	L	L		
South West Africa (35%)	L			s	L	L			s
Austria (98%)	L	L	L	L		L			L
Sudeten area (22%)	L	L	L	L		L	L		
Southern Tyrol (½%)	s	L	L			L	L	L	s
Estonia (1½%)	s		L		s	L	L		
Latvia (3%)	s		s		s	L	L	L	
Hungary (2%)	s	s	s			L	L		
Rumania (2%)	s	s	s	s		L	L	L	s
Yugoslavia (3%)	s	s	s	s		L			
Soviet Union (½%)			s		L		L	L	
United States (1%))			L	s					s
Brazil (1½%)			s	s	s		s	s	s
Argentinia (1½)			s	s	s		s	s	s
Chile (⅔%)			s	L				L	s

The figure given between brackets indicates the percentage the volksdeutsche group formed of the total population of the political unit in which they lived.

for a political movement in favour of the Third *Reich* will be greater.

If we group these factors together in a scheme (see p. 291) then it appears that there was only one area in which *all* these factors were in force: the Sudeten area. By themselves, however, the Sudeten Germans could do no more than disorganise Czechoslovakia, seeing they constituted less than a quarter of the population. The German group was only in the majority, an overwhelming majority even, in the Saar, Danzig and Austria. They formed a third of the white population in South-West Africa. Everywhere else they were a small, or even minutely small minority, varying from 4 per cent to $\frac{1}{2}$ per cent.

These nine 'positive factors' do not give the whole picture, there were also 'negative factors'. To wit:

Absolute isolation. When a German group was completely cut off from Germany no political activities were possible that were part of a German plan. Such was the case in the Soviet Union.

Ban put on by Hitler. When Hitler prohibited getting into touch, with some German group and would not have its discontent fostered then the possibility that the group would develop an active Fifth Column was reduced. This was the case in South Tyrol.

Anti-national socialist influences. When there were religious or political influences at work in a given group bearing an anti-national socialist character, then there too the effect of the 'positive' factors was partly nullified.

This last mentioned 'negative' factor was of great import. In every German group outside of Germany national socialism had to conquer a more or less powerful resistance. There were socialists, communists and liberals who to the very end, even in the Sudeten area, made opposition to the domination of the group by a new body of national socialist leaders. In the Saar a united anti-national-socialist front was formed. In Danzig over a third of the population remained true to the old parties. In Alsace the great majority of the *volks-deutsche* population would have nothing to do with a fresh 'Prussian' ascendancy, however much it might dislike French rule. This caused the big autonomist movement of the twenties to shrink into a national socialist sect only. In Poland Hitler had to intervene personally in order to force the cautious leaders of the German minority to resign in 1937. In Austria the national socialist section of the population was never estimated at more than a third. In Estonia, Latvia, Lithuania, Hungary and Yugoslavia the national socialists did not obtain the upper hand in the German groups there until the end of 1938 and the beginning of 1939. In Rumania the various national socialist organisations that were always violently opposing each

292

other did not unite until 1939. Especially many older people felt more repelled by than attracted to Hitler's doctrines. Young people were sooner drawn to it. That might be observed abroad both among the *Volksdeutschen* and among the *Reichsdeutschen*. There were large groups of *Volksdeutsche*, however, where national socialism was never able to get a noticeable hold, like the strongly religious *russlanddeutsche* groups in Rumania, Canada, the United States, Mexico and the Argentine.

What did Hitler consider the political task of all these *volksdeutschen* groups?

To start with they had to place themselves under national socialist leadership. As a rule the tactics of a united national front were applied, cleverly promoted by incessant German propaganda. It looked 'non-party', in reality it was conducted by national socialists. The formation of such united fronts was usually furthered in secret from Germany. It is no accident that they often did not come about until 1938 and 1939: after the *Anschluss* with Austria and the annexation of the Sudeten area Hitler seemed really invincible. Moreover, when Austria became national socialist it of course became easier to get into touch with the *volksdeutschen* minorities in Hungary and Yugoslavia.

These united national fronts, often after a prolonged internal strife, succeeded in the sense that they were able to get the majority of the group in question to back them, or at least to push all the other *volksdeutschen* organisations into the background, in the Saar, in Eupen-Malmédy, North Schleswig, Poland, South-West Africa, Estonia, Latvia, Hungary, Rumania and Yugoslavia. They failed in Alsace and in the United States. There the national socialist group remained a minority with a conspiratorial nucleus, a sect that was the more aggressive the smaller it was.

As regards the successful united fronts it should be observed that their relations with Berlin were kept strictly secret. Their activities first had positive effect in the Saar, but there the German group after all made up the overwhelming majority of the population, while the watchword proclaimed by their united front—*Heim ins Reich!*—expressed the fondest wish of the whole group from 1918 on. Elsewhere too, the united front tried to enter into the wishes that the group in question had already long been cherishing when Hitler was still unknown. In a sharper form these united fronts claimed the rights and privileges which the group in question had lost after the first World War or earlier. *The danger of all this political activity lay in the fact that thereby weapons were placed in Hitler's hands that he needed for his political game*. He wielded them with absolute mastery. It would lead us too far to describe this in detail. Suffice it to say here that the Austrian NSDAP and the *Sudetendeutsche Partei* were political Fifth Column groups in the highest measure conceivable. The Austrian NSDAP was such from the very outset, the *Sudetendeutsche Partei* became so. Without the activities of these two movments the *Anschluss* of Austria and the disintegration of Czechoslovakia in the way in which they occurred are unthinkable.

When in 1938 Hitler wrote down these formidable victories, there were German groups in ten countries and areas outside Germany which felt oppressed as minorities, and among whom to a greater or lesser extent the other factors were at work which might further the rise of a political Fifth Column: South Tyrol, the Soviet Union, South-West Africa, Memel, Estonia, Latvia, Hungary, Rumania, Poland and Yugoslavia; ten groups that Hitler would have liked to mould first into a political and then into a military Fifth Column. This was not always feasible. Nor did this always fit in with his concrete plans.

The *Volksdeutschen* in South Tyrol had to remain passive. This they did.

The *Volksdeutschen* in the Soviet Union were out of his reach.

The Germans in South-West Africa lived too far away.

The *Volksdeutschen* in the Memel area did get an active role to play. They eagerly promoted the annexation of the Memel territory which Hitler and von Ribbentrop forced through on March 20, 1939.

As regards Latvia and Estonia Hitler did not avail himself of the pressure the *Volksdeutschen* might have exercised on Moscow: in the autumn of 1939 both groups were transferred to Poland.

This leaves four groups of *Volksdeutsche*: those in Hungary, Rumania, Poland and Yugoslavia.

In all four cases the *Anschluss* of Austria and the collapse of Czechoslovakia brought about that national socialist elements, with the support of Berlin, seized the political management of the mass of the minority group in question. Four German political Fifth Columns resulted. Two of the states where they operated became the victims of Hitler's armed aggression: Poland and Yugoslavia.

That these were the only two states where we found indications of military Fifth Column activity on a considerable scale, is by no means accidental. The conclusions reached in our fact-finding survey are confirmed by historical analysis.

294

Conclusion

Fear for a world-embracing Fifth Column did not spread over a large part of the earth, as we indicated in the introduction to Part I, until after and because of the Austrian *Anschluss* and the annexation of the Sudeten area. They were the two greatest, the two only important successes really that Hitler was able to achieve by manipulating mass movements in foreign parts. In both cases they were also due to specifically geographical factors as well as to social, economic and historical ones. The latter were of especial force in the Sudeten area.

Outside Germany people hardly had an eye for these factors. Few felt any need to go into the complicated relations between the German and the Slav peoples in the centre of Europe. One dominant fact had occurred, namely that within a certain state a group of citizens had allowed themselves to be used as tools, as crowbars of Hitler. They were Germans, national socialists. Is it not natural that people in all countries started to harbour suspicions against Germans and national socialists—the more since fresh fuel was added to those suspicions by the fact that these groups backed Hitler continually and consistently? No attention was bestowed on the different historical disposition of the *volksdeutschen* groups, nor on the comparative tepidness with which many of the *Reichsdeutschen* living abroad regarded national socialism. It was not possible for people to see in their right proportion how all these German institutions and offices worked which we sketched in our preceding chapter. People felt menaced. And rightly so! Hitler's policy consisted in a combination of political and military aggression. He made less use of the weapon of the internal *military* Fifth Column than was generally assumed outside Germany; he could do no other; the secrecy, that essential part of his whole conduct of affairs, demanded such. The weapon of the internal *political* Fifth Column, on the other hand, he wielded incessantly from 1933 onwards, and with consummate mastery, diabolic imagination and supreme contempt for stipulations of treaties and rules of decency. That he did not always attain his goal did not lie with him: it was due to the resistance his striving

295

aroused. However much the notions that sprang up during the years 1933–9 about a German political Fifth Column may have been exaggerated or incorrect as to particulars, in essentials they were not beside the truth. In many respects actual events were even worse than people had dared suppose before the second World War started.

Was it not inevitable therefore that when once the war had been unchained by Hitler people should assume at each fresh instance of his aggression that those groups that had for so long backed him politically could certainly not leave him in the lurch when it came to lending military support? The military Fifth Column that people thought they perceived was often, if not wholly then at least for the most part, the transformation of the political Fifth Column. Opponents were arrested and persecuted of whom it was assumed, often rightly so, that they were hand in glove with the enemy and in principle willing to aid him. *Deeds* were often ascribed to these opponents which they had not perpetrated, but the *disposition* whence these deeds *might* have sprung was seen sharply and correctly enough. *Fear for the military Fifth Column was exaggerated, but it was not absurd.*

It must be acknowledged that this fear led people in some countries to subject some groups whose *disposition* was wrongly judged to harsh measures, namely the refugees from Germany and Austria. Many French authorities treated them, once the war had started, with scarcely veiled hostility. The British took the trouble to make an investigation into their political disposition that tried to be fair, and that was both a costly and a lengthy business. That the results of the investigation were after all thrown overboard in a moment of supreme danger and deadly risk, misled as the British were by incorrect reports that came from the continent of Europe, was a hard blow for the victims, but, if we think back to the summer of 1940 and recall how people had seen world events develop since 1933, we do not feel justified to blame the authorities who were responsible for the internment of the refugees. The historian, who, years after the event, when the danger has passed, can weigh up the pros and cons of certain actions in the tranquillity of his study—how easy things are for him compared to the statesman who, at the moment itself and in spite of all uncertainties and surrounded as he is by a thousand threats, has to make decisions on which depend the weal and woe of a whole community! Ultimately only Hitler and all those who followed in his footsteps with conviction should be held responsible for the persecutions, ill-treatment and murders performed on the victims, the guilty as well as the innocent, who were real, potential or only seeming Fifth Columnists.

It would be unfair if we did not also point to what in law might be admitted as extenuating circumstances, for instance in the case of the Sudeten Germans and *Volksdeutschen* in Poland and Yugoslavia. They came to be oppressed as a minority and were sometimes meanly and even harshly treated. This was the result of a development of centuries—a chain of developments, rather, whose separate links were often withdrawn from the view of these minority groups. The same holds good for nations as it does for human beings, namely that what deeply moves the one is usually very little understood by the other. Of what interest was the history of the Czechs, Poles and Slovenes to the Sudeten Germans or *Volksdeutschen* in Poland or Yugoslavia? They felt menaced and neglected, and in their rancour they lent a willing ear to leaders who promised them the recovery of their privileged or supreme position.

Thinking they could undo the wrong inflicted upon them, they got ready to inflict even greater wrong on others. Old and level-headed leaders raised their voices in warning against the dangerous path along which Hitler tried to tempt the *volksdeutschen* groups. Warnings were not wanting in the *volksdeutschen* communities in South America either. After all it was self-evident that all those groups and communities, small islands in an ocean of differently-minded nations, would arouse a wave of hatred if they placed themselves in the service of an ideology that was felt to be a deadly menace by those nations, a wave that would engulf them themselves in the first place. The warnings were of no avail. True, those simple German farmers, industrial labourers and artisans from the Corridor, Eastern Upper Silesia, the Sudeten area, Rumania and Slovenia were truly not every man-jack of them spies, political agitators or guerrilla fighters. Proportionately there were perhaps but a few of them who acted in those capacities. The collectivity became accessories because they allowed those few to continue their practices unchecked. For this reason they became more and more identified—and this counted just as much for the groups of *Reichsdeutschen* living abroad—with leaders who renounced the normal loyalty they owed to the community in whose midst they lived as citizens or guests, and who lent themselves as instruments first of political and later of military aggression.

Very many members of this collectivity, simple souls that they were, did not even realise as much. Born in social surroundings that were not of their own creating, they were swept along in a struggle beyond their understanding and conception and *a fortiori* beyond their control.

Such is the tragedy of history!

Glossary of German terms

ABWEHR (abbrev. of *Amt Ausland-Abwehr des Oberkommandos der Wehrmacht*)—German Office of Military Intelligence.

ABWEHRSTELLE—Regional Office of the *Abwehr*.

AMT AUSLAND-ABWEHR DES OBERKOMMANDOS DER WEHRMACHT—see: *Abwehr*.

ANSCHLUSS—Annexation (of Austria by Germany).

AUSLANDS-ORGANISATION DER NSDAP—Foreign Organisation of the German Nazi Party.

AUSSENPOLITISCHES AMT DER NSDAP—Foreign Political Office of the German Nazi Party.

AUSWÄRTIGES AMT—German Foreign Ministry.

DEUTSCHE ARBEITSFRONT—German Labour Front.

DEUTSCHE GEMEINSCHAFT—German Community.

DEUTSCHE NATIONAL-SOZIALISTISCHE ARBEITERPARTEI—German National Socialist Workers' Party (Sudeten Area).

DEUTSCHE SCHULE—German School.

DEUTSCHE VOLKSGEMEINSCHAFT—German Community.

DEUTSCHE VOLKSGRUPPE—German Minority Group.

DEUTSCHES AUSLAND-INSTITUT—German Institute of Foreign Countries.

EINSATZGRUPPE—Special detachment.

ERFURTER WELTDIENST—Erfurt World Service.

GAULEITER—Gau Leader.

GEHEIME STAATSPOLIZEI—Secret Police.

GEHEIMES STAATSPOLIZEIAMT—Office of the Secret Police.

GESTAPO—see: *Geheime Staatspolizei*.

HAKENKREUZ—Swastika.

HITLER JUGEND—Hitler Youth.

KAMPF- UND SABOTAGETRUPP—Fighting and Sabotage Detachment.

LANDESGRUPPE—Country Group.

LANDESKREIS—District.

LUFTWAFFE—German Air Force.

MERKBLATT—Instruction.

NATIONAL-SOZIALISTISCHE DEUTSCHE ARBEITERPARTEI (NSDAP)—German Nazi Party.

OBERKOMMANDO DES HEERES—German Army High Command.

GLOSSARY OF GERMAN TERMS

OBERKOMMANDO DER KRIEGSMARINE—High Command of the German Navy.

OBERKOMMANDO DER WEHRMACHT—German Armed Forces High Command.

ORTSGRUPPE—Local Group.

PUTSCH—Uprising.

REICHSDEUTSCHE—German Nationals.

REICHSKANZLEI—German Chancellery.

REICHSMINISTERIUM FÜR VOLKSAUFKLÄRUNG UND PROPAGANDA —German Ministry of Information and Propaganda.

REICHSSICHERHEITSHAUPTAMT—German Central Security Office.

REICHSTAG—German Parliament.

SICHERHEITSDIENST—Security Service.

SICHERHEITSPOLIZEI—Security Police.

STÜTZPUNKT—Cell.

SUDETENDEUTSCHES HEIMATFRONT—Sudeten German Patriotic Front.

SUDETENDEUTSCHE PARTEI—Sudeten German Party.

U-BOOT—Submarine.

V-MANN—Secret agent.

VEREIN (VOLKSBUND) FÜR DAS DEUTSCHTUM IM AUSLAND— Association (League) for Germandom Abroad.

VOLKSDEUTSCHE—Minority Germans.

VOLKSDEUTSCHE MITTELSTELLE—Central Office for Minority German Questions.

WEHRMACHT—German Armed Forces.

WINTERHILFSWERK—Winter Relief Service.

Acknowledgments

More than fifty people in thirteen different countries helped the author in getting his facts right. Many of them have been quoted in references. The author is profoundly indebted to all. So he is to Mr. B. A. Sijes and Dr. A. E. Cohen, members of the staff of the Netherlands State Institute for War Documentation, and to Dr. J. Presser, Professor of Modern History at the University of Amsterdam, who were kind enough to offer criticism and advice. So were others. The writing of contemporary history is a co-operative venture. Of course, the author accepts sole responsibility for his conclusions.

Translations from the Danish and the Norwegian were made for this study by Mr. Ernst Valkhoff, Amsterdam, from the Spanish by Miss Lydia E. Winkel, Amsterdam, and from the Polish by Mrs. Miriam Novitch, Paris, and Mr. Willem A. Mayer, Amsterdam.

Books were consulted at the following libraries and scientific institutes, or were received from them for study in Amsterdam:
Rijksinstituut voor Oorlogsdocumentatie (Amsterdam).
Universiteitsbibliotheek (Amsterdam).
Internationaal Instituut voor Sociale Geschiedenis (Amsterdam).
Rusland-Instituut van de Universiteit van Amsterdam.
Vredespaleis (The Hague).
Koninklijke Bibliotheek (The Hague).
Koninklijke Bibliotheek (Brussels).
Bibliothèque de Documentation Internationale Contemporaine (Paris).
Bibliothèque Nationale (Paris).
Archives et bibliothèque de la ville de Strasbourg.
British Museum Library (London).
Wiener Library (London).
Imperial War Museum (London).
Royal Institute of International Affairs (London).
United Nations Library (Geneva).
New York Public Library.
Library of Congress (Washington).
Nationalbibliothek (Vienna).
Universitätsbibliothek (Tübingen).
Universitätsbibliothek (Göttingen).
Bibliothek für Zeitgeschichte (Stuttgart).

ACKNOWLEDGMENTS

The writer would like to express his gratitude to all the above-mentioned persons and institutes for the excellent co-operation he met with. He wants to put on record that his sense of indebtedness is greatest to the Netherlands State Institute for War Documentation, Amsterdam, the Peace Palace, The Hague, and the Wiener Library, London—that magnificent example of what a courageous and conscientious collector may achieve. Only a small part of the books consulted has been quoted in the references. The same holds good for the other sources used by the author. Interested readers might like to know that the Dutch edition of this book (*De Duitse Vijfde Colonne in de Tweede Wereldoorlog*, published by van Loghum Slaterus, Arnhem, and J. M. Meulenhoff, Amsterdam, in November, 1953) contains a 35-page survey of all source-materials used as well as an introduction to these sources.

The writer is grateful to the editors of the *Nieuwe Rotterdamse Courant* (Rotterdam), the *Daily Express* (London), the *Daily Telegraph* (London), *The Times* (London), the *Manchester Guardian* (Manchester), *Life* (New York) and the *New York Times* (New York), who all gave him permission to quote from their columns. And finally he wishes to thank the following publishers, who allowed him to quote fairly long passages from the works cited below:

Athenäum-Verlag, Bad Godesberg—
Hitlers Tischgespräche im Führerhauptquartier, 1941–1942 (1951).

Cambridge University Press, London—
D. Barlone: *A French Officer's Diary (23 August 1939 to 1 October 1940)* (1943).

Gerald Duckworth & Co., Ltd.—
Claire Hollingworth: *The Three Weeks' War in Poland* (1940).

Europa-Verlag, A.G., Zurich—
Hermann Rauschning, *Gespräche mit Hitler* (1939).

Eyre & Spottiswoode Ltd., London—
Hermann Rauschning: *Hitler Speaks* (1939).

Victor Gollancz Ltd., London—
J. L. Hodson: *Through the Dark Night* (1941).

Robert Hale, London—
Hugo Fernandez Artucio: *The Nazi Octopus in South America* (1943).

Hamish Hamilton Ltd., London—
Sumner Welles: *The Time for Decision* (1944).
Alexander Werth: *The Last Days of Paris* (1940).
Alexander Werth: *Moscow '41* (1942).

ACKNOWLEDGMENTS

Harper and Brothers, New York—
Sumner Welles: *The Time for Decision* (1944).
Alfred A. Knopf, Inc., New York—
Alexander Werth: *Moscow War Diary* (1942).
N.V. van Loghum Slaterus Uitg. Mij., Arnhem—
E. P. Weber: *De vuurproef van het grensbataljon* (1945).
John Murray Ltd., London—
Gordon Waterfield: *What Happened to France* (1940).
" Musterschmidt " Wissenschaftliche Verlagsgesellschaft, Göttingen—
Prof. Dr. Walther Hubatsch: *Die deutsche Besetzung von Dänemark und Norwegen, 1940* (1952).
G. P. Putnam's Sons Ltd., New York—
Hermann Rauschning, *Hitler Speaks* (1939).

Index

Aall, Herman Harris, 179
Abbeville, 83
Abetz, Otto, 137
Abwehr. *See Amt Ausland-Abwehr des Oberkommandos der Wehrmacht*
Accao Integralista Brasileira, 30–1
Afghanistan, 281
Albany, 106
Albert Canal, 79, 137, 200
Alien Tribunals, 100–1
Alsace, 7, 203–4, 270; pro-Nazi movement 276; anti-Nazi movement 292, 293
Altmark, 55, 171
Amsterdam, 75, 190
Amt Ausland-Abwehr des Oberkommandos der Wehrmacht, connections with Breton Nationalists, 203; and Alsatian autonomists, 204; generally over-estimated, 220–1; connections with Baltic emigrants, 237–8; and Ukrainians 238; linked with *Auslands-Organisation der NSDAP*, 280; establishment and activities, 286 ff.
    Argentine, 223
    Belgium, 198–200
    Denmark, 159–60
    Eire, 210–11
    France, 202–3
    Greece, 234
    Latin America, 224–5
    Luxemburg, 201
    Netherlands, 183–5, 189–90, 193
    Norway, 168, 173–4, 178, 180–1
    Poland, 152 ff.
    Soviet Union, 237–8
    United Kingdom, 208–10
    United States, 214–17
    Yugoslavia, 229, 232–3
Anderson, Sir John, 101–3
AO. *See Auslands-Organisation der NSDAP*
Arandora Star, 103
Argentine, 28, 30, pre-war fear of Germans, 31–2; fear, 1940–1941, 117; Germans tried, 1942, 120; German Fifth Column examined, 223–6, 227
Armour, Norman, 114
Athens, 121, 234
Auslands-Organisation der NSDAP, seems to introduce new principle 6; congress, 1936, 7–8, 12; Harbour Service, 14; congress, 1937, 15; expands, 1936–7, 16; 'four million members', 137; 'no Fifth Column', 140; total membership, 243; establishment and general activities, 277 ff.

Argentine, 117, 223, 225–6
Brazil, 223, 226, 279
Chile, 224
Denmark, 163 ff., 166
France, 21, 204
Greece, 121, 234
Luxemburg, 202
Netherlands, 190–2
Norway, 177 ff.
Poland, 148
South-West Africa, 9
Spain, 14, 280
Switzerland, 11
United Kingdom, 211–12
Uruguay, 110, 222
Aussenpolitisches Amt der NSDAP, 12, 168 ff., 281–2
Australia, 7, 104
Austria, 5–6, 16–17, 271, 276, 292
Auswärtiges Amt, 152, 215, 285–6
Azores, 213

Backe, Herbert, 275
Baltic republics, 235. *See also* Estonia, Latvia, Lithuania
Bandera, Stepan, 238
Barcelona, 14
Beals, Carleton, 25
Beck, Josef, 36
Behrends, Hermann, 282
Belgium, 20–1, German invasion, 78 ff.; Fifth Column discounted, 139; Fifth Column examined, 197 ff.
Belgrade, 123, 125, 232
Belmonte, Elias, 117
Benes, Edvard, 211
Bergen, 60, 63–4, 175
Bibliothèque de Documentation Internationale Contemporaine, 300
Bibliothèque Nationale, 300
Bloch, Marc, 80
Bloomington, 106
Bohle, Ernst Wilhelm, 15–16, 20, 138, 149; leader AO, 277 ff.
Bolivia, 33, 117
Borjas, Filemon, 117
Boulogne, 82
Brauchitsch, Walter·von, 147, 182, 235
Bräuer, Kurt, 59, 176–7
Braunbuch über Reichstagsbrand und Hitlerterror, 11
Brazil, Integralist rising, 1938, 25, 31; acts against Germans, 30 ff., 108; in 1940, 117, 120; Fifth Column examined, 223; Integralists, 280
Brena, Tomas, 111, 115

INDEX

Breton Nationalists, 8, 203
British Broadcasting Corporation, 97, 111, 128, 213
British Museum Library, 300
British Union of Fascists, 213
Brussels, 79–80
Buenos Aires, 28
Buffalo, 107
Bulgaria, 234
Bund. *See* German-American Bund
Bund der Deutschen in Polen, 149
Bund des Deutschtums in Australien und Neuseeland, 7
Büro Ribbentrop, 286
Butting, Otto, 68, 138, 191, 192

Canaris, Wilhelm, 138–9, 155, 178, 183, 214–15, 225; heads *Abwehr*, 286–7
Canary Islands, 26, 213
Cardozo, José Pedro, 111
Carlson, John Roy, 24
Chamberlain, Neville, 62
Chicago, 277
Chicago Daily News, 63, 136
Chile, 32; fear of Fifth Column, 117, 120; Fifth Column examined, 224, 226
Churchill, Winston, 98, 102, 139, 211
Ciano, Galeazzo, 209 n. 4
Clercq, Staf de, 83, 199, 200
Cleveland (Ohio), 215
Codreanu, Zelea, 290
Cohrs, Heinz, 67, 192
Columbia, 108, 117–18
Columbia Broadcasting System, 69
Cooper, Alfred Duff, 98
Copenhagen, 54 ff., 162 ff.
Corap, General, 89, 205, 259
Cossack, 171
Costa Rica, 118, 120
Courtrai, 79
Crimea, 131
Croatia, 229, 231–2
Cyprus, 104
Czechoslovakia, 7, 18, 250, 294. *See also* Sudeten Germans

Daily Express, 95, 101, 301
Daily Herald, 112
Daily Mail, 102
Daily Telegraph, 95, 101, 301
Danmarks National Socialistika Arbejder Partie, 8
Danzig Free State, 7, 34–5, 43, 155, 270, 276, 292
Darré, Richard Walter, 275
Dautry, Raoul, 197
Degrelle, Léon, 9, 83, 199, 290
Denmark, 8; fear of Germans, 1936, 15; German invasion, 54 ff.; Fifth Column examined, 158 ff.
Derry, T. K., 139
Deutsch-Chilenischer Bund, 226
Deutsche Akademie, 13
Deutsche Gemeinachaft (France), 204
Deutsche Nationalsozialistische Arbeiterpartei, 7
Deutscher Volksbund für Argentinien, 226
Deutscher Volksbund für Paraguay, 226

Deutsches Ausland-Institut, 13, 216, 274, 289
Dickmann, Enrique, 32
Dickstein, Samuel, 24
Dieckhoff, H. H., 219
Dies, Martin, 25, 118
Dirschau bridge, 155–6
Doenitz, Karl, 216
Dollfuss, Engelbert, 5
Donovan, William J., 136–7

Ecuador, 117
Edelman, Maurice, 132
Eden, Anthony, 98
Egersund, 60
Egypt, 20, 104
Eire, 210–11
England. *See* United Kingdom
Esbjerg, 161
Espionage. *See* German espionage
Estampa, 118
Estonia, 271, 276, 292, 293, 294
Eupen-Malmédy, 7, 82, 197–8, 270, 276, 293

Fabritius, Fritz, 276
Falkenhorst, Nikolaus von, 158, 172, 173, 177
Federal Bureau of Investigation, 21, 25, 106, 119, 120, 217, 254
Fernandez Artucio, Hugo, 110 ff., 116, 223 n. 4
Fichtebund, 24, 112
Fifth Column, origin term, 3; Japanese, 249–50, 254; fear in other communities, 250 ff.; fear in first World War, 251–2; origins of fear, 254 ff.; imaginary Fifth Column, 255 ff. *See also* German Fifth Column
Figaro, 21, 263
Finland, 235
Florida, 119, 216
Flynn, John T., 106
Foreign Affairs, 15
Forschungsamt, 288
France, 8; fear of war, 1938, 19; Germans deported, 21; German invasion, 85 ff. Fifth Column examined, 202 ff.
Franco, Francisco, 3, 280
Franco-Prussian War, 253
Frankfurter, David, 11
Freikorps, 276
Fuhrmann, Gero Arnulf, 112, 222

Gamelin, Maurice, 87
Gaulle, Charles de, 211
Geheime Staatspolizei, 12, 284
German espionage, ineffective in Britain and U.S.A., 220–1; by diplomats, 245; largely 'mechanised', 288–9
  Argentine, 223–4
  Chile, 224
  Denmark, 159, 162–4
  France, 202–3
  Netherlands, 67–8, 76, 192–3
  Poland, 152
  Soviet Union, 235
  United Kingdon, 207–8
  United States, 21–2, 216 ff.
  Yugoslavia, 232

304

INDEX

German Fifth Column, fear, summer 1940, vi; popular picture, 1938–9, 20 ff.; fear international phenomenon, 33–4; effect of action as seen in Scandinavia and Holland, 76–7; spread of term, 134–5; fixation of international image, 135 ff.; summing up by Donovan and Mowrer, 136–7; existence denied at Nuremberg trials, 140; definition, 142; political and military Fifth Column, 143; comparison of popular view and reality, 241 ff.; internal and external Fifth Column, 244–5; popular view misunderstood by Germans, 264; causes of fixation of popular view, 265–6; factors furthering political Fifth Column, 291; wartime fear 'not absurd', 296; 'extenuating circumstances', 297
  Argentine, 31–2, 117, 223–6
  Belgium, 79 ff., 87, 96–7, 139, 196, 197 ff.
  Chile, 224, 226
  Czechoslovakia, 287
  Danzig Free State, 155
  Denmark, 57, 62–3, 158 ff.
  France, 87 ff., 202 ff.
  Greece, 121–2, 234
  Latin America, 110 ff., 221 ff.
  Luxemburg, 85–6, 201–2
  Netherlands, 70 ff., 87–8, 95–6, 118, 138, 141, 182 ff.
  Netherlands Indies, 65
  Norway, 61 ff., 167 ff.
  Poland, 43 ff., 147 ff.
  Soviet Union, 128 ff., 235 ff.
  United Kingdom, 97 ff., 207 ff.
  United States, 106, 213 ff.
  Uruguay, 110 ff., 222–3
  Yugoslavia, 103–4, 122–4, 228
German Nationals, few joined NSDAP, 243; influence AO, 277 ff.; identified with Nazi leaders, 297
  Argentine, 120, 225
  Belgium, 82 ff., 198
  Brazil, 226
  Chile, 226
  Denmark, 166–7
  France, 92, 204
  Greece, 121, 234
  Luxemburg, 202
  Netherlands, 70, 72–4, 190 ff.
  Norway, 177 ff.
  Poland, 48 ff., 148–9
  United Kingdon, 100, 211–12
  United States, 119, 218–19
  Uruguay, 115–16, 222
  Yugoslavia, 65, 122, 123, 233–4
German propaganda, 12
German refugees, 11
  France, 92 ff., 204, 296
  Netherlands, 96, 188
  South Africa, 104
  United Kingdom, 100, 101 ff., 212–13, 296
  United States, 219
German servant girls, 191–2, 208

German-American Bund, 23, 25, 118, 119, 216, 219
Gissibl, Fritz, 277
Gjedser, 161
Gleason, S. Everett, 139
Gleiwitz, 283
Goebbels, Paul Joseph, 213, 238, 286
Goering, Hermann, 147, 182, 232, 275, 284, 288
Graudenz bridge, 155–6
Greece, 121–2, 234
Griebl, Ignaz T., 21–2
Grothe, Willy, 277
Guatemala, 118
Gustloff, Wilhelm, 11

Hagelin, Albert Viljam, 168 ff., 174 n. 7
Hague, Frank, 106
Hague, The, 71 ff., 75–6, 188–90, 261
Halder, Franz, 147, 158, 170, 230, 235, 288
Hambro, Carl J., 138, 139, 180
Heimattreue Front, 197–8
Hellman, Florence, S., 136
Henlein, Konrad, 7, 18, 133
Hess, Alfred, 140
Hess, Rudolf, 13, 23, 140, 275, 278, 282
Heydrich, Reinhard, 283, 287
Himmler, Heinrich, 12, 168, 229, 239; supervises *Volksdeutsche Mittelstelle*, 281; heads German police, 283–4
Hitler, Adolf, 13; promotes Bohle, 15–16; annexes Austria, 16–18; denounces pact with Poland, 37; quoted by Hermann Rauschning, 52–3; denies Fifth Column, 104; plans invasion of Poland, 147–8; and actions in Ukraine, 155–6; and invasion of Denmark, 158 ff.; and of Norway, 168 ff.; and of the Netherlands, 182–4; his aggressiveness, 182; plans invasion of England, 207; considers offensive against New World, 213–14; criticizes lack of war-time intelligence, 221; attacks Yugoslavia, 230–1; instructs Yugoslav Minority Germans, 232; attacks the Soviet Union, 235–6; his unsystematic strategy, 242; relinquishes South Tyrol, 276; not interested in *Auslands-Organisation*, 281; instructs *Volksdeutsche Mittelstelle*, 282; low opinion of German diplomats, 285; keeps big business uninformed, 289; avoids intimate co-operation with Quislings, 289–90; intervenes in Poland, 292; wields political Fifth Column, 293; annexes Memel, 294; unable to make intensive use of military Fifth Column, 295–6
Hitler-Jugend, 9, 152, 234
Hitler speaks, 52–3
Hodson, J. L., 81–2
Holland. *See* Netherlands
Hull, Cordell, 109
Hungary, 7, 8, 233, 272, 279, 292, 293, 294
Huntington, Thomas W., 135–6

305

INDEX

I. G. Farben, 139, 289
Imperial Fascist League, 8
Imperial War Museum, 300
Integralists (Brazil). *See Accao Integ-ralista Brasileira*
International Council of Philosophic and Humanistic Studies, v
International Military Tribunal (Nuremberg), 140
Iraq, 20
Irish Nationalists, 209
Iron Guard (Rumania), 8

Jacob, Berthold, 10
Japanese Americans, 250, 254
Jersey City, 106
Jungdeutsche Partei, 36
Jürges, Enrique, 32

Kappe, Walter, 216
Kattowitz, 43, 155
Kaupisch, General von, 54, 158, 159
Keitel, Wilhelm, 147, 182, 230
Kent, Tyler, 208–9
Kleffens, Eelco Nicolaas van, 71–2, 88, 96, 138
Knox, Frank, 136–7
Koestler, Arthur, 91, 92
Koht, Halvdan, 58, 173
Korsör, 161
Kristiansand, 60, 175
Krupp von Bohlen und Halbach, Alfried, 281
Ku-Klux-Klan, 25
Kuhn, Fritz, 290
Kulturbund, 228

La Guardia, Fiorello, 106
Lahousen, Erwin von, 179, 215, 216, 232, 233, 287
Langer, William L., 139
Latin America, pre-war fear of German Fifth Column 25 ff.; German intrigues feared by United States, 108 ff.; fear of Fifth Column, 1940, 110 ff.; after Pearl Harbour, 120; Fifth Column examined, 221 ff.; Nazi-groups before 1933, 277
Latvia, 8, 237, 271–2, 292, 293, 294
League of Nations, 274
Lebrun, Albert, 88
Leopold III of Belgium, 79, 93–4, 200
Lessing, Theodor, 5
Library of Congress, 300
Liebling, A. J., 90
Life, 301
Link, 213
Lithuania, 10, 284, 292
Lodz, 38
Long Island, 119, 216
Lorenz, Werner, 282
Louvain, 82
Lufthansa, 176
Luxemburg, 85–6, 201–2

Mackworth, Cecily, 91
Malmédy. *See* Eupen-Malmédy
Manchester Guardian, 51, 100, 102, 301
Mandel, Georges, 88, 93

Marburg, 233
Marseilles, 203
Marshall, George C., 108, 109, 114–15
Massachusetts, 106
Matchek, Ivar, 231
McCallum, R. B., viii
McCormack Committee, 24
Melnyk, Andrej, 155, 238
Memel Territory, 7, 10, 270, 276, 294
Mexico, 118, 120, 215
Minority Germans, historical development, 267 ff.; factors determining Nazi influence, 290 ff.; identified with Nazi leaders, 297
    Argentine, 225
    Baltic republics, 130
    Brazil, 226, 280
    Chile, 117, 226
    Czechoslovakia. *See* Sudeten Germans
    Denmark, 56, 160–1, 270
    Estonia, 271, 294
    Hungary, 272, 294
    Latvia, 271–2, 294
    Memel Territory, 294
    Poland, 35 ff., 43 ff., 48 ff., 149–50, 151 ff., 270, 292, 294, 297
    Rumania, 272, 294
    Russia, 252
    Russlanddeutsche, 293
    South Tyrol, 292, 294
    Soviet Union, 130–2, 239–40, 272–3, 292, 294
    Yugoslavia, 65, 122–4, 228 ff., 272, 294, 297
Mitrany, David, 139
Mola, Emilio, 3
Möller, Jens, 160
Montevideo, 114 ff.
Moscow, 128
Moscow Trials, 126
Mosley, Oswald, 9, 99, 213, 290
Mowrer, Edgar Ansel, 136
Munch, Peter, 56
Mundo Obrero, 3
Mussert, Anton Adriaan, 9, 68–9, 194–95, 290
Mussolini, Benito, 230, 271

Narvik, 61, 62, 173–4
Nasjonal Samling, 60, 169, 179
Nationaal-Socialistische Beweging der Nederlanden, 19, 66, 185, 194–6
Nationaal-Socialistische Nederlandsche Arbeiderspartij, 8
Nationalsozialistische Deutsche Arbeiterpartei, 275, 276–7. *See also Auslands-Organisation der NSDAP*
Nationalsozialistische Deutsche Arbeiterpartei Nordschleswig, 160
Netherlands, 8, 66 ff.; German invasion, 69 ff.; report on Fifth Column, 138; idem in Anglo-Saxon historical works, 141; Fifth Column examined, 182 ff.; light signals, 1940, 260 n. 1, 279.
Netherlands Indies, 65, 104
Netherlands State Institute for War Documentation, 300–1.

306

INDEX

Netz, Das braune, 12–13
Neurath, Konstantin von, 15, 280, 285
New Republic, 106
New York City, 107
New York Public Library, 300
New York Times, 90, 105–6, 133, 262, 301
New York World Telegram, 106
New Yorker, 90
New Zealand, 7
News Chronicle, 102
Nicaragua, 118
Nisei. *See* Japanese Americans
Noël, Maurice, 263
Norden Corporation, 217
North Schleswig, 7, 57, 160, 293
Norway, 15; German invasion, 58 ff.; Fifth Column examined, 167 ff.
Nuremberg documents, 24 n. 1
Nyborg, 161
Nygaardsvold, Johan, 58

Observer, 95
O'Donovan, Jim, 210
Oncken, Hermann, 275
Operation Cicero, 221
Oslo, 59 ff., 61, 175 ff.

Palestine, 21
Panama Canal, 26
Paraguay, 277
Paris, 91
Patagonia, 32
Paul of Yugoslavia, Prince-Regent, 122–3, 230
Pavelitch, Ante, 229, 231–2, 290
Pennsylvania, 106
Peru, 26
Pétain, Philippe, 88, 94
Peter II of Yugoslavia, 123
Petit Parisien, 12
Pflugk-Hartung, Horst von, 57
Philadelphia, 273
Philip, Percy J., 90, 262
Pierlot, Hubert, 87
Plebiscites after 1918, 274
Poland, pre-war fear of Fifth Column, 34 ff.; German invasion, 39 ff.; Fifth Column examined, 147 ff.; provocations by Sicherheitsdienst, 283–4, 293
Polnay, Peter de, 91
Posen, 44, 47
Putlitz, Wolfgang zu, 194 n. 4

Quisling, Vidkun, 60, 69, 168 ff., 176–7, 179 n. 7, 281, 287, 290

Raeder, Erich, 147, 167, 169, 170, 171, 182
Rauschning, Hermann, 16, 52
Refugees. *See* German refugees
Reichsdeutsche. See German Nationals
Reichsdeutsche Gemeinschaft (Netherlands), 68, 191, 192
Reichssicherheitshauptamt, 229
Renthe-Fink, Cecil von, 56, 159, 163, 164, 166
Rexist Movement, 82–3, 199
Reynaud, Paul, 62, 88, 89, 94, 205

Ribbentrop, Joachim von, 36, 139, 159, 224, 231, 232, 280–1; career 285–6, 294
Ridgway, Matthew B., 109
Right Club, 213
Rio de Janeiro, 28
Rocque, François de la, 9, 290
Rollins, Richard, 24
Roos, Karl, 21
Roosevelt, Franklin D., 4 n. 4, 23, 27, 105, 109, 114–15, 119
Rosenberg, Alfred, 12; contacts with Quisling, 168 ff., 231, 275; heads *Aussenpolitische Amt der NSDAP,* 281
Rost van Tonningen, Meinoud Marinus, 68, 195
Rotterdam, 70–1, 188, 261
Royal Institute of International Affairs, 139, 300
Rumania, 7, 65, 103, 272, 276, 292–3, 294
Russell, Sean, 210–11
Ryan, Frank, 210–11

Saar-Territory, 6, 270, 276, 292, 293
Salgado, Plinio, 30–1
Salisbury, Harrison E., 133
Sandler, Karl, 20
Sarajevo, 123
Scapegoat mechanism, 259
Scheidt, Wilhelm, 169 ff., 174 n. 7, 175–7, 179 n. 7
Schuschnigg, Kurt von, 16–17
Schwarz-Rotbuch, 14–15
Scottish Nationalists, 209
Sebold, William G., 217
Sedan, 85–6
Servant girls. *See* German servant girls
Seton-Watson, Hugh, 139
Seyss-Inquart, Arthur, 17–18
Sicherheitsdienst, 38, 150, 218, 223–4, 229, 238, 283–5
Sieburg, Friedrich, 137
Slovenes, 122, 228, 272–3
Snyder, Louis L., 139
South Africa, 104
South Tyrol, 271, 276, 277, 294
South-West Africa, 7, 9, 21, 270, 276, 280, 293, 294
Soviet Union, relations with Germany after 1933, 125 ff.; German invasion, 127 ff.; Fifth Column examined, 235 ff.; Minority Germans after 1917, 272–3, 292
Spain, 3, 14, 250, 280
Spanknoebel, Heinz, 277
Stark, Harold, 108, 109
Stauning, Torvald, 56, 57
Stavanger, 60, 175
Steierischer Heimatbund, 228
Stowe, Leland, 63, 181
Streicher, Julius, 277
Sudeten Germans, 18; as Fifth Columnists in Poland, 154–5; after 1918, 271; Nazi-party supports NSDAP, 275–6; recruited by *Abwehr,* 287; anti-Nazi opposition, 292; strong Fifth Column, 294, 297

307

INDEX

Sunday Express, 62–3, 101
Sunday Times, 128
Sundlo, Lt.-Col., 15, 61, 174
Sweden, 8, 20, 64, 103
Switzerland, 11, 20, 64, 103, 284

Taborda, Damonte, 117
Temps, 21, 85, 88
Teutonia Society, 277
The Times, 51, 62, 63, 95, 98, 100, 101, 117, 301
Tolischus, Otto D., v, vi, 105–6, 143
Toynbee, Arnold, 139
Trondhjem, 61, 175
Turkey, 104, 235

Ukraine, 130, 239
Ukrainian Nationalists, 153, 155, 238
Undset, Sigrid, 59
United Kingdom, 8; fear of war, 1938, 19; Germans deported, 1939, 20; fear of German espionage, 1938–39, 22; fear of Fifth Column, 1940, 95 ff.; Fifth Column examined, 207 ff.; fear abates quickly, 265
Unesco, v
United States, fear of war, 1938, 19, anti-German trial, 1938, 21–2; pre-war action against Nazis, 23 ff.; counteracts German influence in Latin America, 26–7; fears Fifth Column, 1940, 105 ff.; acts against Nazis, 1940–1, 118–19; Fifth Column examined, 213 ff.; Japanese Americans, 250, 254; German groups, 273; Nazi movement, 276–7, 293
Upper Silesia, 35, 36, 43, 49, 154–5, 270, 272
Uruguay, 33, 110 ff., 222–3

Ustashi Movement, 229

Valparaiso, 225
Vanderbilt, Cornelius, 117
Vargas, Getulio, 31
Venezuela, 280
Verband deutscher Vereine (Brazil), 226
Verein (Volksbund) *für das Deutschtum im Ausland*, 13, 139, 140, 274, 282
Vlaams Nationaal Verbond, 82–3, 199
Volga-German Republic, 131, 272–3
Volhynia, 47, 130, 239
Volksdeutsche, 'untranslatable', vii n. 1. *See also* Minority Germans
Volksdeutsche Mittelstelle, 149, 150, 152, 160, 232, 239, 282 ff.

Waffen-SS, 229
Warsaw, 46
Welles, Sumner, 27, 84, 107, 109
Welsh Nationalists, 209
Weltdienst (Erfurt), 24
Werth, Alexander, 88, 94, 128, 132, 133
Wesemann, Hans, 10
Weygand, Maxime, 88
Wiegand, Karl von, 104
Wiener Library, 300–1
Wight, Martin, 139
Wilhelmina of the Netherlands, 70, 183, 189
Wilson, Edmund C., 114, 223 n. 4
World War I, 251–3

Yenisabah, 104
Yugoslavia, 7; anti-German action, 1940, 65, 103–4; German invasion, 122 ff.; Fifth Column examined, 228 ff.; Minority Germans after 1918, 272, 292, 293, 294

For Product Safety Concerns and Information please contact our EU
representative GPSR@taylorandfrancis.com
Taylor & Francis Verlag GmbH, Kaufingerstraße 24, 80331 München, Germany